AF449202

The Cultures of the Hispanic Caribbean

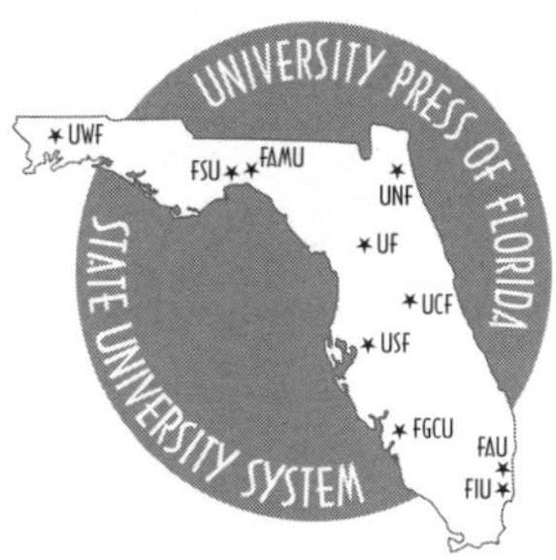

Florida A&M University, Tallahassee
Florida Atlantic University, Boca Raton
Florida Gulf Coast University, Ft. Myers
Florida International University, Miami
Florida State University, Tallahassee
University of Central Florida, Orlando
University of Florida, Gainesville
University of North Florida, Jacksonville
University of South Florida, Tampa
University of West Florida, Pensacola

The Cultures of the Hispanic Caribbean

Edited by
Conrad James and John Perivolaris

University Press of Florida

Gainesville/Tallahassee/Tampa/Boca Raton
Pensacola/Orlando/Miami/Jacksonville/Ft. Myers

Published in the United Kingdom as part of the Warwick University
Caribbean Studies Series by Macmillan Education Ltd., London
and Oxford

Published simultaneously in the United States of America by the
University Press of Florida

05   04   03   02   01   00   6   5   4   3   2   1

Printed in China

Library of Congress Cataloging-in-Publication Data
The cultures of the Hispanic Caribbean/ edited by Conrad James
and John Perivolaris.
p.   cm.
Includes bibliographical references and index.
ISBN 0-8130-1794-7 (cloth: alk. paper)
1. Antilles, Greater—Civilization. 2. Caribbean literature
(Spanish)—History and criticism. I. James, Conrad. II. Perivolaris, John.
F1741.C85 2000
972.9—dc21   99-088123

The University Press of Florida is the scholarly publishing agency
for the State University System of Florida, comprising Florida A&M
University, Florida Atlantic University, Florida Gulf Coast University,
Florida International University, Florida State University,
University of Central Florida, University of Florida,
University of North Florida, University of South Florida, and
University of West Florida.

University Press of Florida
15 Northwest 15th Street
Gainesville, FL 32611
http://www.upf.com

Electra, there is a world out there …

Contents

Preface

The Spanish-speaking islands are essential to any serious study of the Caribbean. Without them there can be no 'Caribbean Studies'. This seems obvious in view of their demographic and geographic dominance and the richness and variety of their cultures (even greater with the inclusion of the nations of the *circum*-Caribbean in the wider definition of the region used in this volume) yet it has been largely ignored in this country with its narrower anglocentric perception conditioned by the imperial legacy and the transatlantic links of the 'Black Atlantic' diaspora. Even in the Caribbean itself there is often little awareness among Anglophone islanders of their Spanish-speaking neighbours.

This narrow view is understandable among those who have never rubbed shoulders with a Cuban, Dominican or Puerto Rican but is less so among academics and those who want an overall view of the region which cannot be comprehended in its variety and complexity except in comparative terms. This is a challenging prospect, requiring competence in a number of languages, an awareness of the inter-relationship between disciplines, a sensitivity to cultural nuances as well as to the differences between political cultures – those unspoken assumptions on which political behaviour is based.

This collection of essays by leading authorities is therefore a welcome and necessary addition to the series, confronting the difficulties of defining and establishing Hispanic Caribbean cultures as a field of study. The use of 'cultures' in the title illustrates part of the problem, as not only are there deep divisions between the Spanish-speaking and other linguistic groups within the region but similar gulfs exist between Cuba, the Dominican Republic and Puerto Rico, each of whose culture has been conditioned by its own particular set of historical imperatives.

The Hispanic islands are distinctive in one crucial respect: they were settlement colonies. As such they have received an uninterrupted flow of immigrants from Spain since the end of the fifteenth until the middle of this century – a longer period of unbroken European links than anywhere else in the non-European world. This explains the persistence of cultural ties both with Spain and Spanish America, as well as the defensive but defiant posture adopted towards encroaching Anglo-Americanism, mirroring in the Americas that confrontation between Protestant North and Catholic South which has been one of the great divides in European history. Coming to terms with being off-shore islands of North, Central and South America has therefore been one of the *leitmotifs* of the Hispanic Caribbean for much of its history, although the growth of a huge Spanish-speaking diaspora in the United States – the 'rise of the Hispanics' – has served to change the nature of past cultural confrontations. The significance of that diaspora is amply illustrated in various contributions to this volume.

If there is one feature common to these three societies which in the past has marked them off from the rest of the region, it has been their slowness in coming to terms with Africanity, which in view of the predominance of peoples of African descent in the Anglophone, Francophone and Dutch-speaking societies has tended to distance them from a shared sense of Caribbeanness. However, once the African contribution to national formation and more particularly to national cultures through music, dance and religion, began to be acknowledged from the 1920s onwards, ties with the rest of the Caribbean at least in cultural terms started to become closer, in recognition of the importance of shared African roots. There is still, however, something of a fissure in the region due to the wide diversity of political systems.

Some of the factors accounting for this are outlined in the Epilogue to this book, which takes as its starting point the War of 1898 which exposed the Hispanic islands to the full blast of Americanization initiating a 60-year cycle of military interventions from which the rest of the region (excepting Haiti) was spared by the protective umbrella of continuing European domination, thus perpetuating the fragmentation, incomprehension and distrust which were features of the pre-independence period.

As globalization threatens the region with even greater fragmentation so the need to draw closer must assume a higher priority than it has done in the past in order to make a reality of that unity in variety which underlines the region's creativity. This collection helps to explain why on numerous occasions the cultural exuberance of the Hispanic Caribbean has had an influence far beyond the confines of the 'American Mediterranean'.

The book owes its origins to the initiative of two final-year PhD students at Cambridge who saw the need for such a venture, organizing the conference on which this volume is based, and attracting to it some of the most eminent scholars in the field. For this they deserve our thanks. A sad footnote is that just after submitting his chapter, Manuel Granados died in exile in Paris.

Alistair Hennessy

Acknowledgements

Thanks are due to the following for their financial and administrative support, as well as their kind encouragement: the Centre of Latin American Studies, University of Cambridge, particularly David Lehmann, and Clare Hariri; Trinity College, Cambridge; the Department of Spanish and Portuguese, University of Cambridge, particularly Paul Julian Smith.

The following promoted and facilitated the production of this volume through all its stages of evolution: Alistair Hennessy, our mentor, Shirley Hamber, Janey Fisher, and the editorial staff at Macmillan.

Finally, but most importantly, we should like to thank the contributors for their participation and support, particularly Manuel Granados, a fine writer, who sadly passed away before being able to see perhaps his last piece in print, in this volume, which is dedicated to his memory.

The contributors and translators

Contributors

Diane Accaria-Zavala is a Professor of Film and American literature at the University of Puerto Rico. She has been a coordinator of the Puerto Rican Film Festival since 1989. She has published articles internationally on Borges and cinema, Luis Rafael Sánchez, Gabriel García Márquez and film, Jean Rhys, and the relationship between the work of Orson Welles and Carlos Fuentes. She has just completed the manuscripts for two books: *Grasping for Shadows in the Flickering Light: García Márquez and the Movies* and *Writing in Shadows: Jorge Luis Borges and the Movies*.

Efraín Barradas is a Professor of Spanish at the University of Boston. He has published extensively from his research in Hispanic Caribbean and Latino cultures. Amongst his major publications are: *Herejes y mitificadores: muestra de poesía puertorriqueña* [Heretics and Myth-Makers: A Selection of Puerto Rican Poetry] (ed. with Rafael Rodríguez, 1980), *Para leer en puertorriqueño: acercamiento a la obra de Luis Rafael Sánchez* [To Read in Puerto Rican: An Approach to the Work of Luis Rafael Sánchez] (1981), *Apalabramiento: diez cuentistas puertorriqueños de hoy* [Coming into Words: Ten Puerto Rican Short Story Writers of Today] (ed., 1983), and *Para entendernos: inventario poético puertorriqueño* [So that We Can Understand Ourselves: Inventory of Puerto Rican Poetry] (1992).

Daisy Cocco de Filippis is a Professor of Spanish at York College, City University of New York, and one of the leading authorities on Dominican literature from Hispaniola and the United States. She has co-organized several international conferences, amongst which are 'The Women of Hispaniola: Moving Towards Tomorrow' (1993), and 'Asian Culture: Traditions and Diaspora' (1993). Her books include *Estudios semióticos de poesía dominicana* [Semiotic Studies of Dominican Poetry] (1984), the co-edited volume, *Poemas del exilio y de otras inquietudes* [Poems of Exile and Other Misgivings] (1988),

Sin otro profeta que su canto, antología de la poesía escrita por dominicanas [With no Other Prophet Except Their Song, Anthology of Poetry Written by Dominican Women] (1988) and *Del desconsuelo al compromiso, antología bilingüe de la poesía de Aída Cartagena Portalatín* [From Grief to Compromise: A Bilingual Anthology of Aída Cartagena Portalatín] (1988).

Lancelot Cowie is a Professor of Spanish at the University of the West Indies, St Augustine, Trinidad and author of works on, amongst other topics, the representation of indigenous peoples in contemporary Mexican and Guatemalan literature, and linguistic issues. In 1996, he compiled a bibliographical work entitled *La Guerrilla en la literatura Hispano-americana: aporte bibliográfico* [Guerrilla Warfare in Spanish American Literature: A Bibliographical Contribution], and is currently preparing works entitled *El proceso político en la novela mexicana* [Political Process in the Mexican Novel] and *Insurrección y novela en la década del sesenta* [Insurrection and the Novel in the Decade of the 1960s].

Arcadio Díaz Quiñones is a Professor of Romance Languages and Literatures at Princeton and a leading authority on Spanish Caribbean literature, culture, and thought, who has published articles, essays, an books on a broad range of issues pertaining to the region. In 1985, he provided a study on racism, history, and slavery as an extended introduction to an edition of Tomás Blanco's *El prejuicio racial en Puerto Rico* [Racial Prejudice in Puerto Rico], and, since then, chapters for numerous edited volumes on the intellectual history of the Spanish Caribbean, including one entitled 'The Hispanic-Caribbean National Discourse: Antonio S. Pedreira and Ramiro Guerra y Sánchez', for the second volume of Alistair Hennessy's *Intellectuals in the Twentieth-Century Caribbean* (1992). In 1993, he published the collection of essays, *La memoria rota* [Broken Memory], which has been acclaimed as the most important book in Puerto Rican cultural theory of the 1990s.

Keith Ellis is a Professor of Spanish at the University of Toronto, a Cubanist, and a leading authority on Nicolás Guillén. He is the author of a key work on this poet, *Cuba's Nicolás Guillén: Poetry and Ideology* (1983).

Juan G. Gelpí is a Professor of Puerto Rican and Mexican literature at the University of Puerto Rico. Apart from numerous articles and chapters published throughout the Americas and Caribbean, he has published two books, *Enunciación y dependencia en José Gorostiza* [Enunciation and Dependence in José Gorostiza] (1984) and *Literatura y paternalismo en Puerto Rico* [Literature and Paternalism in Puerto Rico] (1993). He is on the editorial board of the journal *Nómada* (Puerto Rico).

Gilberto Gómez Ocampo is an Assistant Professor of Spanish at Wabash College, Indiana and author of *Entre 'María' y 'La vorágine': La literatura colombiana finisecular* [Between 'María' and 'The Vortex': Fin de siècle Colombian Literature] (1988). He is an assistant editor of the *Revista de Estudios Colombianos*. His current research interests include nineteenth-century Latin American writers and intellectuals who resided in London.

Roberto González Echevarría is one of the United States' most prominent scholars in Hispanic Studies, with numerous books, articles, and edited volumes to his name. He has published several major works, amongst which are *The Voice of the Masters: Writing and Authority in Modern Latin American Literature* (1985), *Myth and Archive: A Theory of Latin American Narrative* (1990), and *Celestina's Brood: Continuities of the Baroque in Spanish and Latin American Literature* (1993). He is also the Editor in Chief of the *Cambridge History of Latin American Literature* (1997).

Manuel Granados resided, until his untimely death in 1998, in Paris, after emerging as one of the major Cuban writers on the island after 1959. Apart from being a respected critic, essayist, and film archivist, he was a winner of the prestigious Casa de las Américas Prize, for his 1967 novel, *Aidire y el tiempo roto* [Adire and the Broken Time]. He wrote several distinguished novels, such as *El orden del tiempo* [The Order of Time] (1962), *El viento en la Casa Sol* [The Wind in Casa Sol] (1970), and *Expediente de hombre* [Dossier of a Man] (1988). Indeed, he was one of the few Cuban novelists of the post-Revolutionary period.

Alistair Hennessy was formerly the Professor of History and Director of the Centre for Caribbean Studies at the University of Warwick, where he also founded the School of Comparative American Studies. His wide range of major publications includes single-authored works, such as *The Federal Republic in Spain: Pi y Maragall and the Spanish Federal Republican Movement, 1868–74* (1962), and *The Frontier in Latin American History* (1978), as well as edited volumes, such as *The Land that England Lost: Argentina and Britain: A Special Relationship* (1991), and the pioneering two volume *Intellectuals in the Twentieth-Century Caribbean* (1991–2).

Conrad James is a Lecturer at the Department of Hispanic Studies at the University of Birmingham. Research interests include questions of race, gender, and national identity in Latin America and the Hispanic Caribbean. He is also on the editorial board of the Bulletin of Latin American Research.

Jorge Marbán is a Professor of Spanish at the College of Charleston in South Carolina. Amongst his publications, in several genres, he has published *Camus and Cela: el drama del antihéroe trágico* [Camus and Cela: The Drama of the Tragic Anti-Hero] (1973) and *La Florida: cinco siglos de historia hispánica* [Florida: five Centuries of Hispanic History] (1979), and *La vigilia del vigia: vida y obra de Arturo Uslar Pietri* [The Vigilance of the Watchman: The Life and Work of Arturo Uslar Pietri] (1998). He has also published numerous articles on Spanish and Spanish American literature in journals and encyclopedias in the United States, Canada, Venezuela, and England.

John Perivolaris is a Lecturer (Assistant Professor) of Spanish American and Caribbean literatures and cultures at the University of Manchester, with research interests in colonialism, and postcolonialism in the Spanish Caribbean, as well as in diasporic literatures in Spanish and English, and the cultural repercussions of translation. He has published articles internationally on Carlos Fuentes, Luis Rafael Sánchez, Julia Alvarez, Esmeralda Santiago, Hispanic Caribbean and Latin American politics, media, travel writing, ideas, literature, censorship and cinema, and is due to publish a volume entitled *Puerto Rican Cultural Identity and the Work of Luis Rafael Sánchez* in the North Carolina Studies in Romance Languages and Literatures series.

Rodolfo Popelnik is a Professor at the School of Communication, University of Puerto Rico. He has helped coordinate the Puerto Rican Film Festival since 1989. He has just completed the manuscript for a book entitled *Civility Under Siege: Equality and Disenchantment in Technological Society* and his publications include articles on the themes of social class, media issues, and film analysis.

Ian Isidore Smart is a Professor of Spanish at Howard University, Washington, DC and author of *Central American Writers of West Indian Origin: A New Hispanic Literature* (1984) and of *Nicolás Guillén, Popular poet of the Caribbean* (1990). He is also a literary translator, the author of an autobiographical novel, *Sanni Mannitae: A Tall Tale for Our Times* (1994), managing editor and co-founder of the *Afro-Hispanic Review* (1982–87), and vice-president and co-founder of the Afro-Hispanic Institute (1982 to the present). His most recent critical study is *Amazing Connections: Ancient Africa and Contemporary Hispanophone African Literature* (1996).

Doris Sommer is a Professor of Spanish at Harvard University and the author of key works on Latin American and Caribbean nationalism, such as *One Master for Another: Populism as Patriarchal Rhetoric in*

Dominican Novels (1983), and *Foundational Fictions: The National Romances of Latin America* (1991). Her recent research has involved an investigation of politics and nation in Latino popular culture.

Carmen Vázquez Arce is a Professor and ex-Director of the Department of Hispanic Studies at the University of Puerto Rico. Amongst her publications are a book of poems, *Memoria de papel* [Paper Memory] (1992), a pioneering study of the short stories of Luis Rafael Sánchez, *Por la vereda tropical: notas sobre la cuentística de Luis Rafael Sánchez* [Along the Tropical Pavement: Notes on the Short Stories of Luis Rafael Sánchez] (1994), and a cookery book-cum-memoir, *Libro de los afectos culinarios* [Book of Culinary Affections] (1997). The following are in preparation: *Seguiré mi viaje* [I Shall Follow My Course] (poems), *Cuaderno del oso* [Notebook of the Bear] (poems), *Los ensayos de Luis Rafael Sánchez* [The Essays of Luis Rafael Sánchez]. She has collaborated on theatrical productions of Luis Rafael Sánchez's plays and several major Puerto Rican film productions.

Translators

Conrad James. See under Contributors.

Dorothy Marbán is a Senior Instructor of Spanish at the College of Charleston, South Charleston. She is involved in the application of multimedia computer technology to the teaching of the Spanish language and has co-authored computer-assisted lessons on Hispanic culture. She has published translations from Spanish to English, among them writings by the contemporary Spanish novelists Manuel Vázquez Montalbán and Carlos Rojas.

John Perivolaris. See under Contributors.

Nicole Roberts is an Assistant Professor of Hispanic Studies at the University of West Indies, St Augustine, Trinidad, working in the area of Afro-Caribbean poetry. She was a contributor to and translator of the *Encyclopedia of Latin American Literature*, edited by Verity Smith (1997).

Carol Tully has researched into aspects of German and Spanish Romanticism. She translated Thomas Oberender's play *Three Days in May*, performed at the Cheltenham Festival (1995), and Taniana Tsouveli's *In the Lemon Grove*, performed at the Royal Court Theatre, London (1996).

Introduction

Conrad James

The study of the Hispanic Caribbean continues to be undervalued in British institutions. The few Caribbean Studies programmes which exist concentrate on the Anglophone Caribbean with little or no reference to the Hispanophone or indeed the Francophone territories. Within British Hispanism the Caribbean tends to be subsumed within Latin American studies, explored through continental discourse and thus the specificity of the region remains undermined. In 1995, John Perivolaris and I hosted a conference entitled 'Spanish Caribbean Culture: Nationality and Subjectivity'. The principal aim of the meeting was to begin a process of raising the profile of the Hispanic Caribbean within British Hispanism. The meeting brought together academics based in the Caribbean, the United States and Britain who were all involved, in one way or another, in exploring the literature, cultures and politics of the region. The conference crystallized the fact that the Hispanic Caribbean is not easily defined or located. Such processes of location and definition are necessarily fraught with tension: where is the Hispanic Caribbean? What, if anything, is distinctive about this region? What are the challenges which arise when attempts are made to define and locate the region? The essays collected in this volume individually and collectively expose some of these tensions.

The use of the term 'cultures' in the plural in our title is meant to register the dialectic of homogeneity and diversity which Antonio Benítez Rojo (1989) reminds us characterizes the Caribbean as a whole. These cultures do not only exist in Cuba, Puerto Rico, and the half-island of the Dominican Republic but are also located in the coastal regions of continental Spanish America. Equally interestingly, they converge in particularly close ways in New York and to a lesser degree in Miami. The process of defining nationality and homeland began to take on new dimensions after the final exit of the Spanish from the region in 1898 and the establishment of the United States as a dominant political power. Not only have the cultures continued to turn outwards in order to define themselves but they are also constantly enmeshed in struggles to reconcile divisions within and across nations. Therefore, even as the nations of the Hispanic Caribbean pursue the process of finding regional definitions in terms of their 'inner logic and cultural consistencies' (Nettleford 1990: 29), individual nations must come to terms with the various race, class, and gender schisms which complicate unifying conceptions of nationhood. The representation of nations which have common histories of colonialism, slavery, emancipation and rise of nationalisms, yet have very different contemporary political characteristics, is very complex indeed. How to reconcile revolutionary dictatorship in Cuba, democratic authoritarianism in the Dominican Republic, and the continuing colonization of Puerto Rico by the United States? What is the role of tradition within the modern Hispanic Caribbean? What is the function of the intellectual, the writer or other cultural voices within these changing societies? How is the individual subject best positioned in relation to dominant conceptions of nationhood and identity? The chapters in this volume revolve around issues such as these.

Arcadio Díaz Quiñones (Chapter 1) discusses the intellectual beginnings of one of the foremost voices in the construction of Cuban national identity, anthropologist Fernando Ortiz. Ortiz is known mainly for the concept of transculturation, which he introduces in *Contrapuneto cubano del tabaco y el azúcar* [Cuban Counterpoint: Tobacco and Sugar] (1940). Ortiz activates the neologism in an attempt to find an adequate term to describe the complex processes by which Cuban culture is formed, since the Eurocentric binary dialectics inherent in terms such as acculturation rendered them limiting. The introduction of the concept of transculturation constituted part of what Díaz Quiñones refers to as Ortiz's pioneering role in 'rethinking the nation and the ethnic, religious and political dimensions of Cuban society' (Ortiz 1940: 13). It is often suggested that Ortiz's focus on questions of mixture and hybridity signals his moving beyond the constraints of his positivist background, which had lead him to see Blacks as barbaric cultural others and black Cuban culture as pathological, in works such as *Los negros brujos* [The Black Sorcerers] (1906). Díaz Quiñones introduces a fresh dimension to the reading of Ortiz's intellectual formation by highlighting the influence of Allan Kardec and ideas of transmigration on the construction of the concept of the concept of transculturation. Díaz Quiñones suggests a reading of Ortiz which sees spiritualist currents of thought involved in dialogue with positivistic, rationalist categories. His purpose is not so much to critique Ortiz's early criminalization of Africans as to locate it by consideration of the French philosopher. Thus, the African was essentially a criminal because 'his spirit was located in a different position on the evolutionary ladder' (page 21) and atavism represents 'regression in relation to the advancement of the rest' (page 26). Transculturation then, Diaz Quiñones concludes, is inextricably linked to the spiritist tradition.

If Díaz Quiñones is intent on establishing the fact that French spiritist philosophy, as well as Lombrosian positivism, is the source of Ortiz's recasting of the terms of Cuban national identity, Doris Sommer (Chapter 2) focuses on the concern of certain Puerto Rican intellectuals (José de Diego, Antonio S. Pedreira, Margot Arce de Vázquez, among others) with the politics of national self-affirmation, and the professed need for Puerto Ricans to claim their birthright of independence. Sommer uses as her point of departure the startled, if celebratory, response of a Boston-based journalist to the defeat of the 1993 statehood referendum. She links this disbelief at the fact that Puerto Ricans had the courage to say 'no', with the impatience felt among members of the Puerto Rican intelligentsia for the unwillingness of Puerto Ricans to engage in an uncompromising politics of resistance. Antonio S. Pedreira, in his 1934 essay *Insularismo* [Insularism] deplores the supposed docility of the Puerto Ricans, as does René Marqués, in his 1960 essay, 'El puertorriqueño dócil' [The Docile Puerto Rican], while Margot Arce de Vázquez bemoans the weakness of the Puerto Rican voice in 'Esau' (1967). For these intellectuals, whose voices were extremely influential in the establishment of a nation-building cultural project, affirming the nation meant sounding a definitive 'no' both to Spanish colonial coercion (as, Pedreira points out, took place several times in the nineteenth century) and to the impositions of Americanization in the twentieth century.

However, Sommer is more sympathetic to the model of indeterminacy and ambivalence she identifies in the figure of the nineteenth century abolitionist, novelist and intellectual, Eugenio María de Hostos. Sommer critiques Pedreira's impatience with impermanence by holding it up against Hostos's geographical and political transience, which seems to offer an alternative direction and a more useful model for keeping the Island's politics afloat (1934: 36).

The issue of resistance to fixity and attraction to geographical indeterminacy are also central to Juan G. Gelpí's discussion of the nomadic subject in the poetry of Julia de Burgos (Chapter 3). Gelpí examines some of the major aspects of the hegemonic literary canon established in Puerto Rico in the 1930s and some of the associated debates on national culture. Represented by a figure such as Pedreira, the cultural canon reflected an obsession with notions of geographical determinism and a sense of being isolated by the fact of Puerto Rico's being an island. One means through which de Burgos constructs what Gelpí, following Homi K. Bhabha, refers to as a 'counter-narrative of the nation' (page 39) is through the displacement of this geographical determinism by a transgressive nomadism. Not only does she write most of her work outside of Puerto Rico (Havana and New York), but where Pedreira's paternalistic insularism insists on roots de Burgos takes up the life of a wanderer. Additionally, de Burgos resists the masculinist insistence on nationalist themes by focusing on complex women-centred themes. However, Gelpí also points to the fact that, by virtue of her engagement with themes concerning racial mixing and social injustice, Julia de Burgos's texts often distance themselves from the political agenda of the creole women intellectuals of her generation, who were not interested in moving beyond the race and class parameters of Pedreira's insularism.

Like Gelpí, Conrad James (Chapter 4) also explores questions of resistance to containment and control, this time in relation to women's writing in revolutionary Cuba. James's close reading of Excilia Saldaña's autobiographical poem *Mi nombre: antielegía familiar* [My Name: A Family Anti-Elegy] emphasizes her insistence on exploring subjective women-centred themes despite her support for the ideology of the Cuban revolution. While Saldaña is not seen as constructing a counter-narrative to the Cuban nation, James sees her as challenging the official priorities of cultural production in the revolution by bringing into the foreground both racial and psycho-sexual themes.

Like de Burgos and Saldaña, Severo Sarduy also undermines totalizing discourses of nationhood. This is the focus of Roberto González Echevarría's discussion (Chapter 5). He examines the utopianism of traditional discourses on Cuban national identity and maintains that these paradoxically span the socio-political rupture constituted by the Castro revolution, in fact strongly undermining the latter. Against these discourses, he sets the late Cuban novelist Severo Sarduy's explosively subversive work, which employs postmodern pastiche, playful transvestism, parodies of power and sadism, and a promiscuous cosmopolitanism with regard to cultural categories and national origins, as well as experiments in the deconstruction of official languages. In this context, González Echevarría examines Sarduy's exposition of multiple fractured identities, experienced ephemerally at the margins of official yet fragile national and social identities.

Like Juan Gelpí, Carmen Vázquez Arce (Chapter 6) also situates her reading of Luis Palés Matos's *Tuntún de pasa y grifería* (1937) within the

1930s debates on Puerto Rican national culture. Not only was the unified conception of national identity promoted by the 1930s intelligentsia fundamentally masculinist but it was also Hispanophile. For Vázquez Arce, Palés challenged the mainstream Puerto Rican intellectuals by placing in the foreground the Africanist components of Puerto Rican cultural identity. She contends that he struggled against the homogenous conceptions of Puerto Rican cultural identity by affirming the Afro-Antillean. Additionally, her chapter emphasizes that within white culture the body is a taboo subject and that by centralizing the body of the mulatto woman, Palés constructs a transgressive discourse which ultimately reverses the 'bestiality' and 'dirtiness' which white culture attributes to Blacks. Vázquez Arce's redemptive reading of *Tuntún* goes against the grain of much of the criticism of this text and of Palés's poetry in general. His candid eroticization of the black woman is more often seen as both racist and sexist. While the predominance of blood, sweat, and mindless dancing in Palés's famous 'Majestad negra' [Black Majesty] tends to be read by Caribbean critics as evidence of an ideological continuity with what Gilman (1992) refers to as the medieval association of blackness with concupiscence, Vázquez Arce sees the text as forging a space to represent class difference.

Reading Vázquez Arce's chapter alongside Ian Isidore Smart's contribution (Chapter 7) accentuates how contested the issues of race and representation are among Caribbean critics. While Vázquez Arce sees Palés's poetry as constituting a liberatory project for black Puerto Ricans, Smart dismisses their representation by Palés as stereotypically exotic and rejects what he sees as the inauthenticity of his poetry. Smart contextualizes his reading of the poetry of Cuba's Nicolás Guillén within the ideas of Aimé Césaire, Frantz Fanon, and Marcus Garvey, in his attempt to evade 'the whole apparatus of so-called western scholarship' (page 104). For Smart, black writers such as Guillén have entirely fulfilled Afro-Antillean poetry's potential, constructing a truly revolutionary literature. While the dominant colonial culture continued to be obliged to imitate old world models, writers such as Guillén produced a literature which constituted a constantly renewable expression of defiant slave culture. Thus, although Palés Matos's negrism only succeeded in producing 'mumbo-jumbo sounds' (page 107), Guillén, Smart contends, is an authentic African voice.

The fact that Hispanic Caribbean literature in general, and the negrism of the 1930s in particular, is contested terrain is further evidenced in Efraín Barradas's chapter on the Cuban poet Nancy Morejón (Chapter 8). While critics such as Smart insist that Guillén's black poetry ought to be distinguished from that of Palés Matos and other white practitioners of negrism, Barradas mentions the traditional critical framework that tends to view them in the same category, seeing *Tuntún de pasa y grifería* as a high point in a movement initiated by Guillén's *Motivos de son* [*Son* Motifs] (1930), and coming to an end with the Dominican Manuel de Cabral's 1943 *Compadre Mon* [Buddy Mon]. Barradas does not disagree with the linking of these three poets in a single tradition but he distances himself from the idea that negrism has died and discusses a revitalization of black themes in the Caribbean. Concentrating on 'Hablando con una culebra' [Talking to a Snake] (1982), he therefore examines Nancy Morejón's poetry as a re-reading of Nicolás Guillén. The voice of a black woman writing within revolutionary Cuba interrogates and displaces the androcentric perspective of the negrism of the 1920s and 1930s. But Morejón does not only establish a dialogue with Guillén. For Barradas, her poetry might be seen as a re-reading of Cuban history from the margins (symbolized by the snake) and eventually represents a new reading of Caribbean history.

While Smart and Barradas approach the dynamics of race in Cuban culture through twentieth-century poetry, Manuel Granados's poignant testimony places his concerns about race in a diachronic context. Written from the perspective of a black Cuban writer exiled in Paris, Granados's analysis of racial and class politics both in colonial and recent history is extremely scathing. He reminds the reader of the fact that the more bloody periods in the country's nineteenth-century history of race relations were replaced in the republican period by restrictive socio-economic policies which ensured the continuing racialization of poverty. Granados contends that the 1959 revolution did not reverse the system of racial inequality and he points to the disproportionate number of Blacks in Cuban prisons as one source of evidence for his argument. But his essay does not only focus on the marginalization of Blacks by white racism in Cuba, since he also observes the phenomenon of black self-deprecation and the concomitant mimicking of white Cuban culture.

Jorge Marbán (Chapter 10) examines questions of racial separation and mixture as represented by four Venezuelan novelists: Arturo Uslar Pietri, Rómulo Gallegos, Juan Pablo Sojo and Ramón Díaz Sánchez. The novelists attempt to portray the Afro-Venezuelan world at different historical moments from colonial times to the beginning of the twentieth century, and each demonstrates a different attitude to the relationship between a dominant white culture and an oppressed black one. While several of the authors depict African folkloric elements without considering the socio-economic difficulty which characterized the lives of many of black Venezuelans, Marbán reads Díaz Sánchez's *Cumboto* (1950) as an authentic picture of that community.

Like race and gender, the phenomenon of migration has also been pivotal in problematizing concepts of identity in the Hispanic Caribbean. Daisy Cocco de Filippis's essay (Chapter 11) reflects the challenge which migration to the United States has posed for Dominican literature and national identity. In the diaspora, the terms of identity have had to be renegotiated, as Dominicans leave behind old distinctions based on family, class, race and gender. Additionally, the parameters of Dominican national discourse have been broadened, making space for the representation of voices which had been silenced previously in mainstream intellectual debate on the half-island.

Both Keith Ellis and Gilberto Gómez Ocampo (Chapters 12 and 13 respectively) engage with questions of Caribbean modernity. Ellis presents an optimistic defence of Cuban science. The strengths and successes of Cuban science are seen as a demonstration of a wider cultural optimism within that society. Despite the collapse of other communist regimes and the crippling effects of the US embargo, Cuban science continues to thrive, and operates as a 'mainstay of defiant national spirit' (page 173). Ellis also celebrates what he terms the 'social randomness' (page 170) which defines the selection of personnel to work on major scientific projects. According to him, there is a commitment in Cuba to educate all sectors of the society about scientific issues and this symbolizes the overall dismantling of previous, discriminatory traditions. Ellis's essay therefore serves as a counterpoint not only to Granados's contestation of the revolution's claims of egalitarianism but also to González Echevarría's presentation of disassembly by Sarduy of the rhetoric of revolutionary nationhood.

Gómez Ocampo focuses on the criticism of western notions of modernity made by two Caribbean writers, Virgilio Piñera from Cuba, and Héctor Rojas Herazo from Colombia. While Ellis affirms a utopian belief in Cuba as far as local scientific achievements go, Gómez Ocampo shows how Rojas Herazo and Piñera portray dystopic tropical versions of industrialization and progress. The Enlightenment project is represented as a failure and faith in technology is parodied.

John Perivolaris, Lancelot Cowie, Rodolfo B. Popelnik and Diane Accaria-Zavala all interrogate authoritarian versions of Hispanic Caribbean identity, whether from inside or outside the region, through alternative readings or discourses of nationhood, folklore, and popular culture. Perivolaris (Chapter 14) discusses the representation of an informal Puerto Rican nationhood in narratives written by Edgardo Rodríguez Juliá and Luis Rafael Sánchez. He contends that in the work of these two authors, the everyday rituals of life in the colony challenge and reverse meta-narratives of nationalism. In Rodríguez Juliá's narrative, themes of self-sacrifice and the heroic making of history are displaced by a focus on anti-heroic survival in quotidian contexts. And Luis Rafael Sánchez, through homoerotic language, celebrates Caribbean popular culture as a means of decentring nationalist authoritarianism. Reading both authors together, Perivolaris argues that their texts suggest the heterogeneity and ambivalence which underlie Puerto Rican national identity.

Turning to Venezuela, Lancelot Cowie (Chapter 15) studies the representation of the cult of the Virgin María Lionza in contemporary fiction. Followed mainly by the popular classes, the hybridity and dynamism of the cult unsettles the exclusive official versions of national identity. Equally important is the implied resilience of popular folklore within an increasingly modernized Venezuela.

Both Popelnik and Accaria-Zavala (Chapters 16 and 17 respectively) criticize the racist mythification of the Caribbean in the mainstream cinema of the United States. Not only are the cultural specificities of different nationalities confused or ignored but there is a recurrent definition of the region in terms of mindless violence or exotic hedonism. Both essays also allude to the lamentable internalization of racist ideology demonstrated by films made by Caribbean directors. Self-representation thus repeats the prejudicial stereotypes that characterize Hollywood's depiction of the Caribbean. However, for Popelnik the increased production of national cinemas and the expansion of an independent film industry are opportunities for disseminating more diverse images of the Caribbean. As far as Accaria-Zavala is concerned, the process of 'breaking the spell' of discriminatory representation has already been begun by Gabriel García Márquez, through his screenwriting and sponsorship of Latin American film. Thus, she concludes that the creation of a 'truly regional but essentially international film industry' is a possible dream.

Clearly, the essays in this volume are as varied as the cultural terrain which they set out to explore. Yet, like the Caribbean itself, distinct and coherent threads run through them as they all attempt to grapple with the politics of identity in the region.

Fernando Ortiz and Allan Kardec: Transmigration and transculturation[1]

Arcadio Díaz Quiñones

> In every living moment there is a passage between decay and renewal … To be renewed is to die and be reborn so that one can pass away and come to life again. Every living instant is one of creation, one of recreation. It is a connection with the past, of the enduring potentialities incarnated in the individual; and of the present, of the possible circumstances the environment contributes; from this contingent union with individuality the hereafter is born, in all its renewable variation.
>
> Fernando Ortiz, *El engaño de las razas*.[2]

> The two vogues, that of psychoanalysis and that of the occult sciences, have in common their opposition to the ideology and the way of life transmitted by the 'bourgeois society of consumption', in other words, by the Establishment. … They express, each in its own way, the yearning of modern man, and his hope for a spiritual renovation *that would finally give a meaning to and a justification for his own existence.*
>
> Mircea Eliade, *Journal III: 1970–1978*

Fernando Ortiz (1881–1969) is now known principally for his concept of 'transculturation' which passed into currency after the publication of his seminal book *Contrapunteo cubano del tabaco y el azúcar* [Cuban Counterpoint: Tobacco and Sugar] (1940; 1963). Transculturation has become established as a conceptual focus for contemporary cultural and literary debates.[3] Nevertheless, the intellectual beginnings of Ortiz, which are usually treated as a Lombrosian and positivist stage preceding *Contrapunteo*, deserve a separate study in order to understand his extraordinarily fruitful development of that category. These beginnings represent a formative stage in which Ortiz started to explore categories of analysis taken from different disciplines (criminology, law, ethnography, science and spiritist doctrines) and from very distinct political and social practices.

Ortiz quickly managed to become a public figure and intellectual of great influence in Cuba, a status he enjoyed until his death.[4] He had a profound impact on many of his contemporaries, often speaking in the name of the younger generation of post-1898 Cuba in a quite aggressive manner and taking up, in his essays and statements, many of the new ideas of the time. Between 1902 and 1906 he was appointed to the Cuban consular service in Italy and France; in 1906 he was named Prosecuting Attorney (*Abogado Fiscal*) of the High Court of Havana (*Audiencia de la Habana*); between 1908 and 1916 he held the chair of Public Law at the University of Havana; and in 1915 he joined the Liberal Party, and became a member of parliament (*parlamentario*) (1916–26). From 1907 to 1916 he was editor of the prestigious *Revista Bimestre Cubana* [Bimonthly Cuban Review]. In 1926 Ortiz published his *Proyecto de código criminal cubano* [Cuban Criminal Code], the text of a bill submitted to the Cuban government that included a prologue by the Italian criminologist Enrico Ferri (1856–1929). In all these roles, which he undertook within the framework of the new Republic, he was the pioneer of, on the one hand, a certain way of rethinking the nation and the ethnic, religious and political dimensions of Cuban society; and on the other, of the application of criminology and dactyloscopy (the reading of fingerprints) to penal reform and the study of criminality.

Ortiz grew up in Minorca (1882–95) where he studied for his baccalaureate; he returned to Cuba, and during the War of Independence (1895–8) embarked on his law degree in Havana. At the war's conclusion he returned to Barcelona where he graduated as a lawyer in 1899-1900. He then moved to Madrid, where in 1901 he obtained a doctorate in law. From there he returned again to Cuba, earning the degree of Doctor of Civil Law at the University of Havana in 1902. Apart from his institutional career, his marriage in 1908 to Esther Cabrera, the daughter of the influential Cuban intellectual Raimundo Cabrera (1852–1923), was of great importance in enhancing his public profile.[5]

Ortiz returned from Spain with great enthusiasm and began to develop new forms of 'scientific' knowledge, and to establish his authority as a public intellectual. He became known for his critical scrutiny of Cuban culture and politics. (It is worth remembering that Ortiz knew very little about Cuba from first-hand personal experience;

most of his formative years had been spent in metropolitan exile). During the years in which Cuba was emerging from her war against Spain and from the United States occupation, Ortiz forged, with enormous energy, a modern republican discourse. His ambitious intentions can be traced through his early works: in *Hampa afro-cubana. Los negros brujos* [Afro-Cuban Underworld. The Black Sorcerers] (1906), one of his first books, in *La reconquista de América: reflexiones sobre el panhispanismo* [The Reconquest of Latin America: Reflections on Pan-Hispanism] (1910) and in the collection of essays, *Entre cubanos: psicologia tropical* [Amongst Cubans: Tropical Psychology] (1913) in which he challenged the moral complacency of his fellow citizens. His ethical, political and historical concerns culminated in the well-known programmatic speech 'La decadencia cubana' [Cuban Decadence] (1924). Later on, Ortiz became President of La Sociedad Ecónomica de Amigos de Pais [The Economic Society of Friends of the Country] between 1924 and 1933, and a founding member of the Institución Hispanocubana de Cultura [Spanish-Cuban Cultural Institute] to which he belonged from 1926 to 1932 and from 1936 to 1947.[6]

In the intellectual biography that has been more or less fixed by historians and critics, it is usual to present Ortiz's career as one-dimensional. According to this interpretation, Ortiz, under the influence of Cesare Lombroso (1835–1909), started out in criminal anthropology and the analysis of penal systems.[7] During the course of his subsequent research he 'discovered' the notion of transculturation that enabled him to construct a national meta-narrative based on an intense meditation on the concepts of hybridization and mixture. According to this account, the paradigm shift criminology to transculturation 'culminated' in *Contrapunteo*, a book often read as representing his understanding of the history of Cubanness (*cubanidad*).[8]

The trouble with this linear interpretation is that it overlooks Ortiz's interests in certain nineteenth-century spiritualist trends. It fails to take proper account of the continuity of evolutionist perspectives in Ortiz, his persistent zeal for reconciling religion and science, the far-reaching implications of his attention to spiritism, and his interest in the discontinuities of space and time in the formation of Cuban society. Moreover, as well as his complex reformulation of Cuban national traditions (Varela, Saco, Martí and other intellectuals), Ortiz's intellectual origins include his appropriation of 'scientific' criminology and his interest in the new journalistic forms of police narratives.

The complex racist ethnology of the Brazilian Raymundo Nina Rodrigues (1862–1906) became for Ortiz a model of analysis for interpreting the relationships between race, nation and citizenship in

America.[9] However, this model was not sufficient. The scientistic spiritism of Allan Kardec (Hippolyte Léon Denizard Rivail; 1804–69) provided Ortiz with interpretative tools to understand the racial question from the perspective of an evolutionistic theory which articulates a broader framework of national spirituality, law and religion. Spiritist doctrine constitutes a fundamental aspect of the concept of transculturation. Thus, to reduce Ortiz's trajectory to the passage from criminology to transculturation obscures the multiple affiliations, resonances and interweavings that we find in his texts.

In the present essay, therefore, I am interested in raising again the question of Ortiz's beginnings, but with the intention of opening up a perspective in which the Lombrosian versions of positivist, rationalistic categories may enter into dialogue with the spiritualist currents of thought represented by Kardec.[10] In fact, as we shall see, there exists a very subtle relationship between the transmigration of souls – the story of its successive incarnations – and the category of transculturation. Although the work of Kardec has almost disappeared from the intellectual discussion and study of the author of *Contrapunteo*, Ortiz, like other intellectuals in Europe and Latin America, was fascinated by the learned religion represented by Kardec's *Book of Spirits* (1857) and by the possible mediation between science and 'popular religion'.

Ortiz was not only a reader of Kardec, he also dedicated a large part of his intellectual activity to spiritist doctrines. *La filosofía penal de los espiritistas* [The Penal Philosophy of the Spiritists], a work originating in an inaugural lecture Ortiz delivered at the Faculty of Law of the University of Havana in 1912, was first published in the *Revista Bimestre Cubana* in 1914. He considered it so important that he published it as a book in 1915, the same year he published *Los negros esclavos* [The Black Slaves] and *La identificación dactiloscópica: estudio de policiología y derecho público* [Dactyloscopic Identitifation: A Study of Police Science and Public Law]. *La filosofía penal* received considerable attention. Another Spanish edition, for example, appeared in 1924, part of the series *Biblioteca Jurídica de Autores Españoles y Extranjeros* [Juridical Library of Spanish and Foreign Authors]. A third edition was published in 1950 by the Buenos Aires publisher Editorial Victor Hugo, as part of the *Filosofía y Doctrina* [Philosophy and Doctrine] series. In 1919 and at the request of the Sociedad Espiritista de Cuba [Spiritist Society of Cuba], Ortiz gave a lecture entitled 'Las fases de la evolución religiosa' [The Phases of Religious Evolution]. In Havana's Payret Theatre, Ortiz took the bold step of expressing publicly his attraction to spiritism (1919: 16): 'Spiritists! As one who is not able to participate in your mysticism, I calmly say to you: You are the faithful followers of a sublime faith! Perhaps you are those who, with the greatest purity, most closely approximate the ideal of reaching God through love and science!'[11]

Ortiz returned over and over again to what he had written in *La filosofía penal*, reworking it, modifying and extending it. Ortiz's encounter with spiritism was a life-long attraction, as deep as it was intense. It is interesting to note that right up to the 1950s he was still writing about spiritism: 'Una moderna secta espiritista de Cuba' [A Modern Spiritist Sect in Cuba] and 'Los espirituales cordoneros del Orilé [The Spiritual Rope-Makers of the Orilé] were articles published in *Bohemia*, and are very pertinent to a more detailed study of this subject.

Undoubtedly, however, Ortiz defined himself according to the terms of the dual institution of modern science and republican nationality. In 1903 the writer Miguel de Carrión (1875–1929) was already asserting in the journal *Azul y Rojo* [Blue and Red] that the young Ortiz was 'el único de nuestros hombres de ciencia dotado de facultad creadora' [the only one of our men of science gifted with a creative faculty] and a 'positivista convencido' [committed positivist]. At the same time he praised the doctoral thesis Ortiz published in Madrid, entitled *Base para un estudio sobre la llamada reparación civil* [Basis for a Study of So-Called Civil Redress] (1901). Carrión also commented on the 'valioso estudio sobre el ñañiguismo en Cuba' [the valuable study of Afro-Cuban secret societies] which Ortiz would later publish in Madrid (Librería Fernando Fé) under the title *Hampa afro-cubana*.

> There can have been no more arduous task than that of collecting the necessary data for this book, during which process we have followed him step by step. Day by day the researcher came up against the eternal difficulties which make the efforts of the man of science unfruitful in our country: there was no previous work to build upon; it was necessary to start from scratch, organizing the little scraps of isolated and incomplete data that came to his attention and, if that were not bad enough, the conviction of the author was constantly dashed by the apathy of the local scientific community and government circles, who were little concerned in the efforts of a *layabout* to write monographs about the Afro-Cuban secret societies, certainly a trivial matter when compared with the grand concerns of politics.
>
> (Carrión 1903: 5–6).[12]

In *Los negros brujos* Ortiz declared that the 'savage' life could not be silenced, but should be cautiously heeded – and repressed – precisely because the country had to be brought under control and morally educated. Its sensibility should be attuned to modern ethical and political norms. On the one hand, Ortiz was deploying the doctrines of the Italian school of criminology and positivist penal law; on the other, it is already perceptible that the conceptual framework of positivism was proving to be insufficient in his interpretation of the role of religiosity and cultural deracination in Cuban society.

The subtitle of *Los negros brujos, estudio de etnología criminal* [The Black Sorcerers, A Study of Criminal Ethnology], anticipated his condemnation of witchcraft. Ortiz emphatically wrote that:

> The sorcerers' cult is, in the final analysis, socially negative with regard to the improvement of our society, because, given its inherent and totally amoral primitivism, it contributes to keeping the consciousness of uneducated Negroes bogged down in the lowest depths of African barbarism (1906: 227).[13]

He concluded that it was: 'An obstacle to civilization, principally of the coloured population …, since it was the most barbarous expression of a religious sentiment devoid of any moral content.'[14] This analysis of witchcraft was reiterated in his 1919 lecture 'Las fases de la evolución religiosa', where Ortiz interpreted it within the framework of the Cuban *lucha religiosa* [religious struggle] to arrive at the higher spiritual plane of spiritism (1919: 68): In Cuba three religious currents struggle for survival, if not for preeminence: African fetishism, especially of the *lucumí* nation; several derivations of Christianity of varying purity, especially Catholicism, and contemporary religious philosophism, especially spiritism.[15]

At the Spiritist Society of Cuba, gathered together at Havana's Payret Theatre, Ortiz presented spiritism as an improvement on Catholicism and witchcraft (1919: 79): 'Fetishism is the *amoral religion*, Catholicism is the moral religion, spiritism is the *areligious morality*, without dogmas and rituals, nor idols and priests'.[16] Thus spiritism would prove to be 'a vigorous stimulus in favor of the moral improvement of humanity' [*un vigoroso estimulo en pro del mejoramiento moral de la humanidad*] (1919: 65). Looking back over his publications, Ortiz surmised that the honour accorded to him by Cuban spiritists was due to his 'obra acerca del *Hampa afro-cubana*' [work related to *Hampa afro-cubana*] and *La filosofía penal* (1919: 66). With this statement Ortiz was suggesting that his intellectual work made sense as a public service dedicated to Cuban religious evolution. It is important to note that Ortiz conceived his lecture as an act in the service of 'republican survival' [*existencia republicana*]. He was concerned with fortifying the Republic, which led him to accuse 'many of our public men [of] *civic cowardice*' [*muchos de nuestros hombres públicos (de)* cobardia cívica] (1919: 65).

In Ortiz's thinking, the racist ethnology of Raymundo Nina Rodrigues, whom he frequently cites, allowed him to develop a racial theory of the nation: the different 'races' ought 'scientifically' to be situated at unequal stages in the evolutionary scale of culture; consequently, not all races should be expected to adapt themselves to European principles of citizenship. A 'disorderly life' [*mala vida*] was the result of 'psychic primitivism' [*primitividad psíquica*].[17] But for Ortiz it did not suffice merely to establish Cuban racial inequality; rather, he was preoccupied with the possibilities of the spiritual 'progress' [*progreso*] or 'backsliding' [*retroceso*] of the Republic. For this reason, as we shall see later, he turned to Kardecist categories relating to the evolutionist theory of the soul.

There persisted in Ortiz a fear of cultural and intellectual regression [*regresión*] a fear of the effects it could have on society, and a fear of 'contagion' [contagio]. He regarded witchcraft and sorcerers as political adversaries: 'But the inferiority of Negroes, which subjected them to a disorderly life, was due to a lack of an integral civilization, since their morality was as primitive as their intellectuality'.[18] On the other hand, Ortiz spoke from the vantage point of an imperious as well as aggressive idea of progress (1919: 221):

> It is only natural that intellectual progress bring to Cuba, as to the rest of the world, the progressive weakening of superstitions, that it instil more profound faith in ourselves and will eventually debilitate faith in the supernatural, since, as Bain has said, the greatest remedy for fear is science.[19]

'Civilized' knowledge should eliminate 'primitive' practices and penetrate their secret jargon. There should be no area outside the control of a 'civilized', overseeing White intellect. Witchcraft could be liquidated by penal and scientific means, and its materials should be held confiscated in a museum (1919: 235): 'The campaign against witchcraft should have two objectives: the immediate one of destroying the infective centres; the other, the medium-term one, of disinfecting the environment, in order to halt this evil from spreading itself'.[20]

The 'progress' of spirits toward perfection and Kardec's evolutionary ladder were implicit in the revision Ortiz undertook of the Lombrosian concept of *atavism* as it applied to the Cuban case. Although Ortiz does not cite Kardec directly, his historico-spiritualist interpretation of the African's displacement to the Cuban milieu implies more than mere criminological categories ([1906] 1973: 230–1):

> From the criminological point of view, the Afro-Cuban sorcerer is what Lombroso would call a born criminal, and this congenital quality can be attributed to all aspects of his moral backwardness, beyond his criminality. But the sorcerer is not *born* so because of atavism in the strictest sense of the word, that is as the individual's *leap backwards* in relation to the state of progress of the species that forms the social milieu to which he has to adapt himself, instead, it could be said that after being transported from Africa to Cuba it was the social milieu that, for him, unexpectedly leapt forwards, leaving him and his compatriots in the deepest darkness of their savagery, on the first steps of their psyche's evolution. For this, more suitably than according to atavism, the attributes of the sorcerer can be defined according to *psychic primitivism*; he is a *primitive* criminal, as Penta would say. In Cuba, the sorcerer and his adepts are immoral and criminal because they have not progressed; they are savages brought to a civilized country.
>
> (*Los negros brujos*, 230–1).[21]

For Ortiz, the African was essentially a criminal, not so much in the Pentian sense of a 'primitive criminal' (as cited by Ortiz himself), but because his spirit was located in a different position on the evolutionary ladder. When he states that the sorcerer and his adepts are 'immoral' and 'criminal', there remains no doubt that Ortiz is thinking about the problem in spiritist terms – terms that he would later develop in 'Las fases de la evolución religiosa' – and no longer in strictly criminological ones.

Kardec and his belief in successive reincarnations assured Ortiz of a spiritual hierarchy that superseded the framework of 'born criminality' to include 'nation', 'race' and 'progress'. Indeed, his reading of Kardec, to whom he significantly referred as 'that interesting French philosopher' [*aquel interesante filósofo francés*], came early and coincided with his studies in criminology. Ortiz himself stresses the 'simultaneity' of his early readings of Kardec and his initiation in a positivistic epistemology. It seems obvious that Kardec became a major source of inspiration for his thinking, even though Kardec's texts were not legitimized by the academy. As a young student, Ortiz was already fascinated by spiritism (1914, 9.1: 30):

> It is now twenty years ago, when in the lecture halls of my beloved University of Havana I was studying Penal Law and

attending classes with Professor González Lanuza – then the most scientific man in the Spanish dominions –, who was introducing me to the ideas of positivist criminology, whilst simultaneously I was also reading works far removed from the university, which chance had put in my hands or which my investigative curiosity fervently sought out.

It was as a result of the latter that I undertook my religious readings, which then as now delight me especially and arouse my spirit to a singular interest. It was at that time that I became acquainted with the fundamental books of spiritism, written by León Hipólito Denizart Rivail, or Allan Kardec, as he liked to call himself, reviving the name by which, according to him, he was known throughout the world, in a former incarnation during the time of the druids.

And this simultaneity of my university studies in criminology and my accidental philosophical studies of spiritist doctrine deigned that the enthusiasm already awakened in me by Lombrosian and Ferrian theories on criminality should lead me to undertake a special investigation of how that interesting French philosopher, who dared to think of himself as a reincarnated druid, thought about the same penal problems.[22]

A host of questions present themselves. Should his interest be understood as an enthusiasm made possible by the scientific features of spiritism? Is it methodologically acceptable to postulate, as Ortiz does, that the 'penal problems' of criminology and spiritism are 'the same'? Did Ortiz want to legitimize spiritism through positivism? How else then could we reasonably account for his persistent interest in the many births and deaths of the soul?

In the introduction to *La filosofía penal*, Ortiz emphatically declared: 'I am not a spiritist' [*Yo no soy espiritista*]. At the same time he insisted that spiritism shared important premises with 'Lombrosian materialism' [*(el) materialismo lombrosiano*]. It is possible that Ortiz, along with other intellectuals, felt the necessity of distancing himself from other spiritists who were not learned and 'intellectually' inclined. In his correspondence with José María Chacón, Ortiz (Gutiérrez-Vega 1982: 35–6) alluded to 'The so-called spiritist societies of Cuba, who are more concerned with being entertained by more or less serious or grotesque feats of mediumship and by superstitious, parasitic healing practices'.[23] Nevertheless, any attentive reader of his early essays comes away from them with the feeling that Ortiz in fact identifies with spiritism. But there is a certain ambiguity on his part concerning Kardec. In public, he never committed himself entirely to Kardecism, but he does concede him a revered place in both the intellectual world and that of science (1914, 9.1: 30–1):

> And a short time after my mind took that direction I became aware, not without a certain surprise, that Lombrosian materialsim and the spiritism of Allan Kardec notably coincided in not a few matters, and that one could arrive at the same criminological theories both by departing from materialist premises and being lead by the most forthright positivism, or by taking as one starting point spiritist judgements and being carried along by the most subtle idealism.[24]

Ortiz presents Kardec according to one of his favorite rhetorical devices: the *topos* of *coincidentia oppositorum*. As he will later do with tobacco and sugar in *Contrapunteo*, his poetics tries to harmonize opposite forms of thought: 'Opposites meet, one might say, and this is certainly the case in our study' [*los extremos se tocan, pudiera decirse, y ciertamente es así en nuestro estudio*] (1914, 9.1: 33). As Kardec himself indicated, spiritism and materialism share an evolutionist vein. The possibility of finding a complement in the passage from one to the other allows Ortiz to structure his book. *La filosofía penal* is, thus, a book of translation, of passage between doctrines and of transmigration of matter into spirit.

La filosofía penal is also a didactic work: it offers instruction in Kardecist doctrine in straightforward, expository prose. Ortiz assumes the reader's knowledge of positivism, but feels obliged to offer extensive quotations from Kardec. In successive chapters, he analyses the following aspects of Kardecism: the ideological bases of spiritism, the laws concerning the evolution of souls, determinism and free will, the elements of criminality, and the atavism of criminals. In all these chapters he establishes and celebrates the analogies between Kardec and Lombroso.

A central node of the translation of Kardec by Ortiz is the chapter dedicated to 'The ladder of the spirits' [*La escala de los espíritus*] which certainly impressed Ortiz and from where he derives a theory of the elite. Spiritualist evolutionism, with its ladder based on varying degrees of progress, stressed the gradual divestment of imperfections. Those with a propensity for evil are 'imperfect' spirits – in whom matter dominates the spirit. They are given to all the vices and bodily cravings that engender vile and degrading passions, such as sensualism, cruelty, covetousness and sordid avarice. Whatever the social rank they enjoy, they are the scourge of humanity, indifferent to the responsibilities of the nation. For Ortiz they are the equivalent of *born criminals*. They contrast sharply with superior spirits – in whom spirit dominates matter – who are distinguished by their desire to do good. Those pure spirits (with whom Ortiz identifies) bring together science, prudence and goodness, and seem to be the sole bearers of truth and spiritual understanding. Their language is always elevated and sublime: they are the most suited to intellectual life, are competent to make judgments on matters of right and wrong and, therefore, can be entrusted with public responsibilities. When by exception they find an earthly incarnation it is to fulfil a 'a mission of progress' [*misión de progreso*], and they offer us a model of perfection to which humanity can aspire in this world. The possibility of progress through spiritual purification must have seemed very attractive to Ortiz who, in works like his *Proyecto de código criminal cubano* [Cuban Criminal Code Bill] was preoccupied with the formulation of campaigns of 'national cleansing' [*saneamiento nacional*] (1926: XII).

In the chapter entitled 'Basis of Responsibility' [*Fundamento de la responsabilidad*], Ortiz stated that the criminal is an individual in whom a 'backward' spirit has been incarnated. This leads him to develop in a parallel way the notions of spiritual and social punishment: there is a *spiritual*, subjective responsibility based on the law of spiritual progression; there is a *human*, objective responsibility based on social law. Ortiz added (1914, 9.4: 288) that: [t]he law of conservation imposes on society – according to and beyond spiritist philosophy – the necessity of fighting for itself and its integrity, and from this necessity both spiritists and positivists are able to derive the reason for punishment.'[25] In this way, Ortiz managed to lay an absolute foundation for the notion of punishment (1914, 9.14: 289): 'The progress of man, that is, the progress of the spirit, these are the psychological and subjective end of punishment, so it is in this world as the progress of beings is in the infinite universe'.[26] Undoubtedly, Ortiz put high on his agenda the necessity of operating on solid ground in the social organization of the nation.

In *Los negros brujos* Ortiz himself recognized that some repressive propositions could be considered rather threatening or inquisitorial. His extremely problematic position with regard to the figures of the sorcerer and the African demanded the theological foundations of a penal philosophy. That evolutionary theology allowed him to find a humanitarian meaning in the repression of cultural practices harmful to the Republic. Ortiz felt attracted by the moral force of Kardec's principles: there is progress, but it is threatened by the regressive movements of history. The possibility of applying scientific conceptualizations to the moral order ensured the *renovatio* of Cuban society. In a remarkable passage in *La reconquista de*

América (p. 26) he wrote: 'There are no fatally superior or inferior peoples, nor civilizations; there are only advances and regressions, differences in the integral march of humanity'.[27]

Let us now return to *La filosofía penal*. In the chapters on the ladder of the spirits, and free will, Ortiz is particularly interested in the role played by 'prudent' spirits, who come to earth to fulfil a 'mission of progress'. In this conception two opposing projects coincided: one of constructing a space for a learned elite, with all the privileges of full citizenship, and another of opening the gates of progress to other 'backward' spirits who did not have the capacity of articulating their own projects. The political issues are inescapable, of course. The production of citizens for the Republic was possible, though complex, and it had to be based on the science of criminology, surveillance, discipline and the hierarchy of an evolutionist spirituality. *La reconquista de América* offers a particularly forceful – and disturbing – commentary (p. 47): 'White Cubans, those of us who constitute the core of our nationality, should be ever more educated so that we can keep republican life free of Hispanicizing or Africanizing regressions'.[28]

How was the *renovatio* that permitted the ascent of inferior spirits to be achieved? From the theological point of view, the notion of free will contained the possibility of spiritual transcendence. Since the spirit is essentially neither bad nor good, Ortiz found an alternative to the biological determinism of *atavism* in the reincarnation propounded by Kardec (1914, 9.2: 131):

> Just as we have men who are good or bad since infancy, so there are Spirits which are good or bad from the start, with the one capital difference being that the child's instincts are fully formed, whereas the Spirit, once it is formed, is neither good nor bad, but contains all tendencies, and by virtue of its free will can take one or another direction.[29]

Consequently, the spiritist version of *atavism* consists fundamentally of an impasse in the spiritual progress that takes place in the passage from one life to another. While superior spirits continually progress, Ortiz suggests that the *atavistic* ones merely represent a regression in relation to the state of advancement of the rest.

Reversions, however should have no place in the construction of the nation. It is here that the notion of the transmigrating soul becomes crucial. Ortiz's political thinking cannot be understood without reference to Kardec and to the possibility that everyone may form part of spiritual progress. This notion of 'progress' is conceived as an organic part of biological evolution (1914, 9.1: 34):

Spiritist philosophy springs from the existence of a supreme Being, God; creator of all things and of the immortal existence of all the spirits.

But spiritism may be distinguished from other religious credos because it has ended up being an *evolutionist theory of the soul*, certainly an ancient theory, but one whose modern revival is owed to spiritism and theosophy. In effect, spirits are created imperfect, and their existence lived out according to an infinite series of painful trials which awaken it, fortify its faculties and raise it to the higher stages of psychic evolution, in the same way that according to biological materialists – Sergi, for example – the beings who enter their own visual field, from amoebae to the great mammals, progress, are transformed, and become intelligent through the pain of the infinite series of *trials* presented to them by their constant contact with their environment.

The purpose of the spirit is to progress, ascend, always raise itself and approach God. In the natural history of the spirits there are no regressions; there might be impasses, stretches of stillness, but never reversion.[30]

On the other hand, the harmonization of materialism and spirituality is translated into the 'theory of beauty' which Ortiz adopts from Kardec. Kardec explained racial differences by establishing a correlation between physical beauty and the evolutionary ladder of the spirits. His racial aesthetic situated Blacks next to animals. Ortiz cites Kardec (1914, 9.4: 261):

A Negro may seem beautiful to another Negro, in the same way a cat may to another cat, but he is not beautiful in an absolute sense; because his crude features and thick lips reveal the materiality of his instincts; they may very well express violent passions; but they could not adjust themselves to the delicate nuances and modulations of sentiment of a distinguished Spirit.[31]

Thus, in the evolution of the spirit, Blacks would gradually lose the physical features that characterize them to become more similar to Whites.

The embryonic concept of transculturation is found in Ortiz's appropriation of the 'reincarnationist credo'. In his somewhat utopian essay 'La cubanidad y los negros' [Cubanness and Blacks] (1939) he elaborates the theory of the *ajiaco* [Cuban stew] as an emblem of nationality. Ortiz interprets the 'amorous embraces' of *mestizaje* [miscegenation] as 'foreshadowing a universal peace amongst races ... as a possible, desirable and future deracialization of humanity' (p. 6).[32] In the heightened tension of the 1930s Ortiz was rejecting racial hierarchies and rethinking the cultural and public space occupied by Blacks in Cuba. Afro-Cubans were no longer viewed with distrust and hostility. But Ortiz did not abandon the fundamental Kardecist notions of spiritual progress presented here as 'deracialization'. Similarly, he replaced the category of *mestizaje* with the concept of transmigration, in this way enriching its interpretative possibilities (1939: 11):[33]

> We do not believe that there have been more transcendental human characteristics for Cubanness than these continuous, radical and contrastive geographical, economic and social *transmigrations* of populations; than that perennial transitoriness of objectives and than that life always uprooted from its inhabited land, and always out of phase with its host society [my emphasis].[34]

An outline of the notion of transmigration as being spacially and temporally out of phase is already apparent in *Los negros brujos* and *La filosofía penal* where Ortiz applied the spiritist doctrine of the evolution of souls. 'Cubanness' was fundamental in the formulation of the concept of transculturation, and it allowed the development of new forms of interpreting the national culture by profiting from the Kardecist conceptualizations of the spiritual order. In accordance with the spiritual 'regression' developed in *La filosofía penal* or the African's backwardness in relation to his environment in *Los negros brujos*, 'Cubanness' retains the idea of displacement to explain the position of Blacks in Cuban culture. It is worth lingering over the following passage where Ortiz allows one clearly to see the spiritist aspect of his formulation of transculturation (1939: 11, 12):

> With their bodies the Negroes brought their spirits ... but not their institutions nor their implements ... there was no other human grouping undergoing such a profound and continuous *transmigration* of environment, culture, class and con-sciousness. Like the Indians, they passed from one culture to another more advanced one; unlike them, however, they did not suffer on their native land, *believing that after death they would pass to the invisible side of their own Cuban world,* but, in a more cruel twist of fate, they crossed the ocean in agony, *believing that even after death they would have to*

> *cross over it again to live with their lost ancestors over there in Africa.*[35]

Transculturation is inextricably linked to the spiritist tradition. In spite of an absence of explicit references in Ortiz's last texts, we cannot continue to ignore the philosophical contribution of Kardec to his thought. In Ortiz we find the nationalization, historicization and anthropologization of Kardec's theory of the transmigration of souls. This is the *renovatio* that continued to fascinate Ortiz. Transculturation was constructed taking as its point of departure the categories transmigration, displacement, spiritual progress and evolution. I cannot comment here on *Contrapunteo*, but it will not be difficult for the reader to discover how much denser and richer the concept of transculturation becomes in the context of Kardecism. For Ortiz the history of humanity is also a history of souls in transmigration. The lesson Ortiz drew from Kardec silently resounds through his foundational texts of Cuban nationality: the spirit cannot be reduced to the body.

Notes

1 We should like to thank the Institute of Literature and Linguistics of Havana for permitting us to consult the Ortiz archive, and the Fundación Fernando Ortiz for its hospitality. We are profoundly grateful to Cristián Roa de la Carrera and Carlos Rincón for their numerous critical comments concerning this critical study. We are also grateful to John Perivolaris for his translation, and to Paul Firbas, David Carrasco, James E. Irby, Karl D. Uitti and Michael Wood for their valuable suggestions and generous assistance.

2 *En cada momento presente de la vida hay un paso de envejecimiento y de renovación ... Renovarse que es morir y renacer para tornar a fallecer y a revivir. Cada instante vital es una creación, una recreación. Es una cópula del pasado, de las potenciales supervivencias que el individuo trae encarnadas consigo, y del presente, de las posibles circunstancias que el ambiente aporta; de cuya contingente conjunción con la individualidad nace el porvenir, que es la variación renovadora.*

3 For a detailed and important discussion of Ortiz's reception and the evolution of *transculturation*, see the recent prologue by Fernando Coronil to the reprint of the English translation of *Contrapunteo*. A 'postmodern' reading of *Contrapunteo* is offered by Benítez Rojo in his remarkable *The Repeating Island* (1992).

4 For the principal facts and the bibliographic sources, see García-Carranza (1970). See also García-Carranza, Suárez Suárez and Quesada Morales (1996).

5 Cabrera, one of the founders of the Partido Liberal Autonomista de Cuba [Autonomist Liberal party of Cuba], is the author of *Cuba y sus jueces* [Cuba and her judges] (1887). In New York he founded the political, literary and cultural review *Cuba y América* [Cuba and America] (1897–8; Havana 1899–1917) of which Ortiz was a collaborator. Cabrera was, furthermore, a founder member of the Cuban Academy of History (from 1910).

6   A brief history of the *Hispanocubana* and Ortiz's role is provided by Carlos del Toro (1996).

7   Whilst he occupied his consular post in Genoa, between 1902 and 1905, Ortiz was a disciple of the criminologist Cesare Lombroso and Enrico Ferri. As critics have already pointed out, Ortiz proudly traced his intellectual lineage to Lombroso. His first great theme would be precisely marginality, *mala vida* [disorderly life] and religious phenomena. He sought to delimit a scientific object, the *hampa afrocubana* [Afro-Cuban underworld] or the *negros brujos* [black sorcerers], which might also contribute to the development of ethnographic and criminological studies in Cuba. Furthermore, it proves to be very significant that it was in Lombroso's review, the *Archivio di Psichiatria, Neuropatologia, Antropologia Criminale e Medicina Legale*, that Ortiz first published in Italian the articles which were to become his first book: 'La criminalita dei negri in Cuba'; 'Superstizione criminose in Cuba'; e 'II suicidio fra i negri' [The Criminality of the Negroes in Cuba; Criminal Superstitions in Cuba; and Suicide amongst the Negroes]. Later, Lombroso would contribute a prologue to his book. All of this forms part of a series of intellectual relations with the metropolitan centres. In the final decades of the nineteenth century an extraordinary amount of activity in Europe was dedicated to the reform of the penal systems. The debate involved doctors, philosophers, jurists and progressive lawyers, all of whom laid the foundations for penal reform according to the criminological discipline of the time. It is in this context that one can appreciate the great importance of *L'Uomo delinquente* [Criminal Man] (1876; 1878), which was based on a study of inmates in Italian prisons, a book where Lombroso finds the motive for criminality in hereditary 'regression' and also in disorders such as epilepsy. Lombroso's book generated an extensive debate about the notions of 'atavism', the genetic determinism of criminality and 'degeneration'. See, amongst others, Robert Nye's book (1984).

8   See, for example, Jorge Ibarra (1990), where he interprets transculturation as the dialectical surmounting of Ortiz's previous ideas. Also relevant are the essays by Thomas Bremer (1993), Diana Iznaga (1989) and Antonio Melis (1987).

9   For a study of Raymundo Nina Rodrigues, see Ventura (1991).

10 On another occasion it would be necessary to study the broader questions relating to the reception of Kardec by the Latin American intelligentsia. Kardec was extensively translated and published in nineteenth-century Spain and Latin America, largely thanks to the work of the Society of Spiritist Propagation of Barcelona (Sociedad Barcelonesa Propagadora del Espiritismo). Even though it was disseminated in the form of popular texts, the influence of spiritist doctrines spread remarkably in Latin American intellectual circles and in poets such as Rubén Darío and Leopoldo Lugones. For example, see Hess (1991) on the Brazilian manifestation of spiritism, and Gramuglio (1994) for Lugones. On the spiritist dimension of the Mexican intellectual Francisco Madero and the importance of spiritualist currents for José Martí, see Rafael Rojas' study (1995). For Kardec's influence in Cuba, see Argüelles and Hodge (1991). Equally, it would be important to situate Ortiz in the context of the Cuban Race War of 1912 against the Partido Independiente de Color [Independent Party of Colour], when the Black veterans of the War of Independence demanded their own political space and were severely repressed. Aline Helg (1995) includes a study of the journalistic 'sources' of *Los negros brujos* in the period leading to this war.

11 *Espiritistas! Quien no participa de vuestra mística, serenamente os dice: Sois fieles de una sublime fe! Acaso seáis los que con mayor pureza os aproximáis al ideal de marchar hacia Dios por el amor y la ciencia!*

12   *Ningún trabajo más arduo que el de coleccionar los datos necesarios para este libro, durante el cual le hemos seguido paso á paso. El investigador tropezaba día tras día con la eterna dificultad que hace en nuestro país infructuoso el esfuerzo de los hombres de ciencia: nada existía hecho con anterioridad; era preciso crearlo todo, ordenando los pocos datos incompletos y aislados que llegaban á su noticia, y para colmo de males la fe del autor estrellábase contra la apatía del mundo científico local y de las esferas del gobierno, que se preocupaban poco con que un* desocupado *escribiese monografías de ñáñigos, cosa bien trivial por cierto al lado de los grandes intereses de la política.*

13   *El culto brujo es, en fin, socialmente negativo con relación al mejoramiento de nuestra sociedad, porque dada la primitividad que le es característica, totalmente amoral, contribuye a retener las conciencias de los negros incultos en los bajos fondos de la barbarie africana.*

14   *Un obstáculo a la civilización, principalmente de la población de color ... por ser la expresión más bárbara del sentimiento religioso desprovisto del elemento moral.*

15   *En Cuba tres corrientes religiosas luchan por la vida, cuando no por el predominio: el fetichismo africano, especialmente lucumí; el cristianismo en sus varias derivasciones más o menos puras, especialmente el catolicismo, y el filosofismo religioso contemporáneo, especialmente el espiritismo.*

16   *El fetichismo es la* religión amoral, *el catolicismo es la* religión moral, *el espiritismo es la* moral areligiosa *sin dogmas, ni ritos, ni ídolos ni sacerdotes.*

17   Ortiz's formation on the one hand coincided with the context of Africa's imperialist 'discovery', social Darwinism, the modernization of systems of control and surveillance, the development of criminology as a science, and the mixture of aestheticism and violence that characterize the appropriation of the 'primitive' world by modernity. For Lombroso, in the general framework of Darwinism, the concept of atavism postulated the regression to a primitive condition. The term itself comes from Latin: *atavus*, ancestor. It was a leap backwards. Lombroso found certain physical qualities in the *criminale nato* and, above all, a total lack of morality. On the one hand, Lombroso presented the death penalty as a solution; whilst on the other, he suggested a type of reform that would transform the environmental factors affecting the criminal.

18   *Pero la inferioridad del negro, la que le sujetaba al mal vivir era debida a falta de civilización integral, pues tan primitiva era su moralidad como su intelectualidad.*

19   *Natural es que el progreso intelectual traiga a Cuba, como al resto del mundo, la progresiva debilitación de las supersticiones, infunda más fe en nosotros mismos y vaya borrando la que se tiene en lo sobrenatural, pues como ha dicho Bain, el gran remedio contra el miedo es la ciencia.*

20   *La campaña contra la brujería debe tener dos objetivos: uno inmediato, la destrucción de los focos infectivos; mediato el otro, la desinfección del ambiente, para impedir que se mantenga y se reproduzca el mal.*

21   *El brujo afro-cubano, desde el punto de vista criminológico, es lo que Lombroso llamaría un delincuente nato, y este carácter de congénito puede aplicarse a todos sus atrasos morales, además de a su delincuencia. Pero el brujo* nato *no lo es por atavismo, en el sentido riguroso de esta palabra, es decir, como* un salto atrás *del individuo con relación al estado de progreso de la especie que forma el medio social al cual aquél debe adaptarse; más bien puede decirse que al ser transportado de Africa a Cuba fue el medio social el que para él saltó improvisadamente hacia adelante, dejándolo con sus compatriotas en las profundidades de su salvajismo, en los primeros escalones de la evolución de su*

psiquis. Por esto, con mayor propiedad que por el atavismo, pueden definirse los caracteres del brujo por la primitividad psíquica; *es un delincuente* primitivo, *como diría Penta. El brujo y sus adeptos son en Cuba inmorales y delincuentes porque no han progresado; son salvajes traídos a un país civilizado.*

22   *Hace ya unos cuatro lustros, cuando en las aulas de mi muy querida universidad de la Habana cursaba los estudios de Derecho Penal y el programa del Pro. González Lanuza – entonces el más científico en los dominios españoles – me iniciaba en las ideas del positivismo criminológico, simultaneaba esas lecturas escolares con obras muy agenas a la universidad, que el acaso ponía a mi alcance o que mi curiosidad investigadora buscaba con fervor.*

   Entre estas últimas estaban las lecturas religiosas, que antes como ahora me producen especial deleite y despiertan en mi ánimo singular interés. Por aquel entonces conocí los libros fundamentales del espiritismo, escritos por León Hipólito Denizart Rivail, o sea Allan Kardec, como él gustó de llamarse, reviviendo el nombre con que, según él, fué conocido en el mundo cuando una encarnación anterior, en los tiempos druídicos.

   Y quiso la simultaneidad de los estudios universitarios sobre criminología con los accidentales estudios filosóficos sobre la doctrina espiritista, que el entusiasmo que en mi despertaran las teorías lombrosianas y ferrianas sobre la criminalidad me llevase a investigar especialmente cómo pensaba acerca de los mismos problemas penales aquel interesante filósofo francés, que osaba presentarse como un druida redivivo.

23   *las sociedades llamadas espiritistas de Cuba, más entretenidas con mediumnidades más o menos serias o grotescas y con prácticas de curanderismo supersticioso y parasitario.*

24   *Y a poco que mi mente tomó esa dirección hube de percatarme, no sin cierta sorpresa, que el materialismo lombrosiano y el espiritualismo de Allan Kardec coincidían notablemente en no pocos extremos, y que a unas mismas teorías criminológicas se podría ir partiendo de premisas materialistas y conducido por el positivismo más franco, que arrancando de juicios espiritualistas y llevado por el idealismo más sutil.*

25   *La ley de conservación impone a la sociedad – dentro y fuera de la filosofía espiritista – la necesidad de luchar por sí y por su integridad, y de esta necesidad los espiritistas como los positivistas hacen derivar la razón de castigo.*

26   *El progreso del hombre, es decir, el progreso del espíritu, he aquí la finalidad psicológica y subjetiva de la pena así en este mundo como en el universo infinito el progreso de los seres.*

27   *No hay pueblos, ni civilizaciones fatalmente superiores ó inferiores; hay sólo adelantos ó atrasos, diferencias en la marcha integral de la humanidad.* What might seem a curious use of accents in this passage and others of Ortiz was part of common usage in the first decades of this century (eds).

28   *Seamos los cubanos blancos, los que constituímos el nervio de la nacionalidad, más cultos todavía para poder mantener la via republicana independiente de retrocesos hispanizantes o africanizantes.*

29   *Así como tenemos hombres buenos y malos desde la infancia, así también hay Espíritus buenos y malos desde el principio, con la diferencia capital, de que el niño tiene instintos completamente formados, al paso que el Espírtu, al ser formado, no es ni bueno ni malo, sinó que tiene todas las tendencias, y en virtud de su libre albedrío toma una u otra dirección.*

30   *La filosofía espiritista arranca de la existencia de un Ser supremo, Dios, creador de todas las cosas y de la existencia inmortal de los espíritus.*

Pero el espiritismo se distingue de otros credos religiosos, porque viene a ser una teoría evolucionista del alma, *teoría ciertamente antigua, pero cuya revivencia moderna se debe al espiritismo y a la teosofía. En efecto, los espíritus son creados imperfectos, y su existencia se desenvuelve a lo largo de una serie infinita de pruebas dolorosas que lo despiertan, le fortalecen, le fortalecen sus facultades y lo elevan hacia los estados superiores de la evolución psíquica, de la misma manera que según los biólogos materialistas – Sergi, por èjemplo – los seres que entran dentro del campo de su visualidad, desde la ameba a los grandes mamíferos, progresan y se transforman y se hacen inteligentes por el dolor en la serie infinita de* pruebas *que supone el contacto constante con el medio ambiente.*

El fin del espíritu es progresar, ascender, elevarse siempre y acercarse a Dios. En la historia natural de los espíritus no hay regresiones; puede haber estancamientos, situaciones de quietud, pero nunca de retroceso.

31   *El negro puede ser bello para el negro, como lo es un gato para otro, pero no es bello en el sentido absoluto; porque sus rasgos bastos y sus labios gruesos acusan la materialidad de los instintos; pueden muy bien expresar pasiones vilentas; pero no podrían acomodarse a los matices delicados del sentimiento y a las modulaciones de un Espíritu distinguido.*

32   *augurales de una paz universal de las sangres (...) de una posible, deseable y futura desracialización de la humanidad.*

33   Always a compulsive rewriter, Ortiz recycled this paragraph in *Contrapunteo* as part of his discussion of the notion of *transculturation.*

34   *No creemos que haya habido factores humanos más trascendentes para la cubanidad que esas continuas, radicales y contrastantes* transmigraciones *geográficas, económicas y sociales de los pobladores; que esa perenne transitoriedad de los propósitos y que esa via siempre en desarraigo de la tierra habitada, siempre en desajuste con la sociedad sustentadora.*

35   Los negros trajeron con sus cuerpos sus espíritus ... *pero no sus instituciones, ni su instrumentario. ... No hubo otro elemento humano en más profunda y continua* transmigración *de ambiente, de cultura, de clases y de conciencias. Pasaron de una cultura a otra más potente, como los indios; pero estos sufrieron en su tierra nativa,* creyendo que al morir pasaban al lado invisible de su propio mundo cubano; *y los negros, con suerte más cruel, cruzaron el mar en agonía y* pensando que aún después de muertos tenían que repasarlo para revivir allá en Africa con sus padres perdidos. See also the translation by Harriet de Onís, in *Cuban Counterpoint*, pages 101–2.

2 | Puerto Rico afloat

Doris Sommer

Para Roberto Unger, tupi *and* not tupi

'Puerto Ricans Say No', reads the bold-faced title of a *Boston Globe* feature from 15 November 1993. The defeat of the statehood referendum did not really cause disbelief, or just relief, exactly. But the follow-up article does start with frank surprise. 'It wasn't supposed to turn out this way' begins the still startled journalist (Rezendes 1993b). This Boston-based newsman was writing with vicarious triumph and pride, apparently following an insular line of argument against statehood that fears 'normalization' as cultural suicide and prefers the anomalous commonwealth status. 'It's a vote against assimilation', he quotes Miguel Hernández Agosto, president of the Popular Democratic Party, 'a vote in favour of all that the Puerto Rican people love and value' (Rezendes 1993a).

Missing from both articles is any mention of a different decision not to decide, when the same party, the Popular Democratic Party [Partido Popular Democrático], could not get an implicit ratification in 1992 of Spanish as Puerto Rico's official language, the local language that the Party's referendum only months earlier understood to be the lasting vehicle for nominating beauty queens and Olympic champions and the means by which to establish Puerto Rico as an international contender, even if the island did become a regular state of the Union. A 1992 gubernatorial victory presumably *would* have asserted something that the islanders love and value. But opposition candidate Pedro Roselló won instead, promising, among other things, to revoke the law that made Spanish Puerto Rico's official language. Evidently, four centuries of Spanish-only language requirements, centuries of slaves knowing too much when they knew other languages, may have been a caution against restrictive preferences, as Arcadio Díaz Quiñones has argued so poignantly in his piecing together of *La memoria rota* [The Broken

Memory] (1993). Neither this resolution to leave the language issue unresolved, nor any other apparently equivocal move that keeps the island's politics afloat, appears in the northern newspaper. As a result, the *Globe* registers surprise, instead of suggesting a pattern in Puerto Rican politics of pre-empting problems by not presuming to solve them, a pattern imposed, to some extent, by US laws (the Foraker Law of 1900 and its sequels) that leave so little room for manoeuvre.[1] It is a holding pattern that Antonio Pedreira had already deplored in his 1934 essay, *Insularismo* [Insularism] as 'docile' indecisiveness, and that René Marqués would decry a generation later, after Albizu Campos and other militants, not masses, had lost the armed struggle, and docile became a synonym for *aplatanado* [listless] which rhymes with *afeminado* [effeminate]. Pedreira's 1934 publication had coincided with the mass violence that exploded from the sugar-workers' strike, and the founding of Puerto Rico's Communist Party (Flores 1979: 81–2). It was just a couple of years after women began to vote, and Pedreira was apparently nervous about misdirected meddling in Puerto Rico's national construction; he was also convinced that really constructive activity was wanting. The country was stuck, he wrote, 'insular' and undirected, a floating political body internally rent by an indecisive and undecidable mix of races. What the nation needed was to pull up anchor and make headway towards modernity (Pedreira 1942: 16, 79).

The pro-statehood New Progressive Party [Partido Nuevo Progresista] (PNP) must have read the indecisive news in November as a vindication of Pedreira's impatience, even if the party took credit for a near-victory (everybody was claiming victory). But the Boston paper echoed much of the opposition by virtually hailing the defeat as heroic, despite the vote's almost even split between status quo and statehood, and so few voices for full independence. The lure of equal statehood boiled down here to the dubious privileges of voting at presidential polls, and staying on the federal dole.[2] For the decisive half of the voters, these rights would be a mere sop, like the lentil soup that desperate Esau accepted from wily Jacob in exchange for the hungry brother's birthright. The biblical analogy comes from an independentist version of the Bible's cautionary tale. It is a story, by Margot Arce de Vázquez, of unequal twins and tricky legal foundations. In 'Esau' (1967), she recasts Isaac's beloved son, too busy with work to worry about the future, as the beloved and beleaguered island where rights to national recognition have been sold out to tempting convenience. (In his *The Autobiography of an Ex-Colored Man*, James Weldon Johnson complains that he has sold his African 'primitive' birthright 'for a mess of pottage' [1995, p. 211]).

If the *Globe* articles evoke Arce's new Esau, there is no reason to cover over the probable political differences between them. After all, my own text does not pretend to be a seamless argument, much less a procreative patriarchal body like Pedreira's. Unlike Noah, drunk and naked before his sons, one of whom looks upon his nakedness and is punished (and probably disappointed), I have nothing to hide. No pretence of participatory continuity in my spotty readings, and certainly no programmatic presumption about Puerto Rican history. So it is only fair to frame the difference: the news from New England is an outsider's celebration of perceived cultural courage, his applause for the audacity of Puerto Rican pride. And the 'Esau' essay, on the other hand, is an islander's dirge for her disinherited and disheartened brethren; it is also an exhortation to act, to claim the national birthright of independence. Action for Arce, it will be noticed, means the act of claiming, a speech act. She does not lament the loss of military opportunities, nor does she now urge her countrymen to take up arms; rather, she grieves over Puerto Rico's feeble voice. And exactly what message should her countrymen have voiced, instead of submitting to the ventriloquism of Big Brother? The message should have been a thunderous 'No'.

Here, almost mysteriously, the articles from Boston ('Puerto Ricans Say No') and from Borinquen collude.[3] As if by some hidden design, an echo chamber takes shape between texts that could not be talking directly to one another. The liberating speech act that Arce longed to hear the island commit was to fire back a resounding refusal to collaborate in its ignominy. 'The Puerto Rican people did not know how to say a virile "No!" through the mouths of their leaders, and settled for compromise. Instead of cleaving to the principle of our inalienable rights, they sacrificed them in exchange for some reforms which actually meant little in liberalizing the colonial situation.' (1980: 262).[4] That simple and powerful message finally did resonate over the gulf between island and mainland 25 years later, sounding loud and clear at least as far as the pages of a sometimes provincial *Globe*.

Once the echo begins to reverberate, it picks up vibrations form another, unforgettable voice, that of José de Diego. His resonance in Arce's article is no mystery at all. In fact she remembers him lovingly in the sentence just before her lament over a nation unable to say 'no'. Fifty years earlier, after US imperial power had been ratified by Puerto Rican allies, de Diego (1980 [1916]) wrote something truly memorable, nothing short of a masterful manifesto, short though it was. With the intentional bite of concision, he ended simply, 'No'. 'Crisp, solid, decisive as a hammer blow, this is the virile word that should inflame our lips and save our honour in these sad days of anachronistic imperialism' (de Diego 1980: 131). 'Yes' may be useful for some things, he coyly admits after this first sentence, but (131–3):

> In political evolution, in the struggle for freedom, the affirmative adverb is almost always useless and always deadly … The *sí* is noble and good for melody and rhythm, for fantasy and love; but for protest, for impetus, for laying hold, for anger, for anathema, for dry and explosive hatred, the lightning flash *NO* …
>
> We must learn to say NO: arch the lips, relax the chest, tense up all the vocal muscles and powers of will, and shout out that O of the NO! It might resound through America and the world, and to the very heavens, more effectively than the roar of guns.

De Diego had good reason to be confident; Puerto Ricans had in fact already armed themselves against an empire, successfully, by simply saying 'no'. I know this from Pedreira, who celebrates two different occasions when compatriots applied their peace-loving, what *he* called 'passive', nature to a pose of heroic resistance. The nationally legitimating effect of nay-saying in both cases is reported in a section of his book wisely and paradoxically called 'Afirmación puertorriqueña' [Puerto Rican Affirmation]. The first case was in 1810, when an agent of the Spanish army set up a base on the island from which to recruit soldiers to fight against Venezuelan patriots. The very next day he found a flat refusal posted to his door; it was a mixture of outrage at seeing Puerto Rican cordiality misread as cowering, and an unmistakable sympathy for Caracas over Castile.[5] The other heroic 'no' was heard in 1864, when Spain planned to transfer the Puerto Rican Battalion to Santo Domingo, where patriots were routing the imperial army. 'Compañeros', begins the manifesto that obstructed mobilization,

> Until when will we allow the despots from Spain to take advantage of our inaction? … The *jibaros*, sons of Agüeybaná the Brave, have not lost all shame yet and will know how to prove to their executioners … that whilst they are easy to govern as long as they believe they are being treated justly, they will not tolerate being abused with impunity by them.[6]

> (Pedreira 1942: 179–80)

Puerto Rican history was already its own model of heroic refusal. And José de Diego could, as I have written earlier, count on the patriotic resonance of a stalwart (not to say virile) NO. But now I want to suggest another reason for so highly esteeming the simple slogan, an unspoken reason behind de Diego's reasoning about NO being the only word with real political purchase. My literary critical inference has little to do with his specific renunciation of sugar-producing collaborators after he had defended them, and more to do with the general value of 'no' that doesn't get lost in translation from Spanish to English.[7] De Diego suggests as much by pausing to consider the alternative 'sí', its brevity and harmony in Romance languages contrasting with the clumsier Latin equivalents (1980: 131), and presumably with the cacophonic 'yes' in English. It is clear that, from Spanish to English the words of affirmation do not match up, and the asymmetry opens up a space, perhaps, for misinterpretation. When a Spanish speaker hears that English word, does he sometimes wonder at the insistently sibilant 's' at the end, where it might be a hiss of disapproval or the totemic sound of a serpent stalking its prey? And is it possible that an English listener might hear in a Spanish 'sí' not a simple endorsement but an invitation to look at something and thus keep a question open?

'No', by contrast, is as smooth and hard as a bullet; it may in fact be the only politically significant word that is so firm a sound and a substance, so impervious to interpretation, that it alone can safely be used. 'No' is not vulnerable to ventriloquism, nor is it a traffic problem in translations, literally moving meaning from one place to another. Shuttling back and forth is, of course, the more general problem for Puerto Ricans and their language. The imperial relationship keeps an entire population on move, or potentially so, to the extent that Luis Rafael Sánchez makes a hysterical joke about Puerto Rican national identity being grounded in the *guagua aérea*, or air shuttle service that has transported millions of Puerto Ricans between the mainland and the island since the 1950s. Puerto Rico becomes literally a nation of *Luftmenschen*. Mercifully, though, one word, one possession at least, does not tarnish on the trips. NO remains intact and unambiguous.

Is it really safe, though? The very coherence of the word, its traveller-friendly usage, is a kind of betrayal. The problem with 'no' is precisely that it translates so easily, that it is as natural here as it is there, and floats effortlessly between its linguistic homes. The very word that refuses intimacy with empire produces that intimacy. 'No' is a weapon of self-defence that turns out to be a deconstructive trap, a cry of resistance that begins to sound like the moan of irresistible attraction. 'No' treacherously turns its coat, its only clear message, despite de Diego's painstakingly pronounced refusal to collaborate, is its own translatability, the essence of a movable, but not hysterical, politics. I choose not write 'hysterical', a word used against people who are too active to stay put, against women, Jews, blacks, rebellious nations; I choose not to say it because the movement may not be a political disorder at all, but rather a strategy for survival, a strategy that Luis Muñoz Rivera, was calling a *posibilismo* to counterract de Diego's refusal, because it was impossibly dogmatic to fetishize the Spanish or English words for citizenship, autonomy and independence, and more enabling to navigate a practical course between terms.[8]

De Diego himself seems to have had survival in mind, if 'no' is the only right answer to any political question. Even if the word was not destabilizing for him, it was evidently the key to a politics of resistance, not the spirit of positive programmes. Why is it politic only to resist? Are deals never struck, concessions never made? De Diego's posture may come from occupying the already untenable social ground of landowner (a losing ground for coffee growers and slowly deteriorating for everyone else), so that politics always put one in an unequal, and unenviable, relationship. And this is the point, for a privileged Puerto Rican whose historical imagination assumed unfavourable asymmetries. Conditions had evidently not been propitious for an affirmation of nationhood when Spain ruled, nor was an independent project being ratified or celebrated now that the Americans were in power. Where positive pronouncements seemed precarious, the only honourable thing to say was 'no': We want neither unhappy assimilation nor ignominious autonomy. Paradoxically, by saying the opposite, Luis Muñoz Marín's protopopulist and pragmatist father provided the mirror image: saying yes to various possibilities was to profess none of them, to refuse political fetishes.[9] For both de Diego and Muñoz Rivera, national affirmation meant a series of refusals; whereas one denied that a Puerto Rican could be anyone else, the other rejected bold definition, preferring to keep his language loose enough to win some national ground.

These are patterns that Pedreira might have perceived, but evidently deplored too as a lingering adolescence; only children affirm themselves by saying 'no' to adults, or by slipping between the cracks of convention. Puerto Rican politics persisted, for Pedreira, in a reactive binary tension that was unstable and needed a third stage, after colonial infancy and nineteenth-century youthful autonomy. And it needed a third element too, a synthesizing and civilizing intelligentsia that would unravel the racial conflicts and pull the island toward a mature national feeling (Pedreira 1942: 15; Flores 1993b: 21).

This assumes, of course, that politics plays in dialectical rhythms of conflict and synthesis, or in predictable organic patterns of birth, growth and decay; and Pedreira's brand of organicist, naturalist and finally racist thinking has already been the butt of important critiques by Juan Flores (1979; 1993b), Juan Gelpí (1993), and Arcadio Díaz Quiñones (1984; 1992), among others. My question here is whether Pedreira's impatience with impermanence should not be another focus of critique, one that would find him strangely allied to a range of dialecticians and definitive solution seekers. José Luis Gónzalez (1989a) disengages from them, in discursive practice if not in theory, by adding to Pedreira's triadic neatness that dangerous supplement of a fourth floor to national history, a construct now open to unpredictable heights (cf. Flores 1993c).[10] Is there no – perhaps postmodern – politics that acknowledges insoluble tensions as dynamic sites of construction? And is there no particularly Puerto Rican politics of dignified and sophisticated indecisiveness that I am reading out of – or into – responsible nay-sayers? Can we perhaps hear a suggestive resonance with Brazil, where the standard and self-congratulatory terms of political culture would surely translate the demeaning word 'docility' into pragmatic and non-confrontational 'cordiality'. And the contradiction between economic liberalism and cultural conservatism so characteristic of Puerto Rican politics, is that not called pragmatic when it is proposed for the United States by theorists like Daniel Bell in his *The Cultural Contradictions of Capitalism?* If we could hear the theme and variations in the chorus of cautious and committed islanders, from those who aborted the 1810 conscription through to those who frustrated the November 1993 referendum, it would send echo waves directly to the great ideologue of ethical and strategic resistance; that is to Eugenio María de Hostos.[11] This is the Hostos that my colleague Richard Rosa is teaching me to read, Hostos the novelist who kept his autobiographical hero Bayoán floating between dreams of Antillean autonomy and desires for Spanish enlightenment, the man who wrote the pages of his *Diario* with one hand and rewrote and or unwrote them with the other, the ideologue in constant geographical and political shuttles who never landed anywhere because landing was never really satisfying or safe.[12] On one side, generations of unsutured blood-letting in the rest of Latin American was caution enough against armed conflict, before internal bleeding could be diagnosed by writers like René Marqués as the suicidal cost of indignity; and on the other side, a defensive attitude towards the Spanish language limited his hopes for Antillean sovereignty.[13] Black slavery in liberated republics on one side of the sea, and on the other imperial condescension to creative autonomists. Where was one to land? Hostos meditated on this question for a long, long, time, all the while staying afloat.

Notes

1   The Foraker Act was approved by the US Congress in 1900 and established the colonial relationship between the United States and Puerto Rico. According to its terms and to assist US sugar and other commercial interests, the island came under a US tariff system. Nevertheless, the US Constitution was not applicable to Puerto Rico and Puerto Ricans had to wait until 1917 to be granted US citizenship. Subsequently, according to a US Supreme Court ruling Puerto Rico was designated as a 'non-incorporated territory', possessed by the United States but excluded from the constitutional rights of a full state of the Union.

   In 1952, Puerto Rico's colonial status was renovated when the island officially became a 'Free Associated State', or commonwealth territory of the US, enjoying a relative increase in its political and legislative autonomy at a local level, though the US Congress still has to approve all decisions of importance taken on the island [eds].

2   Before the referendum, the *Boston Globe* worried that Puerto Rico would favour statehood out of political and economic laziness, simply in order to retain food stamps and to secure federal funding for development projects.

3   Borinquen is the Taíno Indian name for the island.

4   El peublo de Puerto Rico por boca de sus dirigentes no supo decir ¡ No! virilmente en aquella ocasión; se avino al compromiso. En vez de mantener con firmeza el principio de la inviolabilidad de nuestros derechos, lo sacrificó al logro de unas reformas que, en realidad, no representaban gran cosa para la liberalización de la situación colonial.

5   'This people, who are sufficiently docile to obey their natural masters, will never tolerate that even a single militia should be removed from the island with the purpose of taking him to fight against his brothers the caracans' [*Este pueblo, bastante dócil para obedecer a sus autoridades naturales, no sufrirá jamás que se saque de la isla un solo miliciano para llevarlo a pelear contra sus hermanos los caraqueños*] (Pedreira 1942: 170).

6   *Hasta cuándo permitiremos que los déspotas de España se sigan aprovechando de nuestra inacción? ... Los jibaros de Puerto Rico, hijos de Agüeybaná el Bravo, no han perdido aún la vergüenza y sabrán probar a sus verdugos ... que si son fáciles de gobernar mientras creen que se les hace justicia, no sufren que se abuse de ellos impunemente.* The *jíbaro* is an archetypal Puerto Rican peasant figure, while Agüeybaná the Brave was a legendary Taíno Indian chieftain who lead the earliest resistance against the invading Spanish conquistadores [eds].

7   In his lifetime (1867–1918), José de Diego was one of the principal voices of Puerto Rican independence as well as a lawyer who prospered fighting against workers' rights in the service of the largest North American sugar refinery in the Puerto Rico of his time [eds].

8   Between 1904 and his death in 1916, Muñoz was a co-leader with de Diego of the Union party, the most important Puerto Rican political party of its time [eds]. Of Muñoz's *posibilismo*, Francisco A. Scarano writes (1993: 644):

> Munõz Rivera, the most moderate of the Unionist leaders, persuaded his comrades not to abandon autonomy. Thanks to his intervention, the Party accepted that formula as a means of transition towards independence.
>
> As a result of this action the main Puerto Rican party had rapidly swung to the left. The immediate consequence was a division of the

Unionist ranks between *muñocistas* and *dieguistas*. Muñoz Rivera continued favouring reform of the colonial regime, with or without United States citizenship... . The ever pragmatic leader was thus combatting the resistance to United States citizenship, generated from the independentist wing of the Party led by de Diego.

[*Muñoz Rivera, el más moderado de los lideres unionistas, convenció a sus correligionarios de que no abandonaran la autonomía. Gracias a su intervención, el Partido aceptó dicha fórmula como medida de transición hacia la independencia.*

El principal partido puertorriqueño había dado de pronto con esta acción un giro hacia la izquierda. El resultado immediato fue la división de las filas unionistas entre muñocistas *y* dieguistas *Muñoz Rivera seguia favoreciendo la reforma del régimen colonial, con o sin ciudadanía norteamericana... . El líder siempre pragmático combatía, por lo tanto, la resistencia a la ciudadanía estadounidense procedente del ala independentista del Partido dirigida por de Diego.*]

 9 Muñoz Rivera's son, Luis Muñoz Marín, was the populist leader of the Partido Popular Democrático [Popular Democratic Party], which he founded in 1938 and which dominated Puerto Rican politics until the 1960s. He was the prime modernizer in Puerto Rico's development from an agricultural to industrial economy and a collaborator with the United States in transforming Puerto Rico into the Free Associated State [Estado Libre Asociado], which he lead as its first elected Governor (1948–64) [eds].

10 This open-ended design may be another way that 'the four-storey country' [*el país de cuatro pisos*] exceeds, or falls short of, its Marxist intentions, allied to its emphasis on racial rather than class determinations that Flores notes (1993c: 64).

11 Eugenio María de Hostos (1839–1903). A pro-independence patriot and campaigner for the abolition of slavery, as well as a sociologist, novelist, essayist, historian, critic, and journalist, he collaborated with the Cuban revolutionaries of his day and lived most of his life in exile from Puerto Rico. After disillusioned attempts to reform the conditions of Puerto Rico's colonial status, he eventually advocated the founding of an independent confederation of Caribbean islands. His political work was complemented by his theoretical and practical work as an educational reformer, largely in Chile and the Dominican Republic. There, he held important posts as, amongst other things, an educational administrator and professor of constitutional law. Hostos is one of the major figures of Puerto Rican intellectual, political, and pedagogical history [eds].

12 Bayoán is the Romantic protagonist of his only novel, *La peregrinación de Bayoán* [The Perigrinations of Bayoán]. Hostos's *Diario* is a record of his honest ambivalence as he wrested with the possibilities for his country's future [eds].

13 Marqués noted that Puerto Rico has been the Catholic country with the highest incidence of suicides in the world (1977c: 162).

3   # The nomadic subject in the poetry of Julia de Burgos

Juan G. Gelpí

A literary tradition or paternalistic canon came into being in Puerto Rico during the first half of the twentieth century and was immediately engulfed by crisis. There were two fundamental moments in the development of this hierarchical tradition: the publication in 1934 of *Insularismo* [Insularism], Antonio S. Pedreira's interpretative essay on culture, and the first performance in 1958 of René Marqué's drama, *Los soles truncos* [The Fanlights], which observes the crisis of this tradition.

A basic feature of this tradition is the presence of the metaphor of colonialism as an illness. The seminal works of Puerto Rican literature – from Manuel Zeno Gandía's *La charca* [The Mud Pool] to Luis Rafael Sánchez's *La guaracha del Macho Camacho* [Macho Camacho's Beat] – return over and over again to illness and the crisis of colonialism. On the other hand, when constructing this tradition, the critics – beginning with the Generation of the 1930s, or *treintistas* – chose as a point of departure the work of the doctor and novelist, Manuel Zeno Gandía. According to the *treintistas*, only those totalizing genres – the novel and the interpretative essay – can heal the wound of colonialism. In this scheme of things, lyric poetry assumes a secondary or inferior function, a position assigned to female writers in literary historiography. The obsession with totality also impacts on a hierarchy which accompanies the constitution of the canon: the literature which goes on to form part of this canon is a literature of men, of nation-builders. For them, just as for the nineteenth-century positivists, pleasure and eroticism constitute an excess and a threat, a dissipation. Thus, representations of the body in canonical texts are minimal or non-existent. In short, the body is obscured in this type of text.

Fundamentally nostalgic and geared towards a thematics of the homeland, this literature is also Hispanophile, and one of its obsessive axes is identity; there is neither abundance of nor tolerance towards ambiguity. Historically such literature is linked to the class of landowners whose definitive decline begins with the North American military invasion of 1898. The former estate owners were precisely those who would govern the country when Puerto Rico became established as a North American colony. Some *treintistas*, Pedreira for example, did not belong to this social group, although there is a degree of identification with them in his texts.

Those who created the canon are the heirs of this social class who, even if they could not run the country, could compensate through their literature and criticism for their loss of political hegemony. The literary canon which was created and imposed by the *treintistas* in a colonial society has taken the place of a national constitution and compensated for the lack of an independent nation-state. This canon, therefore, is similar to, though it should not be confused with, the controlling and unifying mechanism provided by the state.

In the early 1940s, the intelligentsia of the Popular Democratic Party – the political organism that would be responsible for sealing the colonial pact with the United States in 1952 under the designation of Puerto Rico as commonwealth territory of its mighty neighbour, and which would be in power until 1968 – appropriated many aspects of Pedreira's national project, as outlined in *Insularismo*. This collection of essays, as well as becoming the authoritative point of reference in the setting-up of school and university literature syllabi, became the hegemonic interpretation of Puerto Rican culture and history until well into the 1970s. The essay 'Alarde y expresión' [Pride and Expression] outlines a series of Pedreira's opinions which would later become 'law'.

In the construction of every canon, hierarchies of genre are established, or modes of representation which allow the privileging of certain types of writing whilst others are disqualified or silenced. All through his essay, Pedreira insists that at the present time a distance must be maintained from poetry of any form, whether *avant-garde* or popular *décimas*.

In *Insularismo*, cultural nationalism institutionalizes an approach to reading which has survived in Puerto Rico more or less to the present day. According to this approach, 'good' Puerto Rican literature should faithfully represent our 'biology' and our 'geography'. Or, what amounts to the same thing, it should seek a 'realistic' representation of the national society and consciousness. A considerable number of recent writers have sought to distance themselves from such dictates of cultural nationalism. In a (1995) essay by Juan López Bauzá, a contemporary short-story writer, the possibility is considered that there already exists a different type of narrative characterized by, amongst other features, a 'disinhibition, a reclamation, which whilst delicately modest is a reclamation all the same, of a more intimate space, and which defends the imagination without trying to deploy it for ideological advantage or assertion'.[1]

Despite the relative power which this cultural nationalism has held until now, it would be reductive to ignore the complex processes of Puerto Rican culture by turning a blind eye to the fact that, by the 1930s, dissident versions of culture were already being produced; positive assertions originating in cultural minorities of the time. One of these minority interventions was constituted by the Afro-Antillean poetry of Luis Palés Matos. Faced with the Hispanophile determinism of *Insularismo*, Palés Matos's poetry defends a *mulato* construction of Puerto Rican culture.

I am interested here in exploring another avenue as marginalized as that of Palés; an escape route constituted by the work of Julia de Burgos, a writer who primarily went into exile in Havana and then in New York. Despite Julia de Burgos's allegiance as a woman to *political* nationalism, in her work may be read – at the cultural level – a version of what Homi K. Bhabha (1994a) terms counter-narratives of the nation: the type of cultural production that evokes and erases the totalizing frontiers of the nation, a type of questioning of the ideological manoeuvres through which nations or imagined communities acquire essential or essentialist identities.

In canonical Puerto Rican literature, the criterion of representativity is foremost. The first person singular, rarely glimpsed in this tradition, only has value to the extent that it forms part of a 'we', of that we which is highlighted in Pedreira's classic; a pronoun which is, nevertheless, part of many national constitutions. If there is a gesture of definition in canonical Puerto Rican works it is generally collective: the questions 'How are we? ... [and] what are we Puerto Ricans, globally considered' [¿cómo somos? ... (y) ¿qué somos los puertorriqueños globalmente considerados?] which open *Insularismo* (1992: 21). These works of cultural nationalism are written by those who are decisively influential within the cultural system of the time. Women – those with the least cultural influence in that decade – were usually relegated to the space of lyrical poetry. This is a genre in which, as has been well observed by Sylvia Molloy (1986), a voice in the first person singular is expected to express its emotions and sentiments in an effusively direct manner.

I propose to re-read the work of Julia de Burgos, and I refer here not only to the political or patriotic poetry which she sometimes produced and in which a break with the cultural status quo of the 1930s and 1940s is most evident. To do this it is necessary to re-examine her work by distancing oneself from the commonplaces to which critics have recurred when considering her poetry as a direct, unmediated expression of the poet's life.[2] Criticism has read her work as the tragic legend of a woman whose exile and alcoholism ended in her death. In recent years, both the poet Anjelamaría Dávila (1984) and the critic Ivette López Jiménez (1979, 1993) have questioned the strategies of a criticism which isolates Julia de Burgos and condemns her to a type of ghetto.[3] Such a ghetto, on the other hand, is alluded to in the pages of *Insularismo*, where Pedreira points to the lyrical genre as that most befitting women.

This critical isolation could be overcome by placing her works in dialogue with those texts by male writers and, as we shall see, those by female writers who, all through the 1930s and 1940s were articulating the Puerto Rican literary canon. This isolation could also be overcome by reading a large proportion of Julia de Burgos's work in the light of what Josefina Ludmer (1984: 53) has termed the tricks of the weak; strategies by which 'from the assigned and accepted place, not only the meaning of that place is changed but also of whatever is situated there'.[4] Here it is worth remembering some of the laws and axes which may be observed in the model of Puerto Rican culture constituted by *Insularismo*: the collective definition of the nation, geographic determinism (the sea which surrounds us isolates us from the rest of the world) and the reduction of women who participate in culture or politics to a stereotype of frivolity.

Much of Julia de Burgos's 'lyric' poetry could be read as a method of resistance, almost a response to the power of that imaginary state which is Pedreira's essay. From the assigned place, that of lyric poetry, Julia de Burgos executes what Gilles Deleuze and Félix Guattari (1988) would call an escape route. One might consider the elaboration of such dissidence as forming the core of her work. Julia de Burgos sets out on her literary journey by speaking in the first person singular, and exploring the conflictive condition of the women of her age. The emergence of her work is very much within the context of the struggles which liberated Puerto Rican women in the first decades of the century: the foundation of suffragist political organizations such as the Feminine League [Liga Femínea] in 1917, and later in 1925, the Puerto Rican Association of Women Suffragists [Asociación Puertorriqueña de Mujeres Sufragistas].[5] Moreover, in the 1930s, the decade in which de Burgos published her first book, women exercised their right to vote for the first time and, in 1934, the needleworkers called an important strike. The form these struggles take in de Burgos's texts is partly that of a conflictive self-definition. The opening text of her first collection of poems, 'A Julia de Burgos' [To Julia de Burgos], is typical of this type of self-definition, in which there is a confrontation between a voice constructed as authentic and one which seems frivolous.

Faced with the geographical determinism and preoccupation with roots which define canonical texts, Julia de Burgos inscribes a symbolic geography characterized by nomadism, amplitude, and dynamism: rivers, sea, air, roads, paths and tracks are some of the spaces negotiated by the subject that construct itself in her poetry. Criticism has not paid enough attention to the fact that the majority of Julia de Burgos's texts refer, in terms of both narrative point of view and images employed, to open spaces, places which eminently lend themselves to the development of a nomadic poetic discourse. Her texts offer, then, a denial or questioning of the insularity Pedreira so vehemently identifies. Geography is, in the case of this poet, the space of freedom and development through which there journeys a nomadic subject whose recurrent act is precisely that of walking.[6] It is worth remembering here the distinction established by Deleuze and Guattari between the subject of nomadic practices and the emigrant subject. The nomadic subject develops in an environment without horizon, like the flat, open space, the steppe, the desert or the sea (Deleze and Guattari 1988: 382). For this subject, 'every point is a relay and exists only as a relay' (ibid.: 380). The migrant, on the other hand, 'fundamentally goes from one point to another, even if that other point is doubtful, unexpected, or badly situated' (ibid.: 385). I insist on this distinction because I am interested in defining the nomadic subject – an effect created in poems – of the woman who wrote the texts and who emigrated both to Havana and New York. Several texts exemplify the construction of this nomadic subject: from 'Yo misma fui mi ruta' [I Was My Own Route], the text which closes her first book, to 'Poema para mi muerte' [Poem for My Death], the final text in *El mar y tú* [The Sea and You], published posthumously in 1954.

Julia de Burgos's corpus spans texts which explore metaphysical questions and poems where metaphysical language merges with that of the clearest eroticism. These lexical and semantic mixtures, which were disturbing to some of the readers of her time, seem very intriguing today. The texts, which combine eroticism and philosophical reflection, perhaps challenge the stereotype of feminine frivolity which appears in Pedreira's text and which later culminates in the misogynist text *par excellence* of our literature: René Marqués's 'En la popa hay un cuerpo reclinado' [A Body Lies Astern].[7]

The poetry of Julia de Burgos, and particularly the nomadic subject that appears in them, questions aspects of the hegemonic cultural discourse of the *treintistas*. In her first book of poems, *Poema en veinte surcos* [Poem in Twenty Furrows] (1938), there is a nomadic subject who visits and alters all the places of that hegemonic discourse. The most interesting aspect of this book is the multiple inflections of its poetic voice. Considering this multiplicity of 'furrows', it is possible to argue that the book is inhabited by a subject who is testing and exploring, in a sort of poetic nomadism, a series of paths within poetry.

Let us examine some of these inflections or routes. The collection is framed by the two poems of conflictive self-definition that open and close it: 'A Julia de Burgos' and 'Yo misma fui mi ruta'. There is also an elegiac text, 'Poema a Federico' [Poem to Federico], dedicated to García Lorca. At the same time we find political poetry written in support of the Republican cause in Spain, as is the case with 'Ochenta mil' [Eighty Thousand]. In others, like 'Desde el Puente Martín Peña [From the Martín Peña Bridge], support is voiced for the struggles of the workers. In the poem 'Nada' [Nothing], there is a somewhat ironic fusion of eroticism and philosophical vocabulary. Similarly, there are texts like 'Ay, ay, ay de la grifa negra' [Ay, Ay, Ay of the Kinky-Haired Negress] which voice a defence of African heritage and celebrate racial mixture in the Americas.

Some readers were worried by the diversity of inflections in this first book by Julia de Burgos. One curious matter ought to be recorded: a little-known critical essay by Margot Arce de Vázquez, published in a commemorative issue of the review *Artes y Letras* [Arts and Letters], which appeared in November 1953, a few years after the poet had died. The critical reading in question tried to 'sanitize' Julia de Burgos's work by disqualifying the diversity of the initial book and praising the last collection, *El mar y tú* [The Sea and You], unpublished at the time the essay appeared. Arce de Vázquez (1953) sees this book as 'the purest and most perfect work' [*la obra más pura y perfecta*]. She underlines and praises the compactness of these last poems, primarily by comparing them with the earlier texts (1953):

> That fury of love and desire, that irate clamour for justice, that impetus, forceful and free like all natural energies, that overflowing, almost animal, joy of youth, have all been pacified and made serene in the crucible of experience, in the discovery that all temporal things feed their roots in the humus of death.[8]

The attempt to 'sanitize' the poetry of Julia de Burgos extends to the approach used in reading *El mar y tú*. Through the exercise of a certain critical sensibility, an attempt is made to erase the suicidal impulse which appears in several poems in the book (Arce de Vázquez 1953):

And the verses go on singing of the amorous union, the unreserved surrender, with an infinite and heart-rending tenderness, with an insatiable appetite to be dissolved in nothingness. But fortunately, in some moments, this suicidal obsession is dissolved by the sheer impetus of love and the ray of God briefly illuminates the shadows.[9]

Thus recourse is made to a religious reading of a book which is not religious.

Returning to the nomadism which I identified in the first book, it is also possible to indicate its presence or repercussions on other levels of the poems. The texts of self-definition which frame the book illustrate a progression with regard to the features relating to metre. The move from a relatively regular metre at the beginning to a clearly polymetric end permits one to argue that, in direct proportion to the development of a nomadic subject, there is a shift toward a greater irregularity of scale or space in which the subject is articulated. Irregularity at the metrical level, then, could be considered a metaphor for the nomadic displacement of the subject. Between the beginning and the end, one of the first texts which breaks with metrical regularity is 'Ay, ay, ay de la grifa negra', a poem in heptasyllables alternating with endecasyllables and alexandrines.

The tendency toward metric irregularity intensifies in the final poem of the book, 'Yo misma fui mi ruta', in which there are verses ranging between six to 16 syllables. This is observed in a poem in which the subject affirms her nomadism right from the metaphor of the title: I am or was a route, or if one recalls the etymology of 'ruta': I am or was an open road. This spacialization of the subject also finds itself reinforced by the scission that occurs at the rhetorical level between the poem's 'old guard' [*troncos viejos*] and other syntagmata linked to the subject: 'new paths' [*senderos nuevos*], 'promissory earth' [*tierra promisora*], and 'intimate liberation' [*liberación íntima*]. In terms of metonymic continuity, the 'old trunks' [*troncos viejos*] also refer to the land.

This is a good moment to move to another level of reading in which all these formal elements can reconciled. Why is an errant poetic subject created in this first book; a nomad who is even characterized by her evasion of metric regularity? There is a rather obvious answer. In the process of transformation produced in lyrical poetry after Spanish-American *modernismo*, it is not rare to find such metrical irregularity or even, as is the case with *avant-garde* texts, a clean break with metre altogether.[10]

A second reading is perhaps more rewarding in terms of interpretative possibilities. The nomadic subject in Julia de Burgos's work is a mark of its difference, of the exile in which she produced a large part of her work, of her literal and imagined exile. She wrote much of her work outside her country of origin and also outside the hegemonic cultural discourse headed by Pedreira. One could equally argue that her work formally and ideologically distances itself from the attitudes toward culture expressed in the 1930s by female creole intellectuals in Puerto Rico. Her work contrasts in more than one sense with that of Margot Arce de Vázquez or Nilita Vientós Gastón, to mention just two examples. Magali Roy-Fequiere (1994) has studied in detail the manner in which issues of class and race have had repercussions on the configuration a female Puerto Rican intelligentsia at the beginning of the century. Female creole intellectuals, whether middle-class suffragettes or women who first had access to university education in the 1920s, considered solidarity as something which fundamentally included women of their own class. Roy-Fequiere adds that these intellectuals negotiated for a space of their own within the intellectual field dominated by men. However, by accepting this state of affairs they renounced the possibility of including a series of elements in their discourse which, curiously and right from the start, form part of Julia de Burgos's nomadic subject. In contrast to what one finds in poems such as 'A Julia de Burgos' or 'Pentacromía' [Pentachromy], these female intellectuals avoided questioning the injustice which underpins the social construction of gender. Instead of the exaltation of racial mixture and solidarity with workers which can be found in some of Julia de Burgos's texts, creole women intellectuals accepted and echoed the limited parameters of race and class proposed by cultural nationalism. Finally, these intellectuals emphasized the importance of femininity, in order to avoid being classed as mannish women. This defence of supposed femininity contrasts with the irony and force of the verses of 'Pentacromía':

> Today I want to be a man. Climb over the walls,
> trick the convents, be a real Don Juan;
> abduct Sor Carmen and Sor Josefina,
> conquer them, and rape Julia de Burgos.[11]

> *[Hoy, quiero ser hombre. Subir por las tapias,*
> *burlar los conventos, ser todo un Don Juan;*
> *raptar a Sor Carmen y Sor Josefina,*
> *rendirlas, y a Julia de Burgos violar.]*

It would be unfair to forget, however, that it was Margot Arce who, in her essays at the end of the 1940s, very astutely indicated the limitations of Pedreira's arguments.

The differences which exist between Julia de Burgos and creole female intellectuals originate, beyond the textual divergences I have mentioned, to the respective spaces they occupied in the intellectual domain of their day. While Margot Arce occupied positions suited to what we might call a 'sedentary' intellectual – a university chair, head of the Department of Hispanic Studies, editor of the *Review of the Association of Graduates of the University of Puerto Rico* [Revista de la Asociación de Graduados de la Universidad de Puerto Rico] (1938–44) – Julia de Burgos travelled through a series of intellectual spaces of a far more provisional nature. She was a kind of intellectual nomad. Let us recall some of the stages of her route.

In 1936, after battling against a series of crippling financial limitations, she qualified as a primary school teacher at the University of Puerto Rico. She began teaching at a country school, and from there went on to write radio scripts for children. She then sporadically attended courses at the university. When she published her first book, she sold it in person from village to village. Shortly afterwards, having moved to Cuba in 1940, she enrolled at Havana University. Her programme of studies reveals a certain disperse and broad intellectual curiosity: she enrolled for courses in Greek, but also sociology; she attended biology classes as well others in mental health. The following year, 1942, she abandoned her studies and moved to New York. Once there she worked as a reporter and interviewer for the weekly *Pueblos Hispanos* [Hispanic Peoples] which, between 1943 and 1944, was edited by the renowned nationalist poet Juan Antonio Corretjer, and which also became an outlet for some of her poems and essays.[12] This multiplicity of contacts made her an intellectual who participated in a great variety of activities. Julia de Burgos's intellectual trajectory is much closer to another nomadic Puerto Rican intellectual, the anarchist Luisa Capetillo; and, in the Latin American context, hers resembles the trajectory of Alfonsina Storni.

I should now like to return to my initial arguments. The texts produced by the hegemonic sector of Puerto Rican culture in 1930s exhibit a profound preoccupation with a thematics of the land. In turn, this preoccupation draws our attention to the change from an estate economy to one of plantations. At a time of great instability, the hegemonic sector of culture – linked by blood or spiritual affinity to the landowning sector – returns insistently to the theme of land, in a gesture of what we might also term a sedentary attitude, and as part of a posture we find in the work of various *treintistas*.

On another level of interpretation, the nomadic subject of Julia de Burgos could be read as another mark of her difference from the sedentary attachment to the land which the hegemonic cultural sector exhibits. Furthermore, if we now turn to the woman who constructed this subject we realize that the land can have very little attraction for someone who never possessed any of it; someone, as Beauchamp (1994) has urged, who belonged instead to the propertyless peasant classes who emigrated to the city in search of better living conditions.

> One returns to the land to recover the lost goodness, harmony, and reestablishment of the old order and the moral as well as spiritual values associated with it, that is to say, the sense of archaic ownership and relations of production. The return to the land, however, is a response which does not correspond to that of peasants who have migrated to the city.[13]

Until now I have highlighted the nomadism found in Julia de Burgos's first book. A reading of her other two books reveals a similar nomadism. In *Canción de la verdad sencilla* [Song of the Simple Truth], her second book, the erotic side of her poetry is developed. The symbolic geography across which the nomadic subject of her first book is displaced becomes, in her second book, the space through which the couple literally and symbolically move. 'Transmutación' [Transmutation] is, in this sense, an exemplary poem. And here, once again, the metre exhibits a great irregularity, switching from a single syllable to verses of 23 syllables.

El mar y tú marks the culminating point of Julia de Burgos's nomadic subject. Two texts from this book exemplify the particularities of that subject: 'Letanía del mar' [Litany of the sea] and the closing poem, 'Poema para mi muerte'.

In contrast to the walking subject of the first two books, in 'Letanía del mar' a subject is presented who defines herself by metaphorically identifying herself with the space of the sea: a multiple and unstable space in which opposites merge: eroticism and death. The poem also elaborates a ritual or trajectory which is founded in that form of subjectivity – I, sea – and ends in the calm smoothness of the universe. On the other hand, the sea is, in this as in other texts by Julia de Burgos, the space of amplitude; a representation that forms a direct contrast to that of Pedreira in *Insularismo* (1992: 116): 'The belt of sea that surrounds and oppresses us is gradually closing off the universal spectacle' [*el cinturón de mar que nos cerca y nos oprime, va cerrando cada vez más el espectáculo universal*].

In a study which forms a dialogue with the theories of Deleuze and Guattari, Rosi Braidotti (1994: 22) has said that the male/female nomad is a manifestation of the type of subject who has given up all idea, desire, or nostalgia for fixity. We find something similar in the last poem of *El mar y tú*. In 'Poema para mi muerte' nomadism takes place across the border between life and death. Precisely for this reason, the subject rejects the possibility of her burial (Burgos 1997: 244):

> Let no one profane my death with sobs,
> nor blanket me forever with innocent earth;
> So that in the moment of freedom I may be left freely
> to have at my disposal the planet's only freedom.

> *[Que nadie me profane la muerte con sollozos,*
> *ni me arropen por siempre con inocente tierra;*
> *que en el libre momento me dejen libremente*
> *disponer de la única libertad del planeta.]*

Here, the subject sees death as a process in which another type of nomadism is initiated: one by means of which her body integrates itself, transforms itself, and molecularizes itself to the point of surrendering itself to a union with other matter (Burgos 1997: 244):

> With what ferocious joy my bones will begin
> to seek little windows in the dark flesh
> and I, giving myself, giving myself, fierce and freely
> to the storm and breaking my chains alone.

> … My defeated smallness made smaller each time,
> each instant greater and simpler the surrender;
> my breast perhaps will curl to give life to a rosebud,
> perhaps my lips will nurture white lilies.

> *[Con qué fiera alegría comenzarán mis huesos*
> *a buscar ventanitas por la carne morena*
> *y yo, dándome, dándome, feroz y libremente*
> *a la intemperie y sola rompiéndome cadenas!*

> *… Cada vez más pequeña mi pequeñez rendida,*
> *cada instante más grande y más simple la entrega;*
> *mi pecho quizás ruede a iniciar un capullo,*
> *acaso irán mis labios a nutrir azucenas.]*

In a final incarnation of her nomadism, the subject imagines her death as an offering to the open space and symbolic geography in which she is constituted.

It is worth highlighting that, in the final moments of her work, this nomadism coexists with another, much more ironic, manifestation of death. This manifestation appears in 'Farewell in Welfare Island', one of the poems written in English by Julia de Burgos in the final months of her life. What is involved here is another type of subject who bids farewell to the world from the space of exile. At the same time we know that these texts of hers written in another language constitute founding texts, alongside those of Bernardo Vega, Jesús Colón, and Piri Thomas, of that other side of Puerto Rican literature: the literature of emigration or diaspora.[14]

Finally, I propose that the nomadism that forms the poetic subject of Julia de Burgos has exceeded the boundaries of her own work. That nomadism is an element which has been transferred by Manuel Ramos Otero from a symbolic geography to the urban space marked out by a homosexual subculture, both in *El cuento de la Mujer del Mar* [Tale of the Woman of the Sea] and the clearly nomadic texts which constitute his last work of fiction, *Página en blanco y staccato* [Page in White and Staccato].[15] The nomadic, transient writing of this narrative writer and poet who, like Julia de Burgos, lived and wrote in New York, is a mark of her legacy to writers of recent years.

Notes

1   *Un desenfado, un reclamo delicado, simple, pero reclamo al fin, de un espacio más íntimo, una defensa de la imaginación sin amarrarla a un propósito o una tesis ideológica.*

    López Bauzá adds 'I sense the sudden emergence of a group of young artists who have decided to assume their national identity without the necessity of defending it' [*siento asomarse de repente un grupo de artistas jóvenes que ha decidido asumir su identidad nacional sin la necesidad de defenderla*].

2   The biographical reading of Julia de Burgos largely draws, for example, on the studies José Emilio González dedicated to her work. Amongst others, see González (1965, 1973–4, 1976).

3   María M. Solá (Burgos 1986: 18–19) has also made the following observation concerning the poetry of Julia de Burgos:

> Route, way, path, words which appear in her verse, come to mind when trying to describe the poetry of Burgos, because in reality her work can represent the testimony of a journey, of a trajectory (…). Considered in their entirety, her books trace the path of this intimate voyage, whose continuous movement is not along a straight line but which involves changes of direction, breakthroughs and regressions. The poetic speaker reveals herself to be a restless being who is never superficial nor easily satisfied. There is only ever this constant movement of inseparable change and struggle.

> *Ruta, camino, sendero, palabras que aparecen en los versos, se recuerdan al tratar de describir la poesía de Burgos, porque en verdad ésta puede representar el testimonio de un viaje, de una trayectoria ....*

> *Vistos en conjunto, sus libros dibujan esa ruta íntima, un movimiento continuo que no es una línea recta, porque tiene vueltas, adelantos y retrocesos. Se va descubriendo la hablante poética como un ser inquieto, nunca superficial ni fácilmente satisfecho. Sólo hay esa constante, el cambio y la lucha, que marchan siempre juntos.*

4 *Desde el lugar asignado y aceptado, se cambia no sólo el sentido de ese lugar sino el sentido mismo de lo que se instaura en él.*

5 On the women who participated in the political struggles for the right to vote, Pedreira says the following (1992: 96): 'They pursue some slight ideas and carry a certain number of secondhand preoccupations in their vanity bags' [*cultivan unas ideas chiquitas y llevan en el* vanity *unas cuantas preocupaciones de ocasión*].

6 On the importance of walking as a motif in Julia de Burgos's poetry, see López Jiménez (1979).

7 In this story, a male narrator feels so dominated by his overbearing mother and materialistic wife, that he murders the latter in a boat and then castrates himself [eds].

8 *Aquella furia del amor y del deseo, aquel clamor iracundo de justicia, aquel ímpetu, pujante y libre como todas las energías naturale [sic], aquella desbordante alegría, casi animal, de la juventud, se han apaciguado y serenado en el crisol de la experiencia, en el descubrimiento de que todas las cosas temporales nutren sus raíces del humus de la muerte.*

9 *Y los versos van cantando la unión amorosa, la entrega sin reservas, con una infinita y desgarrada ternura, con incontenible apetito de disolución en la nada. Más* [sic], *afortunadamente, en algunos instantes, esta obsesión suicida se disuelve en el ímpetu de amor y el rayo de Dios ilumina momentáneamente las tinieblas.*

10 *Modernismo* was an experimental poetic movement of the late nineteenth century, which was influenced by French Symbolism. Its main preoccupations were with a lush elegance of form as well as figurative language, and exotic, often fanciful or erotic, themes and motifs. In its latter stages, a concern with asserting a distinctive Latin American cultural identity emerges, at the same time as the *modernista* poets became more critical of the derivative foundations of their writing [eds].

11 Spanish text from Burgos (1997: 26). English translation by the editors.

12 On this period of her life, see Martínez Masdeu (1992).

13 *A la tierra se regresa para recuperar el bien perdido, la armonía, el restablecimiento del viejo orden y los valores morales y espirituales asociados a ella, es decir, a la propiedad y a las relaciones de producción arcaicas. El regreso a la tierra es, sin embargo, una respuesta que no corresponde con la de los jíbaros emigrados a la ciudad.*

14 One of the best studies of this literature and its founding figures is Flores (1993a).

15 On Ramos Otero as a nomadic writer who consciously identifies with Julia de Burgos, see Gelpí (1993: 137–54). Also see Cruz Malavé (1993), and Sotomayor (1995) [eds].

4 | Women, life writing and national identity in Cuba: Excilia Saldaña's *Mi nombre: anti-elegía familiar*

Conrad James

The masculinist orientation of western autobiography has been challenged consistently by twentieth-century theories and practices. While this traditionally elitist genre once served primarily to consolidate the discriminatory ideology of an ahistoricized, universal, male subject, both western and non-western woman-oriented texts have used autobiography as a means of negotiating a wide range of subjectivities. In this chapter, drawing on Sidonie Smith's ideas on what she terms the autobiography manifesto, I discuss the potential of autobiographical writing to disrupt patriarchal discourses on national identity with an unequivocal projection of woman's voice and subjectivity. Through a detailed reading of *Mi nombre: anti-elegía familiar* [My Name: A Family Anti-Elegy] (1991), I show Excilia Saldaña's engagement in a complex process of negotiation between self-definition and allegiance to the nation. Ultimately what is staged is an essentially woman-centred agenda.

Saldaña (1946–) is a black Cuban woman who has published several volumes of poetry and short stories, including children's stories.[1] Born into a reactionary, middle-class family, the poet's support for the 1959 revolution estranged her from her family.[2] Her autobiographical poetry, particularly *Mi nombre*, recounts this familial rift and the harrowing psychological effects she suffered as a result. Equally important, however, is the poem's expression of a double preoccupation with the authority of woman's voice and the validity of the Africanist aspects of Cuban culture. This double preoccupation is a dominant feature of Saldaña's work, and often finds expression in poems which feature the creative retelling of African myths and legends from a Cuban woman-oriented perspective.

Before turning to the poetry of Saldaña I shall attempt to contextualize the perspectives we find in her work by examining Smith's concept of the autobiographical manifesto and then discussing the way the woman/nation relationship is handled in the work of another black Cuban woman poet, Nancy Morejón. I shall discuss Morejón's construction of an unproblematic revolutionary nation which is devoid of gender conflict. Saldaña's inscription of racial and sexual crisis undermines this construction of homogeneous nationhood and consciously places at centre stage the demands of female subjectivity.

The autobiographical manifesto is a form of resistance narrative which seeks to recuperate memory. It is 'poised against amnesia' and sets out to constitute a future history, to project recollection into the future (Smith 1993: 182). The main thrust of Smith's argument is that the autobiographical manifesto is grounded in questions of agency and serves an emancipatory political function. This form of discourse is 'puposeful, bold, and contentious (p. 157) and works to contest 'the old inscriptions, the old histories, the old politics, the *ancien régime* by working to dislodge the hold of the universal subject through an expressly political collocation of a new "I"' (ibid.).

Unlike some autobiographical practices, then, which are rooted in negative or reductive politics (mimesis and fragmentation), the autobiographical manifesto offers full potential for the staging of resistance. Further, through its constituent aspects of appropriating sovereignty, bringing to light, announcing publicly, performing publicly, speaking as one of a group, and speaking to the future, it enables the subject to insist on identity in service to an emancipatory politics' (p. 157). The poetry of Nancy Morejón which I discuss below might be seen as approximating this emancipatory position. However my thesis here is that for such a discursive practice to be fully liberatory in the context of revolutionary Cuba it must not only celebrate identities authorized by revolutionary culture; it might constantly position the subject in ways which, when necessary, challenge rather than acquiesce in conceptual dictates. Saldaña's poetry forcefully reminds us that specificities of race, gender, and personal history are indispensable in an understanding of the relative meaning that the revolutionary process will have for the individual as well as the demands she or he will make on it.

Whenever Morejón attempts to place the female figure within the context of revolutionary Cuba certain problems arise in terms of the construction of subjectivity. 'Obrera del tabaco' [Woman in a Tobacco Factory] from Morejón's 1982 collection *Octubre imprescindible* [Essential October] is a case in point. The poem has been largely ignored by critics of her work yet it raises issues which are crucial to the understanding of her style and ideological orientation. 'Obrera del tabaco' celebrates the 1959 revolution through the consciousness of a female worker in a tobacco factory (p. 18):

> Una obrera del tabaco escribió
>
> un poema a la muerte. Entre el humo
> y las hojas torcidas de la vega
> dijo ver el mundo en Cuba.
>
> [A woman in a tobacco factory wrote
>
> a poem to death. Between the smoke
> and the twisted leaves of the factory
> she said she saw the world in Cuba.]

What is striking here is the dichotomy between the constraining potential of the subject's employment and the use of it as a site from which an infinite number of possibilities might be constructed. Equally significant is the dismantling of the demarcation between worker and poet. The poem subsequently has the worker's consciousness renounce all the colonialist/imperialist aspect of Cuba's past as well as the seduction of North America (p. 18):

> En su poema, amigos, no había Miami ni reclamaciones;
> no había mendicidad
> no había ruindades
> ni violaciones de la ley laboral;
> no había interés por la Bolsa, no había lucro.
>
> [In her poem, friends, there was no Miami nor demands;
> there was no begging
> there were no mean acts
> nor violations of the labour laws;
> there was no interest in the stock market, there was no lucre.]

Simultaneously the subject's poem embraces the values propounded by the new social order (p. 18):

> En su poema, había astucia militante, lánguida inteligencia.
> En su poema, había disciplina y asambleas.
> En su poema, había sangre hirviendo del pasado.
>
> [In her poem, there was militant shrewdness, languid intelligence.
> In her poem there was discipline and assemblies.
> In her poem there was blood boiling from the past.]

There is no mention, however, of the identity of the 'obrera' as woman. What is celebrated is her identity as worker and defender of the revolution. In this new social order all crises related to the power relations between the sexes will eventually be resolved: 'En su poema, estaban todos los deseos y toda la ansiedad/de un revolucionario contemporáneo suyo' (p. 18) [In her poem there were all the desires and all the anxiety/of one of her contemporary revolutionaries]. Morejón's agenda is clear; she is filtering a specific ideological position which supports the revolution's claim of a commitment to the empowerment of all formerly marginalized groups, including women.

Perhaps another reading of the poem which bears in mind Morejón's disposition towards ellipsis and understatement might see the figure of the woman as silent visionary (she hides the poem which she writes in a volume written by José Martí) and as a suggestion by the poet that the national culture is not yet ready to incorporate or accommodate the female voice. I prefer to read the poem, however, as an example of the truncation of female experience in an attempt to uphold socialist values and maintain a harmonious national rhetoric. Ironically, while a project such as this sets out to declare the liberation of women it fails to construct a liberated female subject. Both in capitalist and socialist societies work is deemed a key element in women's liberation; through feminist ideology in the former and state prescription in the latter. However, the emphasis on collectivity in 'Obrera del tabaco' sabotages female subjectivity and, therefore, while the persona of the poem is linguistically gendered female (*obrera*) the text does not challenge in any way the normative masculinity of the universal socialist subject. It incorporates an ideology of male experience/authority as normative, thus the woman's poem inscribes, paradoxically, all the desires and anxieties of a 'revolucionari<u>o</u> contemporáneo suyo' (p. 18, my emphasis). The hiding of the woman's poem in the volume of José Martí might be read then, as an ironic symbolization of female collusion with, or refusal to react against, the silencing of woman's voice by the male heroes of Cuban nationalism.

This is a recurring feature in the poetry of Morejón. Even in poems which re-create personal family history such as 'La cena' [The Supper] (1967) the priorities of national cohesiveness overtake concerns of subjectivity. Arguably, in 'Amo a mi amo' [I Love My Master] (1986) there is a strong feminist voice which challenges patriarchal systems and claims the right to woman's space and female self-assertion. But the full possibilities of that voice within the context of the revolution are only obtainable through a very subversive reading of the poem as an example of literary and cultural marronage.[3]

Autobiography can be and has been commonly used to serve the same nationalist ideological functions as identified in the poems discussed above. In fact, the autobiographical traditions of Europe, Latin America and the United States have to varying degree demonstrated attempts to present the construction of the individual self as a reflection of the life and ethos of the respective nations. The personal story is thus told as an allegorical re-presentation of the national story.[4] It must be noted, however, that as far as socialist Cuba is concerned, autobiography is not endorsed as a revolutionary genre. This is not to say that there is no place for self-narrative within the discourse of the revolution. In fact self-narrative is a fundamental mode in Cuban revolutionary literature. Fidel Castro's 'La historia me absolverá' [History Will Absolve Me](1953) and the *Diarío del Ché en Bolivia* [Diary of Ché in Bolivia](1968) are key instances in the constitution of this genre within the nation's social text. However, to be deemed ideologically correct the life story has to be presented as *testimonio* since this genre foregrounds the community rather than the individual. As Gareth Williams explains, *testimonios* differ from other autobiographical texts since 'theirs is a life story whose pivotal function is to be found in its explicit desire to engender immediate and collective praxis' (1993: 83).[5]

The Cuban government has given much prominence to *testimonio* and an important cultural institution such as the Casa de las Américas helped to sanction it as a genre by deciding, in 1970, to award a prize in this category. This endorsement of *testimonio* is obviously related to an attempt to promote what José A. Moreno (1971) describes as the change from traditional to modern values in socialist Cuba. Moreno emphasizes that pre-revolutionary Cuba was characterized by hierarchy and individualism but since the revolution a process of change from 'hierarchical elitism to egalitarianism', 'individualism to collectivistic orientation', had begun. It is through *testimonio* that women's lives, in particular, have been most frequently written into the discourse of revolutionary Cuba. In these narratives it is service to community and country which is endorsed and Verity Smith has noted in relation to one such *testimonia, Tania la guerrillera inolvidable* [Tania the Unforgettable Guerrilla Fighter], that it would seem that 'in order to become a hero the woman must first be de-sexed'.[6] Subjectivity would seem to be a hindrance to political commitment. Viewed within this context Excilia Saldaña's consistent exploration of her subjective psycho-sexual crises could be read as potentially subversive and it not surprising that *Mi nombre* was not published in Cuba until 1991, by which time the priorities of the revolution had undergone much revision.

Excilia Saldaña: the autobiographical subject

Mi nombre is an agonized psycho-linguistic journey in which the subject struggles desperately with various aspects of her past, present, and future in an attempt to create meaning and structure out of a chaotic set of impulses. What is compelling about *Mi nombre* is the way a peculiarly woman-centred psychodrama is carefully interwoven with several aspects of Cuba's social and political history. The individual story is not simply a metonymic expression of the country's story; rather woman and nation experience apocalypse and salvation together. The text reconstructs the poet's traumatic upbringing in the straitened environment of a *blanqueada* [whitened] middle-class family.[7] Simultaneously there is the poetic reconstruction of different national crises in Cuba; the dictatorship of Machado, the turmoil of the Batista regime and the struggle preceding the coming to power of the 1959 revolution.

Memory is indispensable to the process of identification constructed in *Mi nombre,* one of his *Elegies* (1948–58). The poem, which has obvious intertextual links to Nicolás Guillén's 'El apellido' [My Surname], is preceded by a double dedication (to Guillén, a symbol of Cuban nationalism, and to the poet's paternal grandmother, Ana Excilia Bregante): 'A Nicolás Guillén/El apellido entero/A mi abuela Ana Excilia/suyo mi nombre' [To Nicolás Guillén/my entire surname/to my grandmother Ana Excilia/hers my name]. The dual dedication signals the double significance, intimate and communal, which memory has in the text. The poem might in fact be read as the struggle between these two forms of memory. Early intimate memories occasion psychological turmoil and correspond to what the North American writer Minnie Bruce Pratt has referred to in a different context as the sensation of being homesick at home (Kaplan 1987: 193).

The first segment of the poem is a demonstration of the resolve to dispense with one kind of memory with its association of repression, inertia, silence, and solitude and establish a concomitant search for an alternative set of memories (p. 4):

> Adiós, boca del sueño sin oficio decoroso,
> realidad
> en el sitio justamente ganado.
> Ejerzo otro idioma. Convoco otra dimensión.
> Indago
> por esta sangre
> de ahora, y aquí
> por esta piel
> a trechos

> manchada y áspera,
> a trechos
> fina como un madrigal
> o
> el suspiro de una niña.
> Me camino
> en todo lo que soy,
> o
> en lo que dejaré de ser manaña.
>
> [Farewell, mouth of the dream without valid duty,
> reality
> in the justly earned place.
> I use another language. I summon up anotherdimension.
> I search deep
> into this blood
> of here and now
> in this skin in places
> stained and sour,
> in others
> as fine as a madrigal
> or
> the sigh of a little girl.
> I walk through
> all that I am,
> or
> what I was not
> through what I will not be tomorrow.]

This play with two contradictory forms of memory, the intimate and the communal, is closely related to the concepts of time which operate in the poem. The coverage of past, present and future in the temporal frame of the text is not strictly chronological, and the dislodging of linearity and chronology indicates the frenetic mental state in which the subject initiates her construction of self. More importantly, however, the play with memory may be understood in terms of its relationship with a wide range of dichotomies which are confronted and overturned in the text: the bourgeois/Eurocentric versus the socialist/Africanist; the *charanga* versus the *guaguancó*; the patriarchal versus the woman-centred; the elitist and restrictive versus the popular and liberatory.[8] Saldaña's dismantling of dichotomies is consistent with the auto-biographical manifesto's agenda of rejecting/contesting sovereign ideologies. This is achieved in *Mi nombre* through direct attack on the family and Roman Catholicism, two of the social institutions through which these ideologies were consolidated in pre-revolutionary Cuba. If home in the poetry of Nancy Morejón is curiously devoid of any tension, *Mi nombre* casts it as a site of torture and torment. In *Mi nombre* all desirable emotions are eroded within the household which is dominated by a debilitating and destructive fear (p. 7):

> Todos tenemos miedo:
> en la casa
> semejamos figuras de un ballet grotesco.
> en puntillas
> y con el dedo temoroso
> estrangulando los besos.

> [We are all afraid:
> in the house
> we are like figures in a grotesque ballet,
> on tiptoes
> and with fearful fingers
> strangling kisses.]

Home then, is an arena of trauma and childhood is a nightmarish experience. Home is also a locus of entrapment from which the subject desperately seeks escape (p. 7): 'Where can I find a locksmith for these bars?' [*Dónde buscar cerrajero para esta reja?*].

The poem reinforces the idea of home as pathological space by contrasting this re-creation of harrowing childhood memories with the amnesia that frustrates the subject's quest for identity: '¿Dónde?/ ¿Dónde está el que soy? ¿Qué olvido me malcría y tutela?' [where?/Where is the person who I am? What oblivion spoils and takes charge of me?] (p. 5). Home does not provide the answers which the subject seeks. She searches for herself in the domestic environment (pp. 6–7) but the confined space of the home exacerbates her crisis of identity and she therefore abandons this domain and the constraints which it symbolizes in order to find solace. But self-assertion in the patriarchal order implies transgression and so the attempt to escape from the household's entrapment is inscribed as an act of delinquency (p. 7):

> Aunque solo yo arrostro el crimen de burlarme de su cerco:
> Cimarrona en los parques,
> apalencada en el colegio.

> [Although only I face up to the crime of mocking its siege:
> Runaway slave in the parks,
> stockaded in school.]

Vertical tropes (upper class/lower class) are explicit in the text. Saldaña stages what must be seen as a redemptive project by constantly reinstating the validity of the 'low' in face of the 'high', and the popular in the face of the 'classical'. This strategy is of particular interest in Saldaña's work in general and in *Mi nombre* in particular because, in contradistinction to a number of black Cuban writers who construct the idea of liberation as a consequence of being equated with the 'mighty fallen' bourgeoisie of the pre-socialist eras, the subject's liberation is achieved through her volitive rejection of the values of the privileged from a position of privilege. The text's redemption of the 'low' involves issues of race and gender as much as it involves questions of class. It entails the inclusion in the woman's story of those 'colourful' figures, the socially abject, who are expunged from traditional autobiographical narratives aimed at reaffirming the autonomy of the universal subject. This is a community-oriented narrative, a kind of 'autoethnography'; but one which explores the interdependencies of national and gender politics.[9]

The complexities involved in moving from 'high' to 'low', then, are seminal to the crisis constructed in *Mi nombre*. Constantly in search of an identity she has been denied and which keeps eluding her the subject pervasively records a sense of stepping 'down' into the 'lower' aspects of Cuban culture. It is here that she finds a multiplicity of forms, predominantly Africanist in character, which serve as a context in which she can engineer/create that identity. This sensibility informs the structure of the poem. The subject's birth is constructed as an inauspicious event. This extends Saldaña's reference, in 'Autobiografia' (1982), to the idea that her birth into the family was an unwelcomed event: 'I was born because the abortions were unsuccessful' [*Nací porque fallaron los abortivos*] (p. 200). Here there is the invocation of the relationship between the loveless environment of the family and the speaker's inability to achieve self-knowledge (p. 6):

En el vaho fatal de Julio se dan cita la guajirita y el proxeneta:
dos cuerpos se presentan
y otro surge.
Error
la más bochornosa tarde de agosto
de este siglo nacido bajo la charanga
y la Enmienda.
No soy yo.
No he nacido:
Sin amor nada se engendra.

[In the overbearing July heat the country girl and the pimp meet:
two bodies show up
and another emerges.
Mistake
on the hottest August evening
this century born beneath the saloon dance
and the Amendment.
I am not myself.
I have not been born:
Without love nothing is engendered.]

Equally important is the linking of the subject's birth to both
European cultural colonization and North American imperialism. The
'charanga' is used here as a metaphor for the family's Eurocentric
values while 'Enmienda' recalls the infamous Platt Amendment to the
Cuban constitution.[10] In juxtaposing the 'charanga' with the oppressive environmental features which accompany her birth the text
effects a further disavowal of the subject's bourgeois family and the
Eurocentric culture which they espouse and this disavowal is
exacerbated in the non-identity of the subject.[11] Throughout the text
the narration of the piercing, often heartrending, story of the household is structured in forms that are similarly Eurocentric. The vocalic
rhyme of the following lines which confront the hypocrisy of the
family and the constraints it places on the grandmother is a case in
point (pp. 25-6):

> Ana Excilia Bregante, criollera,
> ¿cómo fue que me dijiste tu secreto?
> La falsedad del anillo en tu mano,
> el regazo abandonado y desierto.
>
> [Ana Excilia Bregante, creole woman,
> how did you manage to tell me your secret?
> The falsehood of the ring on your finger
> the deserted and abandoned lap.]

Here the use of hendecasyllabic lines with alternating assonance
contrasts with the final section of the poem which celebrates the
subject's accession to selfhood through the use of the anaphoric
structure of the guaguancó to communicate the message and essence of
freedom (p. 31).[12]

> Mi nombre
> de pie y camino,
> mi nombre
>
> Mi nombre
> de yagua y cieno
> mi nombre.
> Mi nombre
> de grasa y humo.
> Mi nombre.
> mi nombre
> de algodón y fuego
> mi nombre
> de alcohol y noche
> mi nombre.
>
> [My name
> by foot and path
> my name
>
> My name
> of palm and mud.
> My name.
> My name
> of fat and smoke.
> My name
> of cotton and fire
> my name
> of alcohol and night
> my name.]

The use of the *guaguancó* symbolizes the quest for that other set of memories, African-centred cultural ones, into which the speaker launches after rejecting the stifling Eurocentricity of the household. The revolution's attitude towards African-Cuban culture remains a question fraught with debate. Saldaña's recourse to the *guaguancó* is, however, symptomatic of her alignment of revolutionary fervour with the reclaiming of the African aspects of Cuban identity throughout the text. It is of equal relevance to the idea of female freedom since in contradistinction to the controlled movement of the *charanga* the *guaguancó* is a dance in which female sexuality is very much a pivotal aspect (see Manuel 1995).

Rejecting the *charanga* and embracing the *guaguancó*, exposing the pathology of the household and affirming the liberating force of the street, stepping from the 'high' down to the 'low', signals the autobiographical manifesto's political agenda of bringing things to light: 'forcing issues into the light of day' (S. Smith 1993: 158). To bring to light is to place at centre stage culturally marginalized experiences thereby confirming a resistance to the pressure to conform to identifications provided by the dominant culture. It is, then, as is effected in *Mi nombre,* the creation of a new perspective, which reveals the falseness of the view from the 'top' and registers a commitment to affirming alternative knowledges gained in the margins.

The pattern of rejecting the 'high'/Eurocentric and embracing the 'low'/African-centred is pervasive in the text. Through the sardonic portrayal of the child's first communion Catholicism is ridiculed and the paternal deity cast as violator (p. 11):

> Dios dentro de mi cuerpo de 10 años.
> Ah, vanidad de vanidades, vanagloria de la teofagia;
> ni mi madre ni la madre de mi padre pudieron devorar
> un dios completo, redondo, blanco, insonoro.
>
> [God in my body of ten years.
> Oh vanity of vanities, vainglory of theophagy;
> neither my mother nor my father's mother could devour
> a whole round, white, soundless god.]

This blasphemy is further developed into a re-inscription of Roman Catholic dogma to reflect a woman-centred socialist ethos. The immaculate conception is parodied, its uniqueness subverted, through the plurality with which it is invested when the subject becomes mother of the future messiahs [*madre de los futuros mesías*] and wife of the all the carpenter Josephs [*esposa de los múltiples Pepes carpinteros*] (pp. 13–14). Santería, on the other hand, is a source of creativity. Poetry provides the opportunity for the subject to structure her life as she realizes that her identity is tied up with language: 'mi nombre-palabra, /mi nombre-poema' (p. 16) [my name word, /my name poem] and this discovery of the gift of poetry is celebrated through the invocation of all the religion's sacred plants (p. 16):

> Siéntate en la copa de la ceiba.
> Dilúyete en el girasol o en un príncipe negro
> Véngate en la compasión del flamboyán.
>
> [Sit down in the crown of the ceiba.
> Dilute yourself with the sunflower or the black prince
> Take revenge on the compassion of the flamboyant.]

The exposure of the pain that is engendered in the household is not the only index that is used to mark its domination. Its excessive indulgence, which is evidenced in the preparation for Christmas Eve, is mocked (p. 20):

> En la cocina
> la vianda hervida,
> el congrí,
> la gallina de guinea,
> el pavo plebeyo,
> los dátiles babilónicos,
> las nueces y avellanas,
> los higos,
> el turrón de almendra o yema.
>
> Prestidigitación invernal de la burgesía.
>
> [In the kitchen
> the warm food,
> the rice and black beans,
> the guinea fowl,
> the plebeian turkey,
> the Babylonian dates,
> the walnuts and hazelnuts,
> the figs, the turrón of almond or egg white.
>
> Winter conjuring trick of the bourgeoisie.]

The attack on the household's conspicuous privileges is inscribed as a rejection of its lack of social conscience and abdication of duty to country. The poem achieves this through bitter satire, juxtaposing obvious social upheaval, 'un pregón abre las ventanas: /un policía y un chivato las cierran' (p. 19) [a shout opens the windows: /a policeman and a stool pigeon close them] with the image of the cloistered, sancti-monious family, 'En la cocina/la sagrada familia y los reyes del oriente' [In the kitchen/the holy family/and the kings of the East] (p. 19). The 'maracas' and the 'bongó', however, are emblems of freedom and what is perceived as authentic national identity (p. 20-1):

> Ay,
> toca las maracas
> mulatón,
>
> Que me muero
> por tu son.

> Ay,
> toca las maracas
> y el bongó
> que mi Cuba
> es un fiestón.
>
> [Oh,
> play the maracas
> my mulatto.
>
> For I die for your *son*
>
> Oh,
> play the maracas
> and the bongo
> for my Cuba is a grand fiesta.]

Abandoning the culture of the home not only allows the subject to enact her own liberation but also enables her to redeem her grandmother, the female figure who is most influential in her formation. Throughout the text Ana Excilia's life, like the speaker's, is intertwined with the social and political life of Cuba. Her entrapment within bourgeois domesticity therefore parallels a period of national self-destruction (p. 11):

> Señora del flan de calabaza,
> abuela y mártir,
> mientras el país se desgaja
> en bombas y muertos.
>
> [Mistress of pumpkin custard,
> grandmother and martyr,
> while the country is torn to pieces
> by bombs and killing.]

Similarly there is an intimation of an earlier romantic attachment that is ruptured through social unrest (p. 25):

> Un sombrero de pajilla está esperándola lejos:
>
> Aquel muchacho muerto en la violencia
> que se encelaba su taconeo.
>
> [A straw hat is awaiting you in the distance:
>
> That young man killed in the violence
> who was filled with jealousy at the sound of your heels.]

The text inscribes the grandmother/granddaughter relationship in contradictory terms; the subject is 'enemiga' [enemy] as well as 'gemela' [twin] (p. 9). The subject's redemption of the grandmother thus becomes a textual resolution of this crisis. Aided by a socialist politics, she is able to re-establish matrilineal ties and thus transcend the vicissitudes of a violent patriarchal history which confounds the potential for female solidarity.

A related issue is the struggle between 'name' [*nombre*] and 'surname' [*apellido*] which is introduced from the very beginning of the poem through the double dedication to Nicolás Guillén and Ana Excilia. In addition to being seen as a reflection of the concern with the personal and communal aspects of the subject's identity, cited earlier, this double dedication might be reconsidered as a reflection of the struggle between the matronymic and patronymic aspects of the woman's identity. The disavowal of the 'father' which is seen throughout the text is clearly complicated by the tension which accompanies the desire to identify with the grandmother. The blame for the destructive aspects of the household experience is therefore never attributed to the grandmother (p. 12):

> No supiste nunca, Ana Excilia
>
> Ni entonces
> ni antes del después,
> cuando la casa dejó de ser el reino de los almíbares
> para convertirse en las ruinas
> del tamarindo.
>
> [You did not know at all, Ana Excilia
>
> Not then
> nor before the afterwards,
> when the house stopped being the syrup kingdom
> and changed into the ruins
> of the tamarind.]

Ana Excilia is unaware of the changing social and emotional circumstances that impinge on the subject's life but this is mapped against her own entrapment in the patriarchal home. She is illiterate, 'without letters nor down strokes' [*sin letras ni palotes*] (p. 25), and her movements are totally controlled by the 'the magic eye of the master' [*ojo mágico del amo*] (p. 8). The subject thus forges an identification with the grandmother confirming her possession of an ability to challenge the strictures of domination (p. 25):

> Sólo tú,
> Ana Excilia,
> comprendes mis campanas,
> campanera tú misma sin saberlo.
>
> [Only you,
> Ana Excilia,
> understand my bells,
> bell-ringer yourself without knowing it.]

And she vows to celebrate the grandmother's name with hands 'blackened with coal' [*renegridas del carbón*] (p. 27). With this in mind, rather than seeing the persona as rejecting her given name (Davies 1998: 25) I would tend to read the poem as her claiming a symbolic association with 'Excilia', not as her total identity, but as the point of departure form which to discover her new name, having exorcised herself of the *apellido*.

The search for the African aspects of Cuban identity which Saldaña's poem constructs is also the theme of Nicolás Guillén's 'El apellido' (1981: 184):

> Yo soy también el nieto,
> biznieto,
> tataranieto de un esclavo.
>
> ...
>
> ¿Seré Yelofe, acaso?
> ¿Nicolás Yelofe, acaso?
> ¿O Nicolás Bakongo?
> ¿Tal vez Guillén Banguila?
> ¿O Kumbá?
> ¿Quizá Guillén Kumbá?
>
> [I am also the grandson,
> great-grandson,
> great-great-grandson of a slave.
>
> Could I be perhaps Yelofé?
> Nicolás Yelofé perhaps?
> Or Nicolás Bakongo?
> Perhaps Guillén Banguila?
> Or Kumbá?
> Perhaps Guillén Kumbá?]

Anxious to recuperate the aspects of his history which do not figure in the official identity imposed on him, the speaker searches for and affirms his African roots. The speaker's name is an arbitrary imposition that is devoid of meaning, an appendage of which he is unable to divest himself. The name does not link him to community and symbolizes an attempt to divorce the speaker from reality. The persona's guess work with surnames is therefore an act of resistance aimed at reclaiming his African patrilineal heritage.

Saldaña also rejects the imposed identity represented by her family name (pp. 30–1):

> Ese talismán fuera de moda,
> esa vieja contraseña,
> ese bastión de familia,
> ¿a quién importarle, sino a mi?
> O a la que dicen que soy
> por pura intuición o maledicencia.
>
> [That out-of-date talisman,
> that old watchword,
> that bastion of family,
> who should care, but me?
> Or who they say I am
> out of sheer intuition or ill will.]

But Saldaña's poem problematizes Guillén's anxieties along gender lines. It is therefore a 'woman version' of his earlier struggle to retrieve identity.[13] Guillén's poem, 'El apellido', is subtitled 'elegía familiar'. Saldaña's antipatriarchal project is signalled, however, in her preoccupation with *nombre* rather than the patronymic *apellido* as well as through her blasphemy against the sovereign ideology of family by composing an 'anti-elegía familiar'. The state of non-identity in *Mi nombre* is not only racialized, as in Guillén's poem. It is also sexualized. The subject inscribes herself in the slave past and in so doing links her critique of patriarchy in the pre-revolutionary Cuba of her childhood with the racial and gender abuse of the plantation economy (p. 14–15):

> Yo habito en un desierto de azúcares turbinadas.
> A través de la mulatez del melado
> oteo un cuerpo:
> me regodeo
> en el cañaveral inédito del pubis,
> en el penacho de la cabeza.
> en el desmoche de las axilas,
> en el breve trapiche de los pechos,
> en las piernas espesas,

en el tacho de bronce del ombligo,
en la centrífuga de los ojos,
en los dientes refinos.

[I inhabit a desert of turbine-pressed sugar.
Through the mulatto mix of cane syrup
I spy a body:
I take pleasure
in the unwritten cane fields of the pubis,
in the crest of the head,
in the cutting of the armpits,
in the small sugar-press of the breasts,
in the thick legs,
in the boiling pan of the navel,
in the centrifugal eyes,
in the refined teeth:]

For Saldaña, restoring a male-centred African ancestral memory is never sufficient as a response to contemporary crises of identity. The gendered aspects of that past must always be interrogated. For example, the poem 'Obba', part of her *Kele Kele* (1987), is a retelling of the myth of the love affair between the Yoruba deities, Changó and his wife Obba, which ends when Changó realizes that she has cut off her ear and given it to him to eat. There are numerous versions of the story but Saldaña's reworking of it focuses the relationship between social deprivation, masculine domination and female self-sacrifice and mutilation. A much earlier poem 'Ogofuyi' (1967) incorporates a reworking of another mythical story in which Oyá a lover of Changó puts Ikú (death) in the corner of her house in order to trap him.[14] The poem does not present the female character as victim. As in *Mi nombre* the woman emerges as victor from a conflictive set of circumstances involving tensions of race, nation and female sexuality.

Mi nombre celebrates the rupturing of traditional gender roles effected in the revolution. The adolescent female subject jettisons the 'encumbering identities' (S. Smith 1993: 16) of the family and its stifling culture in order to discover community, political solidarity and her own worth (p. 25):

Todos quieren que adorne con sus púas
la cintura de mi adolescencia.
Pero
apártense
que voy de pluma.
Pero

apártense
que voy de prisa y vuelo
con un fusil amoroso entre las manos
colmenando la miel que llevo dentro.

[Everyone wants me to decorate with their needles
the belt of my adolescence.
But
stand back
I am off like a feather.
But
stand back
I am in a hurry and I fly
with a loving rifle in my hands/drawing out the honey that I have
inside.]

The rejection of her family name and the affirmation of a new name is an espousal of a communitarian ideal because the subject finds her name in the community: 'in the name of those who have recently found their names/and their memories' [en el nombre de los que recién deciden su nombre y/sus recuerdos] (p. 30). It is partly through this communitarian politics that she derives the power to transcend the objectified status of '*bibelot*' (p. 15) to that of the poet, to move from being 'exiled' [*exiliada*] (p. 23) to being a retriever of African cultural memory. And it is through this communitarian spirit that she retrospectively redeems Ana Excilia Bregante, her grandmother. However, the poem leaves us in no doubt about the woman-centred character of the subject's salvation because, ultimately, she does not discover herself in socio-political involvement but through the birth of her son (p. 29 [my emphasis]):

La casa ya no existe: …
Libre estoy en el espacio
de *la libertad primera*
para encontrarme el origen
en el hijo que me engendra

[The house no longer exists: …
I am free in the space
of the *first freedom*
to find my origins
in the son who engenders me.]

This event engenders her freedom. The birth of the son is also her own re-birth because it provides a new perspective in her own life.

A similarly poignant image of motherhood as the ultimate source of security is presented in Saldaña's *Refranero de la víbora* [The Viper's Refrain] (1989); 'El hijo que no nace/deja a su madre huérfano' [The unborn child/leaves his mother an orphan] (pp. 73–5). It is in this event/image that we find the greatest suggestion of a feminist vision of hope and power. Such a discourse on maternity and power might be considered highly problematic from those feminist perspectives which see motherhood as a major source of women's oppression. Here, however, the relationship between mothering and female agency is unequivocally positive. The birth of her son is contingent on the disappearance of the house, the symbolic destruction of patriarchy. More importantly the narrative expunges paternal power from the woman's story entirely by neglecting to mention a father for the son. This is an extremely positive, revolutionary stance since it signals the woman's final disassociation from the old 'house' and its old male-centred meanings. The woman's new name awaits the son (p. 30):

> Elévate ya,
> estatura de mi hijo;
> mi nombre te espera.
>
> [Rise now,
> my son's height;
> my name awaits you.]

Thus the poem also promises the nurturing of a 'new man' from an anti-patriarchal, woman-centred perspective.

Autobiographical manifestos are not written under the sign of desire, death, or anxiety. While they recall negative and harrowing experiences, by virtue of their empowering thrust, they gesture 'to new spaces for subjectivity' (S. Smith 1993: 163). Thus *Mi nombre* stages the dilemma as well as the hope of a female subject whose struggle against an identity imposed on her by a Eurocentric patriarchal regime ends triumphantly as she creates her 'True True Name' (Mordecai and Wilson 1989).[15] This new identity which the subject forges is very much a disavowal of the old pre-revolutionary order in Cuba. Simultaneously, however, it resists any notion of control or containment in the new order as well. It is the expansive character of the subject's representation of liberation which leads me to make this point. The poetic voice constructs her new identity, precipitated by the birth of her son, in elemental terms 'river' [*rio*], 'sky' [*cielo*], 'thunder' [*trueno*], 'wind' [*viento*]. But also as 'boiler' [*caldera*], 'wound' [*llaga*], 'arch' [*arco*], and 'cave' [*cueva*] – images which remind us of Françoise Lionet's argument that women's autobiographical narratives often have to utilize 'patterns of self-definition which may seem

new and strange' because of the immense difficulty of recognizing themselves in the traditional images that society projects (Lionet 1989: 92).
The poem ends with an image of abundance, amplitude and fluidity
which I can only assume is meant to confirm a defiance of any attempt to
impose boundaries on the woman's concept of self (p. 33):

> Mi nombre
> para precipitarlo como una lluvia sobre el cántaro de mi
> archipélago.
>
> [My name
> to shower it down like rain over the pitcher of my
> archipelago.]

Notes

1   Saldaña's other works include *La noche* [The Night] (1989), *El refranero de la
    víbora* [The Proverb Book of the Viper] (1989), *Kele Kele* (1987), and *Monólogo
    de la esposa* [Wife's Monologue] (1985).
2   See Randall (1982: 197).
3   For a more detailed discussion of this issue see James (1996). Following Linda
    Hutcheon's arguments concerning irony as a forked-tongue discursive mode in
    postcolonial and postmodernist texts I suggests that the poem might be read as an
    instance in which the woman derives empowerment from (finds voice) within the
    revolution and then uses that voice to pose subtle challenges to the vestiges of
    patriarchy within the system.
4   For a discussion of the relationship between national representativeness and
    various Latin American autobiographies See Molloy (1991).
5   For a detailed discussion of the differences between 'testimonio' and autobio-
    graphy see Beverly (1991).
6   See Verity Smith (1993).
7   By this I mean that the family upheld Eurocentric values and aspired to a European
    lifestyle.
8   African cultural memory is a recurring motif in contemporary black Cuban writing.
    Often it is present through the use of folklore or as an emotional quest for the lost
    'motherland'. Two notable examples are Gerardo Fulleda León's *Chago de guisa*
    (1989) and Jesús Cos Causse's moving elegaic poem 'El quijote negro', *Del
    Caribe*, no. 8 (1987), pp. 58–60.
9   Françoise Lionet uses this term in discussing Zora Neale Hurston's *Dust Tracks on
    a Road*, highlighting the text's anthropological positioning of the self within
    history and language. See Lionet (1989: 99).
10 Under the Platt Amendment (May 1901) the sovereignty of the newly independent
    Cuban nation was seriously undermined. Apart from securing the right to set up a
    naval base in Guantánamo the resolution sought and obtained the right to intervene
    at will in the affairs of Cuba. See Aguilar (1993: 21–55, 39).
11 The *charanga* or *charanga francesa* was a popular turn-of-the-century saloon
    dance. The music was orchestral and featured prominently the piano and a number
    of European instruments. See León (1984). In *Campos de Castilla* [Plains of

Castile] (1912), by the Spanish poet Antonio Machado, the 'charanga' is a symbol of a cheap, 'uncultured' Spain. By contrast, in colonial Cuba it became associated with bourgeois culture.

12   The *guaguancó* is one variant of the *rumba* which originated among the Bantu Congo Groups. Like most Cuban cultural forms there are clear areas of Spanish influence in the *guaguancó* such as the lyrical guidelines. The form however, (in which *claves* and three Cuban drums of Congo ancestry are used) is highly polyrhythmic and marked by African liturgical cadences and modes. See Urfé (1984: 170–88).

13   I take this term from Evelyn O'Callaghan. Using a 1960s Jamaican musical development, the 'version', as central trope O'Callaghan suggests a paradigm for reading West Indian Women's Writing as a 'kind of remix or dub version, which utilizes elements from the "master tape" of Caribbean literary discourse (combining, stretching, modifying them in new ways)' and 'announces a gendered perspective'. See O'Callaghan (1993: 11).

14   A translation of the poem has been published under the title 'Ofumelli' in Péres Sarduy and Stubbs' book (1993).

15   Mordecai and Wilson (1989) take the title of their collection of Caribbean women's writing, *Her True True Name*, from Merle Hodge's *Crick Crack Monkey* (1970), a novel which stages the multiple crises of identity which a black female child experiences in post-colonial Trinidad.

The nation from *De donde son los cantantes* to *Los pájaros en la playa*[1]

Roberto González Echevarría

When *De donde son los cantantes* [From Cuba with a Song] first appeared in 1967, and despite the indisputable political, artistic and ideological triumphs of the essay and, indeed, of narrative about cultural identity, the presence of discord was clear between the theories it propounds and Latin American realities. In narrative, which had embarked upon a process of transformation with, for example, the early works of Juan Carlos Onetti, there was highlighted the profoundly urban character of the new Latin American novel. This stood in contrast with that predominantly rural fiction, which, based as it was on primitivist atavisms, seemed to champion pre-Western cultures. In the essay, the magisterial voices of Rodó, Mariátegui, Henríquez Ureña, Reyes, Lezama Lima, and even Paz, seemed to obscure rather than reveal the internal mechanisms of the renewed culture of Latin America. Instead of identity, rather than a fusion of artistic vision and reality, there was a dissonance which these voices muffled with argument and anecdote, the attractiveness of which was indisputable, but which characterized an obsolescent ideology and an exhausted aesthetic. To put it another way, the topic of cultural identity in essays and novels seemed to be devoted to the construction of images, characters, tales and theories whose coherence and capacity to persuade depended on their ability to conceal more than to reveal the active and dynamic nature of contemporary Latin American culture.[2] It need hardly be said that the very nature and existence of these fictions about culture was itself an important element at certain levels of Latin American culture. However, discontentment with both their concepts of 'expression' and 'identity' was indisputable by the end of the 1960s.

National identity has been a constant theme in twentieth-century Cuban literature for various reasons: the lateness of independence, the relatively recent arrival of large numbers of Africans, the threatening proximity of the United States, and the irruption of an acutely nationalist revolutionary movement. Even in the nineteenth century it was an obsessive topic for patriotic thinkers such as José Martí, who constructed the concept of a Cuban nation before it ever existed as such, much less as a state. This anachronism at the origin has endowed Cuban nationalism with an enormous vehemence, which is notable in its literary manifestation as much as in any other. On the island, the most recent essayist tradition concerned with national identity began with Jorge Mañach and his *Indagación del choteo* [Investigation of Cuban Irreverence], of 1927. It continued with Juan Marinello's 1932 essay, 'Americanismo y cubanismo literario' [Literary Americanism and Cubanism], which was, in turn, followed by the work of Fernando Ortiz, above all in his important lecture of 1939, 'La cubanidad y los negros' [Cubanness and Blacks]. The debate was then carried on in *La expresión americana* [Latin American Expression] by José Lezama Lima, published in 1957, followed by *Tientos y diferencias* [Scrutinies and Differences] by Alejo Carpentier, which appeared in 1962. The cycle is completed with *Calibán* [Caliban] by Roberto Fernández Retamar, which appeared in 1971. The text appeared four years after the publication of *De donde son los cantantes*, but in terms of the literary and ideological evolution of Latin American literature should actually be considered a step backward. There then followed other contributions, including those of Gustavo Pérez Firmat in *The Cuban Condition: Translation and Identity in Modern Cuban Literature* (1989) and *La isla que se repite* [The Repeating Island] (1989) by Antonio Benítez Rojo, both of which offer polemical revisions of the tradition from the perspective of exile.

In 1939, Ortiz was courageous enough to proclaim that the most deep-rooted *cubanidad* [cubanness] was that of the island's black population, because, unlike white creoles of whatever origin, they never had the possibility of returning to a much-yearned-for and ever-welcoming homeland. The blacks had to accept Cuba as their homeland. The fact that, today, it is impossible even to contemplate the exclusion of the African element from any discussion of Cuban identity is testimony to the success of Ortiz's social and pedagogical project and is highlighted by the fact that views put forward by Fernández Retamar almost 30 years later do not differ that much from his. All movements towards the formulation of *cubanidad* – including a book like Carpentier's 1946 *La música en Cuba* [Music in Cuba] – were channelled in Cuba by the *Orígenes* [Origins] group, led by Lezama Lima. These efforts achieved their purest doctrinal expression in Cintio Vitier's 1958 work, *Lo cubano en la poesía* [Cubanness in

Poetry]. Based on a providentialist Hegelian framework, Vitier proposes that *cubanidad* constitutes a search for the nation's self through poetry, discovery and formulation of what is autochthonous that reaches its apotheosis in the poetry of the master, Lezama. This is the tradition inherited by Sarduy and which undergoes the most original modification of the last 30 years in his work, finding its final expression in the posthumous 1993 novel, *Los pájaros en la playa* [The Birds on the Beach], which I shall discuss in this context after briefly mentioning those of his previous works which deal with the theme of Cubanness.[3]

Despite having already lived as an exile in Paris for seven years when *De donde son los cantantes* appeared in 1967, Sarduy's takes far greater advantage than any other text, especially those written in Cuba itself, of the historical, political, and cultural rupture constituted by the Revolution. In so doing, he submits the discussion of Cuban and, by extension, Latin American identity, to a deconstructive analysis that stands as a landmark in the Latin American literature of identity (Sarduy 1993). *De donde son los cantantes* is like a vast tapestry which represents the myth of nationality, but viewed as if from behind, examining the seams, the means of construction, even, or particularly, those of which we are least conscious. Sarduy was assisted in this not least by his intense interest in the structuralist and post-structuralist movements and by knowing better than any other Latin American the theories of Lacan and other *maîtres à penser* of the day. The novel highlights all those elements that remained suppressed in preserving the coherence of previous theories of Cuban and Latin American culture. In psychoanalytical terms, which I use only for their familiarity, Sarduy's text illuminates a kind of dense and dark cultural unconscious, liberating that which remained repressed, dramatizing, as if in a *psychomachia*, its cast of figures and phantoms. For example, the plurality and fluidity of the sexual roles conjured up by the language in its sleight of grammatical genders show themselves in the development of the characters who are introduced as transvestites, without the reader knowing what was their 'original' sex. From this point on, the sexual will always appear as simulation in Sarduy. In *De donde son los cantantes*, all culture, beginning with language itself, seems to be motivated by a series of perversions which are created by desire, desire for power, and sadism, but which are at the same time driven by the urge to conceal, dissemble and translate them. Neither does the liberation of the repressed lead to its celebration – it is not a gay literature in the partisan or political sense which the term has today. There is no panacea nor narcissism of that sort in Sarduy's novel, just as there is no folklore. Dissembled components of the Cuban psyche are dramatized, but these appear, in turn, as products of equally perverse impulses. One could, if one wished, term this the Bataille element of Sarduy's work. All culture exists through an interweaving of codes, created to channel these forces and make both the social and its ever dynamic, changeable, and always distortable representation possible, as well as always susceptible to revealing analysis of their hidden mechanisms and structures.

De donde son los cantantes can, therefore, be read as a critique of the *Orígenes* project, despite Sarduy's later declaration (1988) that he was a disciple and even 'heir' of Lezama Lima. Typical of its time, the *Orígenes* group viewed culture strictly in terms of high culture, particularly poetry, which was regarded as the purest form of artistic expression (this is more true of Lezama Lima's acolytes such as Vitier, than of the master himself, for whom culture existed as a whole without fissures, frontiers or hierarchies). The culture depicted in *De donde son los cantantes* is not high, but neither is it popular in the folkloric sense common in the tradition of essays about cultural identity. Sarduy isolates that segment of national culture which we might describe as common or vulgar, where the boundary between the lower-middle and upper-lower classes becomes confused. In this amalgam, nothing is genuine, stable or pure; everything is in a process of transformation, contamination and even degradation. Everything can be assimilated, especially the products of the mass media which alter the nation's culture, depriving it of its autochthonous aura. Sarduy draws the reader into the territory of *kitsch*, of the abject, of everything rejected by official culture in all its forms, including the political. For this reason, *De donde son los cantantes* takes its title from a song by the popular Trío Matamoros and not from a verse by, say, Martí or Lezama Lima.[4] The dynamism of this plebeian culture permits it to be critical, paradoxical and impudent; though essentially urban, it is situated at the margins of city life. It bustles with transvestites, prostitutes, tattoo experts, drug addicts, pushers and other creatures of the night, who, from here on in, are the characters who will inhabit Sarduy's fiction. It resembles the ambience of vulgarity discussed by the great Puerto Rican writer, Luis Rafael Sánchez.

However, the cruellest criticism to be found in *De donde son los cantantes* is that levelled against the basically Catholic, neo-Hegelian providentialism of the *Origenistas*, above all that of Vitier in *Lo Cubano en la poesía*. Cuba's entire history, viewed in the context of the by-products of her Hispanic, African and Chinese cultures, unfolds in a kind of accumulative process in Sarduy's novel, eventually culminating in a lavishly parodic procession in which the characters leave from the province of Oriente, carrying on their shoulders a decaying effigy of Christ (Cristo, but also Castro) all the way to Havana. The effigy gradually rots away during the journey. In a capital improbably buried under snow, they are shot at from helicopters. The conclusion allegorizes the way national culture conceals an irreducible violence which, eventually, always spills over the banks of all the channels that contain it. The white of the shocking snow that covers Havana, and which represents Death in certain Afro-Cuban doctrines, also suggests an end which is not to be seen as an apotheosis of meaning but, instead, of its absence. *De donde son los cantantes* is a never-ending teleology which does not succeed in converting itself into a theodicy. The *donde* [where] – with and without accent in Spanish, question or answer – of 'de donde son los cantantes' [from where the song is/where is the song from?] is that mobile, mutating place represented by the text.

All the elements of his concept of Cuban identity which are present in *De donde son los cantantes* also persist in Sarduy's other work, with some significant modifications. *Cobra* (1970) is Sarduy's most difficult novel and the one which seems to respond least to the dialectic of national identity. There is no doubt that this work reflects the fascination of the *Tel Quel* group for Mao's China. But there are Chinese in Cuba too, an ethnic element neglected by the official Cuban culture that Sarduy emphasized in *De donde son los cantantes*. Yet *Cobra's* probing of language and meaning also has a historical and anagrammatical dimension which refers to Cuba and the theme of identity. First of all, guided by the journey undertaken by the characters through India, we are made aware of a series of allusions which repeat in reverse, as it were, the error made by Columbus in thinking he had arrived in the Indies. 'Las Indias Galantes' [The Gallant Indies], the name of the bar where a few of the characters end up, reminds us that the origin of Latin American history – and by this I mean its discourse – is error, and that the language in which this culture is cast also stems form this error, from this misnaming of the New World. The characters try to control this errancy of language by means of corporal inscription, the tattoo, the ultimate cipher for a symbol continually seeking to detach itself from the point of reference. The tattoo also evokes the pain of inscription, of the imposition of letter and meaning. *Cobra* barely conceals those mechanisms of cultural self-constitution which begin with difference, represented as the inevitable wound of dermic writing. The approximative nature of the language is also revealed in the key motif of the novel which is its very title. The cobra is, of course, a phallic symbol – construction, sexual erection, sign of false materiality, collapsable, the serpent at the origins of so many theogonies. The presence in *Cobra* of a parodic figure of Lacan,

Dr Ktazob, an expert in sexual surgery, suggests that the novel explores the 'imaginary' of Cuban identity, above all the construction of *machismo*.[5] But 'cobra' could also relate to the *cobre* [copper] of the Virgen de la Caridad de Cobre, Cuba's patron virgin, and it could even be a corrupted version of the island's name. Finally, it must be remembered that the characters return to China from exile, and upon reaching the frontier at the end of the novel, they once again encounter snow. *Cobra* seeks a different route to the same elusive whiteness of *De donde son los cantantes*.

But the novel in which Sarduy concentrates most on the theme of Cuban identity after *De donde son los cantantes* is *Maitreya* (1978). *Maitreya* is a geographical allegory in which the characters, in search of the new Buddha, journey from Tibet to Cuba itself, passing through Colombo on the way. From Cuba, they go on (of course) to Miami and New York, and finally end up in Iran on the eve of the Islamic Fundamentalist Revolution. *Maitreya* is, moreover, the biography of Luis Leng, a minor character in Lezama's monumental novel *Paradiso* (he is a cook). There is a strong Afro-Cuban element in *Maitreya*; *Santería* seems to have converted itself into the essence of Cubanness. The range of allegorical journey is appropriately wide: from a Tibet destroyed by the Chinese of the Popular Republic, who employ a western ideology, we arrive in a Middle East shaken by a movement that is striving to obliterate all traces of the West and return to its religion and traditional customs. As in other novels by Sarduy, the characters find themselves in those very environments where national cultures are in the process of global transformation, in which these are recycled by cultural practices emanating from the developed world. The world of *Maitreya* is, on a planetary level, the world of contamination which we have already seen on a Cuban scale in *De donde son los cantantes*, a cosmos in which the detritus of traditional cultures and religions float unbound in a plethora of meaning. Buddhism and *Santería* are jumbled up with Islamic elements. One of Sarduy's great themes takes shape in *Maitreya*: the bankruptcy of Enlightenment promises, amongst them the modern concept of the nation and nostalgia for traditional cultures, which may only be salvaged as degraded fragments, by now incapable of being vehicles of the sacred.

Before dealing with Sarduy's last novels, let us recapitulate the paradigmatic shift carried out in his work, and also what sort of new writing it announces or anticipates. It is not necessary to look for a precise, categorical, and chronological progression. We have already seen how *De donde son los cantantes* is almost strictly contemporary with *Calibán*. Sarduy's work coincides in its infancy with the Boom, but maintained a distance from it from the very beginning. The essay genre and the narrative of identity are based on a model which we could call philological. Adhering strictly to the etymology of this term, we might say that the love of language leads to a search for its origin and centre of meaning, the essence of its being. This essence, this identity, equivalence or homology with other cultural products, manifests itself in two principal means of representation: groups which a) retain more or less intact their cultural traditions, remaining immune to history; and b) which are organized in families with a patriarchal structure.[6] The groups could be peasants of Iberian, black or Indian descent. Mulattoization was possible, but this was considered more as the sum total of characteristics and elements rather than as a dynamic amalgam of these. Octavio Paz in *El laberinto de la soledad* [The Labyrinth of Solitude] (1950), and later Carlos Fuentes in *La muerte de Artemio Cruz* [The Death of Artemio Cruz] (1962) represent the essence of Mexican identity through the 'family romance' of La Malinche and Cortés. García Márquez centres the history of Macondo on the abundant branches of the Buendía family tree, with its recurring names and physical characteristics and its reiterated character traits.[7] *Paradiso* is the history of the Cemí and of the void which the Colonel's death leaves. And so on.

There are hardly ever family groups in Sarduy's narrative, at least not in the conventional sense. Thus the nucleus which composes and conserves the nation and its symbols is abolished. The relationships between characters are of a rather fortuitous nature, and they relate to one another or reproduce in a theogonic form, never in the conventional biological manner. In Sarduy, there are whorehouse matrons, but no mothers; pimps but few fathers. In the *De donde son los cantantes*, for example, Auxilio and Socorro are a pair of Dioscuric Yoruba twins, but they are also united by the pleonastic nature of their names, which almost have the same meaning: Aid and Help. Nor do there appear many common names or surnames. Generally the names are nicknames (or *nommes de guerre*) which highlight, in a humorous fashion, physical or moral characteristics: such as, for example, La Tremenda [Awesome], Cobra, Pup, El Dulce [Sweetie], La Cadillac, La Senecta [Old Dear], El Japonesón [The Fat Jap]. In terms of language, we move from the philological to the linguistic, from words loaded with etymological meaning to words which relate to one another in the present to form an ephemeral *langue*, the slang of the moment, changeable on the spot, which relieves itself of its traditional burden. Sarduy's language is a dynamic system of relations which serves as much to forget as to remember and is never the repository of given or inert meanings. Evidently, the fluidity of sexual roles, their dependence on simulation rather than anatomy (which is eluded, or rather, elided when it presents itself as an obstacle) is another of the fundamental changes in relation to the previous paradigm, which, as has already been said, reproduced (pun intended) the nuclear patriarchal family. The setting in which these *ad hoc* groups operate is no longer a typical landscape but comprises instead towns on the periphery of the West or marginal areas of western towns, which resemble a great city, or rather, a massive citadel, a jumble of cultures in transit and transition, where there could be (and is) a diner in Manhattan called 'Asia de Cuba' [Asia of Cuba].

In *Colibrí* [Hummingbird] (1984), Sarduy's next novel, he writes an inverted – perverted – version of the Latin America jungle novel. It is a text which transposes to a continental context the violated mimetic pact we have seen in his previous works, but at the same time, signals a dispersion of the *Tel Quel* group through its thematic content and the search by Sarduy for a typical Spanish American setting for his novels. The work is fundamental from a strictly biographical perspective for one reason alone: in *Colibrí*, the adolescent, the young man, will succeed in becoming the figure of authority, will reach adulthood and power upon the disappearance of the *Señora* [Madam]. The ending is ambiguous: Colibrí is going to take possession of the *Casona* [The Big House], but by this time it is no longer a gay emporium which stages rigged all-in wrestling bouts. Now it is a lunatic asylum. This is the only instance in Sarduy where the young man assumes the mantle of power and complete identity which will reward him with maturity and power.

Cocuyo [The Glow Worm] (1989), the last novel written by Sarduy before he was diagnosed with AIDS, constitutes a regression, in every sense, which forces him to return explicitly to the theme of Cuban identity by adopting a decidedly personal and reminiscent approach. *Cocuyo* is a kind of autobiography, but in very oblique form, as is usually the case with Sarduy (I allude here to Lezama's concept of oblique experience). In the novel, there is a move from cultural context to individual life, from the whole to the fragment from which that whole can be observed. Cuban history and culture are allegorized in the life of the youth, a version of the author himself. This becomes clear when we compare the novel with essays by Sarduy such as the 1982 *La simulación* [Simulation] and the 1987 *El Cristo de la rue Jacob* [Christ on the Rue Jacob], and is even clearer, of course, to those of us who knew him well. This change of direction is not towards a self founded on and burdened by history, but instead towards a fractured self, broken by the latter. It is a witnessing self, not an actor, the voyeur of its own existence, a sounding board for the actions of adults.

Cocuyo narrates the life of a boy who, in order to take revenge on his family for their mocking remarks concerning his vocation as a writer, tries to kill them with rat poison. He is rescued by a woman who runs what appears to be a home for orphans, goes to work in the chambers of corrupt and perverse lawyers and falls in love with a young girl. However, he soon realizes that La Bondadosa [Generous], the ironic name of the girl's protector, is the accomplice of two shady characters who turn the pupils to prostitution. At the end, they give Ada, the girl Cocuyo loves, over to this fate. Betrayed, Cocuyo decides to poison them all.

Let us tell the novel again but in another key. Sarduy is welcomed by the leading members of the *Tel Quel* group on remaining in exile and adrift in Paris, having fled the ridicule of the establishment of the cultural revolution which institutionalized *machismo* in Cuba. He becomes disenchanted with his protectors when he discovers political, intellectual and moral falsity in some of them. He feels betrayed by the fickleness and inconsistency of his mentors and by their superficiality. Some, the closest, establish relations with others who threaten Sarduy's precarious stability in a world which is not his own. The title of the novel could be read as a play on words of the Franco-Spanish *cocu-yo*, *cornudo yo* [I, the cuckold]. But let us retell it again in yet another key. Cocuyo, the Cuban glow worm, is the fabled metamorphosis of the young man, exploited and betrayed by his associates; that is to say, it is a version of Kafka's 'Metamorphosis', the essential tale of resentment as a process in the construction of the self. Another version: Cocuyo comes from a Cuban province where they still live as they did in the nineteenth century. He endures a Cuban youth – the typicality of his surroundings conveys this – from the large earthenware jars of Camagüey (Sarduy was from Camagüey), to the excesses of the adults, petty clerks and quacks, which allegorize the childhood of the character. Cuban culture, Latin American culture, emerges as a process where the individual is terrorized and sold by his elders; it is a tale of betrayal at all levels: from familial, to the national and continental. The self assembles and disassembles itself in relation – and in reaction – to fear and disgust. Final version: Cocuyo, during his time at the lawyers' chambers, sleeps amongst the files, living in the Archive. The letter represents the law; it is the law, the voice of the father rendered into inscription, which not only marks injuriously but is eternally dangerous, eternally accusing, created by betrayal and oppression.[8]

Clearly, the name of the protagonist suggests that Cocuyo is also a 'portrait of the artist as a young man'. The *cocuyo* is a glow worm which projects light from its interior. It is not necessary to mention the title of the famous book by M.H. Abrams, *The Mirror and the Lamp* (1953), for us to realize that Cocuyo is a budding poet. Furthermore, the mockery which provokes him into attempting to murder his family runs counter to his style of narrative: as he describes to those present the ravages of a cyclone which he observes from a window, and in particular the decapitation of a negro by a flying sheet of zinc, everyone makes fun of his mannerisms and rhetoric. The fear of castration and the jokes made at his expense turn Cocuyo into a voyeur and a masturbator – on two occasions they accuse him of being a *pajero*, Cuban slang for the latter. Fear, narcissism, resentment, these are the components that make the identity of this Cuban artist, for whom the fables of the nation are his nightmare. The national in *Cocuyo* appears, then, as a process of reduction of the individual, of his subjection to the law from which he materializes and seems unable to escape.

One of the most sinister characters in *Cocuyo* is Caimán, and that was to be the title of Sarduy's next novel. But illness intervened and although Caimán figures prominently in the posthumous novel, *Los pájaros en la playa* (1993), the slant of this inevitably changes. The novel both takes stock and bids farewell and thus the themes of identity and the national are necessarily made more dramatic. A kind of *Magic Mountain*, *Los pájaros en la playa* is the tale of a sanatorium for AIDS patients (now known as *sidatorios*) situated on an island, to all intents and purposes one of the Canary Islands, and which is also populated by naturists, nudists, and others dedicated to cultivating their physical health through exercise. The island, with its palm trees, is a reflection or version of Cuba, just as Colombo was in *Maitreya*.

A markedly symmetrical text, *os pájaros en la playa* consists of two interrelated stories. One is that of Siempreviva [Ever Alive], an old Celestinesque, Faustian woman affected by old age only, rather than disease, who wishes to recover her youth.[9] She is attended by two doctors: Caballo, with whom the old woman falls in love and whom she succeeds in seducing, and Caimán, a Cuban herbalist who treats her with plant infusions and concoctions from which he claims to extract the energy of the planet.[10] Whilst those who are ill vertiginously age, Siempreviva becomes ever younger. The other story is that of Cosmógrafo, an autobiographical figure, who is a young man with the AIDS virus who had become an expert on the disease and tries to discover its etiology and a possible cure through reflections on the origins of the cosmos which are similar to those of Sarduy in his 1987 essay 'Nueva inestabilidad' [New Instability]. Auxilio and Socorro (from *De donde son los cantantes*) reappear and there is what amounts to a totemic, or perhaps heraldic, recapitulation of all Sarduy's protagonists: Cobra, Caimán and Cocuyo. The characters, with their emblematic names, move through several levels, one of which is astronomic, where their deeds resemble those of the constellations which some represent.

The title of the novel may derive from a Cuban term. *Pájaro* is one of the derogatory terms used in Cuba to refer to homosexuals, and there is the term *maricón playero* [beach faggot], that is, someone who dedicates himself to the activity known as *flete* (*draguer*, cruising) on the beaches. Reinaldo Arenas, in *Antes que anochezca* [Before Night Falls] (1992), gives an extensive account of this aspect of Cuban life. The title reflects a thinly veiled resentment which is still an echo of *Cocuyo*. Being is self-defining in this work, confined within a perimeter of vexations, threats and rejections, which add to the slow and irreversible physical decline caused by the disease. But 'pájaros en la playa' further alludes to the liminality of the characters and of the world in which they live. Beaches are strips between sea and land, between the island and the sea which surrounds it; the birds move between land and air like reptiles with feathers. On the island, as I already mentioned, there live both those who are ill and experts in physical training who enjoy almost excessive health. The entire text is set up as a combination of binary opposites which is reminiscent of the structure of myth as conceived by Levi-Strauss. Cosmógrafo's interpretation of AIDS can be seen as a counterpart to the cures which are created by the herbalist. Cosmógrafo interprets the illness in terms of the Big Bang theory: the illness heralds a general loss of cosmic energy due to depletion of the initial explosive effect. Cosmógrafo claims to have seen the spark of this original explosion and now believes he can see the beginning of the end, hence his arcane knowledge of the ravages of the illness and his attitude of scepticism and total disillusionment.

A complementary character, the Architect, sets out to construct an underground house, soon obliterated by the sea. He searches for the energy of a supernova in the rumblings of the earth, in the geological depths of the island. But the Architect fails and perishes in his tectonic pursuit, thus annulling all possibility of finding the identity, the essence of the island through his intense bond with the earth. The Architect, the Architext, is for me a representation of Alejo Carpentier, whose first vocation, like that of his father, was architecture, and whom Sarduy always saw as the practitioner of a tellurism typical of the search for identity that was transformed after 1967 in *De donde son los cantantes*. (I never shared this view with my dear friend.) But, in less specific terms, it is precisely this tradition of investigating the national which the Architect represents: even perhaps alluding to the *Orígenes* group, amongst whose members was the architect Mario Romañach, who, in 1957, built a house for the Alvarez family in which he used elements of traditional Cuban architecture, also incorporating materials and colours indigenous to the island, and facing it in such a way as to benefit from the refreshing breezes and shade.

Cosmógrafo gradually loses coherence as the novel progresses and by the end his diary has become a disconnected series of maxims and, finally, of poems. The novel closes with a brief poem by the exiled Soviet, lesbian, mentally ill poetess, Marina Tsvetayeva, whose work Sarduy had translated and edited with Elisabeth Burgos (Tsvietáieva 1991) and which functions as a reflection of himself in a concave mirror. Frantically searching for himself in the turmoil of illness and death, Sarduy gives up his voice to that other condemned artist, Tsvetayeva. The gesture of closing with a fragment from the other alienated exile represented by this Russian woman suggests a final effort to transcend a being which is now defined by a cosmic fatigue with which he blends at the point of death. It is also a final gesture of transvestism and the rejection of an aesthetically pleasing ending to the novel.

The final version of national identity created by Sarduy is that of exile-ex-i(s)le-away from the island, but viewed in cosmic terms. We are fragments of a whole which existed before the explosion that created the universe, and we move, progressively distancing ourselves from each other and from the source of energy. We are not only from the island, but islands ourselves. What remains of Cuban identity in *Los pájaros en la playa* are fragments, reflecting the herbal science of Caimán. *Los pájaros en la playa* seems to suggest that, at the end of this century, the narratives of nations remain mythological fables, deprived of the capacity to confer identity or refer to the sacred. This does not detract from the fact that, to the end, Sarduy has stuck to remnants and memories of Cuban culture, but never to its central fables and even less to official histories from which he saw himself being systematically excluded, as from the *Diccionario de la literatura cubana* [Dictionary of Cuban Literature], edited by the Instituto de Literatura y Lingüística de la Academia de Ciencias de Cuba [Institute of Literature and Linguistics of the Academy of Sciences of Cuba] (two volumes: 1980, 1984). The nation, in the guise of the state, excluded Sarduy from its archive.

The most important vestiges of Cuban identity in Sarduy's last work are the poetic ones. His last poems are mostly *décimas* [ten-line stanzas], the most traditional and rigorously Cuban verse form. In them he treats the most solemn of topics, such as death, with typically Cuban irreverence and takes delight in mentioning Cuban sweets, drinks and fruits. But the national narratives are dead doctrines, aptly placed in that catalogue of broken dogma, ineffective as social norms today, as are the great religions and hegemonic ideologies, whatever might be or has been their actual political agenda, past or future. Most ironically, perhaps, Sarduy's work does not only show the bankruptcy of Enlightenment ideas, but also that its universality lies not so much in its ideas but in the detritus of its products (that is, its by-products), amongst them the spreading of disease. The world is the *rastro* of the West, as much in its etymological sense, in Spanish, of 'trace' as in another of its meanings: 'dumping ground', where, in this case, the scrap of progress, its cosmic waste is emptied.

But there remain at least two more suggestions for readings of *Los pájaros en la playa*. One is that the cosmological vision of this displaced, isolated and oblique Caribbean of the island-sanatorium repeats the true origin of Cuban discourse. In the beginning, the Caribbean was the New World, the *Orbe Novo* of the cosmographer who first tried to interpret it: Pedro Mártir de Anglería (see González Echevarria 1995). Furthermore, the apocalyptic island from which Cosmografo narrates his own demise and that of the universe, suggests that of Patmos, from which Saint John, in the *Book of Revelation*, also narrates the end of all ages. The global binary opposition within which the Caribbean has always swung is that of being both Beginning and End, utopia and apocalypse.[11] The value of Sarduy's later work lies in its liberation of this conflict of oppositions from an origin which hangs over us like some tragic destiny, in a gesture as grandiose as it is pathetic, with recourse to the sacred which it may still contain.

It is fortuitous, in the highest sense, that death interrupted the writing of *Los pájaros en la playa*, confusing the end of the novel with the life of the author, but at the same time highlighting the indissoluble difference between the two: life ends but the novel remains perpetually unfinished, as if waiting for another author, or reader, who might dare to complete it, at the risk of another fatal event intervening to prevent this. These are two different openings to the same infinity where it is useless to set boundaries, in which end or beginning are ephemeral, poignant marks. In *Los pájaros en la playa* the only permanent evidence of these marks is produced by their reiteration; externally, through the apocalyptic gesture first begun by Pedro Mártir de Anglería, the anxious return to a deep and legitimating origin; internally, through poetry, the language of ritual, of liturgical reiteration, ever-bowed before and towards the sacred.

On Severo's grave, in the cemetery at Thiais on the outskirts of Paris, I found that someone had placed a plastic rattle. I don't know who the bearer of that gift might have been, but it occurred to me that there could not have been a more appropriate offering to my dead friend. Like the prayer windmills turning above the snow at the end of *Cobra*, rotating signs against the unanimous and infinite whiteness, that tiny toy, with the endearing *chas chas* of its beads, an elemental rhythm, a prayer offered up to indifferent gods, is like the language of the end of all ages which Severo conceived with the innocence of a child.

Notes

1 An earlier version of this essay first appeared in Spanish in *Cuadernos Hispanoamericanos* (1997), 563: 55–67.
2 I have discussed this point in greater detail in González Echevarría (1985).
3 Although I shall try to expand and improve on what has already been said, the premises of much that will follow, as well as a more extensive exposition of some themes, can be found in González Echevarría (1986).
4 The Trío Matamoros was a popular Cuban musical group founded in the 1920s [eds].
5 On the subject of castration, see René Prieto's brilliant essay, 'The Ambivalent Fiction of Severo Sarduy', *Symposium* (Washington, DC, Spring 1985), pp. 49–60.
6 See Sommer (1991), where it is suggested that there exists a relationship between national projects and family structure in the Spanish American novel of the nineteenth century. These genealogico-patriotic allegories continue and become more complicated in the *criollista* novels and those of the *Boom*.
7 Patricia Tobin (1978) has studied genealogy as a structuring resource of the novel, including *Cien años de soledad* [One Hundred Years of Solitude].
8 I have studied the relationship between law and the origins of novelistic fiction in González Echevarría (1990).
9 I have dealt with 'Celestina's brood', including their manifestation in Spanish American fiction, in González Echevarría (1993).
10 'Caballo' is, by the way, Fidel Castro's nickname amongst Cubans, for, amongst other reasons, the fact that the horse represents the number one in Cuban-Chinese numerology. But this character is also referred to as 'el hombre que parecía un caballo' [the man who seemed a horse], in an allusion to the short story of the same name by Rafael Arévalo Martínez, a Guatemalan writer whose text was one of the most celebrated in the Latin America of the 1930s and 1940s. In however elegant and oblique a fashion, the short story deals with homosexual themes.
11 On this point Lois Parkinson Zamora makes some interesting observations (1989).

6 | # *Tuntún de pasa y grifería*: A cultural project[1]

Carmen Vázquez Arce

I

In this paper, I attempt to examine *Tuntún de pasa y grifería* as an essay in verse form within the context of its publication in 1937. With this book, Luis Palés Matos entered the cultural debate of the 1930s and offered a response to *Insularismo* [Insularism] (1934) by Antonio S. Pedreira, whose discourse put itself forward as a dominant one.

This study is not definitive. It is more a proposal concerning the value of *Tuntún de pasa y grifería* as a text which serves as a reflection on the cultural projects of its generation, and proposes several-hypotheses:

Firstly, with regard to Puerto Rican history and culture, the intellectuals of the 1930s represent the first generation in a broad and diverse foundational movement of nationalism and culture. Intellectuals of the nineteenth century, with the exception of the separatist project, did not try to differentiate themselves from metropolitan culture, but rather tried to establish a Latin American variant. On the other hand, intellectuals of the 1930s proposed a ground-breaking plan which hoped to create a singular identity, distinct with regard to North American culture, while establishing national characteristics whose universal character might reflect their 'soul' and their land, in other words, a Spenglerian model of culture.[2] This movement invents and tries to give form to that which has been taken for granted and which must now be specified:

> The culture in which one grows up is never really 'visible' –
> it is taken for granted and its assumptions are felt to be self-
> evident. It is only through 'invention' ... that the abstract
> significance of culture ... can be grasped, and only through

the experienced contrast that his own culture becomes 'visible'.

(Wagner 1981: 4)

The need to construct a visible cultural model arises in this period as a result of the perception of cultural 'trauma' produced by the North American invasion of 1898.

> Anyone else who is compelled to live in 'new' or alien surroundings, has the taste of this kind of 'shock'. ... We depend upon the participation of others in our lives and upon our own participation in the lives of others ... Culture shock is a loss of the self through the loss of these supports.

(Wagner 1981: 7)

> Culture is made visible by culture shock, by subjecting oneself to situations beyond one's normal interpersonal competence and objectifying the discrepancy as an entity; it is delineated through an inventive realization of that entity following the initial experience.

(Wagner 1981: 9)

The concept of 'trauma' was formulated by Francisco Manrique Cabrera in his *Historia de la Literatura Puertorriqueña* [A History of Puerto Rican Literature] (1956), a fundamental text in the historiography of the 1930s and an intuitive work in the cultural debate.

The idea of a need to invent culture appeared in an essay by Margot Arce de Vázquez, 'Las raíces' [Roots] (1956), whose dedication reads: 'To my comrades in the task of inventing for ourselves a Puerto Rican culture' [*a los compañeros en la tarea de inventarnos una cultura puertorriqueña*]. '"Invention", the "sign" of differentiation, is the obviator of conventional contexts and contrasts.' (Wagner 1981: 43)

From the most diverse fields – history, linguistics, literary creation and criticism, music and politics – the intellectuals of the 1930s gave themselves over to the task of objectifying, delineating and inventing Puerto Rican culture, and also to serving as a compass which might guide the drifting ship of national culture to a port made secure by the satisfaction of development and national progress within a clear concept of what is Puerto Rican.[3]

Another hypothesis I wish to explore is Bakhtin's idea of *heteroglossia* or *plurilinguism* (1991: 102). If we accept that the Puerto Rican intelligentsia of the 1930s was a diverse group, we can understand that there exists within it a multiplicity of discourses, that is, a *heteroglossia* that includes the proliferation of social languages which compete and intersect within the same language. Pedreira's discourse comes across as a unitary discourse, but it does not erase the presence of other discourses which coexist in the field of socio-cultural struggle.

> Every apparently unified linguistic community is characterized by 'many-languagedness' [*heteroglossia*] in which the idioms of different generations, classes, genders, races and locales compete for ascendancy. Every language, then, constitutes a set of languages, and every speaking subject opens onto a multiplicity of languages. All communication entails an apprenticeship in the language of the other, a kind of translation or coming to terms with the meaning on the boundaries of another's set of languages as well as one's own.
>
> (Stam 1989: 59)

It is here that we encounter the transgressive discourse of Palés Matos in *Tuntún de pasa y grifería*.

The presence of *heteroglossia* in intellectual discourse of the 1930s demands a critical re-examination from the perspective of a dialectical debate among its diverse components. Thus, as Lotman and Uspenskij (1979: 67) observe, all historically determined culture generates its own fixed cultural model, which results in it becoming the dominant model; but it does not impede the simultaneous existence of other discourses and practices which point towards heterogeneity in culture and which manifest *heteroglossia*. On the other hand, *Tuntún de pasa y grifería,* as an artistic object, itself shows *heteroglossia*.

Another hypothesis which I uphold is that, from the 1930s, a cultural model was generated whose paradigm is the interrelation between ethnic composition – race – and the environment – nature. This paradigm, used by Pedreira in *Insularismo*, imposes itself as a structural model on the rebellious discourse of Palés Matos and in subsequent official discourses. In the *Prontuario histórico de Puerto Rico* [The Historical Handbook of Puerto Rico] (1935) by Tomás Blanco, however, the structural model of a natural order transmitted by race and nature is changed by proposing a model constructed by the action of historical subjects. In this sense, Blanco becomes another voice of *heteroglossia* and presents himself as an opponent of the ideas proposed in *Insularismo* and even those in *Tuntún de pasa y grifería*.

In order to formulate a cultural model there is a need to convert that model into a universal and homogeneous one, that is, into a dominant culture. Thus we observe that in the construction of the distinct proposals of the intellectuals of the 1930s, some similar structural strategies are used to organize reality.

Pedreira organizes the Puerto Rican world around the figure of the *jíbaro*, or the white Puerto Rican peasant from the mountains, whose image appears to be totally idealized as well as devoid of the traits of inequality, oppression and social marginality of which he has been a victim throughout history. In *Insularismo,* the creole who paradoxically, in the etymological sense, signified 'the slave who was born in the master's house', 'the black born in the colonies' and finally, 'the white born in the colonies' is defined by Pedreira as the result of mixture between whites. From the latter meaning, he defines the mainstream of Puerto Rican culture as creole and lists the distinctive roots of national identity.

The model is structured so as to eliminate or 'to forget' groups and social events such as Blacks, mulattos, independentists and women; and the struggles for emancipation. The mechanism of elimination expresses an internal struggle in the socio-cultural arena and the 'imaginary' created is one of class.

Moreover, *Insularismo* proposes the creation of a collective memory based on that 'imaginary' of class. To create this collective memory he turns to the mechanisms of such a construction. These mechanisms have been described by Lotman and Uspenkij, who distinguish three ways to explain the way memory acquires content (1979: 74):

1 A rise in the volume of knowledge.
2 A redistribution within the structure of what is made to be memorable and the conferring of an hierarchical value to what has been registered in the memory.
3 Omission. A selection of predetermined events and the omission of others.

Palés struggles against elimination, against omission, against a homogeneous view of the heterogeneous, while reaffirming the Afro-Antillean. But in the structuring of his response, definitively antagonistic towards the official world, he uses the same structural methods in the construction of a cultural model and, paradoxically, the same paradigm: race and nature. He also constructs a collective memory using the previously indicated procedure. One of the explanations of this paradox is that anti-establishment discourse is dialectically produced from the discourse of power or the dominant discourse: 'Counter-discourses inhabit and struggle with the dominant which inhabits them' (Terdiman 1989: 18). Also, 'Like all subversive thought, the counter-discourse is intensely – if surreptitiously – parasitic upon its antagonist. ... For in their opposition to the dominant, counter-discourses function to survey its limits and its internal weaknesses (p. 67–8).

Despite this, Palés's proposal continues to be transgressive, in terms of the way in which he structures the differences and the disagreements with the dominant cultural model of the 1930s:

> The general processes of classification which bear most closely upon the identity of the collectivity are indissociable from the heterodox symbolic material of the Imaginary.
>
> The unconscious is to this extent necessarily a political unconscious as Jameson avers, for the exclusion of other social groups and classes in the struggle to achieve categorical self-identity appears as a special dialogism ... within the imaginary of the class in question.
>
> (Stallybrass and White 1989: 194)

The difference between the collective memory of Palés and that of Pedreira is that, for the former, the Afro-Antillean world acquires a superior hierarchical value as a result of attributing to the ancestors a heroical, mythical and primitive aristocracy whose primordial strength displaces the white world and even threatens to devour it. The drama that Palés attributes to the majestic past is much stronger and more convincing than the blandness of Pedreira's *jíbaro* and the Puerto Rican landscape of Margot Arce.

Moreover, *Tuntún* sets out the political criticism of social injustice and oppression by questioning the hierarchies in which the characters of the established social model are placed and the frontiers to which they are assigned:

> The 'poetics' of transgression reveals the disgust, fear and desire which inform the dramatic self-representation of culture through the 'scene of its low Other'. This poetics reveals quite clearly the contradictory political construction of bourgeois democracy. For bourgeois democracy ... had encoded in its manners, morals and imaginative writings, in its body, bearing and taste, a subliminal elitism which was constitutive of its historical being. ... It had engraved in its subjective identity all the marks by which it felt itself to be a different, distinctive and superior class.
>
> (Stallybrass and White 1989: 202)

In this way, Palés assumes an anticolonialist political position and condemns the economic imperialism of the United States in the Caribbean.

Finally, to question the model of culture proposed by Pedreira, one must examine it from the viewpoint of Palés's ironical and parodical approach to sexuality, his metaphors of cannibalism, his primitivism, and the myths and rituals which he constructs in *Tuntún de pasa y grifería.*

II

Tuntún de pasa y grifería was published in 1937, three years after the publication of *Insularismo*. But in all fairness, it must be noted that the initiation of Palés's project of a form of poetry sustained by Antillean culture is prior to the text by Pedreira.

In this sense, the argument of my essay would seem to be totally contrived if it were not for the fact that I maintain that Palés – whose poems were already known in journals and newspapers and by an abundance of oral poets – seemed determined to publish his text in order to present it as part of the reflection on the cultural debate which had been taking place in the country since 1898 and which was continued down to the 1930s.

If we examine some texts published prior to the publication of *Tuntún*, we find a subject through which Palés reflects on and interprets Puerto Rican culture and reality. The method which he uses is that of the essay in prose and his discourse is quite revealing (Palés Matos 1978 [1926]: 207):

> What does not exist is a creole Puerto Rico. The peasant hut, the sentimental and early-rising *jibarita*, the Camagüey cockerel, the sensual womanising singer, all this occupies such a limited space in our lives, that it is already as far removed from us as the Eiffel Tower and Napoleon's white horse.[4]

As we see, Palés openly discards the creole concept of a Puerto Rican world, a concept which would be maintained in the journal *Indice* when on 13 June 1929 it initiated a survey entitled '¿Qué somos y cómo somos?' [What are we? and how are we?], with the evident intention of gauging the opinion of readers for a future programmatic formulation. The responses predictably fitted within the concept Palés himself dismisses.

At the same time, Palés reaffirms his proposal in the San Juan newspaper, *El Mundo,* on 13 November 1932 (Palés Matos 1978: 214):

> I believe in the need for an Antillean poetry and my poetic intention today is aimed toward that goal.
>
> The spiritual life of our islands – Cuba, Santo Domingo and Puerto Rico – which because of their common tradition

and origin are similarly tuned into one accent, one style, one peculiar rhythm, and one homogenous culture, demands adequate expression by its artists and thinkers. This is not merely due to aesthetic necessity but also the essential imperative of a personality which must be protected and reaffirmed so as to fulfil historical destiny.[5]

It must be noted that, in this quotation, Palés conceives culture as a homogenous and specific (different) expression; as *the* culture of the Antilles, employing the same mechanism of constructing cultural models which Lotman and Uspenskij indicate.

In this sense, there is no opposition between Palés's proposal and the way in which the culture projected by *Insularismo* is structured, given that both present themselves as the definitive culture of the nation, that which must be made visible in the face of the Other – the United States – which is seen as a threat. To accept the cultural unity of the Antilles is to accept the 'shock' of the US's expansive capitalism and its threat to interrupt such unity and transform the Antillean world; a fear expressed by Palés, in his 1932 essay, 'Hacia una poesía antillana' [Towards an Antillean Poetry] (1978: 219):

Physically the Antilles also make up one unit: landscape, climate and products are the same; the fauna and flora identical; nuclei of populations are similar: economically, spinning as they are in the orbit of American industrialism, they run the same risks and towards a similar colonial destiny.[6]

In *Tuntún* the Other appears represented and personified in Babbit, a character from Sinclair Lewis's novel of the same name. 'His Highness Babbit/stamped and factory approved' – 'Festive Song for Crying' (Palés Matos 1995: 545): [*Su santidad Babbit Máximo/con sello y marca de fábrica* – [*'Canción festiva para ser llorada'*]. As in the text by Lewis, Palés's characterization results in caricature and parody.

The need to present a new form of cultural expression is also evident because a change has occurred in the dominant social classes, a change which corresponds to the new economic relations which were established as a result of the American invasion (Palés Matos 1978 [1926]: 208–09): 'At the same time, ... the small landowner would disappear, gobbled up by the foreign corporations and the native capitalists (.... The reactionary and fainthearted bourgeosie ... were little by little abandoning their macho attitude.'[7] On the other hand, Palés refutes Pedreira's historical resistance to change, his 'historical omissions' and his whitening of Puerto Ricans:

In a general sense, the fact that the Caribbean has been colonized and populated by the Hispanic race does not signify that after four hundred years, which in itself signifies multiple generations, we continue to be as Spanish as our forefathers.[8]

... The negro lives physically and spiritually with us and his characteristics diffused in the mulatto, are quite evident in the manifestations of our popular life.

... His vitality, his dynamism, his primitive nature ... give us his passion, his exuberant manner of speech, his ease of attitude and his strange magnetism, all of which give the mulatto a type of resounding mystical strength.

... I would say that the Antillean is a Spaniard with Mulatto ways and the soul of a Black.[9]

(Palés Matos 1978 [1932]: 216)

In *Tuntún,* Palés retakes this idea and defines race as that which dictates the form of our Caribbeanness (Palés Matos 1995: 507): .*'Es la raza negra que ondulando va/en el ritmo gordo del mariyandá – 'Danza negra'*. [It is the black race which swaying moves/To the fat rhythm of the *mariyandá*] – 'Black Dance'.]

He also makes fun of those characters who deny their culture so as to assimilate to the fashion of white culture, thus converting themselves in self-parodies, such as the Duque de la Mermelada [Duke of Marmalade] and the green lizard (1995: 559): *'Ahora, en el molde vistoso de tu casaca francesa/pasas azucarado de saludos como un cortesano cualquiera'* – *'Elegía del Duque de la Mermelada'*. [Now, in the colourful mould of your French smock/you pass by sweetened with greetings like a courtier – Elegy to the Duke of Marmalade.]

What places Palés's project into conflict with that of *Insularismo* is his recovery of all that Pedreira's text wilfully 'forgets'. This, in part, explains the reasons why the cultural model proposed by Palés is not favourably received. Palés touches a raw nerve: he draws attention to sectors which are socially and racially excluded; and with them, he discovers the profound inequality and surreptitious racism of Puerto Rican society. Nor does he find support in powerful institutions as occurs with Pedreira's model and its adoption by the Popular Democratic Party [Partido Popular Democrático] and its charismatic leader, Luis Muñoz Marin.[10] Palés's model thus becomes, a marginal and transgressive model, a counter-discourse which clearly demonstrates the racist and anti-democratic values of Puerto Rican society.

In 1932 Palés comes to the defence of his model. He answers his friend José I. de Diego Padró, to whom Palés's vision seems absurd (Palés Matos 1978: 219):

> The distinguished intellectual maintains that my proposal, apart from being unfeasible in the long run, would lack all significant meaning because the Afro-Hispanic elements invoked by me as constituting the dynamic engine of the poetry I envisage, have very relative value as the authentic expression of our culture; ... that in the Hispanic Caribbean, from the psychological point of view, nothing has taken place which justifies the development of this new lyric, given that the white colonizers destroyed the aboriginal Indians and culturally disrupted the enslaved blacks, thereby conserving intact the general lines of their character and thus giving to our Caribbean life a thoroughly Occidental intonation.
>
> ... I have not spoken of a black poetry nor a white one nor a mulatto one; I have only spoken of a Caribbean poetry which expresses our country's reality in the cultural sense of that word.
>
> ... The Hispanic Caribbean – Cuba, Santo Domingo and Puerto Rico – have developed an homogeneous spiritual type and are thus psychologically harmonized.
>
> ... This homogeneity of spiritual type is perfectly different from the common masses of Hispanic peoples and inherent to it is the fact that the negro factor is so tightly woven into the fabric of the Hispanic Caribbean psyche, that it has served as an insulating, or in chemical terms, a precipitating agent.[11]

The social marginality of the Caribbean culture which Palés champions as universal and homogeneous obliges him to become the voice of sectors which traditionally have lacked one. The marginal is a world without a voice, because it has been kept on the margin at the strict limits, or on the border of the sociocultural. Because it is a world at the margins, it is feared because it can become a powerful transformer: 'Only a challenge to the hierarchy of sites of discourse, which usually comes from groups and classes situated in low or marginal positions, carries the promise of politically transformative power' (Stallybrass and White 1989: 201). The poetic voice, as the voice of Antillean culture, the formulation of its distinctive features, transgresses the limits established by white culture.

Transgression is the interrogation of boundaries, 'a realm …
where what is in question is the limit rather than the identity
of a culture'. But cultural identity is inseparable from limits,
it is always a boundary phenomenon and its order is always
constructed around figures of its territorial edge.

> (Stallybrass and White 1989: 200)

Palés places the Afro-Antillean at the very centre of attention.
The marginal is placed in the space of the dominant, thus displacing
it.

To break the established borders, Palés utilizes the lexicon of
white culture and converts it into its opposite. The metaphors of
bestiality and dirtiness, attributed to Blacks by racism are reversed.
The negative becomes positive as in 'Pueblo negro' [Black Village],
and 'Ten con ten' [To and fro] (Palés Matos 1995: 534; 564):

> La negra de las zonas soleadas
> que huele a tierra, a salvajina, a sexo.
> Es la negra que canta
> y su canto sensual se va extendiendo
> como una clara atmósfera de dicha
> bajo la sombra de los cocoteros

> [The black woman from the sun-kissed places
> who smells of earth, savage, sex
> is the black woman who sings
> and her sensual song gradually spreads
> like a clear atmosphere of joy
> beneath the shade of the coconut trees.]
>
> 'Pueblo negro'

> Pasarías ante el mundo
> Por civil y ciudadana,
> si tu axila – flor de sombra –
> no difundiera en las plazas
> el rugiente cebollín
> que sofríen tus entrañas.

> Y así estás, mi verde antilla,
> en un sí que no es de raza,
> en ten con ten de abolengo
> que te hace tan antillana…

[You could pass before the world
in all civility and custom
if your armpit – flower of shade –
did not spread across the plazas
the sizzling spring onions
frying in your guts.

And that is the way you are my green Antilles,
in a yes without race,
in an ancestry all to and fro
which makes you so Antillean…]

'Ten con ten'

The body, a taboo in white culture, is the centre of transgression and desire, the expression of pleasure and power. Images considered by bourgeois culture to be filthy and repulsive are foregrounded. The active body is praised, with its secretions, its sexuality, as occurs in the carnival celebrations theorized by Bakhtin. To speak of the body of the mulata is to construct a space, a social topography, to show the difference between classes (Palés Matos 1995).

Meneos cachondos que el gongo cuaja
en ríos de azúcar y de melaza.
Prieto trapiche de sensual zafra,
el caderamen, masa con masa
exprime ritmos, suda que sangra,
y la molienda culmina en danza.

[Provocative swaying set by the gong
into rivers of sugar and molasses.
Black sugar mill yielding a sensual harvest,
a swaying of hips, every part of her body,
squeezing out rhythms, between sweating and bleeding,
grinding out a dance in the end.]

'Majestad negra' [Black Majesty], p. 536

En tí ahora, mulata…
¡Oh despertar glorioso en las Antillas!
bravo color que el do de pecho alcanza,
música al rojo vivo de alegría,
y calientes cantáridas de aroma
– limón, tabaco, piña –
zumbando a los sentidos
sus embriagadas voces de delicia.

... Todos
los frutos ioh mulata! tú me brindas
en la clara bahía de tu cuerpo
por los soles del trópico bruñida.

[In you now, *mulata* ...
Oh glorious dawn in the Antilles!
wild colour flung from a singing chest,
red-hot music of happiness,
and hot Spanish flies of aroma
– lemon, tobacco, pineapple –
dazzling the senses
with their drunken voices of delight. ...

... All
the fruits, oh *mulata!* you toast me with
in the clear bay of your body
burnished by the hot sun of the tropics.]
                    'Mulata Antilla' [Mulata Antilles], pp. 570–1

Ahí vienen los tambores!
Ten cuidado, hombre blanco, que a tí llegan
para clavarte su aguijón de música.

[Here come the Drums!
Be careful, white man, they are coming to get you
and dig you with their musical spur.]
                    Intermedios del hombre blanco'
                    [White Man's Intervals], p. 567

Palés's cultural project, as we have shown, is built on the race/ landscape paradigm. But, unlike Pedreira who takes it from essayists and European and Spanish American intellectuals (see Juan Flores 1993b), Palés is influenced by primitivist fashions followed by international *avant-garde* movements of his time (see Poggioli 1968). The poetic text functions as an essay in verse. Poetic reflection replaces theoretical reflection but this does not prevent the creation of a visible cultural expression through which he highlights Afro-Antillean cultural features.

In this sense, *Tuntún de pasa y grifería* elaborates on an Afrocentric catalogue of cultural expressions and myth. Through this elaboration, a contrasting image to that of Pedreira's *jíbaro* is formulated, and it highlights precisely that which *Insularismo* rejects. Thus, the characteristics which it explores, have a distinctly oppositional flavour.

Palés initiates his description of the characteristics of the culture by spatially situating it within a Puerto Rican perspective: 'Preludio en boricua' [Prelude in Puerto Rican] is the first poem of the text. At the same time, in this poem Puerto Rican space is fixed within an Antillean context which is described by its spatial components: Cuba, Santo Domingo, Haiti, Jamaica and the Windward islands (1995: 502–3). The poem also marks out the lyrical subject: '¿ Y Puerto Rico? Mi isla ardiente' [And Puerto Rico? My Burning Island] (503); and signals the parodic character of *Tuntún*: 'Puerto Rico, lúgubremente, /bala como cabro estofado' [Puerto Rico, somberly,/bleats like a stewed goat]. These last lines are reminiscent of a passage from *Insularismo*, where Pedreira claims that Puerto Ricans are as docile as lambs (1942: 32). As in the essay, the text shows its metadiscursive function: not only does it speak of other discourses – dialogue with other texts of the period – but it also examines its own discourse and marks out its recipient 'Preludio en Boricua' [Prelude in Puerto Rican], Palés Matos 1995: 503):

> Tuntún de pasa y grifería,
> este libro que va a tus manos
> con ingredientes antillanos
> compuse un día …
>
> [Tuntún de pasa y grifería,
> this book which comes to your hands
> with Antillean ingredients
> was composed by me one day …]

Once the guidelines of the text are established in this introduction, Palés highlights Antillean culture through descriptions of places, objects, food, dance, music, language, religion, rituals, beliefs, customs, beauty and sensuality. Palés's geography has specific names, some of which are real – Cuba, Haiti, Congo, Tortola, Uganda – and some unreal – Mussumba, Farafangana – and some of uncertain origin – Quimbamba. They are the places where myth and men live.

Music, instruments and dance also occupy extensive space in Palés's descriptions ('Numen', p. 516):

> Al bravo ritmo del candombe
> despierta el tótem ancestral:
> pantera, antílope, elefante,
> sierpe, hipopótamo, caimán.
> En el silencio de la selva
> bate el tambor sacramental

y el negro baila poseído
de la gran bestia original.

[To the wild dancing of the *candombe*
the ancestral totem awakens:
panther, antelope, elephant,
serpent, hippopotamus, cayman.
In the silence of the jungle
the sacramental drum beats
and the black man dances possessed
by the great original beast.]

Equally, religion, beliefs, the protective Gods, myths and rituals are described (pp. 517, 521).

Atravesando inmensidades
sobre el candombe su alma va
al limbo oscuro donde impera
la negra fórmula esencial.
Dale su fuerza el hipopótamo,
coraza bríndale el caimán,
le da sigilo la serpiente,
el antílope agilidad,
y el elefante poderoso
rompiendo selvas al pasar,
le abre camino hacia el profundo
y eterno numen ancestral.

[Crossing great distances
on the *Candombe* his soul arrives
at the dark limbo wherein reigns
the essential black formula.
His strength he gains from the hippopotamus,
the cayman toasts him with his shell,
the serpent lends him stealth,
the antelope agility,
and crashing through the jungle
the powerful elephant clears him the way towards the deep
and eternal source of ancestral inspiration.]
                                        'Numen', p. 517

Tenemos el diente del dingo,
Gran Abuelo del Gran Babissa;
tenemos el diente del dingo

> y una uña de lagartija …
> contra todo mal ellos pueden,
> de todo mal nos inmunizan. …
>
> Negros bravos de los palmares,
> venid, que os espera Babissa,
> el Gran Rey del Caimán y el Coco,
> ante la fogata encendida.
>
> [We have the tooth of the dingo,
> Great Grandfather of the Great Babissa;
> we have the tooth of the dingo
> and a lizard's nail …
> they can withstand any evil,
> they immunize us against any evil. …
> Wild blacks of the palm groves,
> come, Babissa awaits you,
> the Great Cayman King, the Devil King,
> before the lighted bonfire.]
>
> 'Candombe', p. 521

The counter-discourse of *Tuntún* is marked out by irony and parody. Palés laughs at the fetishism of white skin in a world which is definitively mixed race. Mulattos materialize in his poetry by means of the images and the words, making visible that which the dominant model tries to suppress. Equally, the image and the word become erotic and burst in on prohibited areas. Irony and the parody are important means of constructing the text as a voice of dissent in the face *Insularismo*.

Palés also counters the concept of Puerto Rican docility with images of a combative Afro-Antillean culture. Its overwhelming presence as well as its future triumph is expressed in images of cannibalism ('Falsa canción del baquiné' [False Song of the *Baquiné*],[12] Palés Matos 1995, p. 155):

> Ahora comamos carne blanca
> Con la licencia de su mercé.
> Ahora comamos carne blanca…
>
> [Now let us eat white flesh
> with the permission of his lordship.
> Now let us eat white flesh …]

Puerto Rican culture is a particular expression of a broader Antillean one and, therefore, it cannot be separated from its mixed-race context ('Ten con ten', Palés Matos 1995, p. 564):

> Y así estás, mi verde antilla,
> en un sí que no es de raza,
> en ten con ten de abolengo
> que te hace tan antillana …
> Al ritmo de los tambores
> tu lindo ten con ten bailas,
> una mitad española
> y otra mitad africana.

> [And that is the way you are, my green Antilles,
> in a yes without race,
> in an ancestry all to and fro
> which makes you so Antillean …
> to the rhythm of the drums
> your pretty to and fro you dance,
> one half Spanish
> and the other half African.]

Tuntún de pasa y grifería breaks out of the restrictions of insularity into a broader, less racially exclusive Caribbean world.

III

The existence of a poetic voice, such as that of Luis Palés Matos in the context of 1930s essay-writing, shows the need to study history and literature from the point of view of cultural studies. Culture is a symbolic as well as practical force which simultaneously produces cohesion and contrast in a specific community. By studying cultural production we can understand the processes of that community.

Palés's voice constitutes one of the expressions of *heteroglossia* in the 1930s. His discourse is doubly antagonistic: on the one hand, he opposes the general world-view developed by his contemporaries; on the other hand, the primitivism which he champions is opposed to the very concept of culture. 'Cannibalism has often been the "name of the other", the ultimate marker of difference in a coded opposition of light/dark, rational/irrational, civilized/savage' (Stam 1989: 125).

Culture rules out the primitive, the savage. Palés's work seems 'impure' and inferior within the ideological categories of his time. Because of this, in Pedreira whiteness is cultured and blackness reminds us of the primitive, the inferior and also the humiliation of slavery. Blackness is dismissed because in its symbolic conception slavery is considered an inherent fact in the black race and not a socio-economic institution. For Palés, on the other hand, it is the primitive, heroic and mythical past which gives strength to Afro-Antillean culture; thus his own poetry becomes the cultured and artistic voice which reclaims a learned culture.

In this sense, *Tuntún de pasa y grifería* is the code for a culture which up to that moment was lacking in letters, and it is a war cry against everything which placed it at an inferior level. The culture which Palés defends denies the criteria and the authorship of a discourse which establishes itself as unique and superior. For this reason, *Tuntún* moves forward to what Bauman (1987: 140) calls a 'postmodern challenge': 'The areas most affected by the postmodern challenge are those philosophical discourses which are concerned with the issues of truth, certainty and relativism, and those which deal with the principles of societal organization.'

By means of his text, Palés maintains and legitimizes an order which he builds by using the same mechanisms as authoritative models of culture. In this act, he is comparable to Pedreira and to the other members of the generation who apply themselves to the same task.

While the cultural projects of the 1930s tended to aspire to unity and cohesion of the community, the 'project' of the dominant classes today only produce segregation. The clearest examples are exclusive programmes of urbanization and restrictions of democratic rights through judicial reform.

The examination of *Tuntún de pasa y grifería* reminds us of the urgent task of resuming the construction of a new cultural project which will serve as a model to present-day Puerto Rican society, a democratically heterogeneous model which will help us to live and to share in peace.

Notes

1   This chapter is dedicated to M. E. R.

2   See Flores (1993b: 45–50), for Spengler's influence on Hispanic and particularly Puerto Rican discussions of culture [eds].

3   Flores (1993b: 20) discusses Pedreira's use of the metaphor of Puerto Rico as a ship adrift [eds].

4   *Lo que no existe es el Puerto Rico criollo. El bohío, la jibarita sentimental y madrugadora, el gallo camagüey, el tiple mujeriego y sensual, todo eso ocupa tan poco espacio en nuestra vida, que ya está tan distante de nosotros como la Torre Eiffel y el caballo blanco de Napoleón.*

5   *Yo creo en la necesidad de una poesía antillana y mi aspiración poética se endereza actualmente hacia tal próposito.*

    La vida espiritual de nuestras islas – Cuba, Santo Domingo y Puerto Rico –, que por su comunidad de tradición y origen pueden sintonizarse en un acento, en un modo, en un ritmo peculiar y homogéneo de cultura, exige adecuada espresión de sus artistas y pensadores. Esto no es ya mera necesidad estética sino imperativo

*esencial de una personalidad que debe protegerse y afirmarse para que cumpla su
destino histórico.*

6   *Fisicamente las Antillas constituyen también una unidad: paisaje, clima y produc-
tos son los mismos; fauna y flora idénticas; núcleos de población semejantes;
económicamente, girando como giran en la órbita del industrialismo americano,
corren iguales contingencias y hacia análogo destino colonial.*

7   *Al mismo tiempo, ... desaparecia enguillido por las corporaciones extranjeras y
los capitalistas nativos, el pequeño terrateniente .... La burguesía reaccionaria y
medrosa que invadió nuestras filas fue deponiendo poco a poco su actitud viril.*

8   *En un sentido general, el hecho de que las Antillas hayan sido colonizadas y
pobladas por la raza hispánica, no significa que después de cuatrocientos años,
que representan múltiples generaciones, continuemos tan españoles como nuestros
abuelos.*

9   *El negro vive fisica y espiritualmente con nosotros y sus caracteristicas, tamizadas
en el mulato, influyen de modo evidente en todas las manifestaciones de nuestra
vida popular.*

   *... Su vitalidad, su dinamismo, su naturaleza primitiva ... nos da su pasión, su
verbosismo exuberante, su elasticidad de actitudes y su extraño magnetismo, que
adquiere en el mulato una especie de fuerza mistíca arrolladora.*

   *... Yo diría que el antillano es un español con maneras de mulato y alma de
negro.*

10   Luis Muñoz Marin (1898–1980) has been Puerto Rico's most influential political
leader, whilst his populist Partido Popular Democrático has been the party of
government for most of the post-Second World war period. On the great influence
of Pedreira on Puerto Rican political rhetoric and thinking, see Diaz Quiñones
(1984; 1993: 162–4) and Flores (1993b: 16–17, 19, 52) – [eds].

11   *El distinguido intelectual sostiene que mi propósito, amén de irrealizable, care-
cería de toda significación trascendente porque los elementos afrohispánicos por
mí invocados para constituir el móvil dinámico de tal poesía tienen un valor harto
relativo como expresión auténtica de cultura ... que en las Antillas, desde el punto
de vista sicológico, no ha ocurrido nada que justifique el desarrollo de esa nueva
lírica, pues el colono blanco destruyó al indio aborigen y disolvió, culturalmente,
al negro escalvizado, conservando él intactas las líneas generales de su carácter y
dándole a nuestra vida antillana una entonación absolutamente occidental.*

   *... No he hablado de una poesía negra ni blanca ni mulata; yo sólo he
hablado de una poesía antillana que exprese nuestra realidad de pueblo en el
sentido cultural de ese vocablo.*

   *... Las Antillas – Cuba, Santo Domingo y Puerto Rico – han desarrollado un
tipo espiritual homogéneo y están por lo tanto sicológicamente afinadas en una
misma dirección.*

   *... Esta homogeneidad de tipo espiritual está perfectamente diferenciada de
la masa común de los pueblos hispánicos y que en ella el factor negroide entrever-
ado en la siquis antillana, ha hecho las veces de aislador, o en términos químicos,
de agente precipitante.*

12   *Baquiné* is the Afro-Caribbean term used in Puerto Rico and the Dominican
Republic to refer to the type of funeral wake reserved for a child [eds].

<table><tr><td>7</td><td>

Discovering Nicolás Guillén through Afrocentric literary analysis

</td></tr></table>

Ian Isidore Smart

Frantz Fanon in the stirring conclusion to his powerful classic *The Wretched of the Earth* (originally published in 1961) urges (1970: 251):

> Let us waste no time in sterile litanies and nauseating mimicry. Leave this Europe where they are never done talking of Man, yet murder men everywhere they find them, at the corner of every one of their own streets, in all corners of the globe.

His 'big brother' and fellow Martinican, Aimé Césaire, had declared earlier in that outburst of a somewhat paradoxical self-deprecating self-affirmation that was and is his *Cahier* (1939): 'Accommodez-vous de moi. Je ne m'accommode pas de vous!' [Accommodate yourself to me. I am not going to accommodate myself to you] (1956: 87). As if hearkening expressly to the Césairian injunction, George G.M. James, who was born in what used to be called British Guyana (BG), penned his one and only tome of quite quaint title, *Stolen Legacy: The Greeks Were not the Authors of Greek Philosophy, but the People of North Africa, Commonly Called the Egyptians* (1954). James may not have read Césaire or any of that posse of young Francophone rebels who launched their *Négritude* in the heady 1930s in Paris, but he certainly knew of Marcus Garvey's injunction to 'do for self' and his guiding principle that 'what man did man can do'. Garvey, of course, was Jamaican.

In the spirit of Garvey this essay repudiates the alleged long chain of reason – what Fanon sees as 'the sometimes prodigious theses which Europe has put forward' (p. 254) – the whole apparatus of so-called western scholarship. For the best way to escape from the maze is not to enter it in the first place. Rejecting the falsehoods of white supremacist scholarship, this approach has been deemed to be lacking in 'global perspective', 'theoretical rigor', to be 'subscribing to fantasy history', or to be 'flamboyant and controversial'. My approach here steadfastly eschews any theoretical framework established with the specific purpose of shoring up the deliberate falsehood of the primacy of so-called white civilization. It proclaims with Césaire, 'Accommodez vous de moi'.

Nicholás Guillén was born of two generations of mulattos in Camagüey, Cuba, in the year in which Cuba developed full-blown neo-colonization, the year of the Platt Amendment, 1902. It is Fanon who provides the best understanding of the cultural context that nurtured the poet. He viewed the colonial world as an essentially polarized, 'Manichean', universe. Amilcar Cabral developed this insight into the Dialectical Theory of Identification, which can be used to great advantage for analysing the evolution of Caribbean culture in general and literature in particular. From the very beginning of the brutal European presence in the region there had been two worlds, two cultures, two literatures, one scribal, the other oral, one proper to the dominant minority, the other emanating from the oppressed majority. The letters and chronicles of the few literate among the marauding multitudes coming from Europe after 1492 constitute the first works of this New World literature. The Colombian man-of-words Manuel Zapata Olivella proclaims: 'America is a product that was "made in the Caribbean"' (1989: 169). Understandably it is this region, the very model after which every society in the Americas was fashioned, that nurtured some of the best known Spanish-American writers: Andrés Bello, José Martí, Rubén Darío, and Gabriel García Márquez.

On the other hand, so successful was the genocide initiated by Columbus that within one generation the new barbaric society had to meet its critical manpower needs with captive African labour. These Africans, degraded to the utmost and unconscionably separated from a literary heritage that dated back to the third millenium BC (cf Hilliard *et al.* 1987), had to content themselves with a merely oral literary practice. And Afrocentric scholars continue to uncover the indisputable organic connection between the post-1492 Africans who came to America as cargo in the infamous slave ships and their ancestors who gave humankind the gift of civilization itself. The language of this oral literature was and still is creole, a blend of a general West African syntax with a specific European lexicon. In the case of the Spanish Caribbean this lexicon would clearly be Spanish. Indeed, there are still extant some examples of this evolving Spanish Creole literature, and they have been conveniently recorded in Rosa E. Valdés Cruz, *La poesía negroide en América* (1970).

Apart from the rare exceptions just referenced, literature written in Spanish emanated from the privileged domains of the ruling minority and was consciously derivative, a slavish imitation of the Old World models, when not Spanish then French or English. Such was the literature of Bello, Darío, Martí, and their ilk. Completely separated in the apartheid conditions of the 'Manichean' colonial universe the new Caribbean natives, the transplanted Africans, graced their existence with the fervent practice of the literary arts, albeit exclusively oral. Their literary expression was also consciously rooted in the secular tradition of their original world. Their imitation was, ironically however, not slavish, for they did not enjoy the luxury of adjudication by the experts back home. True, the African artistic community in the Caribbean of colonial times was constantly invigorated by new entrants fresh from the source. The traffic was one way, however. There was no possibility of feedback to or from the literary elders resident in the Yoruba nation, or the Igbo nation, or the Ashante nation, or any of the others.

Africans, the new Caribbean natives, then, created the most vibrant regional literature in conditions that ensured an intense Caribbeanness, conditions that engendered an unimpeachably *sui generis* expression. This vibrancy could only inform the written literature of the region when the 'Manichean' gap between native and colonizer, between 'orature' and literature was closed. And the 'orature', it must be remembered, was consciously African. It follows, then, that unless and until the scribal literary expression of the dominant minority was touched in some way by the vibrant and African oral literary tradition it could not be Caribbean.

The case of Gabriel de la Concepción Valdés (Plácido) is instructive. He was an almost white Cuban Romantic poet born in 1809 (see Casals 1944). There is little in his work to distinguish him from his Spanish (European) contemporaries and predecessors who were the main luminaries of Romanticism and pre-Romanticism: Manuel José Quintana, José Espronceda, José Zorilla and Francisco Martínez de la Rosa. There was in Plácido's work no overt evocation of the 'real' African cultural heritage. His Africans were 'Moors', straight from the pages of Eurocentric Spanish literature. The criminally repressive Cuban government of the time, however, saw some glimmer of reference in his work to the plight of the hundreds of thousands of real Africans who lived in Cuba. Poor Plácido, the essentially Eurocentric Romantic poet, was executed in 1844 for alleged complicity in a slave uprising. In terms of Cabral's Dialectical Theory of Identification, Plácido did not advance beyond the 'capitulation' phase. At this stage the colonized artist's 'writings correspond point to point with those of his opposite numbers in the mother country. His inspiration is European and we can easily link up these works with definite trends in the literature of the mother country' (Fanon 1970: 179).

Scholars have given some attention to the Spanish-American equivalent of the slave narrative and the anti-slavery novel. Lorna Valerie Williams, for example, has contributed significantly to our appreciation of this literature with *The Representation of Slavery in Cuban Fiction* (1994). Edward J. Mullen's *The Life and Poems of a Cuban Slave: Juan Franciso Manzano 1797–1854* (1981) is a useful tool for research on the topic. All of this literature is Afro-Caribbean in the general sense of the term for it consciously evokes some aspect of the African heritage in the Caribbean. But in the final analysis it belongs to the 'capitulation' phase, and, most significantly it was absolutely contemporaneous with a vibrant oral literature created by Africans who were for the most part brutally enslaved human beings.

In the roaring twenties when an effete Europe sought renewal in things African, when Picasso and his school turned to and even plagiarized traditional West African principles of composition, when white folks went, as Nicolás Guillén put it, to Harlem and Havana to look for jazz and *son*, Luis Palés Matos, a white-skinned Puerto Rican, began to write his so-called *poesía negrista*. The female poetic personae were earthy, sensual, but stereotypically erotic. In his insensitive haste to recreate the spirit of the oral literature and its rhythmic use of repeated strange, non-Spanish words, Palés Matos and his followers (who were many, and almost all white) simply invented mumbo-jumbo sounds. The Cuban Alejo Carpentier is the most important of Palés Matos's aesthetic progeny, but there were many others: Ramón Guirao, José Z. Tallet, and Emilio Ballagas being the best known. The literary expression of this 'Afro-Antillean' school might be deemed to pertain to the second phase of Identification, the 'revitalization' phase.

It was at this precise historical juncture that Nicolás Guillén emerged to take the Afro-Antillean movement to its fullest potential. His art and that of other African-ancestored Cuban contemporaries, notably Marcelino Arozarena and Regino Pedroso, can be deemed to have attained the third phase, 'radicalization'. This is 'the fighting phase [when] the native ... turns himself into an awakener of the people; hence comes a fighting literature, a revolutionary literature' (Fanon 1970: 179). As will be discussed at greater length later on in this essay, the Fanonian model was, however, in Cuba pre-empted by the Marxist-Leninist revolutionary process in which race consciousness is subsumed under the class struggle. Essentially, Guillén and Cuba returned to a version of Afro-Antillean 'revitalization'. Official Cuban culture is locked into this phase, and so even a singularly gifted poet such as Nancy Morejón, who is of pronounced African ancestry, tends to eschew any really radical race consciousness.

The Fanon-Cabral paradigm works for Puerto Rico according to the Puerto Rican scholar Isabelo Zenón Cruz, who, in *Narciso descubre su trasero: el negro en la cultura puertorriqueña* [Narcissus Discovers his Backside: The Black in Puerto Rican Culture], has brilliantly demonstrated that the culture establishment of his native land still slumbers in 'capitulation'. The same, we believe, can easily be demonstrated for the Dominican Republic. Indeed, it is in Panama and Costa Rica where the blossoms of Guillén's art have evolved into real fruit. And these two Central American countries are, of course, as culturally and geographically Caribbean as any of the island nations. Fanon has argued compellingly that 'radicalization' is the sole route to liberation and hence artistic fullness. There is no reason to question the validity of this theory.

The collection entitled *Sóngoro cosongo* which appeared in 1931 was the poet's first after finding the new voice that was sounded with his dramatic passing into the 'revitalization phase', according to the Cabral schema. Conscious of the immense significance of the work, Guillén opened it with a brief prologue defiantly proclaiming his artistically 'born again' poetry to be 'mulatto verses' [*versos mulatos*] permeated with quintessential Cubanness, '*color cubano*'. It is instructive to contrast Langston Hughes's and Guillén's respective ethnic self-concepts. Both were light-skinned blacks; the Cuban, in fact, affirmed in his 'Conversación con Langston Hughes' [Conversation with Langston Hughes] that the North American reminded him of a 'true Cuban mulatto' [*mulatico cubano*] (Guillén 1975–6: 16). Hughes was, of course, the spiritual midwife who assisted at Guillén's artistic rebirth – the two met in January 1930 in Havana and it was in April of that year that the watershed *Motivos de son* sprung up from the Cuban's *sous-réalité*. But whereas for the American the characteristics of Jim Crow Apartheid imposed a brutal clarity, for the Cuban the 'mulatto escape hatch' provided a certain relief from the full stigma of Negritude. Mainstream critics consistently consider the works of this phase to be Guillén's best, and, indeed, these may well be the most representative of his artistic genius. He did, however, evolve into the 'radicalization phase', the fighting phase. The publication of his collection *West Indies Ltd* in 1934 marks his entry into this final phase of development for the native artist. 'Sabás', arguably Guillén's most powerful poem, belongs to this collection. It was written in that very year and was dedicated significantly to Hughes. It begins (1985, 1: 140):

> Yo vi a Sabás, el negro sin veneno,
> pedir su pan de puerta en puerta.
> Por qué, Sabás, la mano abierta?
> (Este Sabas es un negro bueno).
>
> [I saw Sabás, the innocuous negro,
> begging his bread from door to door.
> Why, Sabás, the outstretched hand?
> (This Sabás is a good negro).]

With politically conscious humour heavy with sarcasm the poet seeks to jolt Sabás out of complicity in his own oppression. The next two stanzas are similar in form and content; they are four-line, fully rhyming verses. The stage having been set with this introduction there is a change in rhythm as the poet explicitly exhorts revolutionary action (1972–3, 1: 141):

> Coge tu pan, pero no lo pidas;
> coge tu luz, coge tu esperanza cierta
> como a un caballo por las bridas.
> Plántate en medio de la puerta,
> pero no con la mano abierta,
> ni con tu cordura de loco:
> …
> Caramba, Sabás, que no se diga!
> …
> La muerte, a veces, es buena amiga,
> y el no comer, cuando es preciso
> para comer, el pan sumiso,
> tiene belleza. El cielo abriga.
> …
> Caramba, Sabás, no seas tan loco!
> Sabás, no seas tan bruto,
> ni tan bueno!
>
> [Get up and get your bread, don't just beg for it;
> get up and get your light, your true hope,
> grab hold of the reins, man.
> Plant yourself squarely in the door,
> but not with outstretched hand,
> nor with your crazy good behaviour:
> …
> Come on, Sabás, don't let them
> say it was so!
> …

> Death, at times, can be a good friend,
> and hunger, if eating means having
> to swallow the bread of submission,
> can be beautiful. Heaven protects us.
>
> …
>
> Come on, Sabás, don't be so crazy!
> Sabás, don't be so stupid,
> don't be so good!]

In May 1937 the collection *Cantos para soldados y sones para turistas* [Songs for Soldier and *Sones* for Tourists] was published in Mexico. Entirely consistent with the revolutionary, fighting phase of development it turned out to be the final expression of that particular period of the poet's ongoing artistic evolution. In the very month of May, the poet, again in Mexico, wrote 'España, poema en cuatro angustias y una esperanza' [Spain, a Poem in Four Anguished Voices and One of Hope]. This long work was published in Mexico and then at the end of August in Valencia, Spain. Significantly, there in Valencia that very same year, Guillén formally joined the Communist Party, thereby entering what might be termed the 'post-colonial' phase.

In recent years there has been a major thrust in the United States to validate the category 'bi-racial', sometimes indistinguishable from 'multiracial'. This represents, of course, a radical revision of Jim Crow Apartheid. Even at his most radical stage Guillén, by opting for *mulatez* [mulattoness] over Negritude, fell short of developing what is viewed today as an African consciousness. Furthermore, by joining the Communist Party he officially subsumed his race consciousness – at best a *mulatez* – under a class consciousness, and would later expressly repudiate Negritude, the Afrocentricity of the 1930s. Richard L. Jackson, the first North American scholar in modern times to present a clear understanding of Latin American racism, equates *mulatez*, a form of *mestizaje,* with 'ethnic lynching' (1976: 1). It is clear that the practice of lynching has adapted to the contours of society. We have now 'ethnic' and even, as the infamous Clarence Thomas himself – the token 'Negro' of the nine 'in-justices' who currently sit on one of the most racist institutions in the world, the United States Supreme Court – discerned, 'high-tech', and certainly many other sophisticated ways of 'keeping the N's in their place'.

If, as Derek Walcott – that other great Caribbean poet from St Lucia – would put it, 'the poet never lies', then *Sóngoro cosongo* should not really be different from the work of Guillén, the post-colonial *Poeta Nacional* of Fidel's Cuba. (Walcott made this declaration in his characteristic oracular fashion in the course of an interview he granted me at his house in Victoria Gardens, Diego Martin, Trinidad and Tobago during the summer of 1974.)

Let us take the poem 'Sensemayá', with the subtitle 'Poem to Kill a Snake'. It first appeared in the 1934 collection *West Indies Ltd* and has become a signature work for the poet and for so-called 'Afro-Cuban' poetry. Now, it has been shown to be remarkably similar in form and content to a poem of ancient Kemet [Egypt] that was inscribed indelibly (almost) in hieroglyphs on the walls of a pyramid tomb of Teta, pharaoh of the Sixth Dynasty (cf. Smart 1990: 36–7). It represents one of two instances when the Cuban poet was satisfied with the first version of a work: when he composed the original *son* poems written in the course of one night of true inspiration; and when 'Sensemayá' burst forth spontaneously but based on his recollection of carnival chants he had heard as a youth. Only an Afrocentric approach could lead the scholar to an understanding of this and other 'amazing connections'. Even with Wallis Budge's working translation of the Kemetic poem the reader can appreciate the 'markedly rhythmic expression, the infectious rhythm being created by the repetition of words and images' (Smart 1990: 37). The following are some examples of repeated images (Budge 1973, 1: 142):

a)   'The head is cut, the tail is severed.'
b)   'He hears, the earth hears, thy father Keb hears.'
c)   'If the hand of the deceased seizes thee thou diest, if his hand touches thee thou dost not live.'
d)   'The fingers of the deceased are on thee, the fingers of the Lynx which dwells in the House of Life.'

'Paronomasia' is defined in *Webster's* as 'to call with a slight change of name: a play on words: PUN'. Every one of the examples cited above, even the first, fits the definition. In Kemetic and all other African literary traditions, including the Biblical, the rhetorical strategy labelled parallelism of members is of paramount importance. Guillén's 'Sensemayá' exudes the flavour of the Kemetic poems, echoing not only the content but this characteristic trope as well. The penultimate stanza, for example, reads (1972–3, 1: 148):

> La culebra muerta no puede comer,
> la culebra muerta no puede silbar,
> no puede caminar,
> no puede correr.
> La culebra muerta no puede mirar,
> la culebra muerta no puede beber,
> no puede respirar
> no puede morder.

> [The dead snake cannot eat,
> The dead snake cannot hiss,
> cannot walk,
> cannot run.
> The dead snake cannot see,
> the dead snake cannot drink,
> cannot breathe
> cannot bite.]

The snake cannot be any more dead than the poet makes it; and, clearly, the death of the snake is effected and highlighted in both poems by similar aesthetic processes. Repetition, of course, is the basis of all rhythm, from the beating of the heart to the convoluted intellectual rhythms of, for example, modern free verse. However, the theoreticians of Negritude, Léopold Sédar Senghor for instance, have taken great pains to identify rhythmic virtuosity as the hallmark of black African poetry.

The poem to kill a snake was first published in 1934, and there is no reason to believe that it was written significantly earlier. My first major work on the Cuban and Caribbean Poet Laureate, the PhD dissertation, 'The Creative Dialogue in the Poetry of Nicolás Guillén: Europe and Africa' (UCLA 1975), established the central role played by carnival in any *sui generis* culture of the region. In 1987, Vera Kutzinski published *Against the American Grain: Myth and History in William Carlos Williams, Jay Wright, and Nicolás Guillén.* The section devoted to the Cuban is titled 'The Carnivalization of Poetry: Nicolás Guillén Chronicles', and she presents 'Sensemayá' as a carnival song. Kutzinski is on the right track, but it is one that was signalled in my dissertation 12 years earlier. In my 1990 book on Guillén I sought to establish very clearly the chronology of this carnival-based hermeneutics. In any case, it is clear that neither Kutzinski nor any of her followers from the ranks of Eurocentrism understand the Egyptian origin of carnival. Indeed, much of the material presented in my initial chapter, 'From Kaiso to *Son* and Beyond', in my most recent book, *Amazing Connections,* would be considered radical by all but the most enlightened Caribbean scholars. Errol Hill's *The Trinidad Carnival: Mandate for a National Theatre* (1972), for example, still occupies a privileged position, and he is apparently unprepared to reconsider the favoured doctrine of the Roman origin of carnival. There is every indication, then, that the Guillén poem is connected to the ancient Egyptian one through an oral tradition to which Africans reverted under the circumstances of extreme brutality imposed by barbaric European invaders, marauders, slavers, colonizers, savages.

In marked contrast to the spontaneity of 'Sensemayá' and of course the *Motivos de son*, the poet's 'Elegiá a Jesús Menéndez [Elegy to Jesús Menéndez], written between 1948 and 1951 and finally published in the 1958 collection *La paloma de vuelo popular* [The Dove of Popular Flight), is perhaps his most carefully crafted work. The poem is correctly Marxist-Leninist, rooted in the atheistic contemporary European intellectual tradition. However, the poet gets the best of both worlds, for this modern Marxist hero is a suffering servant, a messiah in the cast of his divine namesake. Furthermore it is quite clear that Guillén consciously incorporates traditional West African religious symbolism into his aesthetic. Jesús Menéndez is presented as a manifestation of Shango, 'the great Yoruba ancestor and military leader who has been raised to the ranks of the *orishas* (divinities) ... becoming ... god of thunder' (Smart 1990: 116).

Henry Louis Gates Jr is one of those contemporary mainstream scholars who have acknowledged the pivotal importance of another Yoruba *orisha*, Legba, the Trickster (1988). Legba's is the discourse of the 'signifying monkey', or in the popular parlance of the contemporary Caribbean: the 'mamaguyer', the 'broad-talker', the 'shit-talker'. It is Legba who inspires those tea meetings in Nevis in the Windward Islands which Roger D. Abrahams depicts as 'a remarkable combination of pageant, mock fertility ritual, variety show, and organized mayhem' (1983: 16). It is clearly Legba who inspired the poem 'Digo que no soy un hombre puro' [I'm No Pure Man I Say] that first appeared in 1968 and was included in the second edition of the 1972 collection, *La rueda dentada* [The Cogwheel]. In this poem 'the artist's purpose appears to be the signalling to the world that the old poet still retains the vibrancy of youth. It is this same purpose that prompted the extreme experimentation of the book *El diario que a diario* [The Daily Daily]' (Smart 1990: 150). Legba's connection to a book like *El gran zoo* [The Big Zoo] (1976) is much more readily grasped. From the dawn of recorded history African civilizations have evinced a deep appreciation for the links between the supernatural and the various parts of the natural world, this latter including the plant, animal and human kingdoms. So African literature throughout the ages is replete with totemic representations of the Trickster: the spider, the rabbit, the land turtle (*jicotea*), the (signifying) monkey, and so on. Some of Guillén's finest expressions of political satire are to be found in the pages of this book penned by the National Poet of a Communist nation.

Diario que a diario (1972), Guillén's final book, is the same kind of work as the 1972 novel *Mumbo Jumbo* by the African-American Ishmael Reed, a consummate parody. According to Gates, 'in six demanding novels [including *Mumbo Jumbo*], Reed has criticized, through signifying what he perceives to be the conventional structures of feeling that he has received from the Afro-American tradition' (1984: 297). Employing the self-same pastiche format, the Cuban's book parodies and signifies on our received notions of his nation's history, and 'is sustained artistically by its irony and sarcasm. It is an experimental work, but the experimental form is not divorced from the content, as the poet is manifestly seeking a new way to express his central poetic vision' (Smart 1990: 91).

Nicolás Guillén is, then, more than just the token 'Black' poet to be trotted out every time the spectre of racism rears its ugly head. He has, in fact, plumbed the depth of his *sous-réalité* to speak *'en negro de verdad'*, in an authentic African voice. In the course of Nancy Morejón's 'Conversación con Nicolás Guillén' [Conversation with Nicolás Guillén], which was first published in 1970, the poet declared: 'my poetry has always been internally consistent' [mi poesia ha sido siempre coherente consigo misma] (Morejón 1974: 57). This, of course, is just another way of expressing the Walcottean declaration.

Caribbean people from the entire region, that is, the region comprised of those islands and lands washed by the Caribbean Sea, are a people oozing culture from every pore. They are a hyper-civilized people precisely because they are African. It has been clear to all honest and serious scholars of North American civilization that its single most creative engine is the one that Africans brought with them. This African creative genius has made the most fundamental defining contribution to popular North American music/literature. At this moment in history under the label of 'world music' other African popular musical/literary forms have begun to impact profoundly on North American culture. One of the most significant of these forms is Jamaican reggae. Caribbean people are far from the 'monkey chasers', the 'ignorant savages' sometimes portrayed in the popular imagination. We are a people with an incredibly rich literary tradition. Our literature, however, will not be appreciated fully until we develop the appropriate analytical tools. I have contended that Nicolás Guillén spoke in an internally consistent, authentic African voice, *en negro de verdad*. It is only through the use of such analytical tools that this great poet will be finally 'discovered'.

8

Nancy Morejon: nation, negritude, and marginality[1]

Efraín Barradas

A view of the siege from the outside

The troubles which Cuba has suffered and continues to suffer at the hands of the economic blockade which has lasted for over three decades dramatically affect not only Cubans but additionally (although to a much lesser extent) those of us from outside the island, who are interested in the welfare of that Caribbean island, including those of us interested in her literature. It is difficult for the researcher of Caribbean literature to remain informed of literary developments in that country. Perhaps with huge gaps and definitely behind the times, but step by step and from the other side of the fence which the blockade has created, we are discovering, as well as helping others discover, the importance of Cuban letters.

Nancy Morejón is one of the female writers from that 'other' Caribbean island who has most effectively broken through the cultural barrier. Her literary production, and specifically her poetry, has been published and frequently studied outside her country. This interest in her work is in part explained by the acknowledgment that, above and beyond her undeniable aesthetic merits, she has helped in spreading an understanding through her own aesthetic perspective, of the history of her country. Thus her poems reflect not only a personal world but also paint a picture of a collective one. For example, some of her pieces have helped in an appreciation of how in recent years, Cuban artists and intellectuals have been reinterpreting their collective lives, how they have been re-reading their past from that which previously was seen as the margins of Cuban society, so as to give us a new version of the Cuban historical process. Her poems such as 'Mujer negra' [Black Woman] clearly show this (Barradas 1980). With this in mind and so as better to understand her, Nancy Morejón's poetry must be read in its Cuban context. Naturally, this does not imply that her work cannot be read as a consummately personal aesthetic project. However, interpreted in a wider context, her work acquires a greater sense of cohesion which in turn gives it special meaning and importance for Caribbean letters in general.

Necessary negrismo *and the need for* negrism

Almost by necessity, the first encounter with Morejón's poetry takes its reader to the world of so-called *negrista* poetry. Whoever reads her closely firstly notices that this Cuban poet assumes her blackness as a central, if not exclusive, part of her work, and consequently contextualizes it in the framework previously established by the first practitioners of this poetic mode, particularly as it was cultivated in her own country. Ballagas, Guirao, and Guillén, among other Cuban poets of the 1930s, produced work whose central focus was the black way of life in Cuba. The importance of the *negrista* work of these poets for the literature of their country, as much as for Caribbean literature and the literature of Spanish America in general, has already been firmly established by critics. But for some scholars who concentrated exclusively on the work produced by the classical poets of the school of Caribbean *negrismo*, this movement was a merely transient fashion which soon died out as a poetic movement of any importance.

Such an interpretation of *negrismo* seemed valid until, from the 1960s, poets all over the Hispanic Caribbean began to create, independently of each other and even without a knowledge of previous work, a new poetry with a black theme which proved that *negrismo*, with a new face and with new ideas, was still alive and valid as a movement. Among these poets, Morejón stands out. She is probably the poet of the Hispanic Caribbean who has most contributed to the revitalization and redefinition of *negrismo* today.

It will be worthwhile to re-examine this point given that it not only assists us better to understand her poetry but also to evaluate more fairly the *negrista* movement in the Hispanic Caribbean. Traditionally, it has been said that our Caribbean *negrista* literature was born as an important cultural movement in the decade of the 1920s and that it reached its zenith the following decade. According to this traditional critical framework, our *negrista* poetry declared its birth with *Motivos de son* [*Son Motifs*] (1930), by the Cuban, Nicolás Guillén, reached one of its greatest achievements with *Tuntún de pasa y grifería* (1937), by the Puerto

Rican Luis Palés Matos, and marked its final moment of importance with *Compadre Mon* [Buddy Mon] (1940) by the Dominican Manual del Cabral. According to such a view, the movement and its central theme appeared and disappeared within a period of 15 years. What existed before and what came after are unknown or are comfortably placed under the broad labels of history or consequence. From the perspective that this view offers, our scarce neo-African folkloric tradition can be seen as a mere archaeological piece of information, without great importance. For these intellectuals, *negrismo* is a passing fashion and nothing more, and thus it is an easily dismissed cultural fact (cf. Fernández de la Vega and Pamies 1973).

But these interpretations err gravely and for very obvious reasons:

1 In the first place, they propose that *negrismo* has died, although they leave the door open for subsequent flowerings.
2 They fail because many label the movement as a mere fashion which has not discovered anything essential for Caribbean literature, beyond serving as a medium through which some poets demonstrate their verbal capacity.
3 These studies err because they visualize our *negrismo* as a limited theme and not as the distinctive perspective from which the artist sees the world and thereby offers a personal vision, one which is as valid as any other.
4 These interpretations also err because they reduce our *negrista* expressions merely to poetry and do not see that the movement shaped and still continues to shape diverse literary forms as well as those of popular culture. To perform an in-depth study of our *negrism*, one must go much further than the poetry of Palés Matos, Cabral and Guillén; one must look, for example, to popular music ('Pintame angelitos negros') [Paint me Little Black Angels], to radio serials (*El derecho de nacer*) [The Right to Be Born], to art (Wilfredo Lam) and, in short, to almost all Caribbean cultural manifestations since then.

Undoubtedly these traditional interpretations err because they do not recognize the profound and widespread penetration of *negrismo*.[2]

The emergence of Nancy Morejón's work, and that of other poets of the Hispanic Caribbean who began to look again at the theme, surprised many and emphatically rejected the verdicts of others who were too ready to administer the last rites to our *negrismo*. Because of them, Morejón's poetry must be juxtaposed with the work of her literary contemporaries as well as some younger writers, figures such as her compatriot Miguel Barnet, the Dominican Norberto James and the

Puerto Rican Mayra Santos, for example; writers who reaffirm with their body of work that *negrismo* is very much alive and well in our Caribbean.

But in addition, Morejón's work must be examined as a re-reading of that of her teacher and mentor, Nicolás Guillén. She herself lends this dimension to her poetry. Proof of this is her extensive study on Nicolás Guillén (Morejón 1982a).

Two models to dismantle

A consideration, however, of Morejón's writing with regard to *negrista* poetry, particularly Guillén's work, obliges us to look for critical models which offer an understanding of this sequence or poetic development without subtracting merit from either of the two poets studied. It is almost an instinctive reflex in Hispanic culture, whether in its Peninsular or Spanish-American forms, to force the Procrustean uniformity of a generational theory on the poetic production of both the older and younger poet (cf. Ortega y Gasset 1923; Marias 1949). But immediately we see that this method resolves nothing or at least almost nothing. If we follow the antiquated ideas of Ortega and his followers, we only achieve a mechanical elimination of the problem, by saying that it is logical and almost natural that Morejón would emulate Guillén given that they do not belong to contiguous generations but rather to completely different generations, which would negate the possibility of any antagonism between them and thus would be more likely to favour imitation or aesthetic continuation. Such an explanation, in the same way as those which we have accepted for years as a result of the imposition of this Ortegan vision of cultural history, is counter-productive. Very little would be achieved if we applied this way of looking at culture to our problem.

On the other hand, to understand the relationship between Guillén and Morejón we are tempted to have recourse to Harold Bloom's ideas, particularly his concept of 'the anxiety of influence' and that of 'misreading' (Bloom 1973, 1975). But this theory, although more meaningful than the previous one, is also not accept-able for exploring in detail the theme, as it covers the relationship between the two poets with superficial psychoanalytic ideas and with useless rhetorical terminology. From Bloom, in this case, I think that we can productively employ the concept of 'misreading', although we cannot accept the totality of his assumed theories. With this critical concept in mind, I propose that we take a look at a specific case where Morejón re-reads Guillén's poetry.

*Before neo-*negrism

In 1934, Nicolás Guillén published *West Indies Ltd,* one of his most important books. This collection of poems represented the culminating first period of Guillén's poetry: after *Motivos de son* (1930) the poet had proceeded to *Sóngoro Cosongo* (1931), thus to end the first poetic phase in 1934 with *West Indies Ltd,* a text which was to consolidate his Caribbean vision. One of the most important poems in this book is 'Sensemayá', a piece which bears the subtitle 'Canto para matar una culebra' [Song to Kill a Snake]. The subtitle immediately takes us back to a previous text with a similar title in which the origin of Guillén's poem obviously lies. This is a folkloric poem which Ramón Guirao includes in his 1938 *Orbita de la poesia afrocubana* [The Development of Afro-Cuban Poetry], but which was known to Cuban intellectuals before the appearance of this important collection. 'Canto para matar culebras' [Song to Kill Snakes], the aforementioned folkloric poem, one of a few texts written prior to the *negrismo* boom, survived and was widely read by Cuban poets in the 1930s.

The poem which Guirao collected reproduces a dialogue between a 'Negrita' [a young black woman] and a 'Diablito' [a little devil] who manages to kill the snake which was threatening the woman. The text is composed of expressions which seem to be African in origin and which were saved through songs and rituals such as the following (Guirao 1938: 9):

> ¡Ni traga ni pica!
> ¡Sángala muleque!
> ¡La culebra murió!
> ¡Sánlaga muleque!
> ¡Yo mimito mató!
> ¡Calabasó-só-só!
>
> [It neither swallows nor bites!
> Sángala muleque!
> The snake died!
> Sánlaga muleque!
> I killed it myself!
> Calabasó-só-só!]

Proof of the importance of this text collected by Guirao is that in 1946, in *La música en Cuba* [Music in Cuba], Alejo Carpentier again picks it as an example of neo-African folklore in his country. In this important volume, the learned musicologist explains the sense and the function of the text. Carpentier notes that the text was part of the carnival music of black Cubans. The text would serve as the musical accompaniment to a procession which represented a giant scorpion or an immense snake which, to the rhythm of the song, symbolically killed itself (Carpentier 1972: 291–2).

The roots of Guillén's poem are thus obvious, but these do not clarify the entire poem, given that in 'Sensemayá' Guillén does not directly copy the folkloric song but rather he creates a parallel text, and one of much more complex poetics (Guillén 1980: 132):

> ¡Mayombre-bombe-mayombé!
> Sensemayá, la culebra…
> ¡Mayombre-bombe-mayombé!
> Sensemayá, no se mueve…
> ¡Mayombre-bombe-mayombé!
> Sensemayá, la culebra…
> ¡Mayombre-bombe-mayombé!
> Sensemayá, se murió.
>
> [Mayombre-bombe-mayombé!
> Sensemayá, the snake…
> Mayombre-bombe-mayombé!
> Sensemayá, does not move…
> Mayombre-bombe-mayombé!
> Sensemayá, the snake…
> Mayombre-bombe-mayombé!
> Sensemayá, died.]

As in the traditional song, in Guillén's poem, indirectly, an ideology or a religious vision is revealed.[3] Both texts accept the good-bad dichotomy which structures so much of neo-African poetry, although it does not necessarily respond to the principles which sustain Afro-Caribbean religions nor African ones which serve as the bases for the texts. The snake in Guillén's poem has a lot in common with the Christian symbolism of evil and does not totally correspond to the neo-African religious representations where the *orishas* [gods of the *santeria* pantheon] and their symbols can be ambiguous and can represent more than one face of the human and divine condition.[4] But the serpent in 'Sensemayá' is the symbol of evil. The poem is a 'song to kill a snake', the music of a ritual to fight against an evil incarnate in this animal. That which is assumed in Guirao's folkloric poem, in 'Sensemayá' is made explicit and is even intensified.[5] Guillén maintains the rhythmical resources and the musical finality of traditional poetry, but the ideological structure of the poem, by emphasizing only one aspect of a very complex symbol, seems to correspond more to the Christian vision than to that of the neo-African. Here a simple dichotomy dominates: good versus evil; the snake versus the human being.

Our sacred conversation

Nancy Morejon's 'Hablando con una culebra' [Talking with a snake] takes us very far from that ideological structure. The poem is obviously a re-reading of the Guillén poem, which is in itself a re-reading of the folkloric one. The main difference between Morejón's poem and that of her teacher, Guillén, is the point of view which the poetic voices in their respective texts adopt when confronted with the snake. While Guillén seems to direct himself to the latter from an aggressive perspective in which the snake is only a symbol of evil, a vision which is maintained in the folkloric poem, Morejón approaches the snake from a wider and more ambiguous personal angle. She begins questioning it with an exemplary compassion (1982b: 40):

> A ti también te dieron con un palo,
> te estrujaron y te escupieron, te pisotearon
> siempre;
> a ti, te mataron con delicia
> y te echaron una maldición que hasta hoy hicieron
> cumplir.

> [They also hit you with a stick,
> they squeezed you and they spat on you, they stamped on you
> always;
> you, they killed you with delight
> and they inflicted a curse on you from which to this day they made
> sure
> you would not be released.]

The first lines of the poem, more so than in Guillén, lead us to think of another great Spanish American poet of the twentieth century, César Vallejo. These lines can be better understood as a re-reading of the well known Vallejo lines (1988: 224):

> César Vallejo ha muerto, le pegaban
> todos sin que él les haga nada;
> le daban duro con un palo y duro
>
> también con una soga.

> [César Vallejo is dead, they hit him
> without his doing anything to them;
> they hit him hard with a stick and hard
>
> with a rope too.]

Morejón approaches the traditional theme of the serpent from a non-traditional angle. The identification with the symbolism of evil herein cannot be read through the musicalization but rather through the identification with the poet herself and her intimate world. As proof of this, note how the poetic voice establishes a parallel between the serpent and the poet's mother: 'you were more possessive than Angelica, my mother' [*fuiste más poseedora que Angélica, mi madre*] (Morejón 1982b: 40).

The relation between the theme of the snake and the poetic voice, a voice which we presume is equivalent to that of the poet given that she mentions her mother, obliges the reader to recall important cultural contexts. The main one is biblical. The poetic voice, which is linked to that of the snake, indirectly echoes the essential problem of *Genesis* given that in the poem, a relationship is re-established between the woman (the poetic voice) and the serpent (the theme and the questioned being). This relationship or tie is a violation of the Christian principles because, as a result of it, the feminine figure is given back the dangerous power of knowledge which is offered to her by the serpent in the Judeo-Christian myth. In this sense, 'Hablando con una culebra' is also a poem which seems to violate certain basic hypotheses in our culture as it restores the origins of an old world.

But more important in interpreting the poem is a return to the Afro-Caribbean cultural context. In the same way as the text eliminates all attempts at the musical re-creation which dominates in Guillén's poem, an intention which was also given prominence in the folkloric text, here there is a complete bridging of any distance between the human being and the serpent. This difference is radical and places the poem in a neo-*negrista* context. If Guillén's poem proposed the revitalization of Afro-Caribbean folklore, then the Morejón poem's point of departure is the very intention of recovering this cultural heritage. Paradoxically, the poem seems simultaneously to negate it. Consequently, the ideological inversion which the poem assumes is complete: the symbol of evil gains the upper hand; the snake is the heroine of the poem. In this sense, 'Hablando con una culebra' is a radically innovative poem. But only its history, a history which is discovered on reading the poem in the light of the other two previous ones which sustain it, reveals this important component.

The false rupture

Why these radical changes? Can these departures categorically separate Morejón's work from that of Guillén and the traditional foundations of his work? What does this poem tell us about the political and ideological location of such an important Cuban writer as Morejón? I shall venture to suggest some ideas which may serve as an answer to the questions which arise from a reading of these three poetic texts.

At the outset, one must be aware that the personal and dramatic differences which seem to distance Guillén's and Morejón's poems from each other, rather than separating them, unite them. This is certainly the case since the work of the younger poet takes the writing of the older poet as one of its principal foundations. But, above all, the two poems remain intimately linked if one does not hold to the conception of *negrismo* as a passing and isolated phenomenon. If we accept that throughout Caribbean culture *negrismo* was a moment when we became conscious of our true cultural constitution, then we realize that Morejón can take up the theme of blackness in her poetic work without declaring it, but only because others before her – here Guillén plays a supremely important role – adopted it in an explicit and even aggressive manner. Morejón can ignore the traditional world – music and ideology – that is present in the text colleced by Guirao because Guillén had already made it clear that that text could not be dismissed, being a primordial element of Cuban culture. Guillén saved the folkloric text and because of that Morejón can now change or even ignore it. But her poem does not ignore Guillén nor the traditional song; the poem takes them on, it takes them for granted, it presupposes them as her starting point, without ever saying so.

History and the serpent

Morejón's text goes further than that of her teacher given that in her 'Hablando con una culebra' there is not only a declaration of independence from Negritude and folklore but also an inversion of traditional ideological parameters: presumed evil is here transformed into good. By proposing this inversion, Morejón coincides with Cuban intellectuals who, after the triumph of the Revolution, re-read their entire national history and also that of Spanish America so as to offer us new parameters by which to understand them. What Morejón does with 'Hablando con una culebra' is exactly the same as Roberto Fernández

Retamar's inversion of the accepted models employed since Sarmiento to interpret the history of Spanish America. In his essay 'Calibán' (1971) Fernández Retamar re-reads Spanish American history from the margins and places at the centre, at least theoretically, the marginalized. If Fernández Retamar establishes that our model is Caliban and not Ariel, Morejón establishes that the old, evil snake is our salvation: her snake is the other face of Caliban.

But the vision of history which I find in 'Hablando con una culebra' is very distinct from that which I encounter in the famous essay. Among others, one reason for this is that Morejón approaches history from both a feminine and a feminist perspective. One of the greatest premises of the feminist movement – the personal is the political – finds itself embodied in the poem when an identification with the snake is established, which consequently comes to represent all marginalized sectors. Morejón does not get caught up in the romantic cliché of self-identification with Satan: neither Southey, nor Sade, nor Baudelaire, nor Kleist, nor the Rolling Stones with their 'Sympathy for the Devil' are models which the poet follows. 'Hablando con una culebra' merely approaches the problem from the margins or from the perspective of the marginalized.

And what happens when the margins become the centre? Is marginality thus eradicated? Fernández Retamar seems to suggest this, and in so doing, he accepts a utopian vision of history. In 'Hablando con una culebra' – but not in any of her other texts: 'Mujer negra' [Black Woman], for example – Morejón seems to negate that optimistic view of history because she takes it one step further than Fernández Retamar. While the latter is only preoccupied with the parameters of the political world, the model of ideological inversion she offers opens on to a wider world, a world which does not exclude the political, but which includes the individual, who is placed at its centre. In her world, there always seems to be a place for the marginalized. Although the poem seems to present the possibility of a utopian world ('And when between sycamores and coco plum trees/you have begun your unredeemed magic') [*Mas cuando entre sicomoros e hicacos/hayas iniciado tu majomia irredenta*], the poet predicts that in that world, absolute peace will never exist. It is for this reason that the poetic voice paradoxically warns the snake: 'shake yourself, beat, bite and kill too' [*sacúdete, pega, muerde y mata tú también*]. All the actions which in the traditional song and in 'Sensemayá' were commands which the respective poetic voices – voices which seem to be associated with a masculine principle given that they were originally spoken by the 'Diablito' in the folkloric poem – gave to man, are now orders that the snake receives. Roles are dramatically reversed.

In the world that this poem creates there will always be victims and victors because there will always be margins and the marginalized. With Fernández Retamar's utopianism in mind, Morejón's good sense, pragmatism and sincerity seem all the more convincing.

Still a view of the siege from the outside

Why this difference? Is it cynicism? Is it irony? Is it lack of faith? 'Hablando con una culebra' does not direct its readers to any of these options. The poem, at least according to this critic, who looks at the text from a distance that the blockade has imposed on it, proves to us that in the Cuban intellectual and artistic world there is still room and need for revisions of its history, a history which only recently had been revised.

That re-reading of Cuban history seems to have been initiated in and by its own margins. Perhaps because of this, one of the best candidates to propose such a revision might be a poet who speaks maternally and sensibly to the snake, by definition the eternal symbol of marginality. But this new and simple song to the old snake represents a profoundly radical reading of Cuban and Caribbean history. And why not of all history?

Notes

1   This chapter is dedicated to the memory of Rafi Rodríguez and Ronnie Torres.

2   One should mention other scholars who offer a broader view of *negrismo*. Mónica Mansour (1973) gives a more credible interpretation of the movement although she tends to see Guillén, Palés and Cabral as the culmination of it, a fact which gives a certain element of closure to the history of our *negrismo*. See also the anthologies of Gonzáles and Mansour (1976) and that of Albornoz and Rodriguez Luis (1980). Additionally one can consult Lourdes Martinez's important volume (1990), although the latter focuses principally on narrative and not poetry. One of the few books which presents the *negrista* movement as one which affects all cultural spheres is Pérez Sarduy and Stubbs (1993).

3   Ian Smart, in Chapter 7 of this book, which deals with Guillén's poetry from Afrocentric perspectives, assures us that this poem is directly rooted in African texts.

4   In describing the founding principles of the Yoruba religion, a faith which served as the basis of many of the neo-African religious currents in Cuba, Robert Farris Thompson says that 'God ... had, according to Yoruba belief, bestowed upon us the power-to-make-things-happen, morally neutral power, power to give or take away, to kill and to give life, according to the purpose and the nature of the bearer' (Thompson 1983: 5–6). Geoffrey Parrinder (1973) studies the multiple meanings, the positive as much as the negative ones, which are attributed to the serpent in

African religions. It is the messenger of death but it also represents water and the rainbow and above all, it is the symbol of eternity. In African religions and, by extension, in the neo-African ones, the serpent, then, does not solely embody evil, as occurs in Christianity and Judaism. Guillén's text thus presents only one face of the myth as well as a very complex symbolism.

5   It must be noted that what we know of the Afro-Cuban tradition (the text by Guirao, for example) is only a poetic fragment of a more complex religious ritual and that this text, as is the case with the entire neo-African culture which we have in the Caribbean, has passed through the devastating process of deculturation which has transformed the culture which was brought from Africa by the slaves (see Moreno Fraginals 1977).

9

Notes on the history of Blacks in Cuba … and may Elegguá be with me

Manuel Granados

In order to talk about Blacks in Cuba I need to draw a few curtains and see what lies behind them, in spite of the political right or left, in spite of Fernando Ortiz, in spite of tourists. On 20 May 1902 Cuba officially became the last colony of Spain in America. But it is not the Spanish flag which, among fanfare and hymns, is lowered in the El Morro fortress in Havana Bay; it is the flag of the United States which vacates its place so that the one with the three blue stripes, the two white ones and the lonely star within the red triangle could fly in the wind. From 1902 to the present this detail has stood out in the social and political history of the largest Caribbean island, which has had quite a different trajectory from the rest of Spanish America.

Cuba's history is one of contrasts and illogicalities which manifest themselves at a national level through the same symptoms shared by psychiatric patients. Both the grandiloquence of the 'patricians' and republican monumentalism cannot be ignored. But neither can the squandering of the so-called high classes who cemented such a recalcitrant aristocracy that that of their peers from other Latin American countries seems petty, even though some of them had more wealth and resources. We only need to look at the social chronicles of newspapers such as *La Marina* or *El País* between 1945 and 1959 in order to confirm this. There we will find mention of noble titles, ladies of noble birth, perfect gentlemen, and extremely lavish saloon events. These sources also verify the pro-fusion of aristocratic private colleges (Catholic and Protestant) which were of equal if not higher standards than their US counterparts. As one would expect this self-projection of the 'higher' classes', as they were called then, with their 'Country Club', Miramar Yacht Club, their special sports and their distinctive ways of entertaining themselves, became a focal point, firstly for the middle classes and then for the lower classes.

This situation could have been viewed as merely an example of the superficial way of life of the privileged classes in whatever society or perhaps, even a little more seriously, as an example of the hierarchical mechanism of third-world societies. But the racial dynamics of this social structure makes it a far more serious concern for me. This racism, which began in Cuba from the period of slavery was consolidated in the First Republic (1902–59). The racism inherent in the social hierarchy meant necessarily that in a multi-ethnic society such as Cuba a large proportion of the population, the Blacks, were second-class citizens. Independence, therefore, did not create social equality. Despite the proliferation of patriotic rhetoric during the new Republic it was impossible to resolve the unquestionable fact that white Cubans, rich or poor, experienced liberation, if not politically, certainly in terms of their lack of racial alienation. They had achieved a consciousness of being at home or at least of belonging to the family. There is a distinct connection here with the concept of the *Madre Patria* (the metropolitan country from which the island had recently detached itself). The ancestors of white Cubans spoke the official language of the colonizer and naturally their descendants followed suit, perpetuating many of its associated myths and legends. On the other hand, the close ancestors of the Blacks who had fought in the war of independence had to learn this language while at the same time disguising their natural universe to assume and copy that of the master.

From a humanistic perspective, I suppose a whole range of conclusions might be drawn. What is certain, though, is that at the level of everyday life it seemed impossible to arrive at a solution to the problem of racial exclusion. The fact that Blacks had paid with blood and death for the liberation of their supposed nation was obviously not sufficient. In 1868 Manuel de Céspedes (known as the father of the nation) proclaimed independence and started to free the slaves he owned (more than anything else, this was due to the fact that certain technological advancements had made slaves less economically viable). An extremely high percentage of these ex-slaves went to fight for the country's liberation from Spain and for me this confirms the haplessness of Blacks at that time. Recently freed but without property or possessions, what other means of survival did they have than to fight? In addition, it is sadly ironic that Blacks had to assume as their country a place where for generations they had been abused and dehumanized in the worst possible ways.

From the inception of independent Cuba black people had to distance themselves from the idea of blackness because on the one hand blackness only brought them misery and difficulty and on the other Whites could only accept Blacks if, under their paternalist tutelage, they mimicked white attitudes and customs. When Blacks refused to follow this path, the Whites who were obliged to co-exist with them regarded them as strange and phrases such as, 'each one in his own place' or 'if he is black we are not equal' marked white reinforcement of racial separation.

It is quite significant that the first place I heard the term *igualón* was in public school while I was still a young boy. After that I heard it constantly in private school. Despite all the years that have gone by I still have not been able to remove from my memory this term and the moment I first heard it. The term was used to refer to a black child who trespassed – went beyond the limits which society had established for him and had the desire to be like others. The worst thing is that there was always a white adult who would use the term to situate the child firmly in his place. In the black family even more astonishing terms existed. *Igualón* is a response to the violation of the white world on the part of the black child and thus becomes either a conscious or unconscious attempt on the part of the establishment to defend itself. But in the black family where there was a desire to protect the child from future trauma the phrases were of a different character: 'We have to conduct ourselves properly because we are black'; or 'you need to stay in your place'. This was obviously a disgraceful approval of the white world.

In the republican period, despite the struggles (usually rhetorical) for racial equality by both black and white public male figures very little success was achieved. In 1912 (a catastrophic year for many Blacks in Cuba, when the nation managed to emulate the cruelty of the Ku Klux Klan of the US South) the free coloured movement, led by Evaristo Estenoz, was formed. The intention of the movement was to find a republican solution to society's deeply ingrained racial crisis. What resulted was virulent repression, which caused the deaths of hundreds of Blacks. Here, the only difference from the methods of the KKK was that this was a tragedy which did not have the usual accessories (such as white hoods, burning crosses, tar).

The extreme lack of worth attributed to blacks in independent Cuba is demonstrated in *Un cuarto siglo de evolución cubana* [A Quarter Century of Cuban Evolution], published in 1924 by the prestigious intellectual and researcher Ramiro Guerra. A collection of 15 essays with a prologue by another distinguished Cuban intellectual, Pedro Betancourt, the book traces the transformation of Cuba since its birth as an independent nation. There is not a single line in which the intellectual writer registers the presence of Blacks or their role in society's evolution.

Nothing was mentioned about Blacks as a basic component of the Cuban nation. Clearly, this could have been regarded as something positive if it were deemed unnecessary to mention them since it was taken as given that they were a part of society. But this was not the case for Betancourt. The example which he uses is that of the Bostonian rebellion caused by the metropolitan imposition of taxes on tea. We are all aware that both legally and economically Blacks were unable either to import or to export anything. We may therefore deduce that the conscientious citizens shaken by the abuse of imperial administration were white citizens. The same analysis may be applied to the Cuban scenario. All economic power was controlled by the Spanish authorities or their white creole descendants. Guerra and Betancourt do not take Blacks into account; when they talk about Cuban people in general they mean white Cubans, the ones who continue to espouse the values and culture of the metropolis. For these Cubans the only difference in perspective with the metropolis concerns the mechanisms of economic development. Their situation is quite analogous to that of a son saying to a father, 'I am now an adult, I am going to run my own business, you are impoverishing me'. Certainly there were cases of Blacks who had some economic power but such cases were isolated and their social influence negligible.

Using the preceding discussion as a point of departure, let us now consider the situation of Blacks in Cuba between 1925 and 1959. As in the earlier period, they had no economic control, not even of small businesses. They were farmers but they did not own land. Fundamentally, they were wage-earners: bricklayers, craftsmen, carpenters. Gradually, in this period, blacks became involved in more specialized jobs, for example as mechanics in the sugar industry. They also worked as casual labourers within that industry. But here a totally different study would be required since most of the labourers within the sugar industry came from Jamaica and Haiti and they went on to form immigrant communities.

In the period after Grau San Martin's government (1944–8) Blacks began to gain a meagre presence in selected professions: medicine; law; teaching. There was a smaller number in professions such as architecture and engineering, where a black clientele did not necessarily exist. These professionals formed societies which tried to become carbon copies of their elitist white counterparts. Aimed at consolidating a black gentry, these clubs were very aristocratic in style and two of the most outstanding examples were the

'Atenas' club of Havana and the 'Sociedad Unión Fraternal' [Union Fraternal Society].

However, owing to the lack of initial capital, and because the island's economic mechanism did not them allow access to this, Blacks basically remained condemned to manual labour and, whether they wanted or not, to being second class-citizens. There were a few exceptions in which Blacks reached the House of Representatives and constituted an elite black aristocracy. It is they who travelled to France, Spain and the United States (to places like New York and other northern cities because at that time Miami remained very Southern in outlook, with all that that implied for Blacks). Completely separated from real black people and victims of their own mimetic alienation, they were aware that they would never be truly accepted within the very strictly delimited national superstructure.

On the margins then, the great mass of black people lived in the poorest neighbourhoods of the country, crammed into shacks, condemned to the hardest forms of labour, earning the lowest wages, and creating a new kind of ghetto. This situation planted ideas about an essential black way of being in the minds of white Cubans. Obviously racist attitudes were upheld by so-called right-thinking and well-adjusted Cubans, whatever their race, who forgot or denied that this 'way of being' was no different to that of any other underprivileged mass in any 'lower class' neighbourhood of any society. Whites who were trapped among the invisible but real fences of these ghettos, then, were also Blacks because they acted like Blacks, lived like Blacks, and thought like Blacks. Like Blacks they were manipulated by the dominant classes, but it must be emphasized that as far as the everyday exercise of power was concerned these whites always held the hope that sooner or later, due to luck or changing conditions, they would escape their impoverished circumstances. No such hope existed for Blacks.

It was the constitutional government of Carlos Prio Socarrás, ousted in a coup in 1952, which issued a presidential decree forcing the large department stores to accept black and mulatto girls to work behind their counters. Many of the girls who took up these jobs had university degrees in law, philosophy or education. Almost all of them had a sponsor from the Atenas Society or another such social club. This guaranteed that the candidate's physical appearance, way of dressing, and hair (which had to be straightened), at least showed a willingness to pass for white. Of course this was the period in which hair-straightening creams were not yet popular in Cuba and black women were obliged to straighten their hair with hot iron combs. All of this so that they could work alongside white girls who, at best, had graduated as stenographers from the Havana Business Academy, but whose conduct followed the aesthetic standard imposed by the dominant classes who, of course, were copying the 'way of life' of their powerful neighbours!

When classified advertisements requested candidates of 'good appearance' it was understood automatically that this meant they could not be black, just like the advertisement – ostensibly for English cooks – aimed at Jamaican applicants. By virtue of being British subjects the Jamaicans were more tolerable than black Cubans to the powerful national bourgeoisie who emerged newly rich after the Second World War.

Thus, it is not difficult to understand the early enthusiasm and support on the part of black people for the coup led by President Fulgencio Batista. In their enthusiasm, Blacks allowed themselves to be led by their knowledge of the social origins of the head of state and his dark skin, which made him black in their eyes. This is something which Batista never, in fact, accepted either in private or in public. More importantly, he definitively denied his blackness through constant attempts to become a part of the white Cuban oligarchy, which rejected him in public and which, aided by Washington (when it was politically expedient), ended up humiliating him.

Once again Blacks had allowed themselves to be dragged along, pledging support to one they believed their own, the honest leader who was going to improve the country and who offered them peace, work and progress. Later on, with Washington's new foreign policy in Latin America, the US government's shameful support for the dictator was withdrawn. This was an opportunity from which the recalcitrant Cuban bourgeoisie profited. Several opposing political factions emerged, among them the 'Directorio Estudiantil Universitario' [University Students Board] and the 'Movimiento 26 de Julio' [26 July Movement], the majority of whom either came from white middle-class backgrounds or had middle-class aspirations.

In such a situation the black majority were faced with two options: apathy (a product of their despair) or involvement with the Batista military regime. In that second category were the so-called neighbourhood Blacks who allowed themselves to be trapped by the demagoguery of the ruling government, the distribution of free Christmas hampers, and low wages for work on different projects. But government propaganda also seduced Blacks by promising a kind of black high life. Thus it placated Blacks by making a section of the beach in the north-east of Havana available to them. They called it the Marbella Yacht Club even though there was not even a boat there. There black Cubans would celebrate wedding receptions, hen parties, and christening showers. Afterwards, pompous reports written in the gushing style of white high society *crónicas* would appear in *La Mancha* or *El País*.

Knowing a little Cuban history and considering the above with reasoned impartiality, it is easy to appreciate the sources of this kind of self-denial. Most of the ladies and gentlemen who attended these splendid social functions would rent their dresses, dinner jackets, gloves and hats from a certain shop on Monte Frente street. The business was owned by a Jew whose characteristic business acumen allowed him to profit from their racial alienation. More interestingly, one block away he had set up a business which sold articles of clothing and ornaments which were used in Yoruba initiation ceremonies. The surprising fact is that he was supported by the same clients at both shops. Of course, the guests at such Yacht Club functions would be the children and grandchildren of domestic servants with the odd exception of a few black independent patricians who might have owned insignificant pieces of land.

Since it was university students, predominantly white, who first showed political non-conformism, and only later secondary school students, of whom there were more Blacks, it was only after the takeover by Castro's revolutionary army that the majority of black people began to take notice of revolutionary discourse. Support for the revolution was easy for most Blacks since they were the only ones who had nothing to lose. Proof of this is the very low number of black-owned properties which were nationalized, both in the city and in rural areas. Not only did they not stand to lose anything but since Blacks had had no formal representation in the previous political oligarchy they were the only ones who did not feel uncomfortable in the new political climate. And they were both surprised and delighted that the populist rhetoric of the revolution seemed to favour their cultural behaviour.

Now, in contradistinction to a few points made earlier concerning the lifestyle and aspirations of middle-class white Cubans, many of the latter also became trapped by a wave of liberal humanism coming out of western European democracies after about 1959. They did not hesitate to divest themselves of the old ways of being and many of them distanced themselves from their families by refusing to accompany them into exile and supporting the revolutionary cause instead. After all, why not? The European intelligentsia had after all got over-excited by the potential of political events in the biggest Caribbean island and offered it moral support. Given that influence and the strong cultural dependence from which Cuba has always suffered, it is entirely logical that liberal intellectuals on the island accepted the fact of the revolution and approached with hope the most brilliant future the nation had ever dreamed of.

What is worthy of note here is that the European intelligentsia half way through the Cold War realized that the perverse politics of the Soviet Union could not be justified. All their dirty schemes had leaked through the Iron Curtain and by 1960 all of Western Europe was wise to exactly what constituted the Communist Paradise of Eastern Europe. That represented absolute frustration for Cubans and, bearing in mind that Algeria gained independence in 1962, it was as though we were caught in a temporary lapse in which there was nothing left to defend.

It was precisely at this moment that a new leader emerged using very big words and espousing a *sui generis* concept of history which was really no more than a tropical version of old concepts. In addition to this the revolutionary youth movements at the end of the 1960s were seeking all kinds of new answers. However they did not dare to think twice regarding the new Caribbean leaders. They had no option but to support the new dawn rising from the region, which was proclaimed by an armed and bearded messiah, who confronted the most powerful nation in the world as it had never been confronted before. The confrontation was thoroughly enjoyed by the European intelligentsia as a question of culture. The barbaric chewing-gum eaters with too much money would not be pardoned. That intelligentsia ingenuously believed the myth which was a product of their own frustrations; a myth that went from Moscow to Peking and from Peking to Havana.

What attitude, then, could we expect from the always-excluded Blacks? What reasons did they have to believe in this revolution? Simple. Given the tremendous oppression they had suffered hitherto, in order to achieve some kind of internal peace they would swallow anything, even a virulent revolutionary slogan.

Regarding Blacks in Cuba, the present authorities have continually mobilized them for their own ends. But they are increasingly approached with some degree of fear since they have had the experience of living in a society ostensibly free from racial discrimination. Attempts are made, as in the time of Fulgencio Batista, to have Blacks work for the regime, forgetting that times have changed and that there is now a strong class of cultured Blacks in Cuba who are extremely well aware of their history. From 'Little Rock' to today many important changes have occurred and these have contributed to black self-recognition.

Before any serious dialogue can be entered into, one question must be answered. What has happened? How is it possible that after

35 years of socialism 90 per cent of the prison population is black? Only a loud and credible answer is acceptable. Blacks are no longer naive. The experiences of history are fresh and painful. It might be worth thinking a little about some of those warm Californian summers when other things inspire greater fear than earthquakes.

10

Transculturation and integration of the Afro-Venezuelan world in the contemporary Venezuelan novel

Jorge Marbán

From the very beginning of the Spanish Conquest of the New World, Spanish America has had the distinctive characteristic of being a land where three diverse cultures, Spanish, indigenous and African, have converged and blended their significantly different traits within a common ground.

Essays on Spanish America initially emphasized the racial factor although there were some early insights into the cultural aspect, such as those of Simón Bolívar.[1] In this century, attention has finally become focused on the relationship between the formative cultures, and certain terms are coined in order to define the resulting ethnic convergence. Acculturation, transculturation, cultural mestization, heterogeneity and cultural superimposition are some of the concepts created to describe the encounter between diverse ethnic groups in Spanish America.[2]

The term 'transculturation' has been frequently used in Spanish American criticism and essays ever since it appeared in 1940 in Fernando Ortiz's published essay *Contrapunteo cubano del tabaco y del azúcar* [Cuban Counterpoint: Tobacco and Sugar]. In this well-known essay, Ortiz underlines the cultural transmutations that occur throughout Cuba's history. He rejects the term 'acculturation' since the process he studies is not limited solely to the acquisition of a culture. It also results in a partial deculturation or loss of the former culture at the same time that other cultural phenomena are created through neo-culturation. For this whole process, Ortiz conceives the term 'transculturation' and states that the history of Cuba is an 'extremely intense, complex and unending transculturation' [*intensísima, complejísima e incesante transculturación*] (1987: 92). He asserts that this concept not only helps us understand Cuba's history, but also that of all America in general.[3] Three decades later, Angel Rama (1982) begins to use this concept in the field of literature.[4]

A propitious area for transcultural research is that of the relationship between Sub-Saharan black African culture and other cultures in America, especially the Spanish and the creole which replace it. One of the most notable aspects in modern ethnology is the preservation of cultural identity by Blacks who settled in America. Frances Bayard emphasizes the survival of many of their customs and beliefs, in spite of the attempt by their white counterparts to strip them of their cultural traditions and human attributes: 'They were sent off in a boat without any ancestral artifacts, then dispersed among cultural groups and families who didn't teach them, and gave them only the most rudimentary religious instruction' (Bayard 1970: 289).

The survival of African culture, nevertheless, does not reach the same level of intensity in all regions of the ex-empires of Spain and Portugal in America. While in the Caribbean Antilles and Brazil it is seen with great vigour and still preserves today many original African religious practices, in Venezuela its presence is much less significant and has less impact throughout the entire country. Juan Pablo Sojo points out some of these differences (1943: 11).

> If we are to believe our historians, the process of racial blending occurred more quickly and was more widespread in Venezuela than in other parts of America. The ritualistic beliefs of both indigenous and black people were dispersed in the recently formed conscience of the mestizo and mulatto.[5]

Although negroid elements are evident in more than half the Venezuelan population, those who promote the idea of 'racial equality' in Venezuela have tended to give less importance to Afro-Venezuelan culture than is given in other Latin American countries.[6] Insistence on the absorbing *mestizo* character of the Venezuelan nation is frequently seen in its intellectuals. Pedro Llaya (1977: 35–6) emphasizes the progressive de-Africanization throughout the history of the country and the lesser impact of the black element in its literature:

> Venezuela is a country of integral, profound and definitive mestization. Our racial mestization is the oldest, most complete and open of all the Americas. In our literature, both narrative and poetry, the influence of 'negroism' is superficial and passing.[7]

Other scholars of this theme have noted the existence of unacknowledged racist attitudes in the minimization of the African component. Winthrop R. Wright observes (1993: 2), for example, that beginning in the last decade of the nineteenth century, the Venezuelan elite tried to promote the whitening of the population through European immigration, cultural assimilation and racial integration.

> Many Venezuelans wanted to dilute the *café* as much as possible with more *leche*. In theory, then, Venezuelans had achieved a society free of racial tensions. At least they thought they had – and claimed as much. But in fact, they accomplished this at the expense of blacks, whom they over-looked as a major class.

Venezuelan narrative, and the novel in particular, offers an interesting area of study of the Afro-Venezuelan theme. The treatment of this topic by various authors illuminates in good part their attitude towards race relations, the value of African culture, transculturation and national integration. The idealization of plantation life (where the majority of Blacks resided until the second half of the nineteenth century) and the diverse consequences of sexual relationships between members of black and white races are common themes in many Venezuelan novels of the nineteenth century, or beginning of the twentieth (Belrose 1988: 175). The study of Blacks within their own social group and an appraisal of Afro-Venezuelan culture did not take place, however, until the 1930s.

Between 1931 and 1950 four novels with a prominent Afro-Venezuelan theme were published in Venezuela. *Las lanzas coloradas* [The Red Lances] (1931) by Arturo Uslar Pietri; *Pobre negro* [Poor Black] (1937) by Rómulo Gallegos; *Nochebuena negra* [Black Saint John's Day] (1943) by Juan Pablo Sojo; and *Cumboto* (1950) by Ramón Díaz Sánchez are novels that deserve special attention because of their literary quality, originality of presentation, or link with authors of notable repute. Although all of them show Blacks in the rural environment of the plantation, each one projects a different approach to the Afro-Venezuelan theme.

Las lanzas coloradas focuses on the years 1813 and 1814 and the war between the Asturian Boves, backed by mestizo plainsmen, against Bolivar's rebellious troops, which were commanded for the most part by white creole officers. Uslar accurately presents this struggle, not as a war for independence between patriots and Spaniards, but as an authentic civil war in which racial hatred functions as a powerful motivator. Presentación Campos, the overseer of the ranch called 'El Altar' [The Altar], is a mulatto who hates equally the Mantuan class of white aristocrats and the black slaves whose subservience and weakness of spirit he scorns. The abyss that seems to separate the races is not as deep as appearances indicate. The legend with which the book begins is in itself a neocultural product which conforms to Fernando Ortiz's concept. The comparisons made by Espíritu Santo, the slave who narrates the tale, reflect the rural influences and syntactic simplicity of the popular language of classic Spanish American works like *Martin Fierro* (Uslar Pietri 1970: 9): 'the sky, black as the bottom of a well' [*el cielo, negro como fondo de pozo*]; 'he marched in the night like a fattened bat' [*marchaba de noche como murciélago cebado*]. Mandinga, an African name for the devil, is one of the main characters in the story. The backdrop of superstitions is a transcultural mix in which are blended supernatural beliefs of Spanish origin with those from Africa. Mandinga's mule is described in the same vein; it reeks of sulphur and exhales fire (Uslar Pietri 1970: 9). Another tale told in Chapter 2 by an old female slave is likewise a clear transcultural product with its distortion of the biblical version of the Slaughter of the Innocents, the African deformation of a royal title ('Miss Carramajestad' for 'Sacra Majestad'), the use of intimate diminutives, and typical African parodic endings (Uslar Pietri 1970: 27–8).

Uslar does not describe in detail the daily life of the slaves. His vision of them is largely negative since what stands out is the cowardly submission of the men, their filthy huts and their general apathy disturbed only by the iron will of the mulatto overseer. Presentación, in fact, burns the ranch, rapes the owner's sister and joins the royal troops that are fighting against Bolívar's followers. He clearly exemplifies the mulatto who is on the fringe and who allied himself with the Spanish foreigners in the early years of the struggle for independence in order to fight against his white compatriots.

In the society portrayed in *Las lanzas coloradas*, the African contingent is not yet fully integrated into Venezuelan life. The novelist does not explore the habitat or the psychology of this important segment of the population. José Marcial Ramos Guédez states that there is no true sociological intent in *Las lanzas* but rather a desire to leave an overly idealistic and dream-like impression (1980: 90). On the other hand, the use of magic realism and surrealistic techniques in this novel exemplifies one of the transcultural processes studied by Angel Rama in which the incorporation of external elements carries with it a new focalization within a traditional cultural structure (Rama 1982: 31).

Pobre negro and the other two novels that follow it (*Nochebuena negra* and *Cumboto*) reveal Afro-Venezuelan culture on the plantation through varied details and within a more traditional novelistic structure. The first two deal with the environs of Barlovento and the last, an area near Puerto Cabello. The festivities, celebrations and customs that are described also demonstrate the final stages of transculturation.

The slave system imposes certain precepts or norms of white culture, like the use of Spanish, adoption of Christianity, celebration of Catholic traditions, fulfilment of assigned tasks, and respect for the social hierarchy. On the other hand, plantation life brings together Africans of different origins who by means of a two-fold process of acculturation and neoculturation tend to create an Afro-American culture that serves as a common denominator for people who were originally heterogeneous. This is a result of the phenomenon of cognitive orientation discussed by Sidney Mintz and Richard Price (Pollak 1994: 12–13). This process establishes a common psychological base which includes distinctive African attitudes towards Nature, the Divine Being, supernatural beliefs, aesthetic pleasures, and so on. Another stage of this process is the mixing of white and Afro-American cultures, which produces syncretic entities of a social and religious nature. One of the most notable Afro-Venezuelan transcultural manifestations is the festival of Saint John or the *Nochebuena* celebrated by Blacks, beginning on the eve of 24 June. The celebration is eminently syncretic: the Spanish contribution represents in itself a transculturation of pagan and Christian elements (Liscano 1973: 11, 25); the Blacks add their dances and songs to the beat of two drums: the Yoruban *mina* and the Mandingo *curbata* (Sojo 1943: 243). The exalted sensuality of the celebration that is highlighted in the last three novels studied can be explained by its seasonal association with the worship of the ancient African gods of fertility and rain (Pollak 1994: 33). This detail clarifies why water acquires greater importance than fire on this side of the Atlantic. Liscano establishes a relevant agricultural connection for this festival: the cultivation cycle for the cacao plantations generally ends around this time of the year (Liscano 1973: 65).

The festival of Saint John is an important hub of the action in each one of these novels. In *Pobre negro* the rape of Ana Julia Alcorta by the slave Negro Malo (which results in the birth of Pedro Miguel, the main character of the novel) takes place to the beat of festival drums in an atmosphere of magic realism (Gallegos 1962: 360–1). In *Nochebuena negra* the decisive events of the dramatic ending occur during the night of Saint John (Sojo 1972: 303–8). The dance performed by the black girl Pascua casts a sensual spell on Federico, the white owner of Cumboto ranch. The sexual relations that expectedly follow have the most significant impact in determining the final outcome of Diaz Sánchez's novel.

Another transcultural entity is found in the animal stories (like Uncle Rabbit and Uncle Tiger) of African origin (Pollak 1984: 268) which are modified by contact with Spanish American culture. In *Pobre negro*, during 'the catechism of the corn cobs' [*el catecismo de las mazorcas*' (a type of *cayapa* which mixes work and pleasures), Father Mediavilla tells his black parishioners stories about the weak rabbit who outwits the more powerful feline (Gallegos 1962: 402–4).[8] In *Nochebuena negra*, Lino Bembetoyo relates the story which describes Uncle Rabbit's herculean tasks, performed at God's request, in order for him to grow bigger (Sojo 1972: 52–4). In *Cumboto*, Venancio describes Uncle Rabbit's and Uncle Tiger's 'endless feats' [*hazañas interminables*] (Díaz Sánchez 1973: 76).[9]

Another transcultural manifestation is the *fulía*: a song originating in the Canary Islands. It is improvised at work but is also sung as an expression of love, at poetry competitions and at wakes (Sojo 1986: 8). In *Pobre negro, fulías* are entoned during the May Cross celebrations (Gallegos 1962: 452). In *Nochebuena negra*, Coínta, a black woman, sings after returning from working in the field, or when alone to express pangs of unrequited love (Sojo 1972: 81–2; 186–9).

The *mampulorio* or wake of the little angels is another transcultural element created by black Venezuelans. Sojo explains that the word is of African origin: *mpangu* is a Congolese word that describes a taboo applicable to children (Sojo 1986: 87). Angelina Pollak points out the probable Murcian origin of a custom that has been modified within the Afro-Venezuelan environment with dances, songs and games of chance (1984: 25). During the wake of a child in *Pobre negro* we see the traditional practice of fixing small sticks to the eyelids of the child so that the eyes remain open (Gallegos 1962: 535). In *Nochebuena negra*, the wake takes on an added folkloric dimension since it includes the game of chance that sometimes accompanies it (Sojo 1972: 231–5).

The Afro-American custom of sorcery is also present in all three novels. In *Pobre negro* a warlock performs a *composición* [spell] in order to make Pedro Manuel fall in love with a certain woman; another sorcerer prepares a *daño* [magic bundle] to the detriment of another person (Gallegos 1962: 495–9). Both attempts turn out to be in vain. It is interesting to note that in the novels that penetrate more fully the Afro-Venezuelan world, the results are different. In *Nochebuena negra* there are numerous acts of witchcraft. The spell that Lino casts on Deogracia to make her fall in love with Emeterio gives her a fever but does not have the desired effect (Sojo 1972: 45–9). On the other hand, other *daños* seem to be more successful. After the *mal de ojo* [evil eye] caused by Lino's first wife, the baby born by his second wife dies. Morocota goes crazy after Coínta's aunt casts a spell to avenge his rape of her niece (Sojo 1972: 230, 288–91). In *Cumboto* a group of black men use a snake in the witchcraft ceremony they organize to avenge the death of Cruz María at the hands of Federico's father. Days later Don Guillermo mysteriously shows up dead, an apparent victim of a rattlesnake bite (Díaz Sánchez 1973: 95–9).

Several other Afro-Venezuelan celebrations are introduced in these novels: the custom of the little demons' dance during Corpus Christi in *Pobre negro* (Gallegos 1962: 528–34), as well as the *tololé*, a ritual song, and the wake of Saint Pascual Bailón in *Nochebuena negra* (Sojo 1972: 119–20; 183).

A backdrop of superstition is common in these works. In *Pobre negro* we see the general acceptance of the effectiveness of *bojotes* [magic objects] and other acts of sorcery. The African origin of some beliefs is seen clearly in episodes like the one in which Negro Malo nervously clutches his magic charm (his umbilical cord) because he fears a supernatural apparition. The African ethnologist John S. Mbiti points out the protective value of this type of charm within an African tribe (Mbiti 1970: 146–147). The belief in Brother Penitente's apparition and in the fatal sign from the *yacagua* [bird] in *Nochebuena negra* (Sojo 1972: 102–3, 228) forms a part of the shared Afro-Spanish background of superstitions that Sojo has indicated in one of his essays (Sojo 1943: 39). In *Cumboto* there are several stories about ghosts, almost all of which belong to oral traditions of the Venezuelan countryside (Piquet 1982: 52; Díaz Sánchez 1973: 48).

The treatment of the Afro-Venezuelan world in these four novels reflects the different purpose of each author. In all of them there is evidently an interest in the transcultural elements of that particular group of people. However, the approach to the theme offers singular contrasts. In *Las lanzas coloradas* Uslar Pietri focuses attention on both the white aristocrat Fonta and the mulatto Presentación Campos as representatives of two opposing classes in a bloody civil war. Uslar does not pause to describe the rhythm of daily life at 'The Altar', nor does he stop to explore slave psychology on the plantation.

Pobre negro reveals a sympathetic approach to Afro-Venezuelan culture and the misfortunes of the black race. The action takes place in the nineteenth century, mainly in the years immediately following the liberation of the slaves (1854), and it concludes with the violent civil war (1859–63) that serves as a catalyst (just like the war for independence) for violent racial hatred. In spite of the relative abundance of Afro-Venezuelan transcultural elements in the work, the author's penetration of that world is nothing more than superficial. The first chapter justifies this assertion. Gallegos describes a Saint

John's Day celebration with stereotypical elements that have nothing to do with the action.

The main focus of the work is on Luisiana's white aristocratic family and the mulatto Pedro Miguel, a product of the sexual liaison between Negro Malo and Luisiana's aunt. The amorous union which occurs at the end between Pedro Miguel and Luisiana, not without its ups and downs, is a symbol of Gallegos' desire to integrate the civilized white element with the uncultured or barbaric *mestizo* for the sake of progress and national unity. 'The white man represents culture and noble deeds; however, the man of colour possesses an inheritance of 'ignorance' and barbaric behavior. ... Only education can save him ... Moreover the white aspects are superimposed on the mulatto ones' (Ramos Guédez 1980: 90–1).[10] One revealing observation is Pedro Miguel's withdrawal from Afro-Venezuelan culture, many of whose customs cause him to feel a strong revulsion. In spite of Gallegos' good intentions, many Afro-Venezuelanists probably agree with the following statements by Raül Agudo Freites (1978: 25): 'Gallegos' black man is a spurious creature, without character in spite of his symbolic contexture, moved by ordinary feelings that lead him in circles to resolve his life where his very misfortunes began'.[11]

The historic frame in *Cumboto* is the last third of the nineteenth century and the first of the twentieth, but the vision of the past is extended to the period of the war of independence by way of confidences and letters. Just as in the previous novel by Gallegos, this work contains a symbolic transcultural goal: the spiritual union of the black world with the white. But the Afro-Venezuelan world is not viewed from the outside as in *Pobre negro*, but through intense interiorization: 'Cumboto aspires to create life just the way black people live it, in other words, the vision of black life comes from within' (Piquet 1982: 43).[12]

Contrary to Gallegos' simple Eurocentric perspective, Díaz Sánchez presents a different vision of the integration of Blacks and Whites. For a traditional landowner like Don Guillermo, Blacks don't deserve to be classified as human beings. For some Whites, like Frau Berza, Federico's governess, they are no more than a passing fancy for satisfying erotic needs. Among the Blacks there are also various viewpoints. For Eduvige, the ranch-house servant, and for Anita, Pascua's grandmother, their destiny is to obey and always remain loyal to their white employers. This slave mentality is one that endures even after the abolition of slavery. For Cervelión, an old farmhand, the life of a black man is a difficult struggle to survive. He cannot expect help from a white man and he says just that to Natividad, the narrator of the novel (Díaz Sánchez 1973: 21): 'We black gotta know thousan trick ta defen us. … You right in with white but you black thru and thru, and dey ain't gonna teach you nuttin dey know; so you gotta bite the bullet if you wanna live like a man.'[13]

For Venancio there is no greater pleasure than remembering the 'matting' days of the civil war when mobs of drunken Blacks raped white women on floors lined with palm mats. The mulatto Fernando Arguíndegui is a clear example of the resentment towards what he describes as a racist society (Díaz Sánchez 1973: 156):

> Your boss … just knows that I'm mulatto, that I descend
> from his family's slaves. When he looked at me, he must
> have asked himself: 'Why is he on the loose around here?'
> He is ignorant of the fact that I have a university degree, that
> I speak several languages and that I have published a book
> on tropical diseases.[14]

The symbolic intent of integration in the work of Díaz Sánchez differs from that of Gallegos: the latter's is political while the former's is aesthetic. Towards the end of *Cumboto* a mysterious young man arrives in Cumboto, many years after Pascua's disappearance. He is Pascua's and Federico's son, and he appears destined to occupy his place as rightful heir to the family patrimony. Like his father, the young man has artistic inclinations and he has been immersed in the world of high culture denied to his mother. The spiritual union of the two worlds of his parents comes to fruition in this young man, capable of playing with the same ability and precision a piece of classical music or one of Afro-Venezuelan beat.[15]

In spite of its superior artistic quality, *Cumboto* has received strong criticism from the well-known Afro-Americanist Maurice Belrose. The critic (1988: 150–1) describes Natividad as 'a black man with black skin wearing a white mask' [*negro de piel negra y máscara blanca*] and he criticizes Díaz Sánchez for having painted a fanciful picture of rural, feudal Venezuela during the second half of the nineteenth century. The second half of this criticism is exaggerated because the picture that Díaz Sánchez unfolds is far from idyllic. As for Natividad, Belrose does not recognize the narrator's psychological development which moves from his initial rejection of Afro-Venezuelan culture to his immersion into its world of beliefs and values.

Nevertheless, in *Cumboto* it is still possible to see the Eurocentric prism of the novels that precede it. *Nochebuena negra*, the last of the novels we have examined, offers the most authentic and complete inner vision of that world. Sojo gives his black characters a sense of dignity and self-worth that are not conditioned by dependency on the white world. Unlike the other novels mentioned, he also places strong emphasis on denunciation.

In this novel one sees all the white man's tricks to deceive or take advantage of the black peasant. White landowners and some officials conspire to exploit some poor soul and turn him into a real serf. They kill Lino's father when he refuses to sell his land adjacent to an Italian landowner's estate. Property titles are falsified and border forces are cut down in order to expel small farmers from their lands. The Blacks who used to be prosperous and able owners of rural ranches have now fallen to the bottom of the economic scale. Don Gisberto, the uncle of the white heroine of the novel (Consuelo), does not hesitate to marry the niece of a black landowner (Crisanto Marasma) in order to better his financial situation. He hides from Marasma the existence of a treasure and eventually becomes the most powerful landowner in the region. Marasma stays on as overseer for his sister's former farm-hand (Sojo 1972: 57, 66, 68–70, 78).

The compulsory recruitment of farm-hands for Juan Vicente Gómez's ranches is also seen in the novel. Sojo uses beautiful images to describe the natural setting that surrounds the part of Barlovento that is the scene of the action. However, far from idealizing the black peon's life, he reveals it in all its severity. The ending of *Nochebuena negra* is in sharp contrast with that of *Cumboto*. Díaz Sánchez provides a symbolic outcome in which two races are united in an artistic union that preserves the best attributes of the two groups. In contrast, Sojo's novel ends pessimistically. The niece of the white landowner and the son of the black overseer never get together. The unlucky day labourer working on one of Gómez's ranches escapes from his servitude only to die from tuberculosis. Ten years after the events described in the novel, the black peons continue 'hunchbacked under their sacks, slaving away from dawn to dusk … cheering themselves up with liquor and drums' (Sojo 1972: 311).[16] These different conclusions make sense when one takes into account that Díaz Sánchez is a light mulatto and defender of the idea of 'racial democracy' while Sojo is a black man who has lived in the region he describes and who has witnessed the hard life experienced by his fellow blacks.

The novels that we have studied constitute an important milestone in the development of Venezuelan literature. They describe the Afro-Venezuelan world from colonial times up to the authoritarian and spoliatory regime of Juan Vicente Gómez. They reveal in great detail the varied transcultural realities that have been created by way of contact between the dominating Eurocentric culture and the subjugated black one. The separation and racial hatred in the first novel we examined is a realistic reflection of a convulsive moment in Venezuelan history. The hope for racial integration in the next two novels we analysed demonstrates appreciation for African folkloric elements. Nonetheless, they avoid mentioning the unfavourable economic conditions in the areas where a majority of coloured people live. The last of these novels, written by a black man, is an authentic picture of the daily life of a rural Afro-Venezuelan, and the only novel that contains a vibrant element of protest.

Distinct sociological and political conditions in Venezuela have prevented the development of the type of *negrista* or militant novel that has been written in countries like Ecuador, Colombia, Cuba, Panama and Costa Rica. *Las lanzas coloradas, Pobre negro*, *Cumboto*, and *Nochebuena negra* serve nonetheless as a spearhead to the introduction of Afro-Venezuelan culture in contemporary narrative. The process of dignifying black culture to which these works contributed, through their prestigious authors and successful publication, provided the impetus for flourishing Afro-Venezuelan themes in the short story of the 1950s and 1960s. Concentration on these subjects also led to more favourable consideration of the African contribution to transculturation in Venezuela. This improved appraisal can be observed in recent comments by a white writer like Arturo Uslar Pietri whose positive approach to African culture has intensified progressively since the publication of his stories of Afro-Venezuelan themes: (Uslar Pietri: 1994, 174, 198) 'The multiple contributions of blacks are evident in the language, proverbs and sense of family and folk-lore. ... We still do not recognize fully enough the presence and contribution of ... the black race...'[17]

In one of his last essays Ramón Díaz Sánchez reacts in a similar fashion by expressing his admiration for the decisive influence of the Afro-Venezuelan in the cultural evolution of the country: 'Everything done in the years following that event (independence) – art, literature, politics and life relationships – will necessarily bear that mark, and everything will vibrate, in somewhat moderating fashion, with an African rhythm' (Díaz Sánchez 1963: 51).[18]

The process of transculturation does not have to mean, as Josaphat Kubayanda fears, a final de-Africanization in Spanish America (1984: 226). The words of Maurice Belrose (1988: 179–80) ought to serve as an epilogue to this study, and as a fair statement of the true meaning that transculturation and integration should convey in Venezuela: 'Africa will continue to be a part of Venezuela's soul unless Venezuela ceases to be what it is, loses its identity, [and] becomes ... the shadow of another nation'.[19]

Notes

1 'We are a world of our own' [*Somos un pequeño género humano*] (Bolivar 1969: 19). It is interesting to note, nonetheless, that Bolívar omits the African factor.

2 Melville Herskovitz is one of the first proponents of the term acculturation. Arturo Uslar Pietri popularizes the concept of cultural mestization (1951: 19). Antonio Cornejo Polar coins the term heterogeneity, a phenomenon based on a twofold sociocultural statute (1982: 67–8). Leopoldo Zea speaks of the superimposition of cultures (1972: 65).

3 Ibid. According to Josaphat Kubayanda and Joseph Schraibman the concept is already seen in 1909 in Ortiz's literary work (Kubayanda 1984: 227 and 238, note 4. On the other hand, if we pay attention to Bronislaw Malinowski's prologue to Ortiz's essay, we have to conclude that the Cuban writer had already created the neologism eleven years before making it public (Ortiz 1987: 3).

4 Rama refers to the article where he uses the term in a note that appears on page 8 of his book *Transculturación narrativa en América Latina* [Narrative Transculturation in Latin America]. While Fernando Ortiz's initial idea has a sociological base, Rama applies it to the field of literature. In this study we will preferentially refer to Ortiz's application.

5 *Si debemos creer a nuestros historiadores, el proceso de fusión racial resultó más rápido y global en Venezuela que en otras partes de la América. Las creencias rituales tanto de los indios como de los negros se dispersaron en la conciencia recién formada de los mestizos y los mulatos.*

   In another book of essays, Sojo incorporates similar considerations: 'Neither Olorún, nor Obatalá nor Yemanyá have any idolatrous meaning in Venezuela [*Ni Olorún, ni Obatalá o Yemanyá significan (en Venezuela) cosa o representación idolátrica*] (Sojo 1986: 29, 31).

6 Frances Bayard says that in the 1960s the black and mulatto population constituted 47 per cent of the total population. Another 32 per cent was integrated largely with mestizos (1970: 329). Angelina Pollak thinks that at least 50 per cent of Venezelans can be considered as Blacks, according to the norms in the United States (1994, 9). It is likely that a considerable number of *mestizos* have some African blood. Racial identification, generally unreliable in the majority of Latin American countries, is not part of the national census.

7 *Venezuela es un país de mestizaje integral, profundo y definitivo. Nuestro mestizaje racial es el más completo, abierto y antiguo de todos los países americanos. En la literatura venezolana, narrativa y poesía, la influencia del 'negrismo' se manifiesta superficial y pasajera.*

8 See the description of a *cayapa* in Pollak (1984: 275).

9 In the novels of Gallegos and Sojo one can observe the local adaptation of these stories (which spread throughout almost all of America). In *Pobre negro*, Mediavilla's stories are based on local social habits: Uncle Rabbit is a humble peasant; Uncle Tiger is a powerful white aristocrat. In *Nochebuena negra*, Lino's story ends with a racist comment against Indians. God decides not to grant Uncle Rabbit's wish because doing so would leave the other animals defenceless. Lino maliciously adds: 'For that reason you shouldn't trust a rabbit or an Indian' [*Por eso no hay que fiarse ni de conejo, ni de indio*] (Sojo 1972: 54).

10 *El hombre blanco representa las tendencias culturales y los hechos nobles; en cambio, el hombre de color posee una herencia de 'incultura' y de comportamientos bárbaros ... Sólo la educación salva ... además lo blanco se sobrepone a lo mulato.*

11   *El negro de Gallegos es un producto espúreo y sin carácter, pese a su contextura simbólica, movido por sentimientos comunes que lo llevan circularmente a resolver su vida en el origen de su mismo infortunio.*

12   Cumboto *aspira a recrear el mundo tal como lo viven los negros, es decir, la visión del mundo negro es desde adentro.*

13   *Lo negro tenemo que conocé mi maña pa defendeno ... Tú estáj metío entre lo blanco pero ere negro por lo cuatro costao y ello no van a enseñate nada de lo que saben; así é que tienej que comé avipa si quierej viví como un hombre.*

14   *Su patrón ... sólo sabe de mí que soy un mulato, que desciendo de esclavos de su familia. Al verme debió preguntarse:"? Cómo es que éste anda suelto por ahi?" El ignora que poseo un grado universitario, que hablo varios idiomas y que he publicado un libro sobre enfermedades tropicales'.*

15   The ideological base maintained at the end of the novel is formulated in the words of an essay published by the author subsequent to this work: 'The human race is marching towards a great coming together through which, one day, it will achieve a homogenization of values which will favour man's soul, not his material needs' [*la especie humana marcha hacia una gran síntesis mediante la cual, algún día, se alcanzará una homogeneización de valores en beneficio del espíritu, no de la necesidad material*] (Díaz Sánchez 1963: 40).

16   *Gibados bajo los sacos, bregando de sol a sol ... alegrando sus vidas oscuras con aguardiente y tambor.*

17   *La contribucion múltiple del negro es inocultable en el lenguaje, en los proverbios y en el sentido de la familia y en el folklore ... Todavía nos falta mucho para reconocer plenamente la presencia y la contribución del ... negro.*

18   *Todo lo que se haga en los años que siguen a ese acontecimiento (la independencia) – arte, literatura, política y vida de relación – estará necesariamente marcado por ese sello y en todo se oirá vibrar, más o menos atemperante, el acento africano.*

In 1934 Díaz Sánchez wrote an essay entitled *Cam* in which Belrose finds some markedly racist remarks like those relating to moral defects of Blacks and their 'indubitable' ugliness (Belrose 1988: 147–9). In 1937 Arturo Uslar Pietri published a series of articles in *El Universal* (Caracas) in which Wright notices a negative view of the black Venezuelan (Wright 1993: 101–2). Wright sees a marked change of attitude in Uslar in the following decade. He attributes that to the weakening influence of positivism and to the diffusion of more favourable and understanding ideas on racial crossbreeding in anthropological and sociological schools of thought led by the Brazilian Gilberto Freyre (Wright 1993: 123). This observation could likewise be applied to Díaz Sánchez.

19   *Africa seguirá presente en el corazón de Venezuela a menos que Venezuela deje de ser lo que es, pierda su identidad, (y) se convierta ... en la sombra de otra nación.*

11

Dominican writers at the crossroads: reflections on a conversation in process

Daisy Cocco de Filippis

Oh, unhappy Antilles, beloved of my soul
wherever my eyes turn now
eager to celebrate you
they are betrayed by debilitating remnants,
past glories of your artistic genius.[1]
        Salomé Ureña de Henríquez, 'Ruins' (1989, 7: 108)

Yesterday I was born a Spaniard
in the afternoon I was born French
by night-time Ethiopian I became
today they say I am an Englishman
Oh! What on earth will become of me?
        Anonymous, in Emilio Rodríguez Demorizi (1978: 17)

The following night I could not sleep. Fighting insomnia, I prepared to write and almost vomited these pages. It was a question of writing a novel whose subject matter would be purely creole.
        Marcio Veloz Maggiolo (1984: 25)

Before there were palm trees,
the sea, the architecture
the girl would question her teacher
once again, betraying a need for further explanation
and a strange howling was heard in the wind.
        Sherezada (Chiqui) Vicioso (1985)

All that remains is singing
and embracing this island, my anchor.
        Miriam Ventura (1987)

Introduction

It is a time-honoured tradition in Dominican letters to begin presentations of consequence with a number of quotations, usually written by learned individuals outside the island, words of wisdom to signal from the outset that the writer is of serious and scholarly purpose, and worthy of respect as regards his or her knowledge of universal letters. I begin my discussion by introducing these words born and bred in a half-island in the middle of the Caribbean sea. I need to quote these words, seldom heard outside the island, for ours is a story that has remained untold. And although we manage to have access to outside sources, albeit in arrhythmic fashion as some of my colleagues are fond of saying, the outside world seldom seems to take notice of our existence as people and as writers. Writing this essay has provided me an opportunity to reflect on who, what, and where we Dominicans are as writers, as we come to the closing of this century.

These pages are part of a project of study, larger in scope, whose possibilities and complexities I have not yet fully explored. Therefore, rather than assertions, I will share *inquietudes*, concerns based on the following considerations:

- In its struggle to find its own identity, beginning with modernism (*la vanguardia*), Dominican writers have oscillated between creating a national literature based on Dominican social and cultural reality known in its first twentieth-century manifestation as *postumismo*, and a universality began with *vedrinismo*, which has produced the replication and insertion of the latest movements from Europe, usually in very esoteric forms and in short-lived literary movements. As a result, positions have been taken that have polarized and impoverished what could have been a more plural and vital literary production. In other words, in looking for Dominicanness, often the universality presented in the Caribbean particularity and specificity has been lost from these texts. The opposite may be said in terms of those whose search for universality has diverted their literary production from the particularity of the Caribbean experience and its readers.
- Although self-publications abound, many writers find themselves at a loss in terms of the validation that can be provided by editors or by the existence of implicit readers for their texts.
- The war of 1965 and the second North American invasion created a generation of writers in the Dominican Republic who are still coping today with the struggle to move beyond the themes generated at the time. The North American invasion of the

Dominican Republic, American support of Balaguer, and its consequence, an economic policy of abandonment of the country's agriculture, massive exodus to the cities, and an urban population explosion, have resulted in an unprecedented index of unemployment and emigration; and the birth of a virtual second Dominican 'nation' in New York city.

- The experience of the diaspora in the United States has brought about the opening of a dialogue on what constitutes Dominicanness; its resulting awareness of the absence of women and persons of colour in many of its publications has brought about the beginning of a rewriting of literary history and of a process, still quite protracted, of reconciliation with these elements.

- The questions to be considered are whether the Dominican diaspora will have a lasting impact on the direction Dominican letters will take in the twenty-first century, and how we will deal with the concept of what a national identity is for Dominicans living in a half-island in the Caribbean, and for the generations to come in the island of Manhattan. That is to say, how temporary or lasting an impact will the diaspora have, and will its impact last long enough to bring about much-needed transformation?

In search of its own voice: Reflections on the twentieth century

By 1900, bankrupt and having buried one of its most brutal dictators, General Ulises Heureux, 'Lilís', the Dominican Republic saw the dawn of a new century; a century destined to bring more devastation, fiscal and natural, to witness two North American invasions, and to experience a brutal dictatorship of 30 years whose atrocities can be exemplified in the murder of 16 000 Haitian workers in 1938 and the assassination of the Mirabal sisters, Minerva, Patria and María Teresa, also known as 'Las Mariposas' [the Butterflies], in 1959. These horrific acts are engraved in the memory of Dominicans and serve as symbols of the brutality endured by both men and women under Trujillo's regime. Today, though he has recently stepped down as president, is in his nineties and suffers from a physical blindness which has yet to produce inner light, Trujillo's trusted man is still the most influential man in the Dominican Republic. For Dominican writers, every election day brings another painful reminder of the nation's legendary recycling of old names, in an ever-spinning, closed circle, devoid perhaps of hope for real change in the future.

Despite its political stagnation, economic hardships and *de facto* official censorship, as indicated by the reversal of the Premio Nacional [National Book Award], first awarded (in 1993) to Viriato Sención and withdrawn when the book's criticism of Balaguer's regime became a topic of discussion, writers have continued to struggle and to fund their own publications and the Dominican Republic has seen an unprecedented number of self-publications in the past three decades. To quote a few statistics from Frank Moya Pons' latest bibliographical database of Dominican literature, let us consider the number of publications of the last 30 years of this century with those of the entire nineteenth century: 723 collections of poetry compared to only 26; 148 novels compared to seven; 51 book-length essays compared to one; 221 theatre pieces compared to six (Céspedes 1994: 21). Such numbers betray, if nothing else, a need to create and to communicate that transcends practical and other considerations.

In his keynote address to the 1993 Congreso Crítico de Literatura Dominicana [Congress of Dominican Literary Criticism], Marcio Veloz Maggiolo defined Dominican culture as lacking in introspection; concerned with the world outside its walls, but shy when it comes to the analysis of the internal process which characterizes it. Veloz Maggiolo established a distinction between this particular moment in the literary dialogue from past experiences where individual and particular visions were shared. The 1993 Congreso Crítico, Veloz Maggiolo explained, was designed to initiate a cycle of conferences to explore what the past 100 years of literary labour has produced in terms of a vision to be distilled, and the relationship between the writers and their readers. For whom, for what, how and why Dominicans have produced art (Céspedes 1994: 11).

Although a number of Dominican answers were presented at the time, none has the poignancy of Andrés L. Mateo's 'Los escritores dominicanos o cómo nadar entre tiburones' [Dominican Writers or How to Swim among the Sharks]. In this essay, Mateo answers Veloz Maggiolo's questions with one of the most pessimistic assessments to date of the condition of the writer in contemporary Dominican society. For Mateo, Dominican writers have been wearing a mask that allows them to deny society.

Writers are not real, Mateo points out, when the sociological existence of a literature derived from three factors, the author, the editor and the reading public, is denied. The current situation is one of few publishing houses, little state support for the arts, and what he terms the 'structural censure' of a writer's work presented by a country whose statistics show 27 per cent absolute illiteracy, added to 45 per cent functional illiteracy, where more than two-thirds of the population are non-readers. Under those circumstances, Mateo concludes, the writer is an unnecessary oddity, a being thrown out of the ideal republic as the degraded *shaman* of the tribe or a wounded being, bleeding and surrounded by sharks, swimming towards a wished-for but very distant shore (Céspedes 1994: 267–73).

Mateo's considerations, however, when coupled with the figures presented by Moya Pons earlier at the same conference, raise a number of questions. If indeed there are no readers for whom to write, if there is no real function for a contemporary Dominican writer, why have so many publications circulated in the past 30 years? For whom are writers like Andrés L. Mateo writing? And why?

The proceedings of the 1993 conference underline the fundamental isolation of these writers, who are as limited by the absence of the necessary dialogue between a writer and his/her editor, as by the separation of experiences prevalent in Dominican literary movements. In a presentation at the 1995 4th Caribbean Women Writers Conference held at Wellesley College, Cuban poet Nancy Morejón (1995) offered a much more complete interpretation of what can be defined as a Caribbean aesthetic:

> Myth, of course, is essential to the poetic aesthetic of the Caribbean. There is no culture that has been able to prosper without a rich mythological subsoil. It entails a reinvention of image and metaphor, organically nurtured by the nature of the region, and the arsenal of wisdom of popular culture. Caribbean poetry is a force that comes out from books and breathes in our plains, our jungles, our mountains, in [a] unique fashion.
>
> But I'd like to talk about myth in [the] plural. The vast scope of ... myths derive from many places. From Europe, that is Spain, France, Portugal, Great Britain and Holland. From Africa and Asia. And from the remains of indigenous cultures wiped out by one of the most [poignant] genocides in history. They are buttressed by the incredible telluric force of our nature and the constant collision of culture and myth that are born of Galicians, Bretons, Celts, Germans, Gauls, Iberians, Yorubas, Congos, Araras, Chinese, and Hindus.

During the 1993 conference in the Dominican Republic, Silvio Torres-Saillant, the founding director of the City University of New York's Dominican Studies Institute, expressed a vision of a future of Dominican letters in terms similar to Morejón's, as he also urged his fellow Dominican writers and critics to consider the importance of what is found on Dominican soil and the fluidity and plurality of our own identity (Céspedes 1994: 61–74).

The 1993 Congreso Crítico had its follow-up in 1994, when the CUNY Dominican Studies Institute sponsored two conferences designed to establish a dialogue between Dominican writers and intellectuals residing in the Dominican Republic and New York. The names given to these conferences: 'Dominican Literature at The Turn of the Century: A Dialogue between a Diaspora and its Nation' (30 June), and 'Dominican Writers in the Context of the Americas: A Dialogue of Literature and Cultural Identity' (4 November) signalled the realization that Dominican letters had arrived at a historical juncture where old terms such as identity, legitimate discourse, history of a people, culture, needed to be discussed and re-written.

On one level, the scheduling of these conferences underlined the fact that the Dominican community had established itself, and was ready to participate in the Latino and Caribbean world of letters in the United States, and to share with other non-Latino, Caribbean and non-Caribbean groups the wealth of its own traditions and cultural heritage. There was a feeling of great pride at having a Dominican institution and organization capable of obtaining grants to support the planning and scheduling of intellectual events of such a high academic and intellectual calibre. This was the official text.

The subtext, however, could have been read as an invitation to established figures in Dominican intellectual and literary circles to come to terms with the fact that no longer were they the only agents privileged to legitimize the discourse on Dominican identity, its history and literary tradition. Because the diaspora had left behind its old differentiations by families, class, race and gender, the time had come to reconsider established interpretations, and to begin the introspective process of self-analysis, dialogue and reappraisal of texts with the aim of including voices that had been traditionally left out.

The June 1994 conference, in particular, will prove to be a useful tool to illustrate some of the concerns facing the Dominican literary community as it scrambles to deal with change, and as it also prepares to meet the new millennium. Early in the programme, it became apparent that precisely because of its thematic emphasis on establishing a dialogue between a diaspora and its land, the conference of June 1994 had to begin by sorting out, albeit not as neatly as one would have thought at first, the representatives of the *diaspora* from those who would be considered the spokespersons for *la madre patria* [literally, the mother fatherland].

The difficulty of making easy assumptions crystallized in the presence of Sherezada (Chiqui) Vicioso, a Dominican-born writer, currently residing in the Dominican Republic after having lived in the United States for 18 years. Her presentation, in fact, owed as much to her Dominican childhood as to her North American experience. It focused on the issue of a young woman's apprenticeship in the world of Dominican womanness. Issues of double standards, sexism and racism were explored from the point of view of a narrator who is at times a young girl, at others a reflective adult, who has dealt with learning the difficult lesson of her world:

> I discovered the geographical limits of my world when I was still quite young. One, two, three, four, five, vertical streets until you reached the main road, la Calle del Sol, with its shop windows, sunny and inaccessible … .

> I discovered also the limits of my grandmother's home which stretched like a worm, long and lanky, eating up slowly all that was green. Each one of us, like the bees, had her own cubicle.
>
> Vicioso (1994)

The narrative continues to trace the gradual realization that there were, in fact, two worlds: 'The entire universe appeared to be masculine then. Boys could go fishing. Boys could stay playing in the street until eleven (we, girls, only until nine). Boys could go out alone … '

These two worlds take additional significance when racial differences are at play:

> I always do things wrong. You should have looked like Juan and Antonia should have looked like Luis …
> But, Mama!
> But, nothing! Imagine yourself a white woman with Juan's green eyes. And Antonia with Luis's blue eyes and blond curls? Wouldn't that have been something! But, Mama!
> To have you turn out like your father. It isn't as if I didn't love him but the boys should have looked like him and Antonia and you like me.

The issue of racial identity is put to rest only when the young emigrant meets the gatekeeper in her new land:

> Your passport …
> Aquí está.
> What is this business of 'india clara'?
> ¿Dígame?
> No buts …

> That is my colour. In Santo Domingo we are classified by
> skin colour. I am 'india clara', that means 'light Indian' …
> Indian is not a colour …
> Pero,
> No buts … Look I don't have time for this kind of hassle …

That day the women participants presented much of what is of concern to a community of Dominican intellectuals who are studying issues of inclusion; who are exploring the means of recreating a history that would present women's lives from the point of view of women, and would begin to address the complex issues of racial identity and to consider a literary discourse legitimized much more by its Dominicanness than by its ability to replicate western discourse. It suffices now to record echoes of women's voices heard that day, such as Marianela Medrano's poem 'El ombligo negro de un bongó' [The Black Bellybutton of a Bongo] (1994: 210):

> In the time set for war, grandmother,
> your stories slid down my skin
> 'black not golden like wheat', grandmother,
> woman, not doll, grandmother.
> My hand moving closer to your bones
> > shakes a sprig of rue
> 'don't be afraid, *abuela*,
> Legba treats you kindly'.

For Dominican writers in the United States the admission of a shared African heritage, as well as their having come to a realization of their position as marginalized members of North American society, brought them to another level of consciousness to be shared with other Dominicans who in the past had accepted anti-Haitian sentiment on the island. As a result of their own experience of exclusion, members of the Dominican diaspora finally understood how it felt to be homeless and black.

The conference of June 1994, however, signalled the conflicts to be faced in tracing the future path or paths in the study Dominican letters. For the members of the audience the disparity between world-views and perspectives presented created at times the impression of having two simultaneously-spoken, mutually exclusive, monologues. On the one hand, there was a progressive call to re-examine roles and rewrite a more inclusive and self-defining history. On the other, the adherence to old paradigms and models signalled the fact that there was much to call attention to a lingering 'malaise' among writers in the Dominican Republic which culminates in what the critic Manuel Mora

Serrano has diagnosed as a case of '*narizparadismo*' [(loosely) a chronically turned-up nose].

Mora Serrano's presentation delineated what he termed 'clues' for understanding Dominican literary history. He cited as its predominant characteristics the following qualities:

1 *La piedad extrema*: an extreme case of pity … as evidenced by the number of authors not worthy of recognition who populate Dominican letters, he explained.
2 *La extraña diáspora*: the strange diaspora … as evidenced by a long history of intellectuals who have chosen to live outside the country, only to live with a chronic case of homesickness.
3 *La fidelidad criollista*: a faithful relationship with the Criollista movement … as evidenced in some of the better known Dominican poetry of the *postumismo* and [the great Dominican poet and novelist] Manuel de Cabral.
4 *Las ínfulas intelectuales*: intellectual affectation of individuals who have undermined Dominicanness with their scorn of popular customs and their rejection of traditions. These intellectual posers, in Mora Serrano's words, have produced and supported quite a number of 'inauthentic' texts by applauding and overlooking any copy or plagiarism, provided that the writer had kept up with the literary movement in style at the moment.
5 *La pasión experimentalista*: a passion for the type of experimentation that would lead writers to an original literary masterpiece. Has taken up much space in Dominican literary texts.

Ironically, Mora Serrano's comments, as critical of current and of past practices as he intended them to be, do not include a reflection on issues of gender or exclusion of other voices and concerns. In fact, as the day progressed, members of the audience finally pointed out to a number of the male presenters that women were also authors and artists. Mora Serrano's comments, nevertheless, serve to illustrate many characteristics of the prevailing position of a group of writers who presentations illustrated quite candidly much of what has ailed Dominican authors in the recent past.

Infused with an urge to overcome a number of the already familiar obstacles for writers striving to achieve international success and fame while having to deal with the limitations imposed on their lives and works by the poverty of the island, much energy has been spent in the Dominican Republic during the better part of the second half of this century in the elusive search for a place in the world 'of universal letters' [*de las letras universales*]. To that end, as Mora Serrano has pointed out, some authors have rushed to imitate and perhaps to plagiarize the works of contemporary writers who have received critical acclaim.

This passion for what is current in western literary circles has, in many instances, brought authors to deny the relationship that must exist between an author and his/her supposed reader. For many, like Andrés L. Mateo, Dominican authors are caught in the silence left by an absence of readers. Since there are no implicit Dominican readers, we assume these authors have taken mental leave of the island in search of hypothetically universal readers. We also know that Dominican books do not travel well, and are seldom found outside the island. Thus, as has been pointed out, the number of writers whose publications remain untouched on the shelves of local bookshops or hidden in the back of one of their rooms at home is understandably quite large.

An encounter with the success of a member of the diaspora does much to dispel the notion that Dominican books do not have a reader at home, as Silvio Torres-Saillant pointed out (1994) in his presentation of *La enana Celania y otros cuentos de Viriato Sención* [Celania the Dwarf and Other Short Stories by Viriato Sención], by referring to the success of Sención's first book, *Los que falsificaron la firma de Dios* [They Forged the Signature of God]. Further, as Torres-Saillant has underscored, it comes as no surprise to realize that the author who has found his way into the hearts and wallets of Dominican readers at home is in fact a member of the Dominican diaspora.

Throughout the conference, however, Mora Serrano's analysis continued to be illustrated in many of the presentations. For Alexis Gómez Rosa and Miguel Aníbal Perdomo, for example, the end of the Dominican civil war of 1965 also signalled the fragmentation and death of many of the aspirations and themes the writers of their generation had embraced. These two poets/critics agreed in their assessment of their generation as a failed one, because of its inability to move from the circumstantial to the transcendental, from the particularity of their moment in Dominican history to the universality of twentieth-century letters.

Perdomo's and Gómez Rosas's search for that elusive encounter with the universality of poetry, finds support in the presentation of a young novelist of the diaspora, Juan Torres, who advises his audience to put aside *Foucault's Pendulum* in favour of *The Odyssey*, to choose the reading of Joyce's *Ulysses* over the headache to be gained by trying to get through a reading of José Donoso's *El obsceno pájaro de la noche* [The Obscene Bird of Night]. Torres's presentation detailed a long journey into the light of the traditional western canon, and served the apparent purpose of separating Torres's hypothetical young writer from the rest of the diaspora; a diaspora of writers who, as he indicated, have only in common their nostalgia for their homeland.

This nostalgia was poignantly presented in Tomás Modesto Galán's reflections on the state of Dominican literature in the United States; one that Modesto Galán denominates as 'Expelled from Paradise', although for him there is no real separation between Dominican writers in the homeland and those in the diaspora. As he explains, 'our generation of writers was not formed in this country' [*no constituimos una generación formada aquí*]. Further, Modesto Galán illustrates his conviction by indicating that 'the diaspora has not landed here' but is merely the farthest extension of a body that vibrates close to the Mona Passage.[2]

The examples cited above serve to illustrate, albeit only on the surface, the fragile state of Dominican writers and letters. The situation is as complex as the lives and works of many of these writers, who are not quite here (the United States) nor there; not quite Dominican nor universal. Nevertheless, as we approach the closing of the century and consider the changes in what constitutes 'Dominicanness', we understand that no longer will geography be the defining factor. The lives and stories of the members of the Dominican community have broken the spell of many years of official silence. Consequently, as Dominicans move from Quisqueya[3] to Washington Heights, and as Dominican geography is expanded, a number of positive changes have begun to take place:

- Racial discrimination against Dominicans has had the positive effect of making Dominicans begin to come to terms with our own racial identity.
- The leading role of women in the migration process has underscored our social inequalities and has resulted in more freedom for women, equal partners in survival. As Miriam Ventura celebrates in her poems:

> There are women who charm the world to make it
> their creditor
> others plan how to question dawns
> those creased in the forehead by years of
> questioning
> for them yeast and happiness ought to go hand in hand
>
> There are women, there are women.[4]

To conclude, for Dominican writers fighting their way to overcome anonymity and economic hardship, the road to travel is still long and hard. We find solace, however, in the tremendous success enjoyed in the Dominican Republic by Viriato Sención's first novel, despite official censorship, and in the mainstream recognition accorded to the publication of Julia Alvarez's novels *How the García Girls Lost Their Accents* and *In the Time of the Butterflies.*

As we begin a new millennium and enter uncharted territory for students and academics interested in Dominican studies, the challenge becomes the writing of the many missing pages in the history of Dominican literature.[5] It is hoped that the diaspora's trials and tribulations, as well as its strength and honesty, will contribute significantly to the creation of a scholarship in the field that will move from the inclusion of voices to a new understanding of the Dominican experience that will necessitate the formulation of a different paradigm to evaluate and encourage future Dominican literary production.

Notes

1   All translations are by the author of this essay [eds].
2   Modesto Galán's contribution is included in the forthcoming conference proceedings.
3   Quisqueya is the Indian name for Hispaniola.
4   Untitled, unpublished, translated by Daisy Cocco de Filippis.
5   The CUNY Dominican Studies Institute has a Rockefeller Foundation scholars-in-residence programme to begin to recreate the missing chapters in the history of the Dominican people, their culture, and literature.

12

The role of science in Cuban culture: Some observations

Keith Ellis

A Caribbean country that makes a commitment to achieve substantial scientific progress embarks on an endeavour which is sufficiently new for it to arouse, even in non-scientists, curiosity about the ramifications not only for science itself but for all the constituents of national life. For the Caribbean countries are searching, or at least hoping, for paths to development. Because we have vulnerable economic and social systems, a quest as dramatic as one for real scientific progress is likely to entail drastic economic measures and have an impact so profound as to affect culture in the broad and durable anthropological sense in which Edward Tylor defined the word in 1871, as 'that complex whole which includes knowledge, belief, art, law, morals, custom, and any other capabilities and habits acquired by [people] as member[s] of society' (Levin 1965: 9). Thus, when Cuba decided in 1959 to emphasize science in its educational system and then in the early 1980s to enter the fields of biotechnology and genetic engineering with the intention of participating at the highest world levels, these decisions had the potential to alter Caribbean experience and to constitute a significant variation in our way of viewing life.[1]

It should be remembered that when Cuba made its undertaking in 1959 science was in the popular western view held in low regard. In that era of widespread testing of nuclear weapons and of the threat of uncontainable nuclear war, the fearsome destructive powers of science, flagrantly unleashed in 1945 on Hiroshima and Nagasaki, seemed decisively to outweigh its positive features, such as the contributions of nuclear energy and nuclear medicine. Indeed, 1959 was precisely the year of C.P. Snow's Rede Lecture entitled 'The Two Cultures and the Scientific Revolution' in which he pointed to the need for scientific education, given the negative attitude to science among literary intellectuals and in contemporary society in general. Six years later, in a special number of the journal *Daedalus*, which soon became the book *Science and Culture*, writers like Oscar Handlin, Eric Weil, Herbert Marcuse, Daniel Bell, René Dubos and Robert Morrison treated science in terms of social philosophy and in the context of the developed, industrialized world. They overwhelmingly endorsed the view of science as a disjunctive force, a source of looming danger. It seemed to them that the narrow focus scientists have tended to employ, combined with an inability or an unwillingness to communicate their special knowledge to non-scientists, exacerbated a very serious kind of social incoherence.

Given these traditional as well as other immediate obstacles to its popular appeal, in order for science to become a major and welcome part of Cuban national life the perception would have to be easily allowed that it was necessary and feasible and that it would play a constructive role while posing negligible dangers. The fact that with the triumph of the Revolution Cuba promptly lost to emigration approximately one half of its medical practitioners, who were already in scarce supply in large parts of the country because of their haphazard distribution, was in a sense a fortuitous circumstance for the promotion of science in the educational system. There are few more compelling needs in any society than for trained medical personnel; and the response to this need, the measures taken to compensate rapidly for the loss and to surpass pre-1959 standards of medical service and public health, carried great appeal. It justified a new emphasis on science in the basic school curriculum and the establishment of pre-university institutions such as the Lenin and Humboldt Schools that gave heavy emphasis to the sciences in the training of some of the island's most gifted students, selected from a pool broadened now by almost full literacy and total attendance as well as by the ambition to be enrolled in schools such as those just mentioned that soon enjoyed great prestige.

The aspect of national emergency converged with factors in the Cubans' early enthusiasm for science, particularly as it applied to the medical field. The prolonged colonial period experienced by the Spanish Caribbean countries put their scientific development at a disadvantage compared with some of the mainland countries. In Mexico, for example, beginning in the late eighteenth century, creole scientists, inspired particularly by Francisco Xavier Clavijero, were defying Spanish directives and taking into account all of Mexican history, pre-Columbian and colonial, in their investigations of the natural sciences.[2] This allowed Mexican scientists to contribute to a predominant sentiment in favour of independence and to enter the independence period of the early nineteenth century with strengths in astronomy, botany, pharmacology and mining.[3] The early enthusiasm for Cuban science was linked to the impulse for autonomy, illustrating the view that the promotion of science is likely to be propitious for the idea of socio-political and economic development and the nurturing of a general revolutionary spirit (Vucinich 1970: i). As director of the Seminario de San Carlos y San Ambrosio in Havana, José Agustín Caballero (1762–1835) initiated the study of scientists such as Francis Bacon and Isaac Newton and carried out experiments in physics at the Seminary. He also drew up in 1811 his 'Proyecto de gobierno autonómico para Cuba' [Autonomous Government Plan for Cuba] and, by so doing, incurred the displeasure of the colonial authorities. Félix Varela, as holder of the Chair of Philosophy and Constitution at the Seminary, proposed a decade later that Spain grant independence to all of Spanish America and spoke of his goal of seeing Cuba as the beloved *Patria* [Homeland], free from slavery, unified and supported by science. In his banishment from the island to the US he translated into Spanish the book *Chemistry Applied to Agriculture*.[4] José de la Luz y Caballero (1800–62), the nephew of José Agustín, and also a holder of a Chair at the Seminary, favoured the advancement of science. These intellectuals, and others such as José Antonio Saco, were instrumental in the 'Sociedad Económica de Amigos del País [The Economic Society of Friends of the Country] founded by royal *fiat* in 1792. But they did not separate the Society's fostering of the teaching of botany, of the introduction of new agricultural tools and machinery and innovative methods of cultivating sugar cane from the desire for progress in the socio-political sphere and above all from a desire for Cuban autonomy. This last issue caused the colonial government to be suspicious of their ideas and led to most of them being banished from the island.[5] Hence political retardation impeded the development of science.

In his banishment from Cuba, José Martí carried out the most systematic promotion of science in the nineteenth century, not only for Cuba, but for all of Spanish America. In fact, his stature as the initiator of Spanish-American Modernism ought to rest not only on his generally recognized literary innovations but also on his quest, which began in earnest with a series of articles published in *La América* in 1883, a year after the publication of *Ismaelillo*, to persuade the Spanish-American and Caribbean countries to adopt scientific education that would enable them to be continuously abreast of and participate in scientific progress.[6] Hence in his essay entitled 'Escuela de mecánica' [School of Mechanics] he explicitly merged the two concerns, the literary and the scientific, revealing his passion for elevating the two in Spanish America in the following words (1963–6, 8: 280):

> And the reform is not completed by adding isolated science courses to literary universities; but by creating scientific universities, without demolishing in any way whatsoever the literary ones; by bringing the love for the useful, and the abomination of the useless, to literary schools; by bringing to bear all the aspects of human thought in the teaching of each problem, and not – and this would be committing dastardly treason – one single aspect; by bringing scientific concreteness, artistic solemnity, architectural majesty and precision to Literature. Such literature should only be worthy of such men!
>
> The literature of our times is ineffective because it is not the expression of our times. …
>
> It is necessary to bring new blood to Literature.[7]

He championed a state of equilibrium between literature that was coherently elevated in form and content and an ethically developmental science functioning within unified societies free not only from slavery but also from racism. Although Martí developed and expressed these potent ideas in the US, there can be little doubt that they were sown in his mind by his tutor Rafael María Mendive, who was educated in the tradition of the leading lights of the Seminario de San Carlos, José Agustín Caballero, Félix Varela and most directly, José de la Luz y Caballero.

The potentially great national achievement in science during that century was Carlos J. Finlay's discovery that the *Aedes aegypti* mosquito was the vector for the yellow fever organism that had plagued Cuba and neighbouring countries for several centuries. He had reported his experiments, observations and conclusions to the Cuban Academy of Sciences in 1881; but in the reigning conditions of colonialism and slavery nothing was done about his findings. Some 19 years later, US troops became victims in Cuba of yellow fever disease following the 1898 intervention. US Army bacteriologist Walter Reed revived Finlay's by then abandoned theory; and Reed's colleague William Gorgas, by the large-scale application of insecticides, brought the peril to an end in Cuba and other parts of the hemisphere. Thus the light of the first great coruscation of Cuban science was deflected to Reed who basked in the glory.[8] There were important lessons in this for Cubans. First of all, Finlay demonstrated native scientific ability of a high order, for in addition to making this monumental discovery he recorded impressive research achievements in a range of infectious diseases, as well as in ophthalmology. Secondly, he targeted diseases that afflicted his compatriots and their neighbours. The fruits of his efforts were therefore primarily national and then international. Thirdly, his case shows how in a country with no control of its own administration, good life-saving science may perish. The Cuban government tried to reclaim Finlay's legacy by establishing the Finlay Institute for Research in Tropical Medicine in his honour early in this century. This initial process of recuperation of Cuba's medical prestige had some positive effects because in his *Viaje a Nicaragua* [Journey to Nicaragua] (1909), Rubén Darío reported with pride that his friend and compatriot, the medical doctor, researcher and poet Luis Debayle, had participated with distinction in the Pan American Medical Congress of which Havana was the worthy host (Darío 1950, 3: 1061). But this recovery was modest and still retarded by an indifferent supervisor, the US, by inadequate standards of literacy and by an unreliable and unsupportive institutional framework that fell far short of what José Martí had advocated in his writings on education.

Yet when science was moved to a role of prominence in Cuba, certain constraints, evident in other countries, in the historical development of science were not significant factors. The old tension between religion and science that had been manifested in the explanation given by a sector of the Church of Finlay's as a revelation, scarcely made an appearance. The Catholic Church, now with a tenuous hold on the population, was not afforded the political support of the State that it enjoyed in the days of the first Republic or the even closer alliance it had with the State in the days of colonialism and slavery. Even so, the foundational role played by such priests as José Agustín Caballero and above all Félix Varela in encouraging science is testimony to a current of rational thinking in the Cuban Catholic tradition. Moreover, Cubans do not overlook the implications for national pride inherent in the fact that Copernicus was forgiven for his 'De Revolutionibus' of 1543, in which he proved the sun to be the centre of the universe, when a fellow Pole finally became Pope four and a half centuries later (in 1992). Besides, the Church would have had to resort to ingenious contrivances to oppose doctrinally the growth of science in Cuba, given its obviously humane justification.

At the same time, the religions with African roots, *santería* in particular, have a marked practical bent, inspiring a sense of satisfaction when there is a realization that efforts are being made to make life better and therefore a predisposition to be friendly to the idea of scientific progress. This attitude allows the viewing with equanimity of the Nicolás Guillén who celebrates the triumph of science in his 1969 poem 'El cosmonauta' [The Cosmonaut], in which he cites fallacies in both African and European religious creeds, a poem that was subsequently taken into outer space by a Cuban cosmonaut. Guillén, also in this period of wide-ranging riches in his poetry, proposes in 'Luna' [Moon] (1966), a poem from his bestiary *El Gran Zoo* [The Great Zoo], an alliance between science and poetry, 'Sputniks y sonetos' [Sputniks and Sonnets], to undermine the complacently accepted mythical stature of the moon; and in his 1969 'Prólogo' [Prologue] to *La rueda dentada* [The Gear Wheel] he employs the mechanical device named in the book's title as an extended metaphor to represent the idea of cooperative work. But Guillén makes other gestures in this period that would enduringly instruct and delight his scientific compatriots. In writing his book of love poems *En algún sitio de la primavera: elegía* [In Some Springtime Place: Elegy] (1994), he engages the acknowledged great writers of love poetry, and debates triumphantly with them, to make an outstanding contribution to the genre.[9] He thus anticipates the basic methodology (surveying the best in the world) and the ambition (superseding those levels) of Cubans in various fields of endeavour, including science, which was prominent in his consciousness.

Several of those who are regarded as founders of modern western science such as Archimedes and Galileo saw themselves as pure observers of natural phenomena and were reluctant to acknowledge their technological achievements. Leonardo da Vinci repudiated this attitude when he declared that 'mechanics is the paradise of mathematical sciences, because with it we reach the fruit of mathematical sciences' (Weil 1965: 201). In the context of countries that are making a serious effort to achieve broad-based development, science as an aspiration is seldom mentioned without technology following as a treasured con-comitant. Cuba is no exception to this and is obliged to be mindful of the fruit of science, to maximize the points of contact between theory and application, and in general to be inventive, not only because of the economic status it shares with these countries, but also because of the chronically urgent need to fill lacunae and discover substitutes for necessities made scarce in part by the long-standing US-imposed embargo. Cuba is in fact freer to attend to this kind of national need because its science is an expression of its sovereignty and does not suffer the constraints and arbitrariness associated with the unintegrated, exter-nally directed scientific activity found elsewhere in the Caribbean and Latin America.[10] For example, what began in the 1960s with technical experts and workers forming teams in their spare time to recover and produce spare parts had grown in the mid-1980s, the country now having thousands of scientists and engineers, architects, chemists, technicians and skilled workers, into a national movement of workers who maintained their focus on utilitarian measures, seeking solutions to problems arising in production and care centres. Their work now culminates in the annual Science and Technology Forum, the ninth of which took place in Havana in December 1994. That Forum acknowledged a preliminary process in which 263 000 persons wrote up projects leading to 256 000 solutions involving a million citizens (Oramas 1995: 3). These numbers already suggest broad-based participation, but there are, beyond, the numbers of co-workers, relatives and friends participating indirectly in or at least becoming aware of projects of invention. Besides, males and females and people of all ages take part. In 1990 I saw the oldest and youngest inventors being interviewed on Cuban television. The former was more than 80 years old, the latter younger than 12. By such means does technology, as widespread capability, become imprinted on the national consciousness and the expectation of efficiency-enhancing inventions becomes normal.

On the specifically medical side, haemorrhagic dengue fever caused many deaths and alarmed the population when it appeared in Cuba, for the first time in the hemisphere, in 1980. It threatened to be an even greater danger when Cuba was obstructed by the embargo in its attempts to obtain insecticides to suppress the carrier of this new fever, the resilient *Aedes aegypti* mosquito. The thorough public health response to the epidemic included instructing the population in the recognition of symptoms and in how to deny the mosquito habitats for their larvae. This became a precedent for dealing with a range of common diseases not controlled by vaccination, and the generally high level of education combined with the more than adequate distribution of doctors throughout the country through the institution known as 'el médico de la familia' [the family doctor] ensures a high degree of medical intelligence.

It was also in the early 1980s that a leap forward occurred that reaffirmed the association of science with the main goal of healing, now at a level of science and technology that was entirely new to the Caribbean. It began in the late 1970s with the selection of two gifted scientists to visit the M.D. Anderson Hospital in Houston, Texas, for training in the clinical application of interferon. By the beginning of the 1980s, six Cuban scientists had spent some ten days at the Central Public Health Laboratory of Finland with Professor Kari Cantell, studying the production of interferon. On their return to Cuba they soon produced, with modest facilities, the country's first biotechnology product: human leukocyte alpha interferon. At that time hopes were high that interferon would be the magic bullet in the fight against cancer. It has not achieved this high goal but has proved to be an effective therapy against some cancers, particularly leukaemias, and against diseases of the liver in general. Its potential scope for application in Cuba had been even greater before scientists there developed a genetically engineered vaccine against hepatitis B. Above all, the initial success in high technology encouraged Cuba to make a full commitment to biotechnology and genetic engineering, and the Centre for Genetic Engineering and Biotechnology was established in 1986. This new institution, headed by Manuel Limonta, one of the six scientists who had produced interferon, represents a level of scientific work done in a complex of buildings that itself brings a new stage of scientific architecture to Cuba, the Caribbean and Latin America.[11] With its state-of-the-art equipment, the Centre has strengthened an interest in science and technology at all levels in Cuba. The feeling of loss displayed by their colleagues when scientists moved from the pure to the applied sciences, such as when the brilliant Agustín Lage went from physics to the biomedical sciences, became attenuated by a recognition of the new high level of science and technology.[12]

Within the short period of seven years, the Centre produced more than 150 biotechnology items that are destined primarily for the nation's health care. Nor had the novelty of the presence of this impressive centre worn off when one was built in Camagüey and very recently another in Sancti Spiritus to be mainly devoted to the veterinary and agricultural sciences respectively. The distribution of such high-level centres of sciences and technology throughout the country is a semiotic index for the population of the national import-ance of sciences. But there are clear benefits to be had from a concen-tration of research institutes and production plants, and in the vicinity of the Centre for Genetic Engineering and Biotechnology in western Havana can be found the new Finlay Institute, the National Centre for Scientific Research, the Centre for Molecular Immunology, the Centre for Medical Surgical Research, the Immunoasy Centre, the Ozone Centre, several other biomedical research centres and eight hospitals, as well as scientific research centres in other fields such as the Centre Institute for Digital Research, whose work in cybernetics aids many other fields of scientific endeavour; and all of them involved in research and production that compete at world levels.

Cuba had for many years been visited by epidemics of meningitis; and the disease remained uncontrolled after most of the traditional con-tagions had been quelled. Scientists at the Finlay Institute took up the challenge; and as a result invented in the late 1980s the world's first and still the only genetically engineered vaccine against meningitis B and C that has not only put an end to the epidemics in Cuba but is proving to be an indispensable shield in other countries, particularly Brazil and Argentina, which have suffered from similar epidemics; this in spite of sedulous efforts on the part of established suppliers of vaccines to keep this invention from the market. Thus products invented in response to local needs are finding a growing place in foreign markets, and scientists are having the additional satisfaction of justifying economically and in good time the substantial outlays allocated to building the sector. By doing, so they also enhance their stature and that of science in society.

The newest of these research and production facilities is the Centre for Molecular Immunology.[13] The theory of the magic bullet that would provide a cure for cancer, which had prompted the quest to produce interferon, has now been invalidated by the finding that cancer is not one but numerous diseases, more than 400 at the present count. This finding has given rise to new strategies for combating these perils that up to now almost inevitably have the catastrophic effects that Nicolás Guillén described so intensely in his poem 'El cangrejo' [The Crab] of *El Gran Zoo*. Each type of cancer is marked by the presence of a specific antigen to which the immune system responds by generating an array of antibodies and T-cells, some of which challenge and engage the antigen. The artificial or genetically engineered production of the antibody most specific to the antigen is at the core of the new strategy; for monoclonal antibodies, as they are called, by having the capacity to encounter a targeted antigen, can be a most effective diagnostic tool. Their activity may also be therapeutic, by boosting a person's immune system or by conveying added forms of medication to the affected cells. The process of identifying, cloning, purifying and packaging, in the most sterile conditions, the appropriate, highly specific, ultra-microscopic antibodies entails research involving all the natural sciences. It also involves laboratory and production practices that meet the highest international standards. A monoclonal antibody of high specificity is a prized item globally. Research centres in Cuba since the early 1980s have been doing monoclonal antibody research and have developed by now more than a hundred of them for use in humans, animals and plants. But at the Centre for Molecular Immunology scientists are in the vanguard worldwide of the study of the molecules involved in immune response and are cultivating large-scale commercial quantities of monoclonal antibodies and other higher cell forms. This new centre is considered to be the most technically complex biotechnology centre constructed in Cuba; and its facilities, its spaciousness and features such as climate control with nine grades of pressure, the circulation of seven qualities of water, its double computer network system, and its on-site waste treatment capacity, make it, in the opinion of many in the field, including the specialist in technology transfer for one of Canada's leading biotechnology firms with whom I visited the Centre, as advanced as any in the world. Augustín Lage, who heads the Centre, explains that Cuba is fully prepared, despite its present economic difficulties, for this new level of work, because in this area of science it has the necessary infrastructure and trained personnel, experience and integrated growth among its social sectors (Losa 1994).

By several indices and certainly by those that have to do with public health, Cuba ranks with the countries that are generally regarded as the most developed. It has the most doctors per capita of all countries. By late 1997 it had achieved an infant mortality rate of fewer than ten per thousand live births, the only country in the hemisphere to do so, apart from Canada and the United States. Its life expectancy of 75 years is approximately the same as that of the United States and eight years greater than the average of the other Latin American countries. It also has a lower illiteracy rate than most developed countries and a high level of skills in the population, the education system providing successive classes of better-prepared professionals. The group of young men and women engineers and architects responsible for the design and building of the technically sophisticated Centre for Molecular Immunology was led by a 26 year old (at the time I met him), when construction had already been going on for a year. The selection of personnel on the basis of interest and competence to work in advanced scientific projects leads to a social randomness that breaks with earlier restricted class, race, gender and age traditions. Thus, in addition to the removal of the barriers of age we have observed so far, we may note that 56 per cent of the workers at advanced levels of science in Cuba are women.[14] And whereas Augustín Lage, the head of the Centre for Molecular Immunology, is from a Havana family with a strong tradition in medicine and research, when the Revolution triumphed in January 1959 the current Head of the Centre for Genetic Engineering and Biotechnology, Dr Manuel Limonta, was a 13-year-old working as an assistant to a Jamaican shoemaker in Santiago de Cuba. Such developments bring science into the consciousness of people in all sectors of Cuban society.

There are other means by which scientific work is divulged to the population. The opening of an institution such as the Centre of Molecular Immunology is a national event, the significance of which is communicated to the population by the President, Fidel Castro. At its opening in December 1996, he addressed, as is his wont, the immediate audience, consisting in this case of scientific and construction workers, so that both groups would have a clear understanding of each other's aims, efforts and achievements, of which he himself is so fully apprised, having taken such a deep and direct interest in all stages of his nation's scientific developments, that he speaks without notes. The rest of the nation is his indirect but equally important audience. The demanding duty he takes on in this case is to explain the science, because this is a new and truly specialized area; in fact the building itself is part of the science. But what is to be done in it is at the core of the people's curiosity. And the President, sensitive to the brevity that the scientific occasion favours, concisely sums up all the salient features in what he calls a 'minidiscurso' [mini-speech], seizing on the key item – monoclonal antibodies. The central difficulty in communicating information about scientific work lies in the narrowness of the semiotic component of scientific language. Fidel Castro surmounts this by introducing metaphor to describe the scientists' efforts (1994a: 4). The antibodies are in one mode (Castro 1994b):

> missiles to diagnose an illness. They are developing a mini-missile that can go directly to where specific substances are being produced, let's say in a tumour, and it's drawn there; so all the studies and all the analyses can be made. However, it doesn't just act as a diagnostic tool. They are already working on monoclonal antibodies to come up with missiles which not only reveal a tumour or reveal certain illnesses, but also to combat them, they already have warheads that seek and destroy malignant cells.[15]

This use of ballistic imagery evokes the field of projectile motion that is at the very origins of modern applied science. This archetype of applied science, that in our day evolved into an instrument of global terror and therefore has universal resonance, becomes a vehicle for conveying the peaceful, life-protecting, generally beneficial, miniscule marvels of contemporary science, which are now impressed on the popular imagination by being antithetically associated with a fearsome militaristic tradition. The metaphor also recalls the resounding '¡armas para la batalla!' [weapons for the battle] with which Martí climaxes his call for development in his essay 'Educación científica'.

Scientific research and the popular imagination also find common ground in another quite different sector of medical care. Use of Cuba's botanical resources as medicines is widespread in the population, some of it sanctified by religious beliefs. In recent years, the numbers of such medicines are growing with the availability of research specialists and facilities to validate known ones and to seek new ones, in pharmacies which boast assortments in which there is happy compatibility notwithstanding their religious or scientific origins.[16]

In 1936 C.P. Snow stated that, 'if science is to play its part in our culture, we have to begin by understanding the mental satisfactions that it can provide' (Hultberg 1991: 3). In the case of Cuba in recent years, the fruits of the system of education, the momentum already gathered by scientific work, the general concern for the best protection and defence against all illnesses, and the likelihood of economic gains have combined to create a movement so strong as to challenge Newton's first law of motion, because even the dissuasive activity of external forces cannot seem to divert Cubans from their constant course toward the highest levels of scientific achievement. Manuel Limonta has explained that those countries that have already missed the revolutions in physics and chemistry, which through electronics and materials development have brought economic and other advantages to the development world, have one last chance: that of taking part in the revolution in biology.[17] Genetic engineering with its capacity for cloning by altering the cells of animals, plants and their fruits, can be devastating to countries that rely entirely on nature by making redundant even nature's most exotic gifts, on the exportation of which some poor countries now depend for their survival, threatening them with conditions of hopeless misery and absolute neglect. By being abreast of world developments in this field and by holding to the ethical standards consistently enunciated by the admired nineteenth-century founders, Cuba has in science a source of mental satisfaction not only for the present but for the future. The avoidance of reckless or cruel experimentation that has eroded trust in science elsewhere – such as the deliberate giving of doses of nuclear radiation to unknowing victims, including pregnant women, or the deliberate denial of treatment to hundreds of black men infected with syphilis in the so-called 'Tuskegee Study' – has strengthened the confidence of Cubans in their scientists. This has positive ramifications not only for biomedicine but for other fields of science in which there is a deep national interest, such as the peaceful uses of nuclear energy.

The science is characteristically Utopian rather than Arcadian, achieving new conquests as it causes obsolescence, fuelled by the view that, as Nicolás Guillén put it, 'any previous era was worse' [*cualquier tiempo pasado fue peor*] (1985, 2: 84). Its cumulative quality inspires a sense of time that is continuous and progressive rather than cyclical, and a greater belief in reasoned effort than in providence. The intellectual openness, the critical attitude towards any present state of knowledge in the quest for progress and the belief in the wisdom of people's rational capacities that characterize scientific endeavour have always tended to make science incompatible with a culture of absolutism. Hence the terrible difficulties Copernicus and Galileo had with the Church in their time (Biagioli 1993). With regard to a different absolutist period and society, that of tsarist Russia, it has been shown that the authorities distrusted the scientific spirit. In examining the period 1861–1917, Alexander Vucinich writes (1970: xi):

The authorities had good reason for their distrust, since nearly all the regime's leading opponents explicitly expected science to play a major role in liberating Russia from the feudal past and introducing an age of civil liberty, social equality, and freedom of thought. Indeed, official ideologues as well as conservative religious philosophers opposed science mostly because of its democratic nature.[18]

In the light of this history, the eager and unwavering promotion of science that is welcomed by the people can be seen as a measure of the democratic character of the Cuban Revolution.

Science is functioning in Cuba as a mainstay of the defiant national spirit, prompting gestures of appreciation from other sectors. It is thus a powerful cohesive force. In 1994, for instance, workers in the tourist industry donated $700 000 from their estimated earnings to the health sector.[19] Science serves as a model and challenge for other areas of Cuban culture, and there is much evidence of the cultural integration of scientific principles.

Alicia Alonso has spoken, echoing Martí, of the necessity to heighten creativity and performance in the arts as science and technology advance, of the balance that needs to be maintained (BBC/Cuban Television 1982). Anyone who has seen performances of the National Ballet of Cuba over the years can attest to the spread of excellence throughout the growing company (in fact compan*ies* because others have been created in Camagüey and Santiago de Cuba). One could always admire the principal dancer in *Giselle*, but more and more the studied technique and mathematical precision of the *corps de ballet* that supports Giselle reflect the absorption of scientific principles into the dancer's art. Technique and precision also attract admiration in the field of sports where in an area such as fencing, heretofore dominated by Europe, the men's world individual champion in 1995 was a 22 year-old Afro-Cuban engineering student, and his only defeat in international competition that year was at the hands of another similar Cuban. Technique and precision must also largely explain the superb results that Cuban track relay teams have been achieving in international competitions by repeatedly coming out ahead of teams from countries whose individual athletes are faster. It is no wonder that the island has more than 500 sports technicians, more than any other country, teaching overseas the science of a whole range of sports, that the manager of the national boxing team has a doctorate in his speciality and that whereas 30 years ago boxers on the national team had an average educational level of grade five, they now achieve an average of second-year university level.[20]

The general familiarity with science and its coexistence with popular belief systems has allowed Juan Carlos Tabío to base in part his extremely successful film of 1990, *Plaff*, on a running joke involving the unnecessary and expensive importation of an easily substitutable Canadian polymer. And several writers have incorporated science in their creative work, particularly in science fiction narrative.[21] Undoubtedly, the admiration for the part women are playing in the field of science has had the salutary consequence that women portrayed in the arts – in popular songs, for example – are treated with a new dignity. The special economic difficulties of recent years have contributed in some unsuspected ways to diffusing scientific awareness among the population. The response to scarce fuel supplies has not been to increase the price of electricity, which for normal usage remains at the price at which it was set in 1959. Rather the task has fallen to secondary school children to visit householders in their neighbourhoods, discuss with them the general subject of electricity and assess with them how much electricity they need to use. The assessment becomes a goal to be bettered, that is to say, to be lowered. The result of this is that Cuba is the only Caribbean country where a normal topic of conversation among people is not how much money they spend on electricity per month but how many kilowatts of electricity they consume, or save. Such a practice, as with the relay runners, the enlightening role played by a young woman scientist in *Plaff*, the dancers in the *corps de ballet*, the poets whose 'yo' [I] readily translates into 'nosotros' [we], and the scientists, technologists and technicians, builds the habit of blending in the people's consciousness the subjective and the national. This process is aided in the case of the scientists by the fact that they are not isolated in their scientific world. The centres in which they do their research and production frequently host lectures by creative writers and experts in the humanities and social sciences as well as performances by artists. One vast area in which the balance that results from all this is illustrated is the attitude to the environment; and it is not surprising that Cuba was recently judged to be one of the four leading countries in the world in the protection of the environment.

The new and accelerating role of science in a cohesive enterprise has been given appropriate administrative recognition. As of the beginning of 1995, a Ministry of Science, Technology and the Environment has been created in Cuba to supplant administratively the Academy of Sciences. The Minister is Rosa Elena Simeón who headed the Academy and she is served by a Vice Minister for each of the three divisions. The mission of this Ministry is to work closely with the others in the task, made more challenging by the persistent and tightening US embargo, of maintaining and strengthening prevailing health-care programmes, such as the 'club de abuelos' [grandparents' club], whose members exercise in parks in any part of the island with all the needed medical supervision, the protection of children throughout the island by vaccines, the most advanced of which are Cuban inventions, or the pre- and post-natal facilities that allow mothers-to-be to arrive confidently at a maternity hospital surrounded by family and flowers.

The high level of scientific work that Cuba has attained and its outstanding inventions readily attract the admiration of those who welcome scientific progress. But when we consider the impeccable ethical character of this activity in Cuba as well as its salutary influence on all the essential aspects of national life we may well conclude that in the annals of scientific endeavour no country has had a more brilliant and auspicious initial period of sustained emphasis on science than has Cuba in these last three decades. Nicolás Guillén called the Cuban literacy campaign and the agrarian reform of the 1960s 'poems'.[22] There is hardly room for doubt that he also would have given this lofty designation to the Cuban realization of the potential of Caribbean science in the 1990s.

Notes

1 Carl Wint (1995) writes eloquently of one of the many cases in which the professed interest is not matched by action.

2 Born in 1731 in Veracruz, Mexico, Clavijero was a Jesuit intellectual who took a keen interest in the indigenous cultures of Mexico and in advancing the natural sciences with a vision of their historical continuity from Pre-Columbian to his own times. He, along with the other Jesuits, was expelled from Mexico in 1767, and settled in Bologna, Italy, where he died in 1787. His remains were repatriated to Mexico in 1970.

3 A very useful study of the role science played in the Spanish-American independence movement is Peset Reig (1987). For a detailed view of the Mexican case see Trabulse (1983–92).

4 This is a translation from the French of Jean Chaptal, *Chimie appliquée à l'agriculture*. Chaptal, who served as a Minister in the government of Napoleon I, had developed the chemical industry in France, and he became very influential in Europe and North America. His *Elémens de chimie* was also translated into English the year after its original publication. Félix Varela's selection of this author for translation is an indication of his desire to place Cuba and Spanish America in touch with contemporary knowledge in the field of the chemicalization of agriculture.

5 Conversations with Angel Augie, Roberto Zurbano Torres, Cintio Vitier, Fina García Marruz, Enrique Nuñez Rodríguez and Josefina Toleda Benedit on this general subject, as well as the latter's book and items on these nineteenth-century figures in the *Diccionario de literatura cubana* [Dictionary of Cuban Literature]

and also Luis Navarro García's *La independencia de Cuba* [The Independence of Cuba] were extremely helpful.

6   See José Martí (1963–73, vol. 8), especially the sections 'Educación Científica' (275–292) and 'Exposiciones' (343–71). Indispensable reading is also Toledo Benedit (1994).

7   *Y no está la reforma completa en añadir cursos aislados de enseñanza científica a las universidades literarias: sino en crear universidades científicas, sin derribar por eso jamás las literarias; en llevar el amor a lo útil, y a la abominación de lo inútil, a las escuelas de letras; en enseñar todos los aspectos del pensamiento humano en cada problema, y no, – con lo que se comete alevosa traición, – un solo aspecto; – en llevar solidez científica, solemnidad artística, majestad y precisión arquitecturales a la Literatura. ¡Sólo tales letras fueran dignas de tales hombres!*

La literatura de nuestros tiempos es ineficaz, porque no es la expresión de nuestros tiempos. …

Hay que llevar la sangre nueva a la Literatura …

8   For a detailed study of this process see López Sánchez (1986: 255–92).

9   For the text of this book along with its translation into English and my study see Guillén (1994).

10   For the problems inherent in externally controlled scientific activity see the essays in Reingold and Rothenberg (1987), especially Wade Chambers (pp. 297–321). For other problems arising from a lack of integration in scientific policy, see Schoijet (1991).

11   Limonta and Victoria Ramírez were the two scientists who had visited Houston. They, along with Pedro López, Silvio Barcelona, Eduardo Pentón and Angel Aguilera, constituted the group that visited Finland.

12   In his excellent book, Ernesto Bravo (1993) has profiled most of those who have become leaders in Cuban biotechnology.

13   Given the pace of developments in the biomedical field in Cuba it is important to point out that this chapter was largely written in 1995.

14   Conversation in Toronto, 1990, with Rosa Elena Simeón, the then president of the Cuban Academy of Sciences.

15   *Proyectiles para diagnosticar una enfermedad. Fabrican el microproyectil ese, que puede ir directamente a donde están produciéndose determinadas sustancias, digamos en un tumor, y es atraído; entonces se pueden hacer todos los estudios, todos los análisis.*

Pero sirven no sólo para diagnóstico, ya se trabaja con los anticuerpos monoclonales en buscar proyectiles que no sólo delaten el tumor, delaten determinadas enfermedades, sino que las combatan, ya son proyectiles de guerra que van a destruir las células malignas.

Among other speeches by the Cuban president on similar occasions are those given on the opening of the Centre of Immunoasy, *Granma* (9 September 1987); on the opening of both the Centre for Genetic Engineering and Biotechnology and the Centre of Studies Applied to the Development Nuclear Energy, *Granma* (29 October 1987), pp. 1–2.

16   The eclectic range is indicated by the fact that, in the high technology sphere, as with the recombinant meningitis B and C vaccine, Cuba is the only country to produce PPG, a medication developed from the sugar-cane molecule that lowers cholesterol, creates a feeling of general well-being and is so free of side-effects that it is sold over the counter in Cuban pharmacies. Cuba was the second country to produce Epidermal Growth Factor, a medication whose effect is to promote rapid skin growth and which represents a breakthrough in burn treatment (its

effectiveness has been demonstrated in the rapid recuperation of the athlete Ana Fidelia Quirot from the severe burns she suffered recently). Cuba is the only country in the world to produce recombinant Streptokinase, a medication that revives people after heart attacks by dissolving blood clots. Also, among the monoclonal antibodies Cuba produces that enjoy exceptionally high specificity are *ior t3*, an efficient immunosuppressor used particularly against rejection in kidney transplant operations, *ior cea 1*, that identifies the carcinoembrionic antigen associated with tumours of the gastro-intestinal tract, and *ior egf/r3*, that identifies antigens associated with breast and lung cancers. At the same time, outside of the high technology field, Cuba has been doing pioneering work in such areas as the use of shark cartilage as an adjunct therapy in the treatment of various cancers. In the botanical field, as of May 1995, the two latest additions to the nationally available products are tincture of guava, applied topically for skin irritations and taken orally for an upset stomach, and tincture of marjoram, resin and rosemary, effective as an expectorant in cases of asthma and bronchitis.

17 Conversations with him in Canada in 1989.

18 The inclusive, egalitarian, and cooperative aspects of Soviet ideology, combined with the chronically urgent need of the Soviet Union to defend itself from externally linked military and other attacks and to be self-reliant, created conditions favourable to the advancement of science. The collapse of the Soviet Union has been accompanied by steep reversals in scientific opportunities and achievement in the former constituent countries.

19 'Tourism Workers Give their Tips to Health Sector', *Granma International* (18 January 1995), p. 9.

20 My source for the latter is Teófilo Stevenson in an interview on Canadian Broadcasting Corporation television, 28 May 1995. It was striking how often the great champion used terms like 'scientific' and 'intellectual' and 'progression in the scientific application of the sport' during the brief interview on the subject of Cuban boxing.

21 Daína Cariano's *Los mundos que amo* [The Worlds I Love] (1979), Agustín de Rojas *Espiral* [Spiral] (1980), and Gregorio Ortega's *Kappa 15* (1982) are a few examples.

22 See Ellis (1985: 196–7) for the speech in which Guillén so describes these revolutionary achievements.

13

Traumas of modernity in the Caribbean: Virgilio Piñera and Hector Rojas Herazo

Gilberto Gómez Ocampo

Virgilio Piñera (1912–1979) wrote some of the novels, stories and plays that are most representative of the absurd in Latin America. Piñera's works continue to receive critical acclaim, although mostly by scholars outside of Cuba.[1] As is well known, Piñera was a member of that group of Cuban poets who produced the legendary literary magazine *Orígenes* [Origins]. Other members of the group associated with *Orígenes* included José Lezama Lima, Cintio Vitier and Eliseo Diego. This group opposed the *criollismo* that was predominant in Cuban literary circles.[2] While Piñera has been recognized for his masterful use of black humour in works of great fantasy, I maintain that the critical relevance of his work goes beyond that categorization and is in need of further clarification.[3] This essay constitutes an attempt to substantiate my position and will draw upon the works found in Piñera's important collection *Cuentos fríos* [Cold Stories], published in Buenos Aires in 1956, which includes stories penned between 1944 and 1954. I will study some of the outstanding aspects of this collection, such as Piñera's particular elaboration of the absurd and his concomitant rejection of the teleology implicit in the philosophy of progress prevalent in western societies. I will then relate this study to the novel *Respirando el verano* [Breathing the Summer] (1962) by Héctor Rojas Herazo, a Colombian contemporary of Nobel Laureate Gabriel García Márquez. While Rojas Herazo, also Caribbean Colombian, a *costeño*, is less well known than Piñera, he is an important novelist, painter and poet. *Respirando el verano* has been considered by some critics as an important Colombian antecedent to García Márquez's *Cien años de soledad* [One Hundred Years of Solitude].[4] It will be argued in this article that the work of Piñera and Rojas Herazo provides the reader with examples of the criticism of 'modern' western culture from the perspective of the Caribbean rim. It is especially because of the manner in which their work criticizes modernity, that it can also be seen to embrace a critique of bourgeois pragmatism. A synopsis of what is understood by the term 'modernity' seems appropriate here.

A reading of a recent work by Bruno Latour, *We Have Never Been Modern* (1993), offers a point of departure which we can use to clarify some of the most salient meanings of 'the modern', contrasting them with the oft-discussed notion of postmodernism. We will note some of them here; in the first place, the notion (often defined as 'postmodernity') that the present moment is characterized by extreme nihilism and scepticism. Although this seems obvious, it acquires greater meaning if we consider the art of the period between the two world wars.

Latour revises the fundamental tenets of the sciences, and re-establishes the principle that human discourse is significant – not just auto-referential. He criticizes the sciences of discourse because they 'retain our discourse and rhetoric but purge our work of any undue adherence to reality – *horresco referens* – or to power plays' (1993: 5). At this point, it will benefit us to remember the words of Derrida concerning formalism: 'Form fascinates when we no longer have the force to understand the force from within itself' (Brooks 1994: xiv). Latour notes that the year 1989, 'The Year of Miracles' (1993: 8), is a less conventional date than others because it would denote not just the fall of the Berlin Wall, but rather a much greater crisis: that of western epistemology. The West had thought itself to be lord and master of matter and nature only to see itself bound by them again: AIDS, ecocide, as well as inconceivable genocides such as those seen in former Yugoslavia and in Rwanda and Burundi. In an almost didactic analysis, Latour writes (p. 10):

> Modernity comes in as many versions as there are thinkers or journalists, yet all its definitions point, in one way or another; to the passage of time. The adjective 'modern' designates a new regime, an acceleration, a rupture, revolution in time. When the word 'modern', 'modernization', or 'modernity' appears, we are defining, by contrast, an archaic and stable past. Furthermore, the word is always being thrown into the middle of a fight, in a quarrel where there are winners and losers, Ancients and Moderns.

Of course, my purpose here is to discuss Piñera and Rojas Herazo, and I need not look for ways to burden the discussion with the concept of 'modernity'. I would refer the reader to the useful surveys of this concept done by Martei Calinescu in *Five Faces of Modernity* (1987), by Stephen Toulmin in *Cosmopolis: The Hidden Agenda of Modernity*

(1990), and by Antoine Compagnon in *The Five Paradoxes of Modernity* (1992). From these (and other) texts, it is clear that the impact of modernity has been reactive in nature, and has existed in contrast with and against that which is negative, that which was before, the past. At the risk of succumbing to historical reductionism, I posit here that the reader of Piñera and Rojas Herazo must consider the time period when they produced their works: the Caribbean in the 1940s and 1950s, a time of accelerated reincorporation into the global economy, which resulted from heightened strategic interest in the region due to the Cold War. It is for this reason, in fact, that Puerto Rico was made a 'Commonwealth' of the United States in 1952. In Cuba, the 1940s were characterized by the new constitution (ratified in 1940). The relative progressivism of Batista's first regime, as well as the adoption of formal democracy and a policy which outlined presidential succession – only broken up by the coup of 1952 – made observers think that a permanently institutionalized republic in Cuba had at last been established. For its part, industry in the Colombian Caribbean took off precisely in this period, and could have led some to think of it as the arrival of a presumed modernity in the tropics.

In their meaning and impetus, Piñera and Rojas Herazo are related to a few other Latin American writers who have been critical of the modern project. However, besides Arlt, Onetti, Cortázar, and a few others, their distaste for modernity has not had many exponents in Latin America. As I indicated earlier, my interest in the work of Piñera and Rojas Herazo stems from the desire to explore their special place in the literature of Latin America. I deem that place to be crucial and their literature almost unique as it labours to dismantle the view that modernity offered of itself. That is to say, both Piñera and Rojas Herazo perceived the vast insufficiency of that cultural project before its failure was fully sensed in the geographical centres of modernity (which came to be known as the 'First World'). I wish to emphasize here the seminal character of their work as well as their virtues of both introspecting *and* prospecting. These two writers created their works in quite different areas of the Hispanic periphery: the Río de la Plata and the Caribbean. It is well-known that Piñera, although Cuban, lived in Buenos Aires from 1946 to 1958. It is what connects them, however, the seminal character of their work, and their ability to look within and without, that is the focus of this essay.

With respect to Piñera, I would like to refer the reader to the work of E.M. Cioran. It seems quite natural to make some general connections between two writers who, although peripheral (one, a Rumanian born in 1911, and the other Cuban, born in 1912), based their works on a clear scepticism of western history and *messianism*. In fact, in 1968 the critic Richard Gilman (pp. 25-7) wrote on Cioran something that, *mutatis mutandis*, may also be said of Piñera:

> For Cioran … history is 'a monster we have called up against ourselves', history is characterized by what he calls the '*idolatry of becoming*', that process of consciousness being transformed into thought and thought into futurity which Nietzsche had in mind when he castigated his own countrymen: poor Germans, 'they never are, but are always becoming.' To wish to become is to be dissatisfied with what is … Against this wish to become Cioran hurls a wish to <u>un-become</u>, to find nothingness, no-action, silence, as plenitudes, inverted spurs to being.

No-action, nothingness and silence are equally characteristic of the work of Rojas Herazo, in which sensualism demarcates/establishes a philosophical horizon of sounds, colours, smells, vertigos, rattles and other natural rhythms of which humankind is merely another component. Humankind is seen here not as a species of superior beings, but as simply another form of life. The significance of this sensualism is greater than it appears: the futility of 'becoming' a different thing from what one is, the plenitude of the present moment when one/a being *is*, when one exists in an eternal present in which there are neither futures nor pre-histories. For example, talking about the bachelorhood of Julia, one of the female protagonists in *Respirando*, the narrator says that the proposals men had made to her were lost:

> Without a trace or an odour … in an undecided calendar that she kept … in co-habitation with the torpor, the vapours of the patios, the isochrony of the untied shoes which she tied again amidst the immemorial buzzing of her inalterable blood.[5]

An identical perception can be found in *La carne de René* [René's Flesh], a novel written by Piñera in 1953, characterized by the assertion – a thousand times repeated – that human existence 'is nothing more than flesh' [*no es más que carne*], that 'there is nothing more than flesh' [*no hay más que carne*], that attempting to find another meaning or dimension to existence other than that which is given to us by the flesh (with its pains and pleasure) is a foolish and futile endeavour.

A reading of Piñera's *Cuentos fríos* confirms his critical perception of modernity. For example, in the story 'La condecoración' [The Decoration] a 15-year-old boy is condemned by his father to walk with an odometer hung about his neck so that, unlike his father, he will know – as a 'justification' for his life – exactly how many kilometres he has travelled in his miserable job as a messenger (Piñera 1956: 95). The teleological distinction between 'function' and 'purpose' is indispensable here for our discussion of this story.[6] The child does not choose the action; rather, the son is the agency of his father's satisfaction – which is both possible and hypothetical, and which the father himself now lacks: this is, knowing with precision the exact number of kilometres travelled in his lifetime. The function of the boy is to satisfy his father, but the child himself does not determine/establish any purpose for his life. Knowing the exact number of kilometres covered in one's lifetime is, moreover, a purpose without any pragmatic consequence, that is to say, without value. In the story 'La caída' [The Fall], two climbers scale a mountain. We are not told why they do it but rather we are told precisely what their motives are *not*: 'not to bury a capsule there at its peak, nor to raise the flag of the bold alpine climbers' (Piñera 1987: 5) [*no para enterrar en su cima la botella ni tampoco para plantar la bandera de los alpinistas denodados*] (Piñera 1956: 9).[7] We are concerned then, with the absence of *telos* or finality: an arduous task that is done happily with no objective. The immediate consequence is a total inversion of order: if getting to the top requires great care and planning, the descent is made literally by accident and in a brief amount of time. In fact, one of the mountain-climbers becomes tangled and thus begins his dizzying fall. Just as there was no purpose for the climb, the descent does not even cause the characters to be concerned with saving their own lives – this doesn't even cross their minds. In effect, the first-person narrator states that 'My sole concern was to avoid losing my eyes …. As for my companion, his only worry was that his beautiful beard … reach the plain intact, not even slightly dusty' (Piñera 1987: 6).[8]

In the story 'Cómo viví y cómo morí' [How I Lived and How I Died], a miserable man describes his affinity for cockroaches, whom he considers his 'equals' to the point of sharing his room with them and not trying to exterminate them: 'I don't know of any cockroach that has done anything constructive. On the contrary, they devour everything within their reach. Why, then, continue fighting?' (Piñera 1987: 132).[9] Again, the implicit point Piñera is making is this: if the cockroaches are going to inherit the earth, what is the *purpose* of human activity? Of course, these brief stories have even greater impact when they are understood as allegories rather than as metaphors: the 'miserable human being' [*miserable ser humano*] who narrates the story is no one in particular, yet he is made to represent all humankind (Latin American or otherwise? – it is up to the reader to decide). The story 'El viaje' [The Trip] is extraordinary in its ability to represent the void in modern life. In this story, a man disgusted with his life decides to 'travel'; he does so, however, in a baby carriage which is pushed by baby-sitters stationed every thousand metres along the road. He wishes to travel in a circular fashion, in a 'lifelong journey' [*marcha vitalicia*] without leaving the country (Piñera 1987: 136; 1956: 104). Of course, this story is about an absurd situation, but to suppose that its absurdity is merely comical would be to miss the potent anti-modern ideological charge of Piñerian discourse. The absurd is intensified further when we realize that Pepe the banker (note the profession of this additional character) has also opted for the circularity of this gratuitous, *repeated, repeatable, non-linear act*. Pepe, in effect, travels in a saucepan driven by chefs who change shifts every half hour: '*Chance* has ordained that at the moment I pass in my carriage, Pepe always faces me as he turns in his pot, obliging us both to call out a ceremonious greeting. *Our faces express our obvious happiness*' (Piñera 1987: 135, emphasis added).[10] The reader finds himself confronted with purely gratuitous acts, acts without an obvious end, which are, in teleological terms, without apparent function. This constitutes a renunciation of that bourgeois utilitarianism which requires action with a purpose. Julio Cortázar, as is well known, would also partake of that critique of 'pragmatic reasoning'.[11]

In 'El gran Baro' [The Great Baro], one of the most powerful stories in the collection, we are offered several interpretive possibilities, all of which are based on a quite complete inversion of logic (an overall characteristic of Piñera's work). In effect, the story presents the reader with the experience of a totally absurd world. A buffoon becomes the virtual leader of a nation. The cardinal and military leaders of this nation, jealous of having been usurped by his 'buffooneries' [*payaserías*] (p. 146), order his execution – not by firing squad, but rather by 'a good clean laugh' [*a risa limpia*] (p. 148). No one, however, finds a way to make Baro laugh, making it impossible to carry out the sentence. In a strange twist, Baro, although able to make others laugh, is himself extremely melancholy and is unable to reap the benefits of his own humour. Finally, 'he is overcome by a scoffing, cynical laugh' [*risa cínica y burlona lo sobrecoge*] (p. 148), at which point he dies and his cadaver is enshrined in the cathedral by Cardinal-Buffoon.[11]

A reading of 'El muñeco' [The Dummy], the last story in the collection, confirms and perhaps emphasizes Piñera's intense sense of the world being diminished through the process of reification of man in modern society. The protagonist of the story, an ordinary, informed 'citizen', becomes alarmed at the continual public appearance of the President of his unidentified country (several contextual details, however, allow us to infer that it is a Latin American country). The good citizen thinks that the President squanders his time and energy in sterile protocol. The citizen, desiring to see the President spend his time pursuing higher goals, concocts a strategy to replace him – with his consent – with a doll that exactly replicates his mannerisms and appearance. This project requires the 'high-tech' of the moment. The consequences of this action are unexpected: all the high functionaries surrounding the President want to have their own doll, by means of which they hope to be liberated from the routine imposed on them by their offices. The doll, however, far from effecting the liberation of the governors, ends up enslaving them. Although it is unclear as to whether it ever truly becomes alive, the doll, like a type of Golem, with all the mathematical calculations and technology implicit in its functioning (miniature gramophones, special rubber that exactly duplicates human skin) surpasses the original human models. The doll is able to learn with great ease the phrase 'law and order' (Piñera 1987: 111) [*ordeno y mando*] (Piñera 1956: 188), and when the doll retires to his rooms the narrator tells us that the President 'slept in a cardboard box' (Piñera 1987: 111) [*durmió en una caja de cartón*] (Piñera 1956: 188). The implications of a story such as this are certainly worth considering in this age of 'artificial intelligence'.

Perhaps the most obscure story in the collection is also the longest and most ambitious one: 'El conflicto' [The Conflict]. In it, Teodoro, a prisoner, awaits his execution. A laconic sentence begins the story: 'He would face the firing squad that coming week' (Piñera 1987: 137) [*Lo fusilarían en la semana venidera*] (Piñera 1956: 105). (Those addicted to the trivial will not fail to note here the similarity between this opening sentence and that of García Márquez's masterpiece *Cien años de soledad*.) The event is presented as something totally devoid of tragedy. On the contrary, the narrator informs us that, for the prisoner – as for the protagonist in Camus' *L'étranger* [The Stranger] – his fate had no importance (Piñera 1987: 137):

> The event in itself had in its chronicity the same flavour as any chronic event …, since, in accordance with the fact that a man is executed every day, at some place on earth, and also with his readings on executions, he had to recognize that it was perfectly natural and logical. That is, faced with the particular case of his impending execution, there was no sense in getting upset or agitated or in making of it the gravitational centre of the universe, since these executions followed each other in time and space with the same inevitability that follows day. … Also, … its anticipated

violence would not be exceptional, for the Chinaman executed the day before one thousand leagues away, and the German sacrificed the year before, and all the men executed up to that moment died with the same equality exhibited by two fresh sausages, due to the insensibility of an exceptionally precise machine.[13]

This is a condemned man whose refusal to save himself questions what there is to live for. Again, the underlying problem in the narrative of Piñera is teleological in nature: What is worth living for? What is the purpose of life? In fact, is life – being alive – a *purpose* or is it merely a biological *function*? The condemned man attempts to delay his own death as merely an intellectual exercise. That is to say, his real interest is not saving his life, but performing an intellectual exercise – these are, we must remember, 'cold stories', as the title of the book tells us. To achieve this, the condemned man acts upon the meaning of 'chronicity', to imply that the nature of successive units of time is arbitrary, ordained by man, and not natural or necessary. In this fashion, he seeks to sabotage the chain of events that culminates or should culminate in his execution. Piñera is interested in demonstrating the inevitable in this story as his character attempts to detain time at the 'point of maximum saturation' (Piñera 1987: 160) [*punto de máxima saturación*] (Piñera 1956: 137), thus allowing the remote (im)possibility that human intercession – a human being as the agent of his future or fate – may alter it, *away from another end or ulterior consequence*, without the intention of saving his own life. This certainly implies 'the breakdown of reason, the purest of values' (Piñera 1987: 160) [*la quiebra de la razón, de los más puros valores*] (Piñera 1956: 117). The text calls it 'scandalous and monotonous chronicity' (Piñera 1987: 164) [*escandalosa y monótona cronicidad*] (Piñera 1956: 121), which could ultimately be altered or sabotaged by a human being acting as the agent of his own life: mixing 'that which happened a hundred years ago with that which would occur within a hundred years' (Piñera 1987: 164)[*lo ocurrido cien años atrás con lo que ocurriría dentro de cien años*] (Piñera 1956: 121). Moments before his execution, Teodoro persuades the official not to execute him, not because he fears death, but in order to impede the realization of an event that seems – as far as common belief holds – totally unavoidable. Impeding this event is the same as avoiding history, sabotaging it.

We have now covered the very basics of Piñera's work as a storyteller. Unfortunately, space is not sufficient here to discuss his poetic and theatrical productions, but we have, I trust, surveyed the basics of his critique of modernity. As we have seen. Piñera presents it as a void which cannot sate the most profound human needs, and is erroneously misguided in its emphasis on those material appetites which characterize the culture of *homo faber*.

As far as this treatment of Rojas Herazo is concerned, his 1962 novel *Respirando el verano* shares with García Márquez's *Cien años de soledad* a focus on succeeding generations, those Babel-like dynasties which perpetuate failure and testify, without intention, to the tenacity of life. Rojas Herazo's novel catches our attention because, despite those deficiencies which are typical of an author's first novel, it excels in conveying the perception of the insufficiency – or irrelevance – of the notion of time – chronism. In fact, in this novel one finds an elaborate narrative in which time itself is a character. Silent and almost invisible, always present yet eternal, time is portrayed in the text as a voracious force that devours all which surrounds it, from human beings to building. But it is a magma, before which it is useless to differentiate between present, past or future, for it homogenizes all in the radiance of destruction and decadence. The temporal structure of Rojas Herazo's novel is altered in order to enhance the perception of time as an indifferent yet powerful magma. The chapters occur at different point along the familial genealogy; each chapter begins with a very specific reference to events in the life of the family. For instance, Chapter 7 begins, 'It was hardly a moment in that June of 1901 (sixteen years before meeting the man from Lebanon)' [*Fue apenas un instante de aquel junio de mil novecientos uno (diez y seis años antes de conocer al libanés)*] (p. 54), and Chapter 17 informs us that Celia, the matron, 'came to the village on the morning of 26 December 1861' [*llegó al pueblo la mañana del veintiseis de diciembre de mil ochocientos sesenta y uno*] (p. 129). Of Anselmo, a child who often serves as a focus of the narrative, we read that, while looking at the roof of his house, 'he prepared himself to face the pain, the destruction, and all the hieroglyphs that time was beginning to inscribe on a wall far beyond his soul' (p. 85).[13] Julia, an older, unwed daughter of the family, read parts of *The Iliad* to her enigmatic father while 'time, having become like the howling of the sea, tore the pages apart, pooled wells of grease beneath her eyelids, and noiselessly decayed the pink bands that hugged her waist' (p. 37).[14]

Rojas Herazo's novel floods the reader's consciousness with the idea that life has no ulterior meaning. Because of this, the reader can easily relate the void of life in Rojas Herazo's characters with those in Piñera's stories. In fact, this rejection of the eschatological is common to both writers, that is, the rejection of creating myths. It can be argued that the profound intensity with which Rojas presents this vision of life is one of the bitter achievements of the novel. Thus, for example, Celia says to Julia:

> 'Your father died first. I buried him and two more children, and I know full well that I'm going to bury this one' (pointing to Horacio, another of her sons). *Everything seems futile ... being born, having children, living, all is futile.* In anguish, she turned her gaze upward and asked, 'My God, why are You leading us on like this? Tell me, what do You want of us?'[15]

(1962: 148; emphasis added)

The narrator adds, 'it seemed to be the eternal image of eternal and human suffering; of the dereliction of all those who have suffered and chewed upon the clods of infinite moments' (p. 148).[16] Further on, Rojas writes 'the only thing that is clear is that we live and we don't know why we do it' [*lo único claro es que vivimos y no sabemos por qué lo hacemos*] (p. 171). At the conclusion of the novel, the narrator says of Eduviges, one of the female protagonists, that (p. 204):

> She felt time running through the hairs of her head, gently licking her cheeks, destroying them as it destroyed the foliage, the wire fencing, the shirts as they were hanging, the flecks of impudent light descending through the mesh of almond tree twigs.[17]

While Valerio, a child looking at the sea (ibid.),

> felt ... that Time had now grasped his arms, his eyes, his entire body, in order to burn for a minuscule fraction and would later continue on in its desolate journey, leaving him – whatever he was then – destroyed, confused, with his entrails ... like one more note in the impossible symphony of destruction and death.[18]

In conclusion, I would like to reiterate my point here: Piñera and Rojas Herazo share many common traits in their criticism of modernity – in fact, they are central to *our* criticism of modernity – especially in terms of criticizing the optimism of 'progress' and the promised redemption of man through science and technology. What Antoine Castagnon has called the 'Religion of Newness' is not for them. On the contrary, in their work modernity is not seen as a superior level or state, nor does it offer plenitude or satisfaction to mankind. For Virgilio Piñera and Héctor Rojas Herazo, modernity should be seen as a collective deception, another chimera, an intricate technological mirage that constantly reflects the void of our existences, disconnected and merely driven by chance. Seen from the vantage point of the years in which they were published, these works propose a serious reconsideration of the divergent national projects in Cuba and Colombia. Bearing in mind Roberto González Echevarria's helpful examination in Chapter 5 of this book of *Los pájaros en la playa*, a posthumous work by Severo Sarduy, Piñera and Rojas Herazo also presented a world which was a veritable dumping ground for the machine of progress, a world that documents the failure of the Enlightenment. Although Piñera and Rojas Herazo offer no antidote for such a painful lucidity, the experience of reading them certainly does bring the pleasure of catharsis.

Notes

1 For a survey of studies of Piñera's work, see García Chichester (1992).

2 *Criollismo* has been seen as a literary movement that sought to capture the cultural 'essence' of Latin America in the first decades of the century, displaying a nostalgia for an agrarian past in the midst of rapid economic expansion, and often overvaluing the autochthonous or 'primitive'. See Alonso (1996).

3 For example, Torres (1989), chooses to highlight black humour in her otherwise very useful essay. Peruvian critic José Miguel Oviedo (1992, vol. I: 341) characterizes Piñera as:

> Without doubt, one of the more unusual and surprising Cuban writers this century. ... In reality, Piñera is a forgotten forerunner of the literature of the absurd in Latin American, since he delved into the absurd a good ten years before it became popular everywhere, under the influence of European theatre.

4 See Menton (1978), Heller (1989), and also Williams (1991: 143–50).

5 *Sin huella, sin olor ... en un calendario indeciso que ella ... iba acumulando en convivencia con el sopor, los hálitos del patio, la isocronía de zapatos desanudados y vueltos a anudar entre el zumbido immemorial de su sangre inalterable.*

6 See Beckner (1967).

7 Shafer's 1987 translation of Piñera's collection of poems *Cuentosfrios* [Cold Tales].

8 *Mi única preocupación era no perder los ojos ... En cuanto a mi compañero, su única angustia era que su hermosa barba ... no llegase a la ilanura, ni siquiera ligeramente empolvada'* (Piñera 1956: 10).

9 *No se sabe de ninguna (cucaracha) que haya hecho algo constructivo; por el contrario, devoran todo lo que se pone a sue alcanc. Entonces, ¿para qué seguir luchando?* (Piñera 1956: 101)

10 *El azar ha querido que siempre, en el momento de pasar yo en mi cochecito, Pepe, girando en su cazuela, me dé la cara, lo cual nos obliga a un saludo ceremonioso.* Nuestras caras reflejan una evidente felicidad (Piñera 1956: 104, emphasis added).

11 See Curutchet (1972), especially Chapters 6 and 7.

12 This story is strangely absent from Schafer's 1987 translation [eds].

13   *El suceso en sí, comportaba en su cronicidad el mismo sabor de los sucesos cróni-cos ... porque de acuerdo con el hecho de que diariamente se fusila un hombre en punto cualquiera de la tierra, y de acuerdo igualmente con sus lecturas acerca de fusilados, se hacía necesario reconocer que la cosa era perfectamente natural y lógica; es decir, que ante el caso particular de su próxima ejecución no cabía alterarse o conmoverse, o hacer de ella un centro de universal atracción, ya que estas ejecuciones se sucedían en el tiempo y el espacio con la misma regularidad con que el día sucede la noche ... También ... supondría violencia quererla referir como cosa excepcional, pues el chino fusilado el dia anterior a miles de leguas, y el alemán, sacrificado el año anterior y todos los hombres fusilados hasta ese momento, morían con esa misma igualdad que muestran dos frescas salchichas gracias a la insensibilidad de un engranaje correctísimo* (Piñera 1956: 105).

14   *Se dispuso a enfrentarse al dolor, a la destrucción, a todos aquellos jeroglíficos que el tiempo empezaba a inscribir en un muro remoto más allá de su alma.*

15   *El tiempo, convertido en bramido de mar, deshacía las hojas, agolpaba bultos de grasa bajo sus párpados, y carcomía sin ruido los lazos rosados que aprisionaban su cintura.*

16   *– Tu padre murió primero. Yo lo enterré a él y a dos hijos más y sé muy bien que voy a enterrar a éste (señala a Horacio, otro hijo suyo). – Todo parece inútil ... nacer, tener hijos, vivir, todo es inútil.*

   Volvió su mirada con angustia hacia arriba ... e interrogó: – ¿Para qué nos traes, Dios Mío?, dime ¿qué quieres de nosotros?

17   *Parecía la imagen eterna del eterno y humano dolor; del desamparo de todos los que han padecido y mordido los terrones de infinitos instantes.*

18   *Sentía el tiempo atravesando sus cabellos, lamiendo suavemente sus pómulos, destruyéndolos como destruía los ramajes, los alambres, las camisas colgando, los flecos con que la luz, desgarrada, descendía por el palpitante varillaje de los almendros.*

19   *Sintió ... que el tiempo, que ahora había escogido sus brazos, sus ojos, su cuerpo entero, para arder en una minúscula fracción y luego reemprender su oscuro y desolado viaje dejándole a él – a lo que ahora era él – destruido, confundido con las raíces ... como un acorde más en la imposible sinfonía de destrucción y de muerte.*

<table><tr><td>14</td><td>

Little stories of Caribbean history and nationhood: Edgardo Rodríguez Juliá and Luís Rafael Sánchez

</td></tr></table>

John Perivolaris

> Doctrines pass, anecdotes remain.
>
> E.M. Cioran
>
> The past is unpredictable.
>
> Post-Cold War Russian saying

Perhaps when you do not have a country, you fall back on little stories: memories, customs, skills, rather than history; rituals of belonging that structure time hospitably in the absence of nation-statehood. Or, if we are talking about larger groups of people, rather than individuals and families, we might use the term nationhood rather than nationality.[1] I shall look at two important Puerto Rican writers' representations of rituals as forms of an informal Caribbean nationhood that emerges every day in the absence of nationality and challenges traditions of transcendental nationalism: Edgardo Rodríguez Juliá's 1984 narrative, 'El cruce de la Bahía de Guánica y otras ternuras de la medianía (25 de julio de 1983)' [The Crossing of Guánica Bay and Other Middle-Age Weaknesses (25 July 1983)], and Luis Rafael Sánchez's 1988 novel-length narrative text, *La importancia de llamarse Daniel Santos* [The Importance of Being Daniel Santos]; and I shall answer the question of what form such a challenge to tradition takes.[2]

History as a swimming race

Rodríguez Juliá's narrative chronicles the participation, on 25 July 1983, of a narrator closely associated with the writer himself in an annual swimming race across Guánica Bay. The date and place are significant since on the same day in 1898 and at the same place invading American troops first landed on the island and took over from the Spanish as the residing colonial power. Furthermore, on the same date are commemorated the Spanish feast day of Santiago, the anniversary of the founding in 1952 of Puerto Rico as an autonomous dependency of the United States, or Free Associated State, and the 1978 assassination of two political dissidents by Puerto Rican intelligence police at Cerro Maravilla. But it is also significant that, instead of joining a political rally held by the Socialists in commemoration of major historical events on the island, the narrator is there for the apparently more trivial reasons of proving his physical prowess at the verge of middle age and of camaraderie with an American companion who joins him. The historical and political concerns of the Socialist rally seem peripheral to or at best just one manifestation of a Puerto Rican nationhood perhaps impossible to unify and define. Indeed, a large proportion of the text is devoted to describing the confusing convergence on the town of cheerleaders' parades, motorcycle and go-kart clubs, child beauty queen pageants, beach excursionists, and sizzling food stalls. Certainly the solemn desire of obeying the call of history on the part of the Socialists is undermined by the myriad little stories of Puerto Ricanness the narrator observes throughout the piece. Also, the narrator's encounters with heroic figures who have played a significant role in Puerto Rican history are resolutely quotidianized, as when, answering the call of nature, he bumps into Juan Antonio Corretjer, a major poet and independentist, in the inauspicious setting of a restaurant toilet.

In his classic essay of 1960, 'El puertorriqueño dócil' [The Docile Puerto Rican], the writer René Marqués concluded that it was a sense of heroic self-immolation in the name of a desperate nationalism that definitively exemplified, and was a compensatory reaction against, the nihilistic docility as well as guilt of a nation which had been frustrated in its attempts to achieve political integrity (1977c: 161–9). On the other hand, most of Rodríguez Juliá's *crónica* is taken up with the quotidian survival of most Puerto Ricans, rather than self-sacrifice, and with all the ambiguities that colonial survival entails; its compromises and modest glories.

That clear-cut divisions between, and affiliations amongst, colonizer and colonized are problematic is illustrated by the central, ironically symbolic, relationship between the narrator of Rodríguez Juliá's text and an older, at times paternal, American friend, Bill Kronyck, who accompanies him on the swim. Theirs is a suitably difficult friendship, founded on genuine loyalty, dependence, hostility and mutual dispossession. Narrated from an individualized perspective, nationality is transformed here from a birthright to a conflictive state of being, whilst this transformation allows the pairing of the two protagonists. Storyck is a Jewish-American anti-hero, or '*yudken* errante' (p. 14), whose unsettled state is suggested by his loneliness, two divorces, and subsequent alcoholism. But Bill's diasporic unsettlement is also quintessentially Puerto Rican and unites him with his friend. His very Puerto Rican Jewishness is indicated by the fact that the narrator comments on his exceptional grasp of Puerto Rican Spanish (p. 15). Such mutual identification accompanies an account of affecting anti-heroism. If nationalism in Puerto Rico has always demanded suicidal self-sacrifice, the two swimmers are physically marked as unglamorous survivors. As well as participating in a type of swimming competition reserved for failed pool swimmers in their forties and fifties (p. 31) the narrator wears contact lenses under his goggles and is almost not allowed to participate because of high blood pressure. Meanwhile, the ageing Storyck's stoicism is etched on 'that face criss-crossed with lines and wounds, broken loyalties with nation and family' [*esa cara cruzada de líneas, heridas, lealtades rotas con nación y familia*] (p. 33). The final prize of such tenacity? A swimming cup made of brass.

But whilst the narrator feels an affinity with Storyck, 'the slight Jew with the sad eyes' [*el judiíto de los ojos tristes*] (p. 14), the kindly and diminutive outsider, his rivalry with Bill the Yankee allows him to act out his love-hate relationship with America in bitter contest. When the narrator states that 'the subtext is clearly understood; for two consecutive years we have crossed the bay of the *americanos*' [*Las claves se entienden; por dos años consecutivos hemos cruzado la bahía de* los americanos] (p. 27), he recognizes that the race is a knotty metaphor for his and Storyck's equivocal relationship to the Americans. The race becomes an act of personal loyalty between friends, one of symbolic historical revenge on the part of two unsettled ethnicities, as well as the re-enactment of colonial conflict between a Puerto Rican and an American. In the middle of the race, the narrator is overwhelmed by an irrationally violent competitiveness against Storyck that shocks him (p. 39). But whilst he states that, at that moment, he wished to 'knock his rival's block off' [*tumbarle la cabeza*], he is held back by 'our somewhat comical loyalty' [*nuestra algo cómica lealtad*] (ibid.), as he becomes aware of the absurdity of grown men in competition.

Following this return to a sense of human mortality, vanity, limitations and compassion, is a detailed and subjective description of the swim through an account of the physical sensations the narrator experiences. Guánica becomes the swimmer's 'metaphor of *my* salvation' [*metáfora de* mi *salvación*] (p. 30), rather than a site of national salvation; a debt of loyalty to a friend and 'an increasingly intimate adventure' [*una aventura cada vez más íntima*] (ibid.). Therein, the material passing of an ageing body's time supplants the abstract passage of history. Meanwhile, as the narrator approaches the coast of Guánica he enjoys the same view as the American invaders; with patriotic emotions that are, however, those of a lonely swimmer who recognizes the beloved roofs of houses he knows. Not for him the appeals to national solidarity of Puerto Rican nationalism. Waiting with the unruly crowds of Puerto Ricans before the race, he confesses that 'I am drawn again to misanthropy' [*me inclino de nuevo a la misantropía*] (p. 30). Nationhood for him cannot be defined by proximity, boundaries and frontiers, spurious anyway in the case of Puerto Rico, virtually half of whose population lives in the United States, but emerges out of the connections and conflicts afforded by personal ritual rather than political allegiance.[3]

History as a song

In Luis Rafael Sánchez's *La importancia de llamarse Daniel Santos*, the idealized collectivity of nationalism is replaced by a Puerto Rican communality that is distinctively both part of a greater Latin Americanism and a dynamic agent of the inevitable divisions of national identity. Travelling to several Latin American towns and cities, a narrator carries out research and interviews fans of the bolero singer Daniel Santos, as part of an investigation into the legend of the historical Puerto Rican artist.

By using a series of popular vernaculars in his chronicle of first-hand reports, the narrator gives free rein to a barrage of enjoyably coarse language, sexual imagery, and an admiring portrayal of Daniel's monumental machismo (for example Sánchez 1988: 124–9, 134–5), all of which have angered some critics.[4] However, I believe that, in fact, the author expresses his sympathies with what, through a low-life brazenness (p. 135), opposes oppressive social inequality and the entrenched official culture that upholds it (pp. 82–3, 109–10). As a popular hero, Daniel, 'the Bohemian …, the Cocksman …, the Disobedient' [*el Bohemio …, el Jodedor …, el Desobediente*] (p. 110), offends by not lending himself to assimilation into the easy categories of conventional virtue misrepresented by corrupt politicians and the exploitative privileged classes to which they belong (ibid.). Moreover, as a mulatto 'outlaw legend' [*mito cimarrón*] (p. 134), Daniel offends the bourgeois myth of *criollo* virtues traditionally promoted by elite powers in Puerto Rico.[5]

Though Sánchez's novel has been accused of deploying a distorting Caribbean masculinity (Figueroa 1989: 198), I believe that his recourse to stereotypes with powerful resonances constitute a strategically offensive position from which to attack the conventional nationalist messianism of Puerto Rican paternalism (Gelpí 1993: 20–5) and the supposedly virtuous *machismo* traditionally promoted by revered writers such as René Marqués. In the same essay I mentioned earlier, Marqués argued that Puerto Ricans' supposed feminine docility, attributed in large part by him to the Anglo-Saxon importation of a supposedly matriarchal social model, should be countered by a patriotic return to the masculine values rooted in a Hispanic tradition: 'Spanish *honra* and the Roman *pater familiae* [sic]' [*la* honra *española y el* pater familiae *romano*] (1977c: 175). That Marqués should condemn modern Puerto Ricans' rejection of tradition has as much to do with certain class affiliations as with a supposed anti-colonialism. Following the 1898 defeat of the Spanish in the Spanish-American War, US colonialism seemed to provide a relatively more liberal framework in comparison with conditions under Spanish rule.[6] Consequently, greater rights, accompanied by growing social mobility for Puerto Rican women and recently emancipated Blacks, as well as the consolidation of emerging working and non-landowning professional classes, constituted a modernizing transformation of social hierarchies. In reaction to the burgeoning freedoms of the groups above, Marqués dismisses their understandable pro-Americanism by attributing it to a reaction against the traditional authoritarianism of Spanish rule (1977: 166n.27). This justified reaction has, according to Marqués, led these groups to be blinded to the injustices of American society (pp. 166–7). With respect to this assertion, Arcadio Díaz Quiñones has observed (1985: 40–4) the unfavourable portrayal of conditions in the US, as compared to those on the island, was a discursive commonplace of a formerly semi-feudal *criollo* elite which attempted to refute the popular classes' antithetically favourable predisposition to the tenets of American egalitarianism.[7]

Clearly, Sánchez's Daniel constitutes a humorous vulgarization of the supposedly noble virility – rooted in a Golden Age or Classical Arcadia – Marqués believed was necessary in the emasculating context of modernizing American colonialism. Meanwhile, Sánchez's concern with bad language, gross sexuality and *machismo* is far from gratuitous. Instead, in ironic dialogue with Marqués, the book portrays a form of popular self-assertion taking the form of histrionic sexual aggression.[8] This *machismo* attempts to compensate for the degrading status of Latin American men who, as third-world, colonized, or tentatively democratized subjects of, in all cases, economically dependent nations, are incapable of measuring up to Marqués's nostalgic and imperially masculine ideal.[9] The singer's *machista* prowess is commemorated by the narrator as a series of tales recounted to him in accompaniment to Daniel's songs (Sánchez 1988:

123), which are heard in countless Latin American bars and billiard halls (pp. 122–3, 124–6). The stage thus set, Sánchez goes on to examine the portrayal of penises in literature and film, from Herodotus (p. 127) to *Empire of the Senses* (p. 128). What takes the place of inaccessible first-world or bourgeois authority is 'a dictatorially absolutist text totalized by the dick and the testicles' [*un texto dictador y absolutista (que) totalizan el güevo y los textículos*] (ibid.). Thus, by highlighting *machismo* as but one, mostly oral, version of a series of cultural texts, histrionic *machista* arrogance is deflated by a pun that underscores *machismo* as a text of economic and political impotence rather than as an unconquerable essence. After all, what does the repetition of the following passage betray if not the haunting desire to keep up a constantly embattled Latin American machismo (p. 126)?:

> To look a man is to fondle militantly one's dick with the various names of offensive instruments – machete, awl, sword of honour, sabre, bludgeon, rod, bar, cudgel, truncheon, prick, harpoon, black beauty, club, bayonet, bat, stake, mallet, sledgehammer, destroyer.[10]

Furthermore, it is clear that an exclusively heterosexual reading is untenable. Certainly, the exhaustive assertion of male physicality may also be read as a homoerotic discourse, where masculinity is staged, takes place and is imitated in all-male environments (pp. 125–6), as a baroque display of *machismo*. Such seductively coded exhibitionism between men is at the very least sexually ambiguous.[11] If, as the narrator informs us, male friendships are defined by a terse restraint from affection (p. 125), 'to look a man demands a rudimentary form of performance' [*parecer varón instruye un histrionismo rudimental*] (pp. 125–6). Therefore:

> If the curve to the nipples shows off the athletic triumphs of the pectorals the shirt is half opened down to the chest. If a rampant hairiness covers the chest, the shirt is unbuttoned down to the navel. If the track of veins between the wrist and elbow show that one is pumping a lot of iron the sleeves are rolled up. If the tightness of one's underpants outlines a worthy size of dick the shirt is tied up in a knot around the waist.[12]

From the reading of Sánchez's novel I have undertaken here I would say that, in his portrayal of popular culture as a defiantly unifying Latin Americanism, he avoids the pitfalls of nationalist authoritarianism, This he achieves by, amongst other means, portraying a positive popular assertiveness that is, firstly, undercut by being identified as a histrionic reaction to the vagaries of oppressive Caribbean and Latin American history. Secondly, the gendered, sexualized nature of popular culture as a disputable space is underlined by the deflation of masculinist terms through possible homoerotic readings of Latin American *machismo*.

However, Sánchez does not fully trust the informal nationhood he recognizes in *La importancia*. In his 1997 essay, 'No llores por nosotros Puerto Rico' [*Don't Cry for Us, Puerto Rico*], he rejects 'postmodernism's' downgrading of nationalism and, by implication a contemporary post-nationalist renovation of Puerto Rican historiography and other intellectual discourses that has attempted to present a more complex picture of Puerto Ricans' affiliations, and in which, paradoxically, he and Rodríguez Juliá have been major figures. They both join others, such as the intellectual historian, Arcadio Díaz Quiñones (1984, 1992, 1993, 1994), the cultural critic, Juan Flores (1993), the writer and literary historian, José Luis González (1989a), the writer and biographer, César Andreu Iglesias (1977), the feminists, Edna Acosta Belén (1980) and Yamila Azize Vargas (1987), and social historians, Angel G. Quintero Rivera (1979, 1986, 1988) and Virginia E. Sánchez Korrol (1993). In opposition to a traditionally nationalist conviction that the modernizing aftermath of 1898 had constituted an emasculating alienation of Puerto Rican society from its essentially Spanish identity, the contemporary intellectuals I have mentioned see their society not as an essence to be defended but as a dynamic complex of class relations. For them, by accelerating the decline of a semi-feudal, and ostensibly white, ruling *criollo* class, North American colonization and its accompanying industrialization gave voice to the previously silenced majority.[13] Countering the traditional elitism of previous Puerto Rican intellectuals, who believed that the very heterogeneity of Puerto Rican society required enlightened leadership from a few great men (Díaz Quiñones 1984: 24–7), this new wave has given rise to a series of biographies and studies of the non-elite classes, the role of women, black Puerto Ricans, and Puerto Ricans' role in a broader Caribbean and Latin American diaspora. The focus of the most recent discussion has broadened to include reflection on sexuality and youth. Such a wide-angle, post-nationalist view is represented by the 1997 study, *Puerto Rican Jam: Essays on Culture and Politics*, edited by Frances Negrón Muntaner and Ramón Grosfoguel.

In the essay mentioned above, Sánchez writes of the necessity, in the face of colonialism, of the nation as a unifying popular culture and shared history (1997b: 208–11):

The nation as a necessity. And a recognition of the necessity of the nation, which postmodern dissolution degrades and theories of the end of history interpret as more pseudo-mystical gibberish. ...

Within the nation converge the bitter sweetness of self-discovery, faces bound together by a series of dates and memories, those experiences which are filtered, sharpened, and woven together over the years like marks of identity. Marks which are shared and recuperated through culture. And here, what I am talking about is everyday street culture without frills. ...

Puerto Ricans respect the American flag but embrace the Puerto Rican flag. Puerto Ricans mouth the American national anthem but sing the Puerto Rican national anthem. Puerto Ricans evaluate American citizenship as the product of a fruitful economic treaty but value Puerto Rican nationality as an essence that is impossible to suppress or subordinate.[14]

Also, in another essay, 'Abrazos, prejuicios y fronteras' [Embraces, Prejudices and Frontiers] (p. 33) [*Puerto Rico tiene un rostro único*], he asserts that 'Puerto Rico has a single face'. In fact, the tension I gauge in this essay relates to, on the one hand, the representation of little stories by both authors as the affirmation of a political attitude and the obligation to appeal to the traditional terms of nationalism, still occasionally in evidence in Sánchez's recent work.[15]

Class is at the centre of global Marxist concerns whereas, in the work of several, if not all, postmodernist theorists class dovetails into and is often superseded by questions of race, gender and sexuality. In this way class becomes only one amongst several elements that fluidly define the specifically located individual or social group.[16] The essays I have mentioned certainly express the Marxist concerns of Sánchez's generation, who reached maturity in the 1960s, in the aftermath of the Cuban Revolution. But these concerns coincide uneasily with conservative Puerto Rican debates about, for example, gender and nationalism, as well as Sánchez's own experience as a working-class mulatto who has come up in the world and who has to navigate the difficult route between the disparate locations he occupies as an Afro-Puerto Rican patriot speaking from a platform that has not traditionally represented the interests of those of his background.[17] This may also explain his occasional backsliding into the nationalist essentialism of the passage above and its approxima-tion to traditional attitudes relating to an authoritatively defensive posture towards Puerto Rican national culture. The latter posture elides the historically generated, black working-class consciousness Sánchez expresses so powerfully in his novel *La importancia de llamarse Daniel Santos*. The fact that such discontinuity occurs in his essays but not in the development of his other work may be a result of writing in a genre that traditionally would attempt to speak transparently in the writer's voice on issues he addressed directly.[18] Therefore, essay writing may reveal more of the writer's uncertainties and divided loyalties. Indeed, it is only the more openly mediated character of fiction and drama that permits Sánchez sufficient dissociation to be able to put these divisions into ironical play in his more dispassionate non-essay work.[19]

Conclusion

It is clear by now that the informal nationhood depicted by the two writers emerges out of a complex dialogue with traditional nationalism, even, in Sánchez's case, an occasional espousal of it, where critique alternates with the obligation to assume the role of a heroic nationalist intellectual. Meanwhile, in both texts, the form of such a dialogue is ritual. And of what does ritual consist if not, simultaneously, actions presided over by authority and actions involving an obsessively informal return to the site and time of trauma with the intention of healing it? In Rodríguez Juliá's narrative text, it is a return to Guánica and the primal scene of 1898; in Sánchez's novel, one to the embattled virility of Caribbean nationalism. In both cases, a dynamically heterogeneous personal as well as popular memory forms the delicate scar tissue that holds Puerto Rican nationhood together.

Notes

1 In later essays, Luis Rafael Sánchez underlines the spontaneous, rather than formally political affiliation entailed by such nationhood when he equates national identity with 'an emotive convergence' [*una convergencia emotiva*] and 'the instinct of belonging' [*el instinto de pertenencia*] (1997b: 208).
2 The following studies of Rodríguez Juliá's work are recommended: Duchesne Winter (1993), Duchesne Winter *et al.* (1992), Gelpí (1993: 45–60), González (1991), Ortega (1991b). Two of the most interesting interviews with this writer are collected in Ortega (1991c). For studies of Sánchez's work, consult Perivolaris (1997).

3   In another book (1989c), Rodríguez Juliá reflects on national history through discussion of a series of family snapshots and others' personal photographs he has found or collected.

4   For example Alvarado *et al.* (1989).

5   González (1989b: 26–9, 35–9; 1989c: 63–4, 73–6).

6   On this point see Carrión (1993: 69–71), González (1989: 27–8, 32–6), Grosfoguel (1995: 6–7), Mattos Cintrón (1993: 201–3), and Scarano (1993: 612–14, 636–42, 649–54). More recently, the work of Kelvin A. Santiago-Valles (1994: 49–62, 204–6) qualifies this view. He suggests that, though by associating themselves with reformist North American movements the groups I have mentioned could claim rights they had never had before, living conditions for most Puerto Ricans during the first decades of North American colonialism were the same, only marginally better, or even worse than before. New rights of expression (Santiago-Valles 1994: 112–15, 119), including eventually the vote for women (Scarano 1993: 654), took place within the context of what Santiago-Valles calls the 'dispossession' of Puerto Ricans in relation to 'inordinately brutal and excruciating' socioeconomic changes (1994: 51, 53–4). Through the establishment of a capitalist system, these substantially deprived Puerto Ricans of the mutual support structures (ibid.: 31, 39) and intimate trade relations of rural pre-capitalism (Scarano 1993: 612).

7   On the other hand, there might be some truth in Eduardo Seda Bonilla's assertion, cited by Zenón Cruz (1974–5, vol 1: 126), that blacks' unprecedented political representation was only made possible by the ironically egalitarian North American assumption that all Puerto Ricans were racially inferior. Hence, the predominance of the degraded *criollo* classes was no longer clear-cut, since in North American eyes they were merely more fully reformed versions of the potentially reformable inferiors in their charge.

8   '*El machismo a todo tren*' [breakneck *machismo*] (Sánchez 1988: 123).

9   Marqués's nostalgic *machismo* is discussed by Barradas (1977). Gelpí (1986) examines Sánchez's confrontation with Marqués's work.

10 *Parecer varón es lisonjearse, belicosamente, el güevo con los nombres variados de instrumentos contusos – la daga, la lezna, el espadín, el sable, el tolete, el jierro, la vara, la tranca, la porra, el cipote, la fisga, el marrón, la macana, la bayoneta, el bate, la estaca, la maceta, el macetón, el* destroyer.

11 Such ambiguity is already present in Sánchez's first novel *La guaracha del Macho Camacho* (1976), as has been pointed out by Efraín Barradas (1981: 141–2 n. 8). On the other hand, the homoerotic display of *La importancia* reconciles *machismo* with homosexuality in a way that circumvents Barradas's discussion (1977: 75) of *machismo*'s exclusion of homosexuality: 'The homosexual, more than the female, is the essential anti-macho. The macho fully reveals himself when he subdues and impregnates the female' [*El homosexual, más que la hembra, es el anti macho esencial. El macho se manifiesta plenamente cuando subyuga y fecunda a la hembra*]. Furthermore, if this is so, what of the non-homosexual machismo attached, in Mexico and Nicaragua, to the active sexual role in male sexual relations that involve an assertion of masculinity?

12 *Si el voladizo de las tetillas configura los triunfos atléticos de los pectorales la camisa se entreabre en los pezones. Si una rampante vellosidad ocupa el pecho la camisa se desabotona hasta el ombligo. Si el tendito de venas entre las muñecas y los codos revela que se está dando duro a las pesas la camisa se arremanga. Si la justedad del calzón perfila el tamaño responsable del güevo la camisa se anuda en la cintura.*

13   See Díaz Quiñones (1985: 25, 34, 72–76), Grosfoguel *et al.* (1997: 4–8), Jiménez Muñoz (1997).

14   *La nación como una necesidad. Ese reconocimiento de la necesidad de la nación, que las disoluciones posmodernas peyoratizan y las teorías del fin de la historia interpretan como otra babosada telúrica.* ...

   En la nación convergen la agridulzura del propio descubrimiento, los rostros encadenados por unas fechas y unos recuerdos, las experiencias que los años filtran, precisan y tejen cual señas de identidad. Unas señas que se esparcen, que se recuperan en la cultura. Hablo de la cultura callejera, corriente y sin elaborar. ...

   Los puertorriqueños respetan la bandera norteamericana pero se abrazan a la bandera puertorriqueña. Los puertorriqueños tararean el himno nacional norteamericano pero cantan el himno nacional puertorriqueño. Los puertorriqueños evalúan la ciudadanía norteamericana como el producto de un benéfico tratado económico pero valoran la nacionalidad puertorriqueña como una esencia de imposibles supresión o subalternidad.

15   Sánchez's attack on 'postmodernism' and 'post-nationalism' may be associated with that of Coss (1996). Coss does not reject outright the validity of postmodernist criticism. Rather, his work is like Sánchez's essay, critical of a 'pessimist' strand of postmodernism that, according to Coss, declares the obsolescence of faith in modernization, historical progress, ideologies and nation-statehood.

16   See Hutcheon (1988: 12, 59, 61–9, 85–6, 134–5, 165–7, 172–7, 195–6, 198–200, 214, 216–17). On the different perspectives of Marxist and postmodern or postcolonial criticism, see Bhabha (1994). On the hostility felt in black quarters, especially by women, towards postmodernism as the movement of a white, male, intellectual elite, see the sceptical essay by bell hooks (1994). See also Waugh (1992) for feminism as a qualified postmodern practice, which attempts to undermine the legitimation of patriarchy and its adherence to supposedly universal truths, whilst at the same time seeking legitimation itself by appealing to freedom, justice and progress.

17   On this aspect of Sánchez's life, see Vázquez Arce (1994: 221–2). On Sánchez's affiliation to the political and intellectual upheavals of the 1960s, see Vázquez Arce (1994: 16).

18   Bringing into the foreground the writer's supposedly authentic voice is frequently signalled by the editorial decision, on the part of the newspapers and magazines that have published many of Sánchez's essays, also to publish accompanying photographs or sketches of the writer. On this point, also see González Echevarría (1985: 16).

19   I deal in greater detail with both *La importancia de llamarse Daniel Santos* and Sánchez's essays, in respective chapters of my forthcoming monograph on the writer's work, entitled *Puerto Rican Cultural Identity and the Work of Luis Rafael Sánchez* (Chapel Hill: North Carolina Studies in the Romance Languages and Literatures).

15

Some critical observations on the cult of María Lionza in contemporary Venezuelan narrative

Lancelot Cowie

I

Venezuelan narrative has always been a fertile repository of spiritual folk-lore, the customs, idiosyncrasies, varying popular beliefs and the magical cosmovision of the people. These visions have been evident in Venezuelan novels from their very origins. In this context, the works of Rómulo Gallegos, particularly *Doña Bárbara* (1929) and *Cantaclaro* (1934), Angel S. Domínguez, *La mojiganga* [The masquerade] (1938) and *El haíton de los coicoyes* [Nest of the Firebirds] (1960), Ramón Diaz Sánchez, *Cumboto* (1920), some works of Guillermo Meneses: *El falso cuaderno de Narciso Espejo* [Narcissus Mirror's Apocryphal Notebook] (1952), *La Misa de Arlequín* [Harlequin's Mass] (1962) and *Diez Cuentos* [Ten Tales] (1968); and Ramón Bravo, *Sobre algún techo comenzará la guerra* [On Some Roof the War Will Start] (1974) stand out.

The magi-religious mosaic is very broad. It embraces daily prayers, incantations, crosses of Blessed Palms, the Way of the Cross, the *Salve* to Saint Isidro, the Saint's Day, the Rosary of the Cross, devotion to Our Lady, fortune-telling, witchcraft, imps, the suffering souls, birds of ill omen, legends, and fortune-telling with cards. All these practices inevitably lead us to ask the question: Why do these kinds of beliefs persist in a society that is so highly developed economically and scientifically? Elena Dorante, referring to the evolution of the magi-religious in Venezuela explains (1981: 170):

> The human reality is, as Jung's study of symbols has shown, mythical-magical, and from this essentially human authentic-ity, man manufactures archetypal images that personify the patrimony of all times and places.

> Mankind needs to maintain some contact with his archetypal images in order to preserve his mental sanity. He cannot be completely rational. He cannot break away completely from the world of magic, mysticism and religion without becoming neurotic.[2]

I would add that spiritual-mental folklore is an important characteristic of the Venezuelan idiosyncrasy. The Catholic Church plays a major role in the promotion of popular Venezuelan culture. All the agricultural festivals and other bring together the elements of Catholic ritual, whether the veneration of the saints or devotion to the Virgin Mary.[3] According to Alí González (1992), 94.2 per cent of the festivals are predominantly Catholic. The history of Marian worship in Latin America dates from the sixteenth century (see Clissold 1972: 123).

If we take a brief look at the works of two Venezuelan authors – José Fabbiani Ruíz and Julián Padrón – we see the fervour that devotion to the Virgin Mary stirs up among the faithful. In Fabbiani Ruíz's short story, 'Una historia vulgar' [A Vulgar Story], the focus is somewhat novel. Francisco Maimone is in financial difficulty and cannot support his household. His conjugal life has become cold, he is suffering from severe depression and seeks refuge by adoring Our Lady of Carmen. She becomes the reflection of his melancholy, of his illusory love (Fabbiani Ruíz 1940: 182–3):

> Today, I did not light a candle to the Virgin of Carmen … . a few moments later, the candle blazed. Time has faded the Virgin; she no longer has a nose, the only remnant of all of her splendour is her eyes. Oh! The eyes of the Virgin! If only she were of flesh and blood, how I would adore her. I would throw myself at her feet, kiss her wonderful eyes. I would embrace her, I would embrace her, I would embrace her … The candle crackled as always. The Virgin looks at me with her beautifully sad eyes, with a sadness that spans centuries … , unconsciously I threw a shoe at the Virgin's candle. Her eyes shone and then were plunged into darkness. I love this woman, I have dreamt of her many times, until I possessed her with the sweetest of possessions. I remember her body, her white flesh, tender yet firm at the same time.[4]

Beyond this story line, there is an implicit message, man creates his own sanctuary to cushion the blows of life.

In *Este mundo desolado* [This Desolate World], Julián Padrón portrays (1957: 1573–4) the Christian-pagan veneration of the Virgin of the Valley:

The merriment over, they went to the square to give thanks
to the Virgin ... the clamour of men, women and children,
the blowing of horns and shells, the pounding of *chicoras* on
the earthen trenches, the usual aggressive prayers in their
grateful voices, is transformed into a song to the Virgin:

> God of the Fields, we give you thanks.
> Evil Spirit, go hang yourself on a tree.
> Virgin of the Valley, shelter me in your bosom.
> Jesus, Our Hope, watch over your flock.[5]

II

When we examine the narrative of the 1960s, we find the same tendency towards religious worship – the veneration of a goddess called
Reina María Lionza. This cult originated in the Yaracuy State and is
concentrated in the Sorte mountains, Agua Blanca and the suburbs of
Caracas and Valencia.

This cult is distinguished from others by its syncretism as Juan
Liscano (1992) points out:

> María Lionza, mother of the aboriginal waters, syncretised
> her ... image in the typically Spanish beauty of Empress
> Eugenia Montijo, wife of Napoleon III. Nowadays, the cult
> of María Lionza is an immense blend
> of acculturation, some of Venezuelan origin, others redolent
> of Cuban santería ritual, some of Yoruba traditions, the
> Shango religion and elements of these found their way
> into the English speaking Caribbean: Haitian voodoo with
> its symbolic drawings, fragmentary practices of Spiritism,
> Buddhism and Fakirism brought by Trinidad coolies or
> travelling gurus, disjointed readings culled from witchcraft
> magazines and manuals.[6]

In Venezuela, cult worship lent itself to sensationalism and spread to
all social sectors, spreading even farther through the press and literature. I think that the phenomenon requires a systematic analysis, given
its recurrence in literature, music and folklore.

In this chapter, I will try to explain briefly the special characteristics of the themes in order to determine
   a) the literary scope of the cult;
   b) the particular focus of the author;
   c) the anthropological bases of the practice of these cults.

I have chosen the following novels for study: José Vincente Abreu's *Las 4 letras* [The 4 Letters] (1969), Adriano González León's *País portátil* [Portable Country] (1969), and Carlos Noguera's *Inventando los días* [Inventing the Days] (1979); as well as Vladimiro Rivas' *Las huellas crecen así* [Tracks Grow Like That] (1972), Alfredo Armas Alfonso's *El Osario de Dios* [The Charnel-House of God] (1969), and the short story 'Las aguas profundas de su cuerpo' [The Deep Waters of her Body] (1980), by Julio Jáuregui. The selection is based on the extent of religious elements that recur in the selected works.

In *Inventando los Días,* religious fervour is demonstrated in the veneration of chosen saints. Mario's mother seeks the intercession of St Theresa, Nena has recourse to Santa Rita de Casia and invokes San Marcos de León in particular circumstances. However, it is La Reina María Lionza who plays the major role in the fiction. Carmen prays to 'the image bathed in golden light and precious stone inlay that was leaning against the little wooden box and she offers La Reinita meat, rice and cheese in exchange for the safety of her husband' (Noguera 1979: 153).[7] These prayers of petition bring together the fundamental aspects of the cult, such as the use of tobacco and invocation of auxiliary figures: Guaicaipuro, Negro Felipe. And they emphasize the extent of the miraculous powers attributed to La Reina (ibid.):

> 'You, O Reina, who know the destiny and who could illumi-
> nate the darkness with a light a thousand times brighter than
> the Star of Bethlehem, because Christ willed it thus ... You,
> who with a single caress of your immaculate hands could rid
> the body of evil spirits, relieve suffering, and heal the sick
> because Christ ordered that it be so: You, who have the grace
> and the cooperation of the powerful Guaiacaipuro, ... of
> Negro Felipe ... the seven African potencies'. She took
> tobacco from the pockets of her gown ... smoking away
> while she held a candle ... and the smoke rose and escaped
> through the vent of the hut.[8]

The apotheosis of María Lionza in Julio Jáuregui's 'Las aguas profundas de su cuerpo' heightens the religious experience with a poetic tone and magical resonance. The healer intervenes to soothe the pain of the peasant, Manuel, who is a victim of his wife's infidelity. He prescribes an esoteric pharmacopoeia and proceeds to invoke La Reina and all the saints of Venezuela, in what seems to be an ironic reference to the ineffectiveness of these divine forces (p. 60):

'In the name of Almighty God and Reina Lionza! I offer you the smoke from this tobacco so that evil spirits will disappear in the magical, delirious night and so that the Reina Corazonada would appear on the eternal pulpit, bringing happiness in this gloomy house where mistaken and treacherous tongues try to divert the rain and sow darkness in beauty's reflection. Ah! Ah! Ah!, with God I wake up, with God, I rise, Miraculous and All-powerful Reina and your Heavenly Court! Show yourself, Invincible Guaiacaipuro, San Juan Retornado, Santa María de la Cabeza, Anima del desertor de Güigüe, Bountiful Negro Felipe, Eternal Father and Divine Son, San Benito del Sacrificio Reservado, Santa Teresa Bendita, Divino San Isidro Labrador, Santo Niño de Atocha, Radiant Virgin of Coromoto, la Niña Guillermina, and San Marcos de León, remove the blood and stones of evil … through the intercession of the Three Cosmic Potencies! May they protect you, cure you, cleanse you'.[9]

The young boy who finds out about the extra-marital affairs of his mother rejects the power of the statue of La Reina (p. 61): 'You let that eye of yours watch over the altar amidst candles and prayers but it was that same static and mute eye that could not follow her into the forest, into the cane field, under the bridge'.[10] The boy invokes María Lionza as an ally of vengeance when he strikes down the adulteress (p. 62):

'Give me the strength I need to bury this pile of ashes and stinking bones, nothing can interrupt this holy plan of the hunter of the ungodly. Hyena of darkness and disgrace; from the tower of my strength, for my father and for the Holy Trinity, we have to make you pay for all the Crowns of Thorns you have sown in our way, open your legs and howl in pain because this Apocalyptic bull is going to leave you pinned to the ground.

– Twenty eight slashes, inspector,
and six deep wounds, three
of them deadly.'[11]

The veneration of María Lionza is not limited to the altar in the home. The spontaneous invocation of the goddess produces a humorous effect in other literary contexts. Enrique Lafourcade relates, in *Tres terroristas* [Three Terrorists] (1976: 100–1), the story of Argenis Vizcana Capproni, a Venezuelan terrorist who while fleeing from helicopters tracking him down, encounters an imaginary snake. On discovering that it is only the dried skin of a snake, he invokes

María Lionza in thanksgiving. 'It's a miracle! I will take flowers and money and some cigars to María Lionza! I was going to do so when I reached Caracas! You saved me María Lionza, you saved your little brother!'[12]

During the interrogation of a prisoner in Marcial Rodríguez's *Relatos de la Revolución* [Tales of the Revolution] (1976 : 62), the leader of the captors sarcastically appeals to María Lionza : 'You should talk, the era of heroes is passed, do you want to become another pin-up? In any case, we'll give you a good bath in cold water and see if the evil spirits leave you, perhaps, María Lionza will open your mind'.

Equally humorous and in an erotic vein is the description, in Adriano González León's *País portátil* (1969: 178), of a statue erected to La Reina in an area of the city where traffic is very heavy:

> It is important to clarify that the statue is an object of swift worship: thousands of vehicles fill her concrete breasts with smoke. The woman rides an elk, as a symbol of ancient freedom. However, they still burn flowers there. Patiently, María Lionza's devotees burn sperm. Some simple but mischievous souls say that at night, when the moon is full, Reina Mora gallops up the highway, bestowing on them fruits and ropes, the best way of getting a woman.[14]

The insipid humour of a policeman is easily perceived in the following passage of José Vincente Abreu's *Las 4 letras* (1969: 201):

> The old woman told me she was certain that the world was going to end on the tenth of November, that I had to get tough with María Lionza that night and ask her permission to move us to an altar, but María Lionza came in the form of a girl who had drunk two bottles of rum and five cans of water and she slept with me in Los Teques and then I found out next morning that it was my mother-in-law and I hit her with the baton … until my brother-in-law arrived and put two plantain branches on my wrists.[15]

The Lionza cult is intermingled with Devotion to Our Lady. In Carlos Noguera's *Inventando los días* (1979: 167), the Virgin is venerated – in a humorous fashion – in the prosaic precinct of a night club:

> La Chinita invoked Our Lady of Coromoto and, in her failed attempt to make the sign of the cross, spilt her rum and Coca-Cola on Zambrano's lap. 'Here's to you!' exclaimed la Negra,

making the most of cleaning her lover. 'Don't you like the place?' she said, passing a paper napkin to him.[16]

In *Las 4 letras* (137–8), Our Lady of Coromoto vies with a trophy (with the National Coat of Arms), to cover a crack in a hut in the suburbs of Caracas. The juxtaposition of these objects in an atmosphere of violence and poverty underlines the value the Virgin has among her followers. The quotation portrays the dilemma while the underlying humour is achieved with a play on the *coromoto*.

She has a statue of Our Lady of Coromoto in her room and next to it – but in the centre of the wall – he has his turtle shell with the National Coat of Arms and its large cornucopias filled to the brim, yielding not only pineapples and mangoes but also oil rigs, blocks of gold, iron gear for industry and success, which he won in a dominoes tournament of the Party. But he doesn't want the shell in the crack and she had to bring the Virgin so that she would be at their side in the face of sin and temptation. If it wasn't the best place for a statue of the Virgin, it certainly was for the Virgin of Coromoto, the Patroness. 'She will know,' she said to herself softly, 'that I am not putting her into the crack out of malice. She is humble and …'
    'I don't like this', he said aloud …
'The Virgin of Coromoto, *moto* … because a *motor*cycle is passing in the street and one hears a shout and a shot: moto'.
    And the man will not let her put his varnished turtle shell with the National Coat of Arms there. 'That is sacred', he says … 'As if the Virgin were not'.[17]

In *Las huellas crecen así* (Vladimiro Rivas 1972: 155), the worship of María Lionza takes on its most profound religious expression. Devotees from different social classes pay homage to La Reina (there are 37 different forms of worship in the novel), to obtain many special favours: good health, wisdom, protection and prosperity. The ritual procedures are vulgarly performed before the statue of María Lionza who emerges mounted on a pedestal holding a trophy with her hands held high and riding an elk. The atmosphere reeks of tobacco, rum, patchouli, lavender, lighted candles and prayers: 'Help me to overcome this difficult period of my life and open the doors to success to me, you who can do all and who are Queen of the wild beasts you protect'.[18]

Although the Goddess is good and generous to those who pay her homage, in matters of love she can be cruel and vengeful. She does not tolerate rivalry or rejection, as the following passage, from *El osario de Dios* (Armas Alfonso 1969: 52), illustrates:

> El Maestro Don, from the Aricagua Mountains was María Lionza's lover, the people say.
> ... Once, El Maestro Don's family was preparing to go to Curiepe to spend Holy Week. Maestro Don told his wife and children to continue walking on ahead while he locked the door.
> Then suddenly, a woman appeared, who was not his wife because she had gone on ahead, and this woman ordered him to stay with her. El Maestro Don disobeyed her. Then the woman took out a stick she was carrying and beat El Maestro Don so badly that he almost died. The woman, they say, was María Lionza.[19]

Conclusion

So far, I have tried to show the importance of María Lionza. From what has been discussed, one can deduce that María Lionza's followers come mainly from the lower classes of society – people from poor areas, peasants, prostitutes, the police and so on. The ceremonies of the Lionza cult are cloaked in a marked Catholicism: the Marian concept, the custom of making the sign of the cross and biblical references. Devotion to María Lionza is shown through prayer. The aboriginal influence is seen in the use of tobacco and the invocation of super-natural beings.

Petitions to María Lionza respond to daily necessities: protection from evil, harmony in married life, and so on. The works highlight the problems that afflict the poor such as marginalization and difficulties with the law. Perhaps the desire to seek refuge in the world of magic responds to the attractions of popular religion with its syncretism and telluric value.

The authors discussed try to explore the psychological back-ground and the naïveté of the followers without emphasizing the miraculous aspects of the cult. It is essentially the humorous element that is evident in these works. In brief, one can conclude that María Lionza is not merely an abstract theme of the novelist. She has passed definitively into the realm of folklore. She is a legend made reality, a Yaracuyan myth transformed into a goddess.

Notes

1   For another viewpoint, see Aretz (1972: 191). For a more detailed report of these phenomena, see Pollak (1968).

2   *Lo humano es, como lo ha demostrado la simbología de Jung, mito-mágico, y desde esta autenticidad esencialente humana, el hombre elabora las imágenes arquetípicas que personifican el patrimonio de todos los tiempos y todas las geografías.*

    El hombre necesita, para conservar su salud mental, mantener un cierto contacto con sus imágenes arquetípicas, no puede totalmente racionalizarse, romper completamente con lo mágico, con lo místico, con lo religioso sin volverse neurótico.

    [All translations are by Lancelot Cowie]

3   For the influence the Catholic Church exerts on Venezuelan festivals, see Alí González (1992).

4   *Hoy no le he puesto su velita a la Virgen del Carmen ... pocos momentos después, la velita ardía. El tiempo ha desteñido a la Virgen; ya no tiene nariz, lo único que ha conservado en todo su esplendor son los ojos. ¡Oh!, los ojos de la Virgen! Si ella fuera de carne y hueso cómo la adoraría, me echaría a sus pies, besaría sus ojos maravillosos, la abrazaría, la abrazaría ... La velita crepita, como siempre. La Virgen me mira con sus ojos hermosamente tristes, con una tristeza de siglos ... , inconscientemente lancé un zapato a la velita de la Virgen. Sus ojos brillaron y se sumieron luego en la oscuridad. Yo quiero a esta mujer, muchas veces he soñado con ella, hasta que la he poseído, la más dulce de las posesiones. Recuerdo su cuerpo, sus carnes blancas, tiernas y duras a la vez.*

5   *Terminado el regocijo, fueron a la plazuela a dar gracias a la Virgen ... El clamor de hombres, mujeres y niños, la guarura de cuernos y caracoles, el golpe de las chicoras sobre la tierra de las zanjas, o las mismas plegarias agresivas de antes, en las voces agradecidas, se transforma en un canto a la Virgen:*

> *– Dios de los Campos, gracias te damos.*
> *– Mandinga malo, ahórcate en el palo.*
> *– Virgen del Valle, sálvame en tu talle.*
> *– Jesús de la Esperanza, guarda tu labranza.*

6   *María Lionza, madre de agua aborigen, sincretizó su imagen ... en la belleza españolisima de la Emperatriz Eugenia Montijo, esposa de Napoleón Tercero. Hoy en día, el culto de María Lionza es una immensa encrucijada de aculturaciones, las unas de origen venezolano, las otras arropadas por la santería cubana, de origen yoruba, el culto a Changó, desrendido de aquella y rondando por las islas caribeñas de lengua inglesa; el vudú haitiano y sus dibujos simbólicos, prácticas fragmentarias de espiritismo, budismoi, fakirismo, traídas por culíes trinitarios o por gurúes itinerantes, lecturas desordenadas de revistas o manuales de brujería.*

7   *La imagen dorada de luces y pedrerías que se recostaba contra el cajoncito de madera y la ofrenda a la Reinita, la carne, el arroz y el queso por el retorno a salvo de su esposo.*

8   *Tú, Reina, que conocías los destinos y podías iluminar la oscuridad con una luz mil veces más poderosa que la estrella de Belén, porque Cristo así lo quería ... Tú, que con una sola caricia de tus inmaculadas manos podías curar los malos espíritus del cuerpo, aliviar los llantos, curar las enfermedades porque Cristo así lo había dispuesto; Tú, que tenías la gracia y la colaboración del poderoso*

Guaiacaipuro, ... del Negro Felipe ... de las Siete Potencias Africanas, ... Extraía el tabaco de los bolsillos de la bata ... y chupa y chupa mientras agarraba candela ... saliendo el humo por el alto respiradero de la choza.

9   *'¡En el nombre de Dios Todopoderoso y a la Reina Lionza! Ofrezco los humos de este tabaco para que los espíritus malignos se pierdan en la noche delirante y mágica y la Reina Corazonada amenazca en el púlpito inmemorial, despertando la felicidad en esta casa oscura donde lenguas equivocadas y pérfidas intentan desviar la lluvia y sembrar la sombra en el espejo de la belleza. ¡Ah! ¡Ah! ¡Ah! ... ¡Con Dios me acuesto, con Dios me levanto, milagrosa Reina de Todos los Poderas y tu corte celestial! Hazte presente, Invencible Guaiacaipuro, San Juan Retornado, Santa Maria de la Cabeza, Bondadoso Negro Felipe, Eterno Padrey Divino Hijo, San Benito del Sacrificio Reservado, Santa Teresa Bendita, Divino San Isidro Labrador, Santo Niño de Atocha, Esclarecida Virgen de Coromoto, la Niña Guillermina y San Marcos de León, aparten la sangre y las piedras de la maldad ... ¡Por las Tres Potencias Cósmicas! Por ésta te proteges, por ésta te sanas, por ésta te limpias ...'*

10   *Veratas ese ojo vigilando en el altar entre velas y oraciones pero era un ojo mudo y estático que no podía seguirla hasta el bosque, en los cañaverales, bajo el puente ...'.*

11   *'¡Oh! ¡Milagrosa Reina, María Lionza! ... Dame la fuerza necesaria para sepultar este cielo de cenizas y de huesos malolientes, nada podrá interrumpir el santo designio del cazador de impíos, hiena de la oscuridad y de la infamia; desde la torre de mi fuerza por mi padre y por la Santísima Trinidad te hemos de hacer pagar por todas las coronas de espinas que has sembrado en el camino, abre las piernas y ruge porque este toro del Apocalipsis te va a dejar clavada sobre la tierra'*

> *– Veintiocho cortadas, inspector,*
> *y seis heridads penetrantes, tres*
> *de ellas mortales.*

12   *'¡Qué milagro! ¡Iré a ponerle flores y dinero y algunos habanos a María Lionza! ¡Eso iba a hacer llegando a Caracas! ¡Me salvó María Lionza, hermanito!'*

13   *'Debes hablar, los héroes, los héroes están completos; ¿quieres convertirte en un afiche? ... De todos modos te daremos un baño de agua fría para ver si te salen los malos espíritus, quizás María Lionza te abre el entendimiento'.*

14   *Es importante aclarar que la estatua es objeto de un culto veloz: miles de automóviles le llena nde humo los senos de concreto. La mujer cabalga en una danta, como símbolo nde una antigua libertad. Sin embargo, aquí arden flores todavía. Pacientemente, los devotos de María Lionza queman esperma. Algunas almas sencillas, pero jodedorcitas, dicen que en las noches, cuando hay una luna llena, por supuesto, ella, la Reina Mora, avanza a pleno galope por la autopista y concede, lanza frutas y cordeles, la mejor forma de conseguir una mujer.*

15   *La vieja me dijo que ella tenía seguridad de que el mundo se iba a acabar el diez de noviembre, me tenía que poner duro con María Lionza esa noche y pedirle permiso para mudarnos en un altar, pero María Lionza vino en el cuerpo de una muchacha que se bebió dos botellas de ron y cinco latas de agua y se acostó conmigo en los Teques y cuando pude ver esta mañana era mi suegra y le di duro con el rolo ... hasta que llegó mi cuñado y me puso en las muñecas dos ramas de llantén ...*

16   *La Chinita invocó a la Virgen de Coromoto y, en el fallido intento de santiguarse, derramó la cuba-libre en el regazo de Zambrano.*

– ¡Salud! – exclamó la Negra, que aprovechara de limpiarlo bien a su amor.
– ¿No le gusta el sitio? – pasándole una servilleta de papel.

17   *Ella tiene una Virgen de la Coromoto en el cuarto y él tiene al lado – pero en el centro de la pared – su concha de tortuga con el Escudo Nacional de grandes cuernos de la abundancia que no sólo arrojan piñas y mangos sino torres petroleras, ladrillos de oro, engranajes de hierro de la industria y el progreso que se ganó con un torneo de dominó del Partido. Pero él no quiere colocar la concha en la grieta y ella tendrá que traer la virgen para que se encuentren con ella cuando vengan a la tentación y pecado. Aunque no es el mejor lugar para una virgen, más si lo es [para] la Coromoto que es Patrona.*

– Ella sabrá – se dice en voz baja – que no es por nada mal que la ponga en la grieta. Ella es humilde y …
– No me gusta eso – dijo en voz alta …
– La Virgen de Coromoto, moto … porque pasa una motocicleta por la calle y se oye un alto y un tiro: moto …
Y el hombre no dejará que ella coloque allí su concha de tortuga con el Escudo Nacional barnizado.
– Eso es sagrado – dice.
– Como si la virgen no lo fuera.

18   *'Ayúdame a vencer el duro trance que vivo y ábreme las puertas del éxito, ya que lo puedes todo y eres Reina de los animales feroces a quienes proteges'.*

19   *El Maestro Don, de la Serrania de Aricagua, murmuraba la gente que era amante de María Lionza.*

… Una vez se dispusieron a irse a Curiepe, a pasar la Semana Santa. El Maestro Don les dijo a la mujer y a los muchachos que se fueran andando adelante mientras él aseguraba la puerta.

Entonces se le presentó de improviso una señora que no era la suya porque Ia suya se había ido andando adelante y lo mandó a quedarse. El Maestro Don Ia desobedeció y entonces la señora sacó un palo que llevaba y golpeó al Maestro Don tan desconsideradamente que el Maestro Don por poquito no se muere. Según, esa señora era María Lionza.

16 Cultural ethnocentricity in commercial cinema: representation and self-identity

Rodolfo B. Popelnik

One major complaint heard about the representation of minorities in feature films relates to a demonstrable under-representation. With Hispanic Americans, the argument further states that during a period when we are the fastest-growing minority group in the United States, comprising around 10 per cent of the population, representation of less than 1 per cent in films is certainly asymmetric (Greenberg 1980: 3–12). While this question of numbers is important, it should not be, in itself, sufficient cause for alarm. Another complaint, I believe of more substance, has to do with the kind of representation Hispanic Americans have had in commercial cinema. On this issue, the belief that existing roles perpetuate long-standing stereotypes dating back to the last century is paramount (Woll and Miller 1987: 243). Something similar happens with the representation of Caribbean islanders who appear mostly in stereotypical characters. Jamaican Blacks, for example, are easy-going, music-loving, pot-smoking hospital aides (*Whose Life is it Anyway?*, 1981) or cyclists (*Thelma and Louise*, 1993). Cuban and Puerto Rican male characters are notable as ruthless criminals and these roles are often filled by non-Hispanics, as with De Palma's preference for Al Pacino in the leading roles of *Scarface* (1983), a remake of the 1932 classic updated by making the lead character a Cuban refugee in Miami involved in drug-dealing instead of bootlegging, and *Carlito's Way* (1993), where another professional criminal is depicted in a story-line that presents the futility of escaping a life of crime. It is common knowledge that most Hispanic roles were played by non-Hispanic actors and actresses for many years, a condition that changed somewhat during and after the Good Neighbor Policy years (1939–45), although remnants of it are still evident as the earlier examples of Pacino as a Cuban or Puerto Rican gangster attests. Indeed, pseudo-Latins have continued to play leading Latin roles such as Alan Arkin did in Arthur Hiller's *Popi* (1969), a charming story of poverty in the barrio that nevertheless celebrates the land of plenty that embraces anyone who is willing to assimilate, or *Che!* (1969), where Omar Sharif plays the starring role and Jack Palance plays Fidel Castro in a film that renders comic-book treatment of the famed revolutionary. Recent films that also have non-Latins in leading Latin roles are *Q & A* (1990) and *The Mambo Kings* (1992), where Armand Assante plays respectively a Hispanic drug-lord and a striving Cuban musician in New York.[1] During the Depression years Paul Muni became Warner Brother's resident Latin while Lupe Vélez portrayed 'Chinese, Eskimos, Japanese, Indian squaws, Hindus, Swedes, Malays, and Javanese', but seldom a Hispanic (Woll and Miller 1987: 246).

Although this pattern was partly a response then, as now, to marketing strategies within the Star System that defines Hollywood cinema, there are manifest undercurrents of a discourse that perpetuates stereotypical portrayals, marginalizes and devalues the presence of minorities, and in so doing affirms views and conceptions that, in formulaic fashion, repeat the errors, and the horrors, of a mistaken depiction of these groups. Such is the case of a Puerto Rican actress who has become a darling of film critics – Rosie Pérez – who nevertheless seems always to give the same performance. Her characters are loud, street-smart, brassy and foul-mouthed Brooklynites with a short fuse and big dreams, as may be seen in movies as different as *Untamed Heart* (1993), *White Men Can't Jump* (1993), and *It Could Happen to You* (1994). Another example may be seen in the film *Moon over Parador* (1988), which presents a generic Latin American country that seems recycled out of every farcical cliché ever created by Hollywood about the region. The 'fictional' country, film critic Roger Ebert properly notes, is led by bemedalled buffoons, ruled by nepotism, tamed by a corrupt army, inhabited by raging mobs of chanting peasants, entertained by countless national holidays, and given solace by hot-blooded women. These perceptions of the Other are so deeply ingrained in the collective psyche, that anti-establishment directors also concur in these practices. A case in point is Oliver Stone's *Born on the 4th of July* (1989), which shows us Puerto Rican actress Cordelia González as a Mexican prostitute, and her screen presence is limited to the nude scene without the more substantive scenes the actress filmed and which were edited out of the final product. While many more examples can be mentioned, the above may suffice to suggest that stereotypes and misinformation, wilfully or not, serve well as prerequisites of an imperial process perpetuated by the film industry which advances the lack of understanding that feeds the rhetoric of domination, colonization and appropriation, which for so long has defined its character. The Good Neighbor Policy, which promoted a larger number of Hollywood productions with Latin American themes portraying Hispanics with what Ana López (1991: 407) has called a 'new-found sensibility', was to be a short-lived phenomenon which responded to specific economic and political policies of the Roosevelt era.[2] While surely this period is not without criticism, the depiction of Hispanics was positive when compared to earlier periods when films like *Barbarous Mexico* (1913) presented insensitive, bloodthirsty revolutionaries without addressing the political questions of the Mexican Revolution. After the Good Neighbor Policy years, representation lacked any overt political direction and can indeed be said to be again populated with many stereotypes which are questionable.

Certainly, no group monopolizes virtues or defects except in Hollywood, where these constructions so often take place. And here intention is secondary to result. When a film shows a certain type of minority engaging in certain kinds of actions yet these actions are devoid, as Ward Churchill writes (1992: 235), 'of all cultural grounding and explanation', how is meaning to be interpreted? While his argument is specific to Native-American cultures as these are defined by Eurocentric values, it seems clear that viewing audiences are a complex group and do not necessarily have the referential elements needed to gain insight into the culture and values exhibited. Even if the depictions were to be more-or-less accurate, these may 'appear irrational, cruel, unintelligent or silly when displayed in film' (Churchill 1992: 235).

As it happens, the above is a best-case scenario. We all know that filmic images do not necessarily reflect these constructions accurately. Like media representations in general, they simultaneously reflect and create a reality we all share and thus become important referential and self-defining elements for minority groups who surely view themselves as collectivities that share meanings and values. Inasmuch as many of these meanings and values are defined cinematically, they impinge on the social interaction of these groupings, both among themselves and between them and the dominant groups who have a hand in the construction of these identities. Among the views propagandized by Hollywood films regarding minorities, a constant reference seems to be the us/them dichotomy which is supported by systems of signification pertinent to the cinema, where the cinematic and the ideological tend to converge to present a form of control assumed as natural. As John W. Adams argues (1979), the success of ideology in narrative must convince us that characters, their motivations and actions, are 'perfectly natural'. The scheme of things presented in commercial cinema tends to reify a conception of the world that defies alternative interpretations and in so doing, reaffirms identities far removed from the social praxis yet wholly believable as cinematic representations that appear to exhibit a modicum of verisimilitude. From pirate films starring Errol Flynn to westerns to spy movies to romances, our regions and our identities are subject to the most mythical definitions by Hollywood film-makers but, interestingly, they conform to many of our own expectations. Thus racism, and ignorance of culture, language and religion, are endlessly perpetuated by the powerful medium of communication that Hollywood cinema is.

Although at times certain films have attempted to reaffirm nation-hood and identity, as with *Juárez* (1939), *Viva Zapata!* (1952) or *Salt of the Earth* (1953) – all dealing specifically with Mexicans – in the case that interests us here, the cinema has mostly been used to present Hispanic Americans in one of two veins: one pejoratively called 'greaser', who early on in this century replaced the Latin or Mexican with a generic, violence-prone Hispanic, or a non-committed, happy-go-lucky individual whose singing and dancing defined a national character. It generally did not matter from what country they came from or in which country the action took place. And just as ethnicity is interchangeable, so is music. To define a national character, especially for the Caribbeaner, music takes a direct role within the cinematic language. Misconceptions abound and whether the rhythm is samba, salsa, merengue, calypso, bachata, cumbia, plena, bomba, mambo, rumba or any of many others, the enormous diversity and prodigious history that makes these various groups and their cultural manifesta-tions possible remains an enigma to be explained. While certain attempts at explanation do take place from time to time, an overview of filmic genres and specific films and scenes tends to support the view that we are mostly portrayed not as we are, but as we are *imagined* by Eurocentric conceptions. Indeed, in this regard it is illuminating to mention that when filming *The Fugitive* in 1948, John Ford 'expressed surprise when he discovered that real Latins were far more industrious than the siesta-prone caricatures that Hollywood had been portraying for years' (Woll and Miller 1987: 250).

But just as these stereotypes have permitted a way of imagining us, such conceptualizations reached beyond the dominant group and became familiar and acceptable self-defining concepts for the minority. One film that exemplifies this is *El Mariachi* [The *Mariachi*] (1993). It was shot on location in a Mexican border town with mostly Hispanic actors and technicians by a young film-maker – Robert Rodríguez. The film tells the story of a young *mariachi*, a rambling guitar player, who arrives one day looking for work. He is dressed in black and carries a guitar case. All he wants to do is sing and play his guitar. On the same day and dressed in a similar outfit, a killer arrives in town. Mistaken identities soon provide the story-line and *el mariachi* is thrust onto someone else's blood feud. A sexy barmaid listens to his story, believes it, and they fall in love, yet she is the object of the local warlord's unrequited lust, which adds another soap-opera kind of complication. The film is peopled with every stereotype imaginable and yet it is somehow believable. It is as if, excepting brief moments of reflection, our view of ourselves is pregnant with the ideology promulgated by Eurocentrism. Perhaps Fanon's admonition in *The Wretched of the Earth* (1970) is still valid and our identities are trapped within the definitional power of the oppressor, drifting endlessly in other-defined categories, stranded in a pastless/presentless/futureless vacuum. National identity is thus transmogrified through hegemonical dominance which replaces troops and guns finally as the relevant tool of colonization.

The issue of race is an interesting case in point. Who for example has not heard of 'la rubia superior' [the superior blonde] to market beer in Mexico, or the colloquialism 'no seas indio' [don't be an Indian] to show disdain for unwarranted behaviour or modes of thought. How about the Xuxa phenomenon in Brazil, where there is near-worship of her atypical blond, blue-eyed appearance.[3] Any stroll among boulevards or streets, colonias or urbanizaciones, arrabales or favelas, will present an opportunity to see how many Miss Clairol blondes populate our societies. Can it be that truly 'blondes have more fun'?

If misrepresentation did begin with the *oppressor*, it now has evolved into a rhetoric of domination that defines national identities and preferences from within. Indeed, the accurate analysis of the function of stereotypes Walter Lippmann presents in his seminal work *Public Opinion* ([1922] 1956) strengthens this view when he writes that a 'pattern of stereotypes is not neutral. … They are the fortress of our tradition, and behind its defences we can continue to feel safe in the position we occupy' (p. 96). Thus, it may well be that once stereotypes are embedded in our psyche, they give form to our self-image, even if distorted, devalued, questionable and untrue, and yet, with the capacity to invoke a consensus of what we are like for others, but more important, to ourselves.

While the films mentioned at the beginning of this chapter are all Hollywood productions that transgress under the guise of entertainment, it is worrying to find that our own production efforts appear to exploit these stereotypical depictions too. Witness, for example, Darnell Martin's independent production *I Like It Like That* (1994), which opens with a Puerto Rican couple engaged in ardent sex while a throng outside their window in the streets of New York's *El Barrio* enthusiastically cheers the would-be record-breaker for lengthy, uninterrupted copulation.[4] Written and directed by Puerto Rican Martin, a first-time woman director who was previously an assistant director for Spike Lee, and with mostly a Hispanic cast, the film has elements of soap opera and sitcom. It is a story fraught with flagrant stereotypes which we all associate with the macho culture of Hispanics. There is the stud, Chino (who, with more class, would be upgraded to Latin lover), married to Lisette for 10 years and pursued by the lustful Magdalena who may have borne his child. When he steals a stereo and is put in jail, Lisette is resolved to raise the money for bail. She finds a job as an assistant to an Anglo producer specializing in Latino music, and when a rumour reaches Chino that his wife is cheating on him with her new boss, Chino (now out on bail) retaliates with Magdalena. Not much of a story-line here but the 'required' elements – sex, jealousy, music, thievery – are all present. Similarly, a recent Caribbean independent film project, *Rice, Beans and Ketchup* (1994), is a Puerto Rican production also full of unrealistic portrayals, where depictions are far removed from reality and most characters are caricatures in a film that is no parody. It is a romantic comedy that purports to show the American Dream from the vantage point of a young man who leaves his native Dominican Republic and arrives in New York to fulfil his ambition in the land of plenty. He soon finds that it is a dog-eat-dog world out there; yet he knows how to move and dance and with these attributes, and a few lessons from his Anglo teacher, he is able to obtain his moment of glory *à la* John Travolta in *Saturday Night Fever*. Even the marketing poster for the film emulates Hollywood Cinema as it shows the young, handsome, dancing couple in a beautiful shot against the New York skyline reflected on the Hudson. Together with *Nueva Yol* (1995), *Shortcut to Paradise* (1994), and *La guagua aérea* [The Flying Bus] (1993), all are recent examples of a regional cinema that reifies long-standing conceptions. They may be funny or nostalgic, intriguing or entertaining, more or less subtle, but they all are 'nails in the coffin' that present an obstacle to true representation, for how is Hollywood cinema to correct its ways if our own films promote such myopic views?

The previous discussion amidst filmic examples suggests that identity is a question related to representation and perhaps some words are required to explain this assertion. Self theory as a paradigm for the interpretation of processes which define one's self-concept and behaviour places great importance on the roles played and the statuses occupied by the individual, and takes into account the reference groups upon which we model ourselves (Hickman and Kuhn 1956: 45).

Equally important is the notion that referential elements in the culture allow certain types of performances and preclude others. We call this role-playing and it forms our persona, one that defines us to others as much as to ourselves. Summarized, the argument states that 'behaviour is socially determined by the actor's definitions, particularly self-definitions ... on the basis of internalized prescriptions and proscriptions' (Meltzer *et al.* 1975: 62), which I submit come from film as much as from any other referential element we use in the construction of our reality. Peter Berger and Thomas Luckmann (1967), among others, have suggested that the social construction of reality is a historically grounded process that necessarily implies particular kinds of power relations in a given society. As they write (p. 119): 'power in society includes the power to determine decisive socialization processes and, therefore, the power to *produce* reality'. In a region where European and later on American hegemony has prevailed in the form of colonial dominance, these 'prescriptions and proscriptions' certainly were the result of power arrangements at the service of the colonial power, where stereotypes were created, fed and maintained in order to obtain a certain ordering of an otherwise incomprehensible culture for the transposed colonizers. Surely a lot can be said about the uses of stereotypes to create marginalized categories, define outcasts and legitimize a dominant value system, a process that certainly allows the group with power to impose their definitions at the expense and devaluation of those who lack it. Furthermore, the psychosocial process whereby a person develops his or her identity is related to the way others see that person. In this light, it can be said that we are a reflection of what others think we are and *our self-image need bear no relation to objective facts.*[5] Given that filmic images of minorities publicize a certain representation which mostly responds to the perceptions dominant groups have of them, perceptions which are coloured by ethnocentric views, it is not unwarranted that minorities devalue themselves and praise the dominants. Indeed, white domination has been so complete that Indian children play at being 'cowboys', which is as if Jewish children played at being Nazis (Churchill 1992: 240). In order really to grasp the meaning of this statement, let us imagine the costumes worn by children when playing 'Cowboys and Indians' and what they do to each other. Surely they emulate the practices learned from the images seen and accordingly tie, scalp, torture, shoot and pillage. What would this be like in a 'game' of 'Nazis and Jews'? Would uniforms, helmets and swastikas be one costume and striped outfits, numbered tattoos and stars of David the other? How about make-believe gas chambers and ovens? Certainly the mere thought of this is repulsive to us all, and yet 'Cowboys and Indians' as children's play is not. Obviously, white domination reaches so far in diverse institutional settings that cinematic representation is just one more outlet for it. The composition of expectations one believes others hold toward him or her become a defining self-concept that can be roughly equated to dominant standards.

Lakoff and Johnson's (1980) view that perception and actions are based on conceptual systems and these in turn are founded on certain 'metaphors we live by', suggests that what is read within a culture (including definitions of Self) is the product of subjective appraisals that give form and specificity to it.[6] If that form and specificity is fed and nurtured by cinema as much as by other socializing agencies, then cinematic representation should be scrutinized in great detail to understand better the relation between representation and identity.[7] Indeed, one way to approach the issues of identity, as these are mediated and represented in Hollywood cinema, is by looking not only at the economic aspects of an industry that is sometimes excused of its offence by recognizing that film is a commodity and as such, responds to laws unrelated to historical accuracy or social responsibility, but by focusing also on the psycho-social aspects of an enterprise that, on the basis of an Eurocentric view, has helped define the American character and American hegemony for most of this century. This definition includes a certain construction of those not American as well – the 'Other'. On the ideological power and hegemonical constructs present within Hollywood films, Mexican writer Carlos Fuentes has said (Holmberg 1982):

> Movies are the bearers of the collective unconscious, the warehouse of modern myths. Hollywood manufactures the archetypes we need to understand our collective life. … American pop archetypes have permeated the world from the mountains of Tibet to the jungles of Brazil.

In this same vein, Carlos Monsiváis reminds us that however one chooses to define popular culture, and many possible definitions abound, 'what is certain is that in the invention or preservation of customs, the cinema is the most powerful influence' (1993: 144). Since movies can and do project distorted images, there is no such thing as neutrality of portrayal; a message is always there and it responds to and supports a value system, one that by definition reflects the power structure of a given society. Attempts to deny this obvious function of the movie industry are often heard. Surely, the much-quoted piece of advice that depicts the unapologetic commercialism of Hollywood film studios during their heyday, which stated: 'Pictures are for entertainment, messages should be delivered by Western Union', in Sam

Goldwyn's words,[8] testifies to this. A belief in entertainment, however, as the ultimate goal of the industry could only be the fantasy of studio moguls who either did not comprehend the power of their product or did not care about the repercussions their filmic constructions had on the psyche of audiences worldwide. To think that Hollywood was not in the message business is a naïve view few hold today.

Images in the media certainly relate to issues of power in society, and the fact that minority groups are present in feature films in positions that may be questionable to many of us, may be related to how little power these groups hold in society and in the industry that puts forth these productions. Of course, history and the tales that nurture it must, of necessity, be ambiguous. From the earliest times the official story has always been used to legitimize those in power and sustain a certain interpretation of facts and reality. But when these stories have the strength that accompanies visual images, they seem self-evident, and hence, defining elements for a certain kind of perception. Walter Lippmann (1922: 88–9) has said that stereotypic thinking 'precludes reason', and 'as a form of perception [it] imposes a certain character on the data of our senses'. Ellul poignantly adds (1985: 210–14):

> When we glimpse a picture, a process whereby images recall one another is immediately set off. These images cause us to go from one idea that is represented in this manner to others that have no necessary relationship between them. ... Visual means of communication set in motion an overall mechanism of apprehension. ... The growth of prejudices and mental stereotypes ... is not a transposition of discourse and words, ... [but] is truly the mental reception of images in the material sense: posters, photographs, ... ready-made images received as is, from outside. ... Thought based on images can be neither abstract nor critical. Of necessity it is thought related to the milieu.

What is this milieu? It is one inundated by one-dimensional images that conform our psyche by reifying a conception of the world as *is*. The discourse put forth in commercial cinema seems to point unquestionably towards an uncontested first-world hegemony that embeds a definition of self that precludes major differences among Hispanics or Caribbeaners, while establishing generic categories that loosely fit us all. It should not be surprising, for example, that the Caribbean is mostly seen as a *geographical* concept devoid of cultural differences except in the common traits which the Eurocentric view concedes to the region – voracious lust and sexual acrobatics, heated arguments and ardent contests, endless corruption and troublesome instability, abundant drinking and exuberant dancing, all in a carnivalesque spectacle of uncontrollable primal passions. The Caribbean as a *cultural* concept transcending the limits of its geography is certainly evident in the African element of our common formation. Ancestral Blacks came from the same regions, the same nations, the same tribes – and in the new continent shared common traditions, but also gave rise to distinct cultures. The continual portrayal of an undifferentiated, stereotyped Other can only feed on itself and promote the solitude which characterizes so vast a region as ours. It is a scheme that begs to be broken if Pan-Americanism is to be more than an idea. Orlando Senna makes an observation that is equally applicable to the common man in the Caribbean or the rest of Latin America. He writes (1990):

> The average Brazilian, the man in the street, knows very little about Latin America and (the) Caribbean, but he knows what is happening in Europe and can describe the behaviour of North American citizens, based principally on what he has learned from the cinema produced in Hollywood.[9]

Any analysis of ethnic and dominant representation in films – as in other media – shows a lack of commitment to history and to truthful depictions that would advance the understanding we now lack.

Certainly our regions exemplify at once paradoxical features such as the tension between the apparent stability of post-colonial political structures, and the fragility of civil society, between presumably democratic forms and the realities of arbitrary rule, between the professional advancement of women and deeply rooted sentiments of male superiority, between the development of an acquisitive lifestyle and the exporting of labour migrants, between the growth of tourism and the displacement of refugees, and between the flourishing of modern media of communication that bring new values and the resilience of traditional forms that confront them. Yet many of these complex paradoxes are the result of specific historical conditions and political constructions that produced particular forms of power, self-identity, exclusion and subjection, in a process that still constructs, groups together and devalues customs and behaviours by placing these in subordinate opposition to Eurocentric practices and points of view. When our region and our identities are depicted as to conform to the *image* constructed of us, it not only asserts the dominant powers' interpretation but imposes this interpretation on audiences.[10] And although it is possible to view media texts as sites of constant ideological struggles where meaning is not fixed but constantly in flow, the fact remains that these struggles do not necessarily result in a favourable resolution of the issues discussed. How many stories could be told about our region's history, replete with fascinating mythologies and legends, about the course and the curse of our development, about fantastic cities and empires that existed long before Europeans ever set foot in this continent, about the tragic loss of life and land, about the daily lives of a people who confront problems and solve them, about rapidly changing social conditions and a breathtaking capability for adaptation, about struggles for independence and dreams waiting to be fulfilled? As García Márquez remarks (1982: 55):

> The history of the Caribbean is full of magic, a magic brought by the black slaves of Africa, but also by the Swedish, Dutch and English pirates, who were capable of setting up an opera house in New Orleans and load their women to the teeth with diamonds. The blending of humanity and the contrasts of the Caribbean are nowhere else in the world to be seen. I know all its islands: honey-skinned *mulatas*, with green eyes and crowned with golden head-scarves; Chinamen crossed with Indians who launder clothes and sell amulets; green Hindus who come out of their ivory shops to shit in the middle of the street; hot and dusty villages whose houses are shaken apart by cyclons, as well as skyscrapers of tinted glass reflecting a rainbow of colours.[11]

Back in 1943, actress Lena Horne made a plea regarding media portrayals of African-Americans which fits our current condition. She said (Ellison 1981: 181): All we ask is that the Negro be portrayed as a normal person. Let's see the Negro as a worker at union meetings, as a voter at the polls, as a civil service worker or elected official.' It is perhaps time to confront what seems to be a persistent problem with commercial cinema – the simplification of the Other, making him or her palatable, conforming to expectations without the need to decipher the intricacies that define this Otherness, and which negates the possibility of bridging cultures. The distortion of our self-concept runs deeper than we would like to imagine. On the issue of identity Garcia Canclini (1995: 238–9) quotes what a resident of the northern Mexican territory says:

> 'When they ask me my nationality or ethnic identity, I cannot respond with one word, since my "identity" has multiple repertories: I am Mexican but also Chicano and Latin American. On the border they call me "chilango" or "mexiquillo"; in the capital "pocho" or "norteño", and in

Europe "sudaca". Anglo-Saxons call me "Hispanic" or
"Latino", and Germans have more than once confused me
with being Italian or Turkish'.[12]

To perceive oneself in a rootless fashion is certainly tragic for it
embodies an ideology that diminishes a sense of worth. For the
dominant groups this view confirms a superiority that stands in the
way of true understanding.

On the wider concerns of mediation and representation in film and
the force of images, we should remember that Sukarno of Indonesia
considered the Hollywood film industry profoundly revolutionary
(McLuhan 1967: 257). To suppose that the industry will respond to the
concerns here exposed is unwarranted and illusory. An alternative way
must be found to assert the realities of the so-called New World Order
whose cultural pluralism is an undeniable condition waiting to be
addressed. The cinema's role in this is clear: it either maintains things
as they are, supporting a value system that is questionable, or confronts
its own shortcomings to present a sound depiction of our region and
our selves beyond the dramatic performances so common today. What
we certainly do *not* need are more portrayals that support the us/them
dichotomy that, once internalized, distorts history and is conducive to
neglect, apathy, ignorance and rejection. The advent of independent
film productions, those unrelated to major studios, might prove to be
an avenue worth exploring. In an age when the independent film industry is rapidly expanding, be this due to financial need or artistic desires,
this window of opportunity, if taken advantage of, may have the effect
of broadening a viewing audience perspective, of rediscovering our
own stories and re-telling our history, one that is full and rich and
complex, although long suppressed by the Hollywood Establishment.[13]
We can certainly hope for an increased production of national cinemas,
but in an age when Latin American film production is markedly
reduced by economic urgency, and a growing dominance of the film
market and film technique resides in Hollywood, it may be an uphill
battle. Hollywood's capacity to impinge on all national cinemas, as in
many independent productions attempting to be successful in the
market place, thus raises the spectre that a truly valid portrayal of
minorities, while long overdue, will not be coming soon.

I should like to end with an anecdote that I find significant. When
a Mayor of San Juan, Héctor Luis Acevedo, was Puerto Rico's
Secretary of State, and in charge of organizing the festivities leading to
the celebration of the Fifth Centennial of the Discovery of America
and Puerto Rico, he made a plea for emphasizing the positive aspects
of the colonization. Among the things he proclaimed (Medina 1986),

the following are noteworthy for their profound implications: 'at the time of the Europeans' arrival, the original inhabitants of America did not know meat ... nor had tools for farming or a written language'. We know they did, but not from the tales told in our popular culture, or in the official discourse. Native cultures numbered hundreds and had varying degrees of technological development, political organization and economic systems. Several had attained high levels of sophistication in engineering, architecture, astronomy, medicine (including surgery), market systems and empire-building. On the magnificence of these cultures, all we need to do is read Bernal Díaz del Castillo, whose account, in his *True History of the Conquest of New Spain*,[14] clearly demonstrates a complexity other indigenous cultures also shared. Yet so common a view as that espoused by a distinguished Puerto Rican is indicative of the very devaluing process that hegemonical constructs promote. Filmic images in commercial cinema, inasmuch as they publicize an illusory Otherness, are partly responsible for the continuation of this state of affairs.

Notes

1   Beyond the issue of stereotypical portrayals, controversy over the casting of so many non-Hispanic actors in Hispanic roles certainly continues today as was recently noticeable with *The House of the Spirits* (1994), based on the homonymous novel of Isabel Allende, or the romantic comedy *The Perez Family* (1995). Both films are prime examples of what still seems to be a pattern characteristic of the industry. There is certainly no shortage of talented Latino actors as *My Family* (1995), a film released at about the same time, demonstrates.

2   A dormant policy was resurrected and Nelson Rockefeller headed the newly created State Department Office of the Coordinator for Inter-American Affairs (CIAA). He was responsible for directing the effort to promote inter-American understanding, and films were seen as a good vehicle for this purpose. A Motion Picture Section was created which, together with the Hays Office's newly appointed Latin American expert, pressured the studios to present Latins in a favorable light. For more on this policy and how Hollywood responded see Woll (1977).

3   For more on this the reader may wish to see Simpson (1994).

4   Martin received the coveted 1994 New York Film Critics Circle Award for Best New Director and Best First Film with this movie.

5   For more on this the reader may wish to see the work of George Herbert Mead, particularly *Mind, Self and Society from the Standpoint of a Social Behaviourist* ed. with an introduction by Charles W. Morris (Chicago: University of Chicago, 1934).

6   See particularly pages 115–46 for a detailed discussion on the need for metaphoric definition of our conceptual systems, the human compulsion for categorization, and the processes we incur to establish meaning. While their analysis relates expressly to linguistic usage of metaphors and how these provide specific meanings to our everyday experience, I feel strongly that their discussion lends itself to other

readings, particularly when so much of our metaphoric understanding of the world now comes from the visual experiences we obtain in commercial cinema, with images that span the world and reinforce, over and over again, a view of that world responsive to the popular culture industry which produces it.

7 The Caribbean as playground or paradise where passions roam freely in Carnival-like displays among happy, laid-back people, is a common metaphoric rendering of our region that finds placement in film and in the marketing strategies of the tourism industry. Witness, for example, how the concept of the carnival is used for identification of fun vacations with Carnival Air Lines or Carnival Cruises, both operating in the region. The same stereotypical imagery is evident in successful advertising campaigns such as that for Corona beer.

8 *Oxford Dictionary of 20ᵗʰ Century Quotations* (Oxford: OUP, 1998), p. 130.

9 *El hombre común brasileño, el hombre de la calle, conoce muy poco de América Latina y [el] Caribe, pero sabe lo que está pasando en Europa y puede describir los comportamientos de [los] ciudadanos norteamericanos – principalmente por lo que ha aprendido en el cine producido en Hollywood.*

10 In the Cultural Studies tradition, a body of literature suggests that audiences confront media messages in an assertive manner and can produce meaning and create their own identities through specific cultural processes that operate in spite of, or in resistance to, attempts at cultural domination through the communication media. This view, as explained by Jesús Martín Barbero, states that messages are mediated through culture and everyday life activities in which people constitute and reconstitute their identities. For more on this, the reader may wish to see Martín Barbero (1993). Another author who shares this conception is Stuart Hall (1980), who discusses the ways in which an audience may create meaning and see in a text alternative or subcultural readings.

11 *La historia del caribe está llena de magia, una magia traída por los esclavos negros de Africa, pero también por los piratas suecos, holandeses e ingleses, que eran capaces de montar un teatro de ópera en Nueva Orleans y llenar de dia-mantes las dentaduras de las mujeres. La síntesis humana y los contrastes que hay en el caribe no se ven en otro lugar del mundo. Conozco todas sus islas: mulatas color de miel, con ojos verdes y pañoletas doradas en la cabeza; chinos cruzados de indios que lavan ropa y venden amuletos; hindúes verdes que salen de sus tiendas de marfiles para cagarse en la mitad de la calle; pueblos polvorientos y ardientes cuyas casas las desbaratan los cyclones, y por otro lado rascacielos de vidrios solares y un mar de siete colores.*

12 *Cuando me preguntan por mi nacionalidad o identidad étnica no puedo responder con una palabra, pues mi 'identidad' ya posee repertorios múltiples: soy mexicano pero también soy chicano y latinoamericano. En la frontera me dicen 'chilango' o 'mexiquillo' en la capital 'pocho' o 'norteño' y en Europa 'sudaca'. Los anglosajones me llaman 'Hispanic' o 'Latino' y los alemanes me han confundido en más de una ocasión con turco o italian.* (García Canclini 1990: 302)

13 Distribution channels and marketing, while important issues closely related to the focus of this analysis, are beyond the scope of this chapter.

14 Bernal Díaz del Castillo, *The Conquest of New Spain* (Harmondsworth, Penguin, 1963).

Breaking the spell of our *hallucinated lucidity*: surveying the Caribbean self within Hollywood Cinema

Diane Accaria-Zavala

> In that state of hallucinated lucidity, not only did they see the images of their own dreams, but some saw the images dreamed by others.[1]
>
> García Márquez 1970: 50–1

A brief incursion into mainstream films which are about Caribbean islanders, or about our region, takes us into the already suspect world of false constructs. Yet the insistence of these constructs, the recurrence of the same stereotypes, misrepresentations and myths, the depth of ignorance about the region these films show within their images, remain truly frightening. A film such as Richard Lester's *Cuba* (1979), for example, opens with a crude array of cinematic metaphors which intend to define quickly life in pre-revolution Cuba. Afro-Cuban music sets the beat while we are shown a quick sequence of shots against the backdrop of a luxury-hotel pool, beautiful women in suits one knows are too tiny for the time-set of the film, a close-up of a woman's wet breast followed by another close-up of a musician's maracas, a fully decked *generalísimo* lasciviously eyeing the woman, counterpointed, of course, with the gushing rush of champagne overflowing from its bottle. Crude indeed. Cuban music, the heat of the tropics, and the ways of a people are all linked to the idea of free sex and enterprises, extreme and ludicrous behaviour. A more recent production, Darnell Martin's *I Like It Like That* (1994) also opens with the same note of constructed association. A couple is ferociously engaged in heated sex. A crowd outside their window cheers the fellow on (they all know he wants to break the world-record for a pro-longed erection). Their small children are pounding on the bedroom door while Mom and Dad threaten to beat them amidst gasps and sexual spasms. A clock ticks and finally an alarm goes off, all to show that he indeed has had the longest erection and orgasm yet. A central film sequence in Arne Glimcher's *The Mambo Kings* (1992) is a brilliant montage of music (the famed Tito Puente and a handsome Armand Assante are fire on the drums), fast shots tuning us into a 'normal' night in a Caribbean nightclub. Music, drinking and revelry are suddenly halted by a knife-yielding stud who is shot after trying to score another man's woman. In Woody Allen's *Bananas* (1971) a generic Caribbean island seems to engage rather happily in guerrilla warfare and revolution. No one's life is safe, we are told, especially that of a stumbling, innocent gringo. Again, sex with an uncontrollable hot-blooded female is the highlight of the gringo's island experience. Rita Hayworth's sizzling dance accents a tropical *fiesta* in a film with an already charged title, *Fire Down Below* (1957). In this film alcoholism, laziness and a high tolerance for petty and not so petty crime are the way of life in the islands – for natives and drifting Americans alike. In *The Black Swan* (1942), a pirate film featuring Errol Flynn, we find a Venezuelan woman belly-dancing to the beat of what is supposed to be native Caribbean music. A village feast in Irving Cumming's *Down Argentine Way* (1940) adopts the trappings of a tropical island fiesta. A strange array of drums, pampadress, and Mexican sombreros are the constructs depicting the 'true Argentine way'. And yes, even as early as 1940, free love is part of the deal for those who dare come down under.

When viewing these films, one easily sees that throughout the decades of mainstream cinema production the silver screen comes alight once more with images of Caribbeaners immersed in the stereotypically tropical: heated sex, heated arguments, knife-fighting, gunfighting or revolutionary fighting but always fighting, thieving, copulating, or dancing, always dancing, tapping feet or drums, conforming to the *image*, performing the perfect role of the flamboyant or slimy, harmlessly irresponsible, fun-loving tropical bunny (or should I say tropical snake). The audience can thus relax, secure in the cunningly implanted knowledge that they are seeing the tropically real within the reels of cinema, all sitting back and relaxed within the proper order of things, everything as it should be. Meanwhile, despite the pleasurable hallucinatory sensations engendered by this narcotizing facade, on go the perpetual transgressions, Caliban's tortured self victimized and *admiring* the victimizer, constrained of thought and action, alone and isolated from all others, the endless haemorrhaging of our region and our regional self goes on and on, unconstrained by public outcry, hidden safely out of sight and mind by the seemingly harmless weapon of celluloid.

I

These images reflect the ills of cultural imperialism and political colonialism. Here lies the implied assumption that distinctions between cultural groupings of Caribbean people are either non-existent (denoting ignorance) or irrelevant (denoting arrogance). The weird confluence of different and distinct traits, Cubans, Venezuelans, Puerto Ricans, Jamaicans, amalgamated into one bastardized *tropical identity* shows Ward Churchill's conclusions regarding Native-American stereotyping in Hollywood films, in his *Fantasies of the Master Race* (1992: 239), are painfully true for us all:

> It is elementary logic to realize that when the cultural identity of a people is symbolically demolished, the achievements and very humanity of that people must also be disregarded. The people, as such, disappear, usually to the benefit – both material and psychic – of those performing the symbolic demolition. *There are accurate and appropriate terms which describe this: dehumanisation, obliteration or appropriation of identity, political subordination and material colonization are all elements of a common process of imperialism.* This is the real meaning of Hollywood's stereotyping (emphasis added).

Edward Said's *Culture and Imperialism* (1993: xix–xx) also points to the need we have of taking a second look at the image made of the third world in the work of many film-makers. Even those who take a liberal political stance (Said offers examples such as *Apocalypse Now, Salvador* and *Missing*), remain inheritors of 'residual imperialist propensities' (Said 1993: xix–xx):

> These works, which are so indebted to Conrad's anti-imperialist irony in *Nostromo*, argue that the source of the world's significant action and life is in the West, whose representatives seem at liberty to visit their fantasies and philanthropies upon a mind-deadened Third World. In this view, the outlying regions of the world have no life, history, or culture to speak of, no independence or integrity worth representing without the West. And when there is something to be described it is, following Conrad, unutterably corrupt, degenerate, irredeemable. But whereas Conrad wrote *Nostromo* during a period of Europe's largely uncontested imperialist enthusiasm, contemporary novelists and film-makers who have learned his ironies so well, have done their

work *after* decolonisation, *after* the massive intellectual, moral, and imaginative overhaul and deconstruction of Western representation of the non-West world, *after* the work of Frantz Fanon, … *after* the novels and plays of Chinua Achebe, … Gabriel García Márquez, and many others.

Mainstream cinema is clearly a source of often subtle, at times blatant, biased and false, construction. Worse yet, and the point of true pre-occupation underlining this study, is that some of the most biased images made are *not* Hollywood creations. The 'Duracell-still-going' sex-scene described from *I Like It Like That* was conceived by African-American and Hispanic Americans in an independent production. Now that there is an open door (small as it still is) for marginal groups (such as African-Americans, Native Americans or Caribbean people) to use the cinema as a voice, a tool of acknowledgement, expression, and reappropriation, many of the constructs which should be rejected and done away with are being endlessly and detrimentally perpetuated. By focusing on the image of the Caribbean self the cinema is feeding us, we discover that we are not too far from that first distorted image with which Prospero described us, during the euphemistic discovery of the New World. The images with which the cinema imbues the colours of Caribbean identity are not at all far from the descriptions within the notes of Columbus' fleet surgeon, Dr Diego Alvarez Chanca, in 1493: 'The way of life of these *caribe* people is bestial' (Hulme and Whitehead 1992: 33). A testimony taken nearly 100 years later (ibid.: 40), in 1580, on the island of Puerto Rico, concerning the injuries done to Luisa de Navarrete, a captive of these 'bestial Caribs' [*bestiales caribes*] also subscribes to the image of the hot-tempered tropical war- and sex-fiend we still seem to be, prone to cruelty, drunkenness, and long endless nights of carnal and musical revelry (ibid):

> When they want to make wine they make Christians chew cassava at night and make it, with which wine they get drunk, take the females captive and force them, knowing them carnally, making them do as they wish, … and when the said Indians want to eat others that they have captured they make their areytos [ritual songs] and call to and speak to the Devil.

Inevitable, it seems, to the process of a re-encounter with a native self, some of the most distinguished Caribbean novelists include in their texts the falsity of identity ensured within this ongoing mis-representation process. Antonio Benítez Rojo, in his impressive study of the Caribbean within the postmodern perspective, *La isla que se repite* [The Repeating Island] (1989), describes the tendency some of the region's novels have of presenting the fictional world they subscribe to in the form of a 'performance' or a spectacle, of lights and music, revelry and dance, and a constructed sense of self as consummate 'performer'. He reminds us (p. 15) of the opening of Cuban-born Cabrera Infantes' *Tres tristes tigres* [Three Trapped Tigers] (1965):

> *Showtime!* Señoras señores. *Ladies and gentlemen.* Muy buenas noches, damas y caballeros, tengan todos ustedes. *Good evening ladies and gentlemen. Tropicana*, el cabaret MAS famoso del mundo … ≪*Tropicana*≫, *the most fabulous night-club in the WORLD* su *Nuevo* espectáculo … *its new show* … en el que artistas de fama continental … *where performers of continental fame* … se encargarán de transportarlos a ustedes al mundo maravilloso … *They will take you all to the wonderful world* … y extraordinario … of supernatural beauty … y hermoso … *of the Tropics.*

In the Puerto Rican Luis Rafael Sánchez's *La guaracha del macho Camacho* [Macho Camacho's Beat] (1976), characters take on the roles they are expected to perform by a warped sense of self fed by commercial films and other media. Darnell Martin's Puerto Rican stud-virtuoso in her *I Like It Like That* is all too close to Sánchez's character, Senator Vicente Reinosa, a man who relies on his perpetuation of movie Latin lover fame for his own sexual transgressions (1981: 17–18):

> Senator Vicente Reinosa … Is tied up, held up, caught up … In a traffic jam as phenomenal as life, *Made in Puerto Rico*, … lateness will impose haste on fornication. And hasty fornication is a procedure that, for my part, has never been to my liking. And my established credentials as a tempestuous lover and my widespread fame as a meticulous wooer: *a sort of fucking superstar*, will suffer the consequences of a haste for which I am not responsible. Situations like the one I'm going through and enduring now are attacks on the maintenance, propagation, and perpetuation of the continental tradition of the *Latin lover*. And attacks against the unattainable cult … of the genital deeds of Ricardo Montalbán and me, Fernando Lamas and me, … Jorge Negrete and me, Mauricio Garcés and me.[2]

La China Hereje, Vicente's lover, wants to be the TV and film bombshell Iris Chacón; Graciela, his high-class wife, wants to be Liz Taylor, and his son is the movie-type, spoiled-rotten child of the rich: glamorously lazy, irresponsible, no intellect (and proud of it). These 'performances' of the Antillean character, these 'show-time' portrayals of countries under siege by economic need and tourism (and we must recall Puerto Rico's advertisement in travel-ads: 'Come to Paradise. ... Come to us, the "showcase" of the Caribbean') are here as our novelists attempt to serve us with a looking-glass in which to see ourselves, to see how we have masked ourselves with these stagnant myths created 500 years ago. Of this Caribbean discourse Benítez Rojo writes (1996: 220, emphasis added):

> The masquerade that the Caribbean discourse often puts on is nothing but a concession to the bungling of Christopher Columbus, who took the Caribbean for Asia and the *'indios'* for Indians. The West's idea of the Caribbean is a product of these and other mistakes and inventions. Acceptance of certain forms of Caribbean culture – such as music, dance, literature – in the great cities of the Western world owes substantially to these forms' playing the roles of the 'native', or the 'picturesque Indian maiden', the 'blithe Negress', the 'sensual *mulata*', the 'baroque creole', that is, *roles belonging in the farcical libretto that Europe has written about the Caribbean for five centuries.* Except that behind the words in that libretto, behind the 'Good evening ladies and gentlemen', behind the picturesque steps of the 'one-two-three-hop', *there lie codes that the Caribbean people alone can decipher. These are codes that refer us to traditional knowledge, symbolic if you will, that the West can no longer detect.*[3]

By applying Benítez Rojo's wisdom to the images we see on the commercial film screen, we begin to understand just what is wrong with the picture made of us. We begin to note that the inaccuracies instrumental to our cultural demise and to our confusion about national identity are inaccurate only by degrees, small but deadly degrees which force us into the typically tropical, and which the film-maker all too often takes as insignificant. The generic Caribbean is a place of carnivals, music and dance, for the West does not see (or want to see) the nuances which truly define us and make our region distinct within our myriad varieties. All carnivals in island-based film-texts seem necessarily Brazilian, and the Brazilian carnival dancing beat, the *batucada* takes the place of Cuba's *mambo* or of Puerto Rico's *plena* (*Moon Over Parador* [1988], *Captain Ron* [1993], *Fire Down Below* [1957]). Santo Domingo's *merengues* are heard on the streets of San

Juan, danced with boys who wear Rastafarian hairstyles and shirts (*Captain Ron*); African-American tap-dance to what is supposed to be a tropical beat, and the Mexican dance, the *charanga*, forms the steps within Argentinian fiestas (*Down Argentina Way*), Rita Hayworth sensuously dances a weird mixture of steps to the somewhat-offish beat of drums (*Fire Down Below*); a Venezuelan mulatto woman dances (and is dressed) in the belly-dancing tradition of the Orient (*The Black Swan*); islanders who live in New York are dressed and dance in the tradition of the Spanish Flamenco (*West Side Story*, 1961). All off, all inaccurate, but only to the eyes of the native who is familiar with the true codes of his or her distinct culture within the Caribbean region.

The point of the argument made here is not that the Caribbean is bereft of influences and should be portrayed in absolute purity, for there *is* no such thing as purity in our region. Our music is a reflection of what we are. Therefore, it necessarily involves a myriad of influences (going from African tribal beats to European Romanticism); in fact, *salsa* means mixture, a well-tuned concoction of diverse rhythms and beats. However, commercial cinema transgresses in that it claims specificity in its attempt to create the mood, the true atmosphere and movements of the Caribbean nations, only resulting in a messy array of the non-specific, misleadingly defining us by pushing together what *seems* tropical, recreating the sounds that *sound* Spanish. Where the real danger of this lurks is when we begin to take notice of the films made by natives and all too often see that too many of these inaccuracies are believed, or are convenient means of denoting the Caribbean self. When does the native stop identifying the codes that refer us to traditional knowledge? The process of misreading or misrepresenting cultural identities may, at times, be done out of innocence or unawareness. They are still deadly in the consequences they deliver.

One may follow the argument that we, the Caribbean natives, can tell the difference, know what is specific to our national traits, and what is shared on the regional level. It does not matter that Hollywood only thinks it knows us when we know ourselves. But do we? Do we know the specifically Jamaican and that which Puerto Rico shares with her sister island? Do we know what the Dominican responds to, what are the problems which assail Haiti? The truth of the matter is that we do not know ourselves, perhaps just as much as we are not known. In spite of our very similar cultures and the sharing of a history and an ocean, there is little solidarity among us. We do not question the fact that our own ground is utilized for military exercises which will be applied against our own people (Grenada, Haiti and Santo Domingo have all been invaded from US military bases in Puerto Rico). The fact is that we are each alone and isolated from each other within our exotic shores, misunderstood by our neighbours and misrepresented by the rest of the world. In fact, one of the strongest voices the Caribbean has is that of Gabriel García Márquez, and he has made isolation and solitude the unifying theme throughout his work: 'In reality, one writes only one book. ... You'll see that I am not writing the book of Macondo, but the book of solitude' (1982: 57).[4] Each of his texts tell us, in one way or another, that the spell which is binding our region within this isolation must be broken. There is a way out of the labyrinth caused by our unknowingness and solitude, this labyrinth maintained and perpetuated by a film industry for the sake of entertainment, of complacency, and maintenance of the status quo. The key with which to open the gates of this entrapping labyrinth lies, perhaps, within the very work of García Márquez, a writer with close ties to the cinema. The Nobel laureate once told a fellow journalist: 'I must try and break through the clichés about Latin America. Superpowers and other outsiders have fought over us for centuries in ways that have nothing to do with our problems. In reality, we are all alone' (Simons 1982: 7).

II

One of the most memorable attempts to delineate the depth, and warn of the danger, of the estrangement from ourselves is found in Macondo, a mirror of our region, a mythical place which, at one point, suffers from a strange illness in the famed novel *Cien años de soledad* [One Hundred Years of Solitude] (García Márquez 1981: 50–1):

> They had indeed contracted the illness of insomnia. Ursula, who had learned from her mother the medicinal value of plants, prepared and made them all drink a brew of monkshood, but they could not get to sleep and spent the whole day dreaming on their feet. In that state of hallucinated lucidity, not only did they see the images of their own dreams, but some saw the images dreamed by others.[5]

This state of 'hallucinated lucidity', where the Buendías see their dreams and the dreams of others, as if they lived within a perpetual cinematic projection (where the projector is turned on and off erratically), reminds us of the playful imagery depicted by Adolfo Bioy Casares in *La invención de Morel* [The Invention of Morel]

(1940). Yet, in Macondo, this 'hallucinated lucidity' is not in any way playful in its connotation. The tragic spell which assails the people of Macondo will cause them to lose not only the memory of who they are but also of everything that is, was, and will be. This, in a sense, is the curse of a seeping non-existence, a slow but steady voyage into total annihilation. What seems quite interesting is the fact that the magician Melquíades has chosen the new machine of photography (perhaps the author's playful recreation of a Latin American Meliés) to try and restore order in Macondo. If such technology helps bring Macondo into modernity, it will take the more primal art of magic to break the spell and restore order. Melquíades soon realizes that his image-machine recreates everything but only on a parallel plane. Macondo's real life is still fated to disappear. Once he breaks the spell with a magic potion Melquíades will dedicate himself to writing the history of Macondo in an unknown tongue which will eventually be deciphered by the last Buendía. Melquíades knows that if these 'one hundred years of solitude' are forgotten they will only be fatally repeated.

Despite a hundred revolutions, the bloodshed, the new decades with new dictators, everything remains fatally the same. In an act of revitalizing the word over the image, for the images in our region are easily lies, García Márquez tells the story of Macondo so that we may see ourselves. The real plague which besets Macondo is the plague of indifference, greed, a thirst for power at all costs, and an over-whelming solitude which leaves no room for love or solidarity. It is the same plague that assails much of the Caribbean today. Just as Aureliano deciphers Melquíades' parchments and lives through the destruction of Macondo, we too witness our own death, which is paraded before us.

El otoño del patriarca [The Autumn of the Patriarch] (1975) is yet another warning against living with the constructs and illusions fed us. From the moment Saenz de la Barra comes into the patriarch's life, the man who controls everything begins to lose control over his own identity. A mercenary hired to keep the patriarch's power intact, Saenz de la Barra sees fit to manipulate the image of the dictator. And the more his image is manipulated, the more the real patriarch loses his identity, and the image takes over. Significantly, the patriarch is shown films which depict his wildest dreams, beautiful tales where love conquers all, even death (García Márquez (1976: 223):

> The all-worthy who knew everything never knew that ever since the time of José Ignacio Saenz de la Barra we had installed ... a closed-circuit television system so that he would see the movies arranged to his taste in which no one

died except the villains, love prevailed over death, life was a breath of fresh air, we made him happy.[6]

And they were not deceiving him in order to please him … but to keep him the captive of his own power.[7]

(1976: 239)

He who knew everything knew not himself. Power is not possessed even by patriarchs in the Caribbean. Again, as in *One Hundred Years of Solitude*, García Márquez uses celluloid and its manipulative potency as a metaphor for the life of mirages which exists throughout the Caribbean and Latin America. However, as the patriarch dies (along with his gullibility in believing everything) so too dies the wicked spell of corruption and the rule of mirages with which we have been complicit. Contrary to the apocalyptic whirlwind that destroys Macondo at the end of *One Hundred Years of Solitude*, in this novel about a fallen patriarch, we are given hope. If García Márquez was able to restore hope this time, perhaps for those of us who continue to believe, there might be a second chance for our region, a possible resurrection. This is a theme which will underline his best work to date. From the simple, yet remarkable story of love conquering death in his screenplay for *Milagro en Roma* [Miracle in Rome] (1988) to the more complex revival of Bolívar's notions of unity in his novel *El general en su laberinto* [The General in His Labyrinth] (1989), García Márquez wishes to confirm the idea that if Bolivar's body could not possibly come back to life physically, he could be immortal in the resurrection of his dream of solidarity.[8] And here lies the magical potion, the solution we must seek to leave our labyrinth of solitude. For if we have believed the manipulative lies told about us and our region, if our cultural identity has been symbolically demolished, appropriated and changed into a largely uncontested construction of a performed and bastardized self, it is time now to use the most powerful weapon offered us – cinema – to contest and reappropriate, to humanize our identity, to break the spell of this 'hallucinated lucidity' with an endeavour defined by love and human solidarity.

III

It is truly the dream of solidarity which forges the creation and extremely difficult economic subsistence of the Foundation for New Latin American Cinema [Fundación del Nuevo Cine Latinoamericano], established, with the help of García Márquez, in Cuba in 1985. García Márquez is its mentor, its international spokesman, fund-raiser, a major economic contributor, adviser, best friend. He occasionally teaches screenwriting at the Fundación's film school. His style, his sense of imagery, and his unique sense of story-telling all lead young film-makers to the desire of telling their own stories by creating their own constructs. 'What we have to do now', he tells *Variety*, 'is struggle for an identity and for the reaffirmation of independence. ... We need to make films that our own audiences like – not those we make now to try to win at Cannes' (1996: 55) It was not coincidental that the film series *Amores difíciles* came about when García Márquez was researching for his novel *El general en su laberinto*. During the day, he found himself crafting scripts, while he pored over letters, books and documents about Simón Bolívar all through the night. Before long, García Márquez found himself deeply moved, touched by the splendour of this statesman's ideals. As if to recreate Bolívar's efforts at unifying America, García Márquez led production of the six films of *Amores difíciles* [Difficult Loves], working with well-known directors from Brazil, Colombia, Mexico, Cuba and Venezuela, for what was to be the first Foundation project. The writer was now finally indulging in his life-long passion for the movies, appropriating the very language he knew could be capable of creating the most dangerous of travesties. In a *New York Times* inter-view, when asked about this particular film project and the film school these come from, García Márquez said: 'The principal problem we have in Latin America is finding our identity. That is what we are looking for here. Who are we? What are we like?' (Rohter 1989: 9). He continued to say (ibid):

> The only thing I have ever studied almost to completion in my entire life is the cinema. ... *The idea of the foundation is to forge a unitary Latin American cinema, recognizing that each nation has its own characteristics and culture, but taking into account the common features.* I think the reason our cinema has not flourished until now is this continental division, with nothing but dispersed efforts. Obviously, all of this forms part of a bigger idea I have, which is the total integration of Latin America, as Bolívar saw it (emphasis added).

In love with film since, as a child in Aracataca, he saw the first Tom Mix Westerns, García Márquez has now become something of a towering figure in the world of cinema. He calls upon film-makers, screenwriters, and producers such as Robert Redford, Francis Coppola (both investigated by the CIA for possibly violating the US trade embargo against Cuba), Sidney Pollack, Jonathan Sanger, or Ruy

Guerra, to give of their time and creativity to teach a younger generation of artists, and they respond wholeheartedly. Of his efforts in getting the best film-makers from around the world to help with the Foundation's film school, the writer says: 'Despite all the problems they have with the immigration service to come here, they still do it. They're helping us' (Wolin 1990: 19).

The fact that the Foundation is on Cuban ground, and that its film school has an agenda (although it is not the one most would think), has caused concern among right-wing politicians, journalists and Hollywood professionals. Merle Linda Wolin, in her article 'Hollywood Goes Havana' reports: 'the Cubans and their friends are using a cultural project to legitimize one of the last bastions of Stalinist rule – and then roping in Hollywood to do the PR' (p. 17). In fact, the film school takes a critical stance through comedy, it laughs at the many ways in which the Caribbean nation tries (in many ways, unsuccessfully) to decolonize its own sense of self, but at the same time, it shows how independence and survival are possible with little or no resources.

Plaff (1990) opens with a shot of two lovers kissing on a living-room sofa, but the shot is projected upside down. After a couple of seconds, a voice-over requests patience and tolerance with their broken-down equipment but good intentions, and the camera-shot is corrected. We are later informed that the film opened with the wrong sequence as the order of the reels was mistaken. The point of the story, however, if not its sequence, remains the same. Following the cue of an earlier film movement – Brazil's Cinema Novo – *Plaff* indulges in the very knowledge that the film (much like its country) can *never* be like its Hollywood counterpart; romance is imbued with bad-breath and hair-rollers, cars are smoking, engines backfire and gadgets break down, the sound goes off, the lights go off, glamour is non-existent, and actresses forget their lines, but there is a ferocity in the belief that with all the limitations and ills which assail the island they will survive. And survival comes best through self-knowledge, acceptance, and the dignity and strength these instil.

An earlier film, Puerto Rico's *La Gran Fiesta* [The Big Feast], directed by Marcos Zurinaga in 1985, attempted, by its clever staging, to demystify a dark page of Puerto Rico's colonial history, a moment of decision concerning our acceptance of American military intervention and economic dominance. This is done without scenes of violence, no blood is shed, no bombs under tables go off. Rather, the film recreates a very modern, physically non-violent colonization by the US. To recreate this complex process the film frames its story metaphorically within a dance, the last dance Puerto Rican elite families would have in the Casino de Puerto Rico, in 1942. In the midst of a fearful war looming over Europe (but feared in the Caribbean as well) that night the Casino is 'voluntarily transferred' by those in power to Uncle Sam's 'benevolent' protection and rule. The film presents the story of a country under siege, but the siege takes place through the use and manipulation of an instilled fear and the paralysis such fear, and lack of self-knowledge, imposes.

Music is used metaphorically to present the story. A young political idealist is threatened with the destruction of his family if he chooses the wrong girl to marry (a country and an ideal both symbolically transposed to an intelligent, beautiful and very independent woman). If his family is to remain on the island and in control of their business, if he wishes to maintain the easy lifestyle he has become used to, the woman he loves has to be sacrificed. With the help of an astutely chosen musical score the story is dramatized. In a crucial scene, while he deliberates on his final decision, the song 'Summertime' is being crooned in the background. The young idealist makes his choice as the beautiful woman he loves (symbolically the ideal of a free nation) walks away, doors closing behind her, in favour of the benefits non-resistance and complacency may offer, namely military security and economic welfare. Another key scene in this film shows an impertinent youth, the poet-son of a wealthy family (Raul Juliá), momentarily take over the Casino's stage, drowning out the music, halting the dance, to correct daringly the conveniently inaccurate double-talk (and the action it implies) used to describe the overtaking of the Casino by the American military. What is taking place is not a *traspaso* [transfer] he points out, rather, this should be called *la entrega* [surrender]. Finally, in a poem he passionately recites for the audience, with his flashy style and deeper wit, he ends his very Antillean 'performance' by declaring his refusal to acknowledge weakness, fear, incapacity, and paralysis as the characteristics of his people and the country they are born to: 'Lo imposible *no es* Boricua!'.

Indeed, this acknowledgment that 'the impossible is not Puerto Rican' is one the entire Caribbean region must adhere to. As Caliban did before us (in making French, Spanish, English or Dutch his own), we must take this new tool the modern Conqueror continues to dominate with, and make it our own, appropriate the machine's language, speak with our own images of flickering shadows and light. We must recognize the importance film and television have in our time, as accessible media with powerful possibilities. As these last cinematic examples have shown us, this is not an impossible task. Many do not know, or choose to ignore, that our region is a highly fragmented movie market, for governments typically impose protectionist limits on film distribution from neighbouring countries (other than the US, for Hollywood's business interests rule). The goal must be to change all this, to help create good features, as well as a market which unifies instead of divides, to offer a much needed counterpoint to the cinema created or defined by Hollywood, and all this should be geared towards aiding the understanding of our common history as well as our common goals. And breaking with the images which lie about us, as well as rocking the boat of complacency for the mass audience of cinema, certainly should be common goals. A news release on García Márquez's most recent film project *Edipo alcalde* [Mayor Oedipus] (1996), a film co-written with Orland Senna and Stella Malagnon and directed by Jorge Ali Triana, describes it as 'the kind of tragic vision of a continent that must make the tourist authorities quake in their boots'. So it seems that the writer turned film-maker remains adamantly set on rocking that boat.

After our initial incursion into the cinema of, or about, the Caribbean, certain questions loom. When will the spell of our 'hallucinated lucidity' be broken? When will we know ourselves, find what truly defines us? Until we answer these, we cannot, and should not, expect the rest of the world to know us. It is now our turn, it is now in our hands, to correct the many misconceptions which still abound. Images based on García Márquez's men with wings, resurrected children or women who cook with rose-petals may be used to tell the people of Macondo (as did the word before it), that our fate is one with the fate of others; that which assails one island today may assail another island tomorrow. Perhaps it is through the creation of a truly regional (but essentially international) film industry that we may be granted life again, resurrect and forge the America men such as Bolívar or Martí died dreaming of. Melquíades' camera-box may break the spell after all. With united efforts, the dream of solidarity may once again be found, a flickering projector's light leading us out, this time, of the dark labyrinth of solitude, if only with one single expression, voiced in our cinema. Indeed, *Lo imposible no es Caribeño* [The impossible is not Caribbean].

Notes

1   In the translation by Gregory Rabassa. [*En este estado de alucinada lucidez no sólo veían las imágenes de sus propios sueños, sino que los unos veían las imágenes soñadas por otros.*] (García Márquez 1967: 46.)
2   *El Senador Vicente Reinosa ... está atrapado, apresado, agarrado ... por un tapón fenomenal como la vida, made in Puerto Rico, ... la tardanza impondrá la precipitación del fornicio. Y el fornicio precipitado es un procedimiento aficionado por mi parte nunca recurrido. Y mi cartel establecido de amante tempestuoso, y mi fama pregonada de cortejo meticuloso: a sort of fucking superstar, sufrirán las*

consecuencias de una prisa de cuya razón no soy yo el responsable. Situaciones como esta que ahora vivo y padezco atentan contra el sostenimiento, propagación, y perpetuación del latin lover. Y atentan contra el culto ... a las hazañas genitales de Ricardo Montalbán y yo, Fernando Lamas y yo, [...] Jorge Negrete y yo, Mauricio Garcés y yo (Sánchez 1976: 27–30).

3   *La mascarada que en muchas ocasiones dibuja el discurso caribeño no es otra cosa que una concesión a la chapucería de Cristobal Colón, que tomó al Caribe por Asia y a los 'indios' por indios. La imagen que tiene el Occidente del Caribe as producto de esa y otras tergiversaciones e invenciones. La aceptación de ciertas formas de la cultura caribeña – digamos, la música, el baile, la literatura – en las capitales del mundo occidental se debe, en buena medida, a que éstas interpretan de alguna u otra manera el papel de la* 'nativa', *de la* 'india pintoresca', *de la* 'negra jaracandosa', *de la* 'mulata sensual', *de la* 'criolla barroca'; *es decir,* **el libreto farseco que Europa ha escrito sobre el Caribe a lo largo de cinco siglos** *Sólo que tras las líneas de ese libreto, tras las palabras de gentlemen, tras los pasos pintorescos del* one two three hop, Good evening, ladies and **hay códigos que sólo los caribeños pueden descifrar. Son códigos que remiten al conocimiento tradicional, simbólico si se quiere, que Occidente ya no puede registrar**. (Benítez Rojo 1989: 246–7, emphasis added).

4   *En realidad, uno no escribe sino un libro ... Verás que el libro que yo estoy escribiendo no es el libro de Macondo, sino el libro de la soledad.*

5   *Habían contraído, en efecto, la enfermedad del insomnio. Ursula, que había aprendido de su madre el valor medicinal de las plantas, preparó e hizo beber a todos un brebaje de acónito, pero no consiguieron dormir, sino que estuvieron todo el día soñando despiertos. En este estado de alucinada lucidez no solo veían las imágenes de sus propios sueños, sino que los unos veían las imágenes soñadas por los otros.* (García Márquez 1967: 46).

6   Translation by Gregory Rabassa. *El benemérito que todo lo sabía no supo nunca que desde los tiempos de José Ignacio Saenz de la Barra le habíamos instalado ... un circuito cerrado de televisión para que sólo él viera las películas arregladas a su gusto en las cuales no se morían sino los villanos, prevalecía el amor contra la muerte, la vida era un soplo, lo hacíamos feliz con el engaño* (García Márquez 1975: 225)

7   *Y no lo engañaban para complacerlo ... sino para mantenerlo cautivo de su propio poder.* (García Márquez 1975: 242)

8   *Milagro en Roma* [Miracle in Rome], directed by Lisandro Duque Naranjo (1988). This screenplay, written by the director and García Márquez, is one of six features in the film series *Amores difíciles* [Difficult Loves]. The other features are: *Un señor muy viejo con alas enormes* [A Very Old Man with Enormous Wings], directed by Fernando Birri; *La bella palomera* [The Beautiful Dove-Keeper], directed by Ruy Guerra; *Cartas del parque* [Letters from the Park], directed by Tomás Gutiérrez Alea; *Yo soy la que buscas* [I am the Woman You are Looking for], directed by Jaime Chavarri; and *La señorita Forbes* [Miss Forbes]. All six films are based on scripts, novels, tales, or ideas by García Márquez and all explore various aspects of love.

Epilogue: 1898 and all that

Alistair Hennessy

The understandably obsessive concern of Cubans, Puerto Ricans and Spaniards with the intervention of the United States at the end of the Cuban War of Independence, which had lasted nearly 30 years, generated a spate of centennial conferences on both sides of the Atlantic, resulting in revisions, re-interpretations and new perspectives.[1]

For those unaffected directly by the war, 1898 had no deep resonances but for Cubans and Puerto Ricans it was an emblematic date as the war's consequences were enshrined in an inequitable peace treaty at the deliberations for which they were not represented. Anomalous constitutional provisions embodied in the Platt Amendment of 1901 restricting Cuban sovereignty, and the semi-colonial incorporation of Puerto Rico into the American union, marked the end of an era. From now on power and cultural relations throughout the Americas would be completely transformed. The new century ushered in decades of armed intervention by the United States in both the Caribbean and Central America.

The war had global repercussions, especially in the Pacific, and presaged the passing of global hegemony from Britain to the United States, but it was in the rest of Spanish America that its effects were to be most apparent. Overwhelming American victory, accompanied by imperial pretensions, reminded Spanish Americans of the warnings of José Martí in 1889 of the threat from the United States to the rest of the continent which at that time had gone largely unheeded. The events of 1898 provoked two contradictory impulses: on one side it accelerated the process of Americanization and the onset of modernity in Cuba and Puerto Rico (and to a far lesser degree in the Dominican Republic which had been independent since 1821). On the other side, it contributed to the Latin Americanization of the Hispanic Caribbean, strengthening a sense of cultural and economic solidarity against the enroaching power of the United States which was to reach a climax in the Cuban Revolution of 1959. The already deep gulf between the Hispanic islands, enveloped in an overarching Spanish American cultural universe, and their neighbours protected by the carapace of colonial rule was further deepened.[2]

Neither the French nor British West Indies were greatly concerned with the threat of the intrusive presence of the United States. The French islands had been assimilated politically into the French republican tradition and were linguistically and culturally impervious to American influences. They remained oriented, as they had been since 1635 and still are today, towards metropolitan France. For their part, the British had, by the end of the century, abandoned their forward-looking policy in the Caribbean and with imperial interests shifting to India and Africa had reluctantly accepted the Monroist principle. It was of little concern to them who ruled in Spain's ex-colonies provided political stability was assured. In any case, the British, alone of European powers, considered the 'splendid little war' a 'good thing' as they shared with the United States the *fin de siècle* mood of Anglo-American providentialism, with its echoes of the Black Legend which had clouded Anglo-American perceptions of Hispanic people for three hundred years. Nothing but good, in this view, could come from exposure to American ideas and the invigorating influence of Protestant missionaries who avidly seized opportunities to proselytize in both Cuba and Puerto Rico. Furthermore, influenced by events in Haiti the British, whose racialism had hardened under social Darwinist influence, tended to share the contemptuous view most Americans had of Cuba's black population.

The cultural threat of de-hispanicization posed by American occupation and influence was, of course, much more overt in Puerto Rico. In Cuba, with its nominal independence, qualified by the Platt Amendment, the threat was more insidious and contradictory. American reconstruction of the devastated island left Cubans with ambivalent attitudes – admiration for US technology tempered by a grudging gratitude. Cuba became the first showpiece outside the United States of American modernity, drive and efficiency, as well as becoming a major field of endeavour for overseas investment now that the continental frontier had 'closed'. Although American occupation restored the countryside to a semblance of normality the price paid was high in terms of national self-esteem, but it was one which the Cuban elite was prepared to pay in order to have American protection in the event of a threat to their survival.

Americanization, however, was matched by an unexpected surge of hispanicization. In spite of the savagery of General Weyler's concentration policy, a grim portent of the total wars of the twentieth century, Spaniards were welcomed back to the newly independent Republic. Immigration from Spain was actively encouraged at the same time as black immigration was forbidden by decree. In this way it was assumed that the population would be 'whitened'. This exemplified the dilemma which had haunted Cuban nationalists. What constituted the essence of nationality? Was the new Republic to be white, Hispanic and exclusivist as the theorists of *cubanidad* in the 1830s had envisaged or would it be realization of Martí's *Cuba Libre* vision of a racially harmonious and integrated society where there would be no Whites or Blacks, only Cubans, and where the plantation would be replaced by a society of small landowners in a diversified economy? United States intervention effectively killed off Martí's *Cuba Libre*. For the white elite, many of whom through years of exile in the United States had come to share the American racist views which were to become widespread during the military occupation of 1898–1902 and again in 1906–9, reluctantly accepted the Platt Amendment, permitting US intervention in the case of threats to property or from black radicalism with its support among the predominantly coloured ex-veterans of the Liberating Army.

Discriminatory practices in the early years of the Republic, in the police, in education, in land distribution and in the bureaucracy, excluded Blacks from the spoils of office and led to the forming of the *Partido Independiente de Color* and finally erupted in the 'Race War' of 1912, the largest rising of its kind in the twentieth-century Caribbean. This was provoked, in large measure, by the Morúa Law, forbidding the organization of parties based on colour in an attempt to encourage racial integration, but it badly misfired.[3]

It was not until the 1920s when the 'Other' became fashionable that a new inclusive nationalism slowly emerged, based on recognition of the Cuban African heritage as a key component in national identity and influenced by the theories of Fernando Ortiz, the poems of Nicolás Guillén and later by the novels of Alejo Carpentier.

The assertion of an African dimension in Cuban nationhood was one aspect of the burgeoning anti-imperialist sentiment of the early 1920s, on the collapse of the war-induced sugar boom and under the influence of the Mexican and Russian Revolutions. These events had found intellectual legitimization in Spengler's *Decline of the West* which had been published in Spanish in 1922. His view of the rise and fall of civilizations in circular progression challenged the Eurocentric linear interpretation of history and gave an impetus to the belief that after the debacle of the 'European Civil War' the Americas would become the cradle of a new civilization.

The major carriers of a new Cuban nationalist spirit engendered by these factors were the students of Havana University under the influence of the University Reform Movement which had originated in the Argentine University of Córdoba in 1918 with its notion of a democratized university where power was shared between professors and students. This would serve as a model for society in general with students arrogating to themselves the role of a regenerating elite, nourished on the idea of the incorruptibility of youth. The foundation of the FEU (*Federación de Estudiantes Universitarios*) in 1923 under this influence institutionalized the rumbustious tradition of student activism with its roots in the independence struggle when Havana University had been a bulwark of nationalist views. Until tamed after 1959, students were to be key actors as an oppositional force in revolutionary politics. Nothing could have been further from the political university than the University of Puerto Rico, established by the Americans in 1903.[4] Modelled on the Land Grant College, with English as the language of instruction, it had a pragmatic orientation, concentrating on business and education. Downgrading the dominant role of Law Faculties in the traditional Hispanic university was a deliberate way to prevent the new institution from becoming a nationalist forum. The absence of a university in Puerto Rico during the colonial period may have been one factor in hindering the development of a national consciousness comparable to what had happened in Havana. However, the University of Puerto Rico would make up for lost time in the 1960s when, under the influence of the Cuban Revolution, it was in the vanguard of nationalist agitation.

In Spanish America, the critical Spenglerian view of Europe was not felt to apply to Spain which had remained neutral during the war, so that the process of re-evaluating the Spanish heritage which had begun in the early 1890s was given an additional boost. This changing attitude, in such marked contrast to the condemnation of everything Spanish after the loss of the mainland empire in the 1820s, was partly due to the effectiveness of Spanish propaganda and partly to the writings of the Generation of 1898. One aspect of the centennial conferences in Europe has been a reassessment of the concept of the Generation. One does not have to share the view that it was a 'mischievous term which has been endlessly masticated, like a piece of chewing gum, passed from mouth to mouth until it has lost all its flavour' to appreciate the significance of the emergence of intellectuals as the nation's moral guardians and as a regenerating elite, echoing the role of the dreyfusards in France.[5] For the first time both the quantity and quality of Spanish writers guaranteed a serious readership throughout Spanish America.

Nevertheless these writers were deeply divided over prescriptions for regeneration. The issues they raised were sharpened and their views criticized – particularly their political quiescence – by José Ortega y

Gasset. Although he was to found the *Liga de Educación Política* in 1913 it had little immediate effect and his influence was not destined to lie in political leadership but in his writings and editorial work, particularly through the *Revista de Occidente*, founded in 1923 (and still extant) which became a pace-maker for journals throughout the Hispanic world, and in his wide-ranging comments on Hispanic and European culture generally.[6] Many must have learnt about European and particularly German thinkers for the first time from the pages of the *Revista*.

Attempts to foment a sense of pan-Hispanic solidarity during the Primo de Rivera dictatorship (1923–30) could not obscure the deepening divisions at home which Primo's rule had failed to resolve. These were to be given freer and more vocal expression during the Second Republic.

Historians have so far failed to study the Hispanic world adequately and comparatively in the twentieth century and yet Spanish American republics were facing similar problems in the 1930s.[7] All experienced the consequences of the economic recession which exacerbated issues which were common to them and to Spain – agrarian reform, civil-military conflict, church-state hostility, the polarization and factionalism of politics. The failure to resolve these issues resulted in the outbreak of the Spanish Civil War in 1936. No Spanish American republic remained unaffected, not least Cuba, whose links with Spain were closer than any other republic. Once the war broke out Cuba contributed more republican volunteers per head of population than any other foreign power as well as sending the largest delegation of writers to the International Congress for the Defence of Culture in 1937, in which the most significant Cuban was Nicolás Guillén.

The Civil War marks a crucial stage in Guillén's intellectual development. He joined the communist party in Spain; his views on Afro-Hispanism were confirmed, and he linked the Abyssinian resistance to Italian invasion with the fascist and anti-colonial struggle, something which the European left found embarrassing in view of the feudal nature of the Abyssinian regime. However, for Guillén as for Blacks generally Abyssinia, as the oldest independent black state in Africa, was held in particular affection as evidence of the longevity of African civilization, becoming a source of inspiration for Marcus Garvey, Rastafarians and other Afrocentric thinkers.

In Cuba, the war had a profound political effect, contributing to the rehabilitation of Batista and facilitating the emergence of the communists as a respectable political party, with long-term consequences for the later consolidation of Castro's revolution. Many of the ideas which underpinned the revolution were of Spanish provenance.

For Franco, the defeat of 1898 was avenged by the Cubans' defence of their national sovereignty against the United States after 1959, a view reflected in the unexpected but pragmatic relationship between Castro and Franco, both pariahs, the one in Europe, the other in the Americas, but both united in their scorn for the United States and resentful of its intervention in Cuba in 1898.[8]

In Puerto Rico and the Dominican Republic, the Civil War's impact was more diluted, although in the former support for the Republic from the younger generation clashed with the *hispanidad* of Albizu Campos who, in the 1930s, was the acknowledged nationalist leader with his support for traditional Hispanic values.[9]

In the United States, opinion towards the War was deeply divided because of the power of the Catholic lobby which was to have repercussions during the McCarthy period. In cultural terms, however, the War was to have a lasting positive effect. Through the diaspora of exiled republican intellectuals Hispanic Studies received a boost comparable to that of German exiles fleeing Nazism and to that of the later diaspora of Cuban exiles. The rise of the Hispanics in the United States of which these two diasporas were such a significant part enriched the culture of the Hispanic Caribbean as many of the essays in this collection testify, reflecting the complexities and tensions between diaspora and homeland – that experience common to all Caribbean societies.

Exile for political reasons has been a common experience for many in the Hispanic Caribbean, from Martí and Hostos to the present. While in exile an awareness of a shared Caribbean identity is often aroused, overcoming insular attitudes perpetuated by colonial legacies which continued to exist in the islands in spite of the homogenizing influences of slavery and plantation-based economies. A major factor marking off Hispanic societies from the rest of the Caribbean was that they were settlement colonies in which migrants from Spain were creolized to an extent that rarely occurred in the predominantly plantation colonies of Britain, France and the Netherlands, whose officials and planters, with few exceptions, were birds of passage with no deep roots in the soil. In these colonies creolization was mainly confined to slaves, ex-slaves and coloureds.

In these latter colonies, with their population of predominantly African descent, black ideologies such as *négritude*, Fanonism, Garveyism, Pan-Africanism and Rastafarianism are in marked contrast to the Hispanic Caribbean where there has been no equivalent of 'Back to Africa' movements. In Cuba, for example, in spite of black intellectuals arguing in the early 1960s for a specifically African-based foreign policy it was not until the 1970s that such a policy was initiated with interventions in Angola and Ethiopia and increased aid programmes.[10]

A further differentiating factor is the contrast between Catholic and Protestant societies – the former permitting no latitude in religious practice, the latter tolerating dissenting sects. The established Church was the prop of the plantocracy whereas the sects were allies of the oppressed. Where there is no sect tradition there can be either a flight to secular ideologies as in French republicanism and utopian socialism or to metaphysical alternatives, as in Spanish Krausism.[11] Through their educational work Krausists were a major influence on the development of modern Spanish liberalism affecting both José Martí and Eugenio Mariá de Hostos when they were students in Madrid. Without the dissenting voice of any sect, abolitionism was slow to develop in Spain, and when it did so it was due to Julio Vizcarrondo, a Puerto Rican Protestant married to an American abolitionist. Similarly, when abolitionism revived in France in the 1820s it did so under Victor Schoelcher, also a Protestant.

In the British West Indies, Protestant missionary sects – Methodists, Moravians, Presbyterians, Baptists (black and white) were robust in their opposition to the plantocracy. Their success in conversions contrasted with the Spanish experience in Cuba where earlier missionary zeal had been blunted in the gold-rush atmosphere of the sugar revolution. In addition to spearheading abolition, Protestant sects encouraged literacy, giving access to the Bible, and after emancipation they settled ex-slaves in 'free villages', promoting a counter-plantation proto-peasant culture.[12] The presence of black Baptist missionaries from America as early as the 1780s presaged the Africanization of Christianity and later co-operation between black Americans and West Indians in 'Back to Africa' colonization movements and missionary projects.[13]

These early contacts with Americans were followed by others when West Indians began to migrate in search of work, first to Panama and Costa Rica, later to Cuba and then, during and after the First World War, to the United States itself, specifically to Harlem. These migrant waves differed in one crucial respect. In the former, migrants were subjected to racial abuse by white American overseers. In the latter, they created a predominantly black environment where their education and skills – entrepreneurial, cultural and political – gave them the edge over less skilled, less well-educated migrants from the Deep South many of whose self-confidence had been sapped by segregation.

West Indians made a positive contribution to the Harlem Renaissance and in Garveyism provided the inspiration and leadership of the largest black movement until the 1960s with followers throughout the British Caribbean, in Central America and Cuba as well as in

Africa itself.[14] There was no comparable black Hispanic migration and Hispanic diasporas were slow to develop (the period during the Cuban War of Independence excepted) apart from Puerto Ricans until, during and after the 1960s when they were joined by the enormous predominantly white Cuban migration and a lesser flow of Dominicans.

The success of West Indians in the United States was due to common ties of language, to their educational, religious and family background and to the shelter of the ghetto, which shielded them from the humiliation of racial abuse (although American Blacks could resent their success). A long-term effect was to dispel residual anti-American feeling and to strengthen ties with the United States to such an extent that in a Jamaican poll in the late 1970s some 60 per cent expressed a wish to settle there permanently and even 43 per cent considered Jamaica would be better off as the 51st state of the Union.[16]

The centrality of the African issue in Cuba was intimately related to the inexorable expansion of sugar plantations. The most pungent and influential attack on the threat of this expansion to national identity was Ramiro Guerra y Sánchez, *Azúcar y población en el Caribe* (1927) in which he held up the *patricios*, the old original families, as the founders of Cuban nationality.[17] However, they had been ruined by the growth of impersonal foreign-owned sugar corporations which depended on imported black labour from Haiti and the British West Indies. These were, in Guerra's view, the major threat to Cuban nationality. In the face of the need for labour as plantations expanded into Oriente after 1913 the decree forbidding black immigration had been waived. Over the next 20 years as many as 300,000 *braceros* or *antillanos* were introduced, creating in the view of the press another 'Africanization of Cuba' scare, recalling that of the 1850s, just at the moment when intellectuals like Fernando Ortiz were promoting Afro-Cubanism.

Elsewhere, peasants were regarded as the bed-rock of national identity, but in Cuba the *guajiros*, small-holding peasants, often Canary Islanders and squatters, were marginal to the economy and did not become the embodiment of national virtues or idealized heroes, as they often collaborated with planters as slave-catchers. In contrast, in Puerto Rico where sugar did not dominate the economy Africans were not felt to be a threat nor were they regarded as an element defining Puerto Rican nationality until José Luis González's daring best-seller *El pais de cuatro pisos* (1980). In his view the African population defined Puerto Rico as a people. Previously the *baros*, peasants of predominantly Hispanic stock, living in the interior, were idealized by the aristocratic elite who embraced an ideology of *Hispanismo* in opposition to American democratizing tendencies. This was to shade into

Hispanidad with Albizu Campos' admiration of *franquista* traditionalism.[18]

In the Dominican Republic, where slavery had been abolished in 1821, sugar plantations did not develop until the 1870s, employing a predominantly Haitian labour force. This, together with memories of the Haitian occupation, contributed to establishing Manuel de José Galván's romantic novel *Enriquillo* (1882) as a founding text. Idealizing an Amerindian chieftain who became hispanicized both legitimated historical claims to the land predating the introduction of slaves and bolstered the *Hispanismo* which had been such a distinctive aspect of elite ideology among cattle *caudillos*, who, opting for 'civilization' against 'barbarism', had invited Spain to annexe the country in 1861.[19] Although Spain had been compelled to withdraw after a war of resistance and in spite of their misrule, *Hispanismo* remained the dominant strand in nationalist ideology until the recent migration of Dominicans to the United States, where the success of black baseball players was a contributory factor to changing perceptions. The new view of Blacks reached a point that the major challenge to Joaquín Balaguer's strangehold over the presidency was a black candidate.

As the three islands have come to terms with assimilating what was previously considered to be unassimilable, so ties with the rest of the Caribbean, at least in cultural terms, have become closer in recognition of the centrality of the African contribution to the whole region's culture. In political terms, though, the gulf remains, not only with regard to the rest of the Caribbean but between Puerto Rico with its anomalous constitutional position and US-style political system, the Dominican Republic with its strong *caudillo* tradition (now being modified, since Trujillo's assassination in 1961, by democratic reforms), and finally Cuba with its one-party system.

In spite of a common language, religion, a Hispanic *modo de ser* and a common colonial overlord, each country has its own political culture, rooted in a distinctive history. Although proposals had been made by both creoles and Spaniards during the nineteenth century for some form of federation or confederation they came up against intractable opposition.[20] For centuries, the islands had been backwaters of empire, staging posts to service the trans-atlantic *flotas*, and bastions against threats from other colonial powers.

It was the crisis of empire in the opening decades of the nineteenth century which accelerated their divergent development. Cuba experienced the strains of rapid social change connected with the sugar revolution; Hispaniola was embroiled in the Haitian independence struggle, having to submit to a 20-year occupation by the Haitians; Puerto Rico was fortunate to remain on the margins. Cuba and, to a far lesser extent, Puerto Rico had to bear the burden of loss of empire by admitting Spanish refugees from the mainland and, more significantly, a constant stream of immigrants from Spain anxious to escape from civil wars and economic backwardness to the haven of peace and riches offered by Cuba. Independence was not a serious option given Britain's forward policy in the Caribbean, annexationist ambitions of the Southern States of America and the possible threat of a slave rising.[21] Hence the reluctant acceptance by Cubans of rule by Special Laws and Captains-General.

On the collapse of Spanish power in 1898 both Puerto Rico and Cuba were left politically rudderless. With the failure of proposals for granting autonomy, creoles had had no experience of self-government nor was there any unequivocally clear and established Spanish model of government to adopt – nothing comparable to the Westminster system or the French republican tradition.[22] The reason for this lay in the bankruptcy of Spanish liberalism which had failed to establish stable government in Spain itself where, being a minority creed, it was forced to depend on a symbiotic relationship with the military and the corrupt *cacique* system for its survival.

After 1898, therefore, political options were wide open with decisions being influenced by American rather than Spanish political practice. Puerto Rico was perhaps more fortunate in experiencing a workable form of parliamentary government which for all its deficiencies, leaving Puerto Ricans without political dignity, nevertheless was to ensure 24 uninterrupted elections. This was a remarkable record although not one to mollify nationalists in the face of the island's lack of sovereignty.[23]

The case of Cuba was quite different. Nationalism produced a devastated country, American intervention and the spectre of *caudillo* rule, quite apart from strengthening and extending the plantation system – precisely what Martí had most feared. Under American influence, during the first occupation the US-style political model was copied (down to a replica Congress building), incorporating a spoils system which contributed to instability. With the export-import trade concentrated in the hands of Americans, together with their land occupancy and control of sugar plantations, and with internal commerce controlled by the swelling number of Spanish immigrants, government became a major source of income for Cubans – hence the incessant factional conflicts to reward followers, with the possibility of appealing to United States to intervene under the Platt Amendment should electoral decisions be disputed.

The impact of recession after the First World War and the Great Depression resulted in the dictatorship of Gerardo Machado and Fulgencio Batista respectively – the latter an ex-army sergeant who came to power after the failure of the 1933 Revolution. Batista's populist regime up to 1940 constituted the prelude to a return to elections and parliamentary politics but corruption undermined its legitimacy, providing an excuse for Batista to return once again to power and for Fidel Castro to launch his campaign to overthrow him. This struggle revived the guerrilla tradition of the War of Independence, invoking the establishment of Martí's *Cuba Libre* which in Castro's view had been prevented through the American intervention.

The role of *líder máximo* which Castro adopted had been sanctified by Cuban tradition and legitimated by reference to Martí's teachings.[24] Inspirational though his life and writings might be, Martí's prescriptions were largely irrelevant in the conditions of the 1960s.

With the assistance of the United States embargo Castro continues to occupy the moral high ground, supported by UN resolutions; but paradoxically, by excluding the grosser aspects of Americanization the embargo has enabled him to pursue revolutionary goals which, however faded, can still impress by their commitmment to a vision of a society where the health, education and eradication of poverty among the *damnés de la terre* continues to be given the highest priority in defiance of economic profit. Should the embargo be removed, could these revolutionary goals survive?

Cuba is differentiated from Puerto Rico and the Dominican Republic not only by its size, wealth and political and social structure but by the myth of heroic resistance to Spanish rule embodied in the rural guerrilla and a revolutionary tradition stretching back to 1868, and in the case of African resistance through Maroons, further back still. Lacking such a myth or a comparable revolutionary tradition it is easy to understand the reasons for the Puerto Ricans' sense of inferiority which has conditioned Cuban attitudes towards them and their low-key heroism of compromise. Particularly savage has been Cuban condemnation for those who submitted to the American promotion of the Puerto Rican model as an alternative to the Cuban way.

Nor have the Dominicans been able to generate a comparable national myth of resistance. Haitians withdrew peacefully after the occupation of 23 years and the Spaniards in 1865 after their four-year failure to reannex. Many veterans of the war against them were soon to depart to fight with the rebel army in Cuba, one of whom, the Dominican veteran Máximo Gómez, became *generalísimo*.

In the Dominican Republic itself, regional *caudillos* continued to dispute control until Ulises Heureux established a 17-year domination between 1882 and 1899, when he attempted to create a national state by building up the bureaucracy and promoting economic development – but at the price of mortgaging future revenues, forcing the United States to intervene to collect debts and manage the customs, partly to avoid European creditors from doing so.[25] A further intervention between 1916 and 1924 provoked a guerrilla resistance but when the marines withdrew they left a supposedly politically neutral constabulary which in fact provided the base for Trujillo to seize power in 1930 and establish one of the most repressive dictatorships in the region's history. His assassination in 1961 provoked yet another intervention in 1965 to forestall a Cuban-style revolution. Since then there has been a gradual process of democratization.

Although the political record of Cuba and the Dominican Republic raised deep distrust and suspicion among democratic politicians elsewhere there is a powerful thrust, through the Association of Caribbean States, cutting across ideological barriers towards greater integration in the face of globalizing tendencies.[26] However, the continuing United States embargo of Cuba bolstered by the extra-territoriality of Helms-Burton and the banana dispute between peasants and plantation calls into question the nostrums of free-marketeers and exposes the continuing dependence on the United States.

What of the future in the age of globalization? Faced with the fissiparous tendencies of Caribbean politics and the threats to the region from its vulnerability to climatic changes and the predators of the age – drugs barons, money launderers, sexual adventurers, property speculators, multi-national companies, banking agencies, fundamentalist sects and fanatics fired by millennial visions, the prospect is not reassuring. There is, however, the compensation for intellectuals, writers, musicians and artists that they are heirs to a rich and varied culture. How that culture is defined has given rise to an academic industry, providing a testing ground for social and cultural theories, one of which emphasizes the central role of the Caribbean in the development of the post-Renaissance world.

Through the establishment of the sugar plantation, the Caribbean became the harbinger of modernity. The 'factory in the field', with its relentless work-discipline, foreshadowed the factories of the Industrial Revolution in Europe, to which slave trade and plantation profits made a substantial contribution.[27] With globalization the Caribbean may now be seen as an exemplar of post-modernity with its embrace of hybridity, and the diversity of its peoples drawn from all the continents through migration – forced, free and indentured – to create an *ajiaco*.[28]

In the making of this stew the Spanish contribution has been ambivalent. Historically the Hispanic Caribbean has been oriented towards Europe through the constant ebb and flow of Spanish migrants. There is scarcely a Spanish family which cannot show some connection, however small, with the Caribbean, especially Cuba. The surge of patriotism in 1898 was not simply press-induced but reflected the unease of many humble people who saw the possibility of a vanishing future, cut off from one of the few societies to which they could migrate without being forced into competition with more highly educated and better qualified foreigners, and where also there was a black labouring class to whom they could feel superior.[29]

If there is one feature which stands out it has been the slowness of the Hispanic Caribbean to come to terms with Africanity and to recognize that what binds the Caribbean together has, to a great extent been the resilience, exuberance and creativity of its people of African descent and, as essays in this collection make clear, interest in African culture has been very much a concern of writers trying to come to terms with the complexities of Caribbean culture. When salsa rules the dance halls of the West, octogenarian Cuban musicians can pack the world's concert halls and reggae has revolutionized popular music, one recalls the observation of the much-quoted and perceptive eighteenth-century traveller Père Labat: 'I have travelled everywhere in your sea of the Caribbean ... It is no accident that the sea which separates your lands make no difference to the rhythms of your body',[30] sensing the rhythms of music, song and dance as unifying factors overriding the impositions of status and race.

Because of the range and diversity of their imperial past the British, Dutch and French have experienced the phenomenon, absent from Spain, of an imploding imperial frontier, bringing back a flow of migrants from the ex-colonies, and creating multi-racial societies which are challenging accepted notions of national identity. Lacking a similar black diaspora as well as having had no equivalent to the huge African colonies of Britain and France, Spain is marginal to the 'Black Atlantic' community.[31]

Meanwhile in the ex-colonies the wheel has come full circle. The events of 1898 temporarily severed Hispanic Caribbean links with Europe, providing a space to renew cultural contacts and be re-incorporated with continental Spanish America. Adopting a defiant stance towards the United States took one form in the assertion of the superiority of Hispanic spiritual values against the materialist values of North America in the Caliban-Prospero-Ariel metaphors so beloved by Spanish American cultural commentators. But with political turbulence and economic imbalances throughout the region, political exiles and economic migrants moved to the United States where they have made a major contribution to the melt-down of the 'melting pot'. The 'Rise of the Hispanics' reflects the new reality of cultural pluralism which must be a sweet revenge for past humiliations and the travails of the long march since 1898.

Notes

1   For a collection from one of the conferences in Britain see Angel Smith and Emma Dávila-Cox (eds), *The Crisis of 1898: Colonial Redistribution and Nationalist Mobilization*, Macmillan, London, 1999. Further volumes will come from conferences in Manchester and London.

2   The concept of a Hispanic American culture is associated with the Dominican critic Pedro Henríquez Ureña (1884–1946) who spent most of his life outside his homeland. For an analysis of his life and ideas see Arcadio Díaz Quiñones. 'Pedro Henríquez Ureña: modernidad, diaspora y construcción de identidades' in Gilberto Jimenez and Ricardo Pozas (eds), *Modernizacíon e Identidades*, UNAM, Mexico 1994 and the centenary Henríquez Ureña issue of *Casa de las Americas*, No. 144, 1984, May–June.

3   For long the 'Race War' was glossed over in Cuban historiography but see now the detailed and excellent study by Aline Helg, *Our Rightful Share: The Afro-Cuban Struggle for Equality, 1886–1912,* University of North Carolina Press, Chapel Hill, 1995. Santiago Morúa, an ex-slave, was President of the Senate and an integrationist in the Martían sense. He was one of the black intellectuals to come to prominence in the 1880s. For his novels see William Luis, *Literary Bondage: Slavery in Cuban Narrative*, University of Texas Press, Austin, 1990.

4   Arthur Liebman, *The Politics of Puerto Rican University Students,* Austin, 1970. Spanish did not replace English until 1948. The elite tended to boycott UPR. The total university population of Puerto Rico in 1989 was in the region of 200,000 in comparison with the University of the West Indies which had only 12,000 although the population of Puerto Rico and Jamaica, Barbados and Trinidad was approximately the same. For the Spanish American context see Joseph Maier and Richard Weatherhead (eds), *The Latin American University,* Albuquerque, 1978. There were many cultural forms of black resistance in Cuba although the preponderance of Whites militated against a Maroon phenomenon comparable to Jamaica and Surinam. Until recently, however, little research has been done on Cuban Maroon communities – ancestors of the rural guerrilla. See the classic Miguel Barnet, *Autobiography of a Runaway Slave: Esteban Montejo,* Introduction by A. Hennessy, Macmillan, London, 1993. African culture was perpetuated in *santería, abakúa* and the *cabildos* which after their prohibition in 1888 became masonic-style mutual aid societies in which African names were replaced by those of popular Catholic saints. See M. Barnet, *The African Presence in Cuban Culture,* 2nd Rodney Memorial Lecture, University of Warwick, 1986.

5   Sebastian Balfour, 'The Solitary Peak and the Dense Valley': Intellectuals and the Masses in Fin de Siècle Spain', *Tesserae I,* 1994–5. See also E. Inman Fox, 'El año de 1898 y el origén de los intelectuales' in his *La Crisis Intelectual del 1898,* Cuadernos para el Diálogo, Madrid, 1976. For the Caribbean see A. Hennessy (ed.), *Intellectuals in the 20th Century Caribbean*: Vol. II, *Unity in Variety,* Macmillan, London, 1992.

6   A useful overview is Andrew Dobson, *An Introduction to the Politics and Philosophy of José Ortega y Gasset,* Cambridge, University of Cambridge, 1989.

7   A rare attempt to do so is Mark Falcoff and Frederick B. Pike (eds), *The Spanish Civil War, 1936–9, American Hemispheric Perspectives*, University of Nebraska Press, Lincoln, 1982. For Cuba see chapter by Hennessy.

8   This is discussed in A. Hennessy and G. Lambie (eds), *The Fractured Blockade: West European-Cuban Relations during the Revolution*, Macmillan, London, 1993, especially Chapter 8.

9   For this see Luis Angel Ferrao, 'Nacionalismo, Hispanismo y elite intelectual' in the important collection edited by Alvaro Curbelo and Maria Elena Rodríguez Castro, *Del nacionalismo al populismo*, Huracán, Río Piedras, 1992. For Albizu Campos see Antonio M. Stevens-Arroyo, *Catholicism as Civilization: Contemporary Reflections on the Political Philosophy of Pedro Albizu Campos*, CISCLA Working Paper, Inter-American University, San Germán, 1992.

10 The most pungent analysis of Cuban Blacks' discontent with Castro's policy and the African policy alternative of Walterio Carbonell is Carlos Moore, *Castro, the Blacks and Africa,* University of California, Los Angeles, 1988.

11 Krausism is the best example of the switch from French to German philosophical influences and illustrates the way in which in peripheral societies (which Spain was in the 19th century) little-known figures often exert undue influence – Kardek is perhaps another case in point. For succinct analyses of French Caribbean ideologies see R. Burton, 'The idea of difference in contemporary French West Indian thought: Négritude, Antillanité, Créolité' in Richard Burton and Fred Reno (eds), *French and West Indian: Martinique, Guadalupe and French Guiana*, Macmillan, London, 1993; and Michael Dash's introduction to Eduoard Glissant, *Caribbean Discourse: Selected Essays,* University of Virginia, Charlottesville, 1992.

12 The superb book by Richard D. E. Burton, *Afro-Creole: Power, Opposition and Play in the Caribbean,* Cornell University Press, Cornell, 1997 is a suggestive and subtle interdisciplinary analysis of the interplay between religion, carnival, cricket, and slave culture and its legacies. The chapter on cricket is particularly apposite as it is a key indicator of cultural differentiation between the anglophone Caribbean and the rest. The main focus of the book is on Jamaica.

13 For a brief overview see Vincent Franklin, 'Caribbean intellectual influences on Afro-Americans in the United States', in A. Hennessy, *Intellectuals*, Vol. 1.

14 Garvey and Garveyism can be studied in the indispensable and exhaustive ten volumes of Robert A. Hill (ed.), *The Marcus Garvey and Universal Negro Improvement Association Papers*, University of California, Los Angeles, 1983. There is considerable material on Cuba and Costa Rica. Garvey like Albizu Campos was much influenced by Irish nationalism but, unlike him, for its secular not Catholic implications.

15 Over 20 per cent of Cuban exiles in Florida in the 1890s were black compared with under 5 per cent today. Martí went out of his way to work with black exiles. The fundamental book for West Indians' political influence in the United States is Winston James, *Holding Aloft the Banner of Ethiopia*, Verso Books, London, 1998. From Hubert Harrison in 1900 to Stokeley Carmichael in the 1960s West Indians were in the vanguard of black radical movements in the United States. Claude McKay was a key literary figure in the Harlem Renaissance. An important link was established between the Renaissance and Guillén by Langston Hughes who visited Havana in 1930.

16 Carl Stone, *The Political Opinions of the Jamaican People (1976–81)*, Blackett, Kingston, 1982. There had even been talk of annexation among planters in the 1880s to protect their economic interests and again in 1898, fearing tariff discrimination from US-owned plantations in Cuba.

17   For a very suggestive comparison with Pedreira see A. Díaz Quiñones in Hennessy, *Intellectuals,* Vol. II.

18   *Hispandid* was the traditional right-wing form of *Hispanismo* popularized by Ramiro de Maeztu, *Defensa de la Hispanidad (1934).* The key book for Hispanism is Frederick B. Pike, *Hispanismo, 1898–1936: Spanish Conservatives and Liberals and their Relations with Spanish America,* Notre Dame University Press, Notre Dame, 1971.

19   The nature of Dominican *caudillismo* is analysed in H. Hoetink, *The Dominican People, 1850–1900,* Johns Hopkins University Press, Baltimore, 1982 and the ethnic question in Michiel Baud, '"Constitutionally White": The forging of a National Identity in the Dominican Republic', in Oostindie, *Ethnicity in the Caribbean,* Macmillan, London, 1996.

20   Hostos and Betances from Puerto Rico and Labra and Pi y Margall from Spain were the main proponents for federation.

21   Annexationism was integral to the Manifest Destiny ideology of the 1840s reflecting the aim of the Southern states to add another slave state to the Union and so change the sectional balance in the South's favour. Opinion in Cuba was divided between those who saw annexationism as a way to escape from Spanish backwardness and those who feared it would destroy all sense of Cuban identity.

22   The problem of being cast adrift by the *madrastra* (Spain) is well illustrated by Bolívar ransacking the political theories of Europe and the United States to find the perfect solution. The end result was the Bolivian Constitution of 1826, which was totally unworkable. The 'corporatist school' of political theorists and historians represents an alternative to liberalism but it can easily lead to fascism.

23   There is a huge literature on the Puerto Rican constitutional problem. See Juan Manuel García Passalaqua, 'The Role of the Puerto Rican People in the Caribbean' in J.I. Domínguez, R. Pastor and R. Delisle Worrell (eds), *Democracy in the Caribbean,* Johns Hopkins University Press, Baltimore, 1993. Anthony Maingot's original discussion is in his *The United States and the Caribbean,* Macmillan, London, 1993. For a sophisticated historical analysis see Raymond Carr, *Puerto Rico: A Colonial Experiment,* New York University Press, 1984.

24   The difficulty with Martí is that he was so eclectic in his writing that almost all political persuasions can find some justification in his writings.

25   This illustrates the fear of European intervention in the Caribbean during the Great War. There was considerable German property in both the Dominican Republic and Haiti. The Dominican guerrilla resistance by *gavilleros* parallels that in Haiti of the *cacos* during the same period. The resistance was a stimulus to the writings of Jean Price-Mars whose vindication of Haitian Blacks needs to be compared with Fernando Ortiz – see Richard Morse in Oostindie, *Ethnicity in the Caribbean.*

26   A penetrating, concise study is Andrés Serbin, *Sunset over the Islands – The Caribbean in an Age of Global and Regional Challenge,* Macmillan, London 1998.

27   Eric Williams, *Capitalism and Slavery,* first published in 1944, is still the classic view. It focuses on the British experience and does not question why slavery did not fuel an industrial revolution in Spain. Research on this needs to be done. Catalan industry was partly stimulated by the Cuban connection.

28   *Ajiaco* is a simmering stew combining 'The African name for an Indian condiment (*aji* or green pepper) with the Spanish suffix – *aco*'. See Morse in Oostindie, *Ethnicity in the Caribbean,* p. 31.

29 With *compadrazgo* ties and regional and extended family links Spanish immigrants were a tight group, organized in regional *centros*. It was one of the reasons for the Cubanization Law during the Revolution of 1933 limiting Spaniards to a 50 per cent stake in shops and businesses.

30 Quoted in Antonio Benítez-Rojo, *The Repeating Island, the Caribbean and the Post-modern Perspective,* Duke University Press, Durham, 1922, p. 35. The Caribbean can never be the same again after reading this extraordinary book.

31 Paul Gilroy, *The Black Atlantic: Modernity and Double Consciousness,* Verso Books. This does not touch on Spain or indeed Brazil.

Bibliography

Abrahams, Roger D., 1983. *The Man-of-Words in the West Indies: Performance and the Emergence of a Creole Culture* (Baltimore: Johns Hopkins University Press).

Abrams, M.K., 1953. *The Mirror and the Lamp: Romantic Theory and the Critical Tradition* (Oxford: OUP).

Abreu, José Vincente, 1969. *Las 4 letras* (Caracas: Centauro).

Acosta Belén, Edna, 1975. 'Spanglish: A Case of Languages in Contact', in *New Directions in Language Learning, Teaching, and Bilingual Education*, ed. H. Dulay and M.K. Burt (Washington DC: TESOL), pp. 151–8.

—— (ed.), 1980. *La mujer en la sociedad puertorriqueña* (Río Piedras, PR: Huracán).

—— 1996. 'Rosario Ferré's Crossover Writing' [Review of Ferré's 1995 novel, *The House on the Lagoon*], *Latino Review of Books*, 2.2: 30–1.

Adams, John W., 1979. 'Representation and Context in Ethnographic Film', *Film Criticism*, 4.1 (Fall): 89–100.

Agudo Freites, Raúl, 1978. 'Cincuenta años de *Nochebuena negra*', *Revista Nacional de Cultura* (Caracas), 238 (Sept–Oct): 23–32.

Aguilar, Luis, 1993. 'Cuba 1860–1930', in *Cuba: A Short History*, ed. Leslie Bethel (Cambridge: Cambridge University Press), pp. 21–55.

Alí González, Enrique, 1992. 'Estadísticas de lo divino', *Revista Bigott*, 21 (Jan.–Mar.): [n.p].

Albornoz, Aurora de, and Luis Julio Rodríguez, 1980. *Sensemayá: la poesía negra en el mundo hispanoparlante* (Madrid: Orígenes).

Alonso, Carlos J., 1996. 'The "Criollista" Novel', in *The Cambridge History of Latin American Literature*, ed. Roberto González Echevarría and Enrique Pupo-Walker, 3 vols, (Cambridge: Cambridge University Press), ii, pp. 195–212.

Alvarado, Ana D., María Milagros López and Wanda E. Ramos, 1989. 'Celebrating Life and the Rearticulation of Mytho-Misogyny: Women Unearthing the 'Machosaurus', *Sargasso* (San Juan, PR), 6: 1–7.

Alvarez, Julia, 1984. *The Homecoming* (New York: Plume/Penguin).

—— 1992 [1991]. *How the García Girls Lost Their Accents* (New York: Plume/Penguin).

—— 1994. *In the Time of the Butterflies* (New York: Plume/Penguin).

—— 1995. *En el tiempo de las mariposas*, trans. Rolando Costa Picazo [First Spanish translation] (Buenos Aires: Atlántida).

—— 1995. *En el tiempo de las mariposas*, trans. Rolando Costa Picazo and revised by José Alcántara Almánzar and Juan Ducoudray (Santo Domingo: Taller).

—— 1996. *The Other Side/El otro lado* [Poems] (New York: Plume/Penguin).

Alvarez-Borland, Isabel, 1994. 'Displacements and Autobiography in Cuban-American Fiction', *World Literature Today*, 68.1: 43–8.

Aparicio, Frances, 1988. 'La vida es un Spanglish disparatero', *European Perspectives on Hispanic Literature in the US*, ed. G. Fabre (Houston: Arte Público), pp. 147–60.

Arce de Vázquez, Margot, 1953. 'Los últimos versos de Julia de Burgos', *Artes y Letras* (San Juan, PR), 1.5: 5.

—— 1956, 'Las raíces', *El Mundo* (San Juan, PR), 16 June.

—— 1980 [1967]. 'Esau', in Zavala and Rodríguez (1980), pp. 259–72.

Arenas, Reinald, 1992. *Antes que arochezca (Barcelona: Seix Barral)*, tr. Dolores Koch as *Before Night Falls* (London: Viking, 1993).

Arévalo Martínez, Rafael, 1915. *El hombre que parecía un caballo* (Guatemala City: Arte Nuevo).

Aretz, Isabel, 1972. *Manual de folclore venezolano* (Caracas: Monte Avila).

Argüelles Mederos, Aníbal and Ileana Hodge Limonta. 1991. *Los llamados cultos sincréticos y el espiritismo* (Havana: Editorial Academia).

Armas Alfonso, Alfredo, 1969. *El osario de Dios* (Caracas: Monte Avila).

Arteaga, Alfred, 1997. *Chicano Poetics: Heterotexts and Hybridities* (Cambridge: Cambridge University Press).

Azize Vargas, Yamila, (ed.), 1987. *La mujer en Puerto Rico: ensayos de investigación* (Río Piedras, PR: Huracán).

Bakhtin, Mikhail, 1982. *Estética de la creación verbal* (Mexico City: Siglo XXI).

—— 1991. *Teoría y estética de la novela* (Madrid: Taurus).

Barkan, Elazar, and Ronald Bush (eds), 1995. *Prehistories of the Future: The Primitivist Project and the Culture of Modernism* (Stanford: Stanford University Press).

Barradas, Efraín, 1977. 'El machismo existencialista de René Márques: relecturas y nuevas lecturas', *Sin Nombre* (San Juan, PR), 8.3 (Oct–Dec): 69–81.

—— 1980. 'La negritud hoy: sobre la poesía de Nancy Morejón', *Areyto* (New York), 6.24: 33–8.

—— 1981. *Para leer en puertorriqueño: acercamiento a la obra de Luis Rafael Sánchez* (Río Piedras, PR: Editorial Cultural).

—— 1996. 'La difícil tarea de ser Julia Alvarez' [Review of *The Other Side/El otro lado*], *Latino Review of Books*, 2.2: 24–26.

Bauman, Zygmunt, 1987. *Legislators and Interpreters* (Ithaca, NY: Cornell University Press).

Bayard, Frances, 1970. 'The Black Latin American Impact on Western Culture', in *The Negro Impact on Western Civilization*, ed. Joseph Roucek and Thomas Kiernan (New York: Philosophical Library), pp. 287–335.

Beauchamp, Juan José, 1994. 'La literatura de la crisis social y cultural de la identidad nacional puertorriqueña (1925–49): un ensayo de apertura (Parte II)', in *22 conferencias de literatura puertorriqueña* (San Juan, PR: Librería Editorial Ateneo), p. 346.

BBC/Cuban Television, 1982. 'Classically Cuban: Alicia Alonso and the Cuban National Ballet', dir. Michael Dibb.

Beckner, Morton, 1967. 'Teleology' entry in his *Encyclopedia of Philosophy*, 8 vols (New York: Macmillan), viii, pp. 88–91.

Bell, Daniel, 1996. *The Cultural Contradictions of Capitalism* (New York: Basic Books).

Belrose, Maurice, 1988. *Africa en el corazón de Venezuela* (Maracaibo: Universidad del Zulia).

Benítez Rojo, Antonio, 1989. *La isla que se repite. El Caribe y la perspectiva posmoderna* (Hanover, NH: Ediciones del Norte). Tr. James E. Maraniss as *The Repeating Island: The Caribbean and the Postmodern Perspective*

(Durham, NC, and London: Duke University Press, 1992. 2nd expanded ed., 1996).

Berger, Peter, and Thomas Luckmann, 1967. *The Social Construction of Reality* (New York: Anchor Books).

Beverly, John, 1991. 'The Margin at the Center: On Testimonio', in *De/Colonizing the Subject: The Politics of Gender in Women's Autobiography,* ed. Sidonie Smith and Julia Watson (Minneapolis: University of Minnesota), pp. 91–114.

Bhabha, Homi K., 1994a. 'DissemiNation: Time, Narrative and the Margins of the Nation', in his *The Location of Culture* (London: Routledge), pp. 139–70.

—— 1994b. 'How Newness Enters the World: Postmodern Space, Postcolonial Times and the Trials of Cultural Translation', in his *The Location of Culture,* pp. 212–35.

Biagioli, Mario, 1993. *Galileo Courtier: The Practice of Science in the Culture of Absolutism* (Chicago: University of Chicago).

Bioy Casares, Adolfo, 1940. *La invención de morel* (Buenos Aires: Losada), tr., with other stories, Ruth L.C. Simms as *The Invention of Morel, and Other Stories* (Austin, Texas: University of Texas Press, 1964).

Blanco, Tomás, 1981 [1935]. Prontuario histórico de Puerto Rico (Río Piedras, PR: Huracán).

—— 1985 [1942]. *El prejuicio racial en Puerto Rico* (Río Piedras, PR: Huracán).

Bloom, Harold, 1973. *The Anxiety of Influence: A Theory of Poetry* (Oxford: OUP).

—— 1975. *A Map of Misreadings* (Oxford: OUP).

Bolívar, Simón, 1969. *Discurso de Angostura* (Caracas: Gobierno de los EEUU de Venezuela).

Braidotti, Rosi, 1994. *Nomadic Subjects: Embodiment and Sexual Difference in Contemporary Feminist Theory* (New York: Columbia University Press).

Bravo, Ernesto, 1993. *¿Desarrollo en el subdesarrollo? La biomedicina en Cuba* (Buenos Aires: Centro Editor de América Latina).

Bremer, Thomas, 1993. 'The Constitution of Alterity: Fernando Ortiz and the Beginnings of Latin-American Ethnography out of the Spirit of Italian Criminology', in *Alternative Cultures in the Caribbean. First International Conference of the Society of Caribbean Research,* ed. Thomas Bremer and Ulrich Fleischmann (Frankfurt: Vervuet Verlag), pp. 119–29.

Brooks, Peter, 1994. *Reading for the Plot: Design and Intention in Narrative* (New York: Knopf).

Budge, Wallis E.A., 1973 [1911]. *Osiris and the Egyptian Resurrection*, 2 vols (New York: Dover).

Burgos, Julia de, 1986. *Yo misma fui mi ruta*, ed. María M. Solá (Río Piedras, PR: Huracán).

—— 1997. *Song of the Simple Truth: Obra poética completa/The Complete Poems of Julia de Burgos*, ed. Jack Agüeros (Willimantic, CT: Curbstone Press).

Cabrera Infante, Guillermo, 1965. *Tres tristes tigres* (Barcelona: Seix Barral). Trans. Donald Gardner and Suzanne Jill Levine as *Three Trapped Tigers* (New York: Harper and Row, 1971).

Calinescu, Matei, 1987. *Five Faces of Modernity, Avant-Garde, Decadence, Kitsch Postmodernism* (Durham, NC: Duke University Press).

Carpentier, Alejo [1946], 1972. *La música en Cuba* (Mexico City: Fondo de Cultura Económica).

Carr, Raymond, 1984. *Puerto Rico: A Colonial Experiment* (New York: New York University Press).

Carrión, Juan Manuel, 1993. 'The National Question in Puerto Rico', in Meléndez and Meléndez (1993): pp. 67–75.

Carrión, Miguel de, 1903. 'El Doctor Ortiz Fernández', *Azul y Rojo* (Havana), no. 24 (14 June): 5–6.

Casals, Jorge, 1944. *Plácido como poeta cubano* (Havana: Ministerio de Educación, Dirección de Cultura).

Castro, Fidel, 1994a. 'Este es un Centro del que puede sentir orgullo el país', *Granma International* (7 Dec): 2–5.

—— 1994b. 'This is a Centre of which the Country Can Be Proud', *Granma International* (21 Dec): 7–9.

Césaire, Aimé 1956 [1939]. *Cahier d'un retour au pays natal* (Paris: Présence Africaine).

Céspedes, Diógenes (ed.), 1994. *Ponencias del Congreso Crítico de Literatura Dominicana* (Santo Domingo: Editora de Colores).

Churchill, Ward, 1992. *Fantasies of the Master Race* (Monroe, ME: Common Courage Press).

Clissold, Stephen, 1972. *The Saints of South America* (London: Charles Knight & Co. Ltd).

Compagnon, Antoine, 1992. *The Five Paradoxes of Modernity* (New York: Columbia University Press).

Cornejo Polar, Antonio, 1982. *Sobre literatura y crítica latinoamericana* (Caracas: UCV).

Coss, Luis Fernando, 1996. *La nación en la orilla: respuesta a los posmodernos pesimistas* (San Juan, PR: Punto de Encuentro).

Coss Causse, Jesús, 1987. 'El quijote negro', *Del Caribe*, 8: 58–60.

Cruz Malavé, Arnaldo, 1993. 'Para virar al macho: la autobiografía como subversión en la cuentística de Manuel Ramos Otero', *Revista Iberoamericana*, 162–3; 239–63.

Curutchet, Juan Carlos, 1972. *Julio Cortázar o la crítica de la razón pragmática* (Madrid: Nacional).

Darío, Rubén, 1950. *Obras completas* (Madrid: Afrodisio Aguado).

Davies, Catherine, 1998. 'Cross-Cultural Homebodies in Cuba: The Poetry of Excilia Saldaña' in *Theory and Crisis: Feminist Readings in Latin American Literature*, ed. Catherine Davies and Anny Brookbank Jones (Oxford: OUP).

Dávila, Anjelamaría, 1984. '"Un clavel interpuesto": (apuntes sobre la imajen [sic] de Julia de Burgos)', *Claridad* ('En Rojo' supplement, 24 Feb–1 Mar) (San Juan, PR): 15.

De Diego, José, 1980 [1916]. 'No', in Zavala and Rodríguez (1980), pp. 131–3.

Deleuze, Gilles, and Félix Guattari, 1988. *A Thousand Plateaus: Capitalism and Schizophrenia* (London: Athlone).

Díaz Quiñones, Arcadio, 1984. 'Recordando el futuro imaginario: la escritura histórica en la década del treinta', *Sin Nombre* (San Juan, PR), 14.3: 16–35.

—— 1985. 'Tomás Blanco: racismo, historia, esclavitud', introduction to Blanco (1985), pp. 13–92.

—— 1992. 'The Hispanic Caribbean National Discourse: Antonio S. Pedreira and Ramiro Guerra y Sánchez', in *Intellectuals in the Twentieth-Century Caribbean*, 2 vols, ed Alistair Hennessy (London: Macmillan) (*vol. 2, 'Unity in Variety: The Hispanic and Francophone Caribbean'*), pp. 99–121.

—— 1993a. *La memoria rota* (Río Piedras, PR: Huracán).

—— 1993b. 'La política del olvido', in Díaz Quiñones (1993a), pp. 137–66.

—— 1994. 'Pedro Henríquez Ureña: modernidad, diáspora y construcción de identidades', in *Modernización e identidades sociales*, ed. Gilberto Giménez and Ricardo Rozas (Mexico City: Universidad Nacional Autónoma), pp. 59–117.

Diáz Sánchez, Ramón, 1963. 'Perspectivas históricas de la cultura venezolana: lo español y lo africano', *Revista Nacional de Cultura*, 161: 35–51.

—— 1973 [1950]. *Cumboto* (Barcelona: Plaza y Janés).

Diccionario de literatura cubana, 1980–4. 2 vols (Havana: Letras Cubanas).

Dorante, Elena, 1981. *Venezuela, magia y ficción* (Cumaná, Venezuela: Editorial Universitaria de Oriente).

Duchesne Winter, Juan, 1993. 'Multitud y tradición en *El entierro de Cortijo* de Edgardo Rodríguez Juliá', *Revista Iberoamericana*, 59: 162–3 (Jan–Jun): 221–37.

Duchesne Winter, Juan, Rubén Rias Avila, María Elena Rodriguez Castro, Juan Gelpí, Aurea Maria Sotomayor, and Yvoune Sanavitis, (eds) 1992. *Las tribulaciones de Juliá* (San Juan, PR: Instituto de Cultura Puertorriqueña).

Ellis, Keith, 1985. *Cuba's Nicolás Guillén: Poetry and Ideology* (Toronto: Toronto University Press).

Ellison, Mary, 1981. 'Blacks in American Film', in *Cinema, Politics and Society in America*, ed. Philip John Davies and Brian Neve (New York: St. Martin's Press).

Ellul, Jacques, 1985. *The Humiliation of the Word* (Grand Rapids, MI: William B. Eerdmans).

Fabbiani Ruíz, José, 1940. 'Una historia vulgar', in *Antología del cuento moderno venezolano, 1895–1935*, ed. Arturo Uslar Pietri and Julián Padrón (Caracas: Escuela Técnica Industrial/Taller de Artes Gráficas), pp. 182–4.

Fanon, Frantz, 1970. *The Wretched of the Earth*, trans. Constance Farrington, 2nd ed. (Harmondsworth: Penguin).

Fernández de la Vega, Oscar, and Alberto N. Pamies, 1973. *Iniciación a la poesía afro-americana* (Miami: Universal).

Fernández Retamar, Roberto, 1971. *Caliban: apuntes sobre la cultura en Nuestra América* (Mexico City: Diógenes).

—— 1989. 'Caliban: Notes toward a Discussion of Culture in Our America', in *Caliban and Other Essays*, trans. Edward Baker (Minneapolis: Minnesota UP), pp. 1–45.

Figueroa, Armando, 1989. Review of *La importancia de llamarse Daniel Santos*, *Revista Hispánica Moderna* (Columbia University), 2: 197–9.

Flores, Juan, 1979. *Insularismo e ideología burguesa en Antonio Pedreira* (Havana: Casa de las Américas).

—— 1993a. *Divided Borders: Essays on Puerto Rican National Identity* (Houston: Arte Público).

—— 1993b. 'The Insular Vision: Pedreira and the Puerto Rican Misère', in Flores (1993a), pp. 13–57.

—— 1993c. 'The Puerto Rico that José Luis González Built', in Flores (1993a), pp. 61–70.

Fuentes, Carlos, 1962. *La muerte de Artemio Cruz* (Mexico City: Fondo de Cultura Económica), tr. Sam Hileman as *The Death of Artemio Cruz* (New York: Noonday; London: Collins). Also tr. Alfred MacAdam (New York: Farrar Straus and Giroux, 1991.)

Gallegos, Rómulo, 1962 [1937]. *Pobre negro*, in his *Obras completas*, 2 vols (Madrid: Aguilar), ii, pp. 337–642.

García Canclini, Néstor, 1990. *Culturas híbridas: para entrar y salir de la modernidad* (Mexico: Grijalbo). Tr. Christoper L. Chiappari and Silvia L. López as *Hybrid Cultures: Strategies for Entering and Leaving Modernity* (Minneapolis: University of Minnesota Press, 1995).

García-Carranza, Araceli, 1970. *Bio-bibliografía de don Fernando Ortiz* (Havana: Biblioteca Nacional José Martí).

García-Carranza, Araceli, Norma Suárez Suárez and Alberto Quesada Morales, 1996. *Cronología. Fernando Ortiz* (Havana: Fundación Fernando Ortiz).

García Chichester, Ana, 1992. 'Superando el caos: estado actual de la crítica sobre la narrativa de Virgilio Piñera', *Revista Iberoamericana de Bibliografía*, 42. 1: 132–45.

García Márquez, Gabriel, 1967. *Cien años de soledad* (Barcelona: Plaza & Janes). Tr. Gregory Rabassa as *One Hundred Years of Solitude* (New York: Harper & Row; London: Jonathan Cape, 1970).

—— 1975. *El otoño del patriarca* (Barcelona: Plaza & Janes). Tr. Gregory Rabassa as *The Autumn of the Patriarch* (New York: Harper & Row, 1976).

—— 1989. *El general en su laberinto* (Bogotá: Oveja Negra). Tr. Edith Grossman as *The General in His Labyrinth* (New York: Knopf, 1990; London: Jonathan Cape, 1991).

—— 1996. 'On the Lot with García Márquez', *Variety*, 362.8 (25 March), p. 55.

García Márquez, Gabriel, and Plinio Apuleyo Mendoza, 1982. *El olor de la guayaba: conversaciones con Plinio Apuleyo Mendoza* (Bogotá: Oveja Negra).

Gates Henry Louis, Jr, 1984. *Black Literature and Literary Theory* (New York: Methuen).

—— 1988. *The Signifying Monkey: A Theory of African-American Literary Criticism* (New York and London: Oxford University Press).

Gelpí, Juan G., 1986. 'La cuentística antipatriarcal de Luis Rafael Sánchez', *Hispamérica*, 15.43 (April): 113–20.

—— 1993. *Literatura y paternalismo en Puerto Rico* (Río Piedras, PR: EDUPR).

Georges, Eugenia, 1990. *The Making of a Transnational Community: Migration, Development and Cultural Change in the Dominican Republic* (New York: Columbia University Press).

Gilman, Richard, 1968. 'The Revolt Against Becoming', *New Republic* (May 18): 25–7.

Gilman, Sander, 1992 [1986]. 'Black Bodies, White Bodies: Toward an Iconography of Female Sexuality in Late Nineteenth-Century Art, Medicine and Literature', *Race, Culture, and Difference*, ed. Ali Rattansi (London: Sage), pp. 171–97.

González, José Emilio, 1965. 'Algo más sobre la vida y la poesía de Julia de Burgos', *La Torre*, 13.51: 151–74.

—— 1973–4. 'La individualidad poética de Julia de Burgos', *Río Piedras* (San Juan, PR), 3–4: 47–59.

—— 1976. 'Julia de Burgos: la mujer y la poesía', *Sin Nombre* (San Juan, PR), 7.3: 86–100.

González, José Luis, 1989a. *El país de cuatro pisos y otros ensayos*, 7th ed. (Río Piedras, PR: Huracán).

—— 1989b. 'El país de cuatro pisos: notas para una definición de la cultura puertorriqueña', in González (1989a), pp. 11–42.

—— 1989c. 'Literatura e identidad nacional en Puerto Rico', in González (1989a), pp. 43–84.

González, José Luis, and Mónica Mansour, 1976. *Poesía negra de América* (Mexico City: Era).

González, Rubén, 1991. 'Las tribulaciones de Jonás: La historia detrás de la historia', *La Torre*, 5.18: 133–55.

González Echevarría, Roberto, 1985. *The Voice of the Masters: Writing and Authority in Modern Latin American Literature* (Austin, TX: University of Texas Press).

—— 1986. *La ruta de Severo Sarduy* (Hanover, NH: Ediciones del Norte).

—— 1990. *Myth and the Archive: A Theory of Latin American Narrative* (Cambridge: Cambridge University Press).

—— 1993. *Celestina's Brood: Continuities of the Baroque in Spanish and Latin American Literature* (Durham, NC: Duke University Press).

—— 1995. 'Pedro Mártir de Anglería y el segundo descubrimiento de América', *La Torre* (Río Piedras, PR), 9.3: 29–52.

Gonzalez León, Adriano, 1969. *País portátil* (Barcelona: Seix Barral).

Gramuglio, María Teresa 1994. 'Estudio preliminar' of Leopoldo Lugones's *El ángel de la sombra* (Buenos Aires: Losada), pp. 7–21.

Greenberg, Bradley S., 1980. *Life on Television: Content Analyses of US TV Drama* (Norwood, NJ: Ablex).

Grosfoguel, Ramón, 1995. 'Puerto Rico in the World System: The Different Modes of Incorporation in the Twentieth Century (1898–1995)', paper presented at the 19th Annual Conference of the Society for Caribbean Studies, Institute of Commonwealth Studies (London), 5–7 July.

Grosfoguel, Ramón, Frances Negrón-Muntaner and Chloé S. Georas 1997. 'Beyond Nationalist and Colonialist Discourses: The *Jaiba* Politics of the Puerto Rican Ethno-Nation', in Negrón-Muntaner and Grosfoguel (1997), pp. 1–36.

Guillén, Nicolás, 1972–3. *Obra poética*, 2 vols (Havana: Instituto Cubano del Libro).

—— 1975–6. *Prosa de prisa 1929–1972*, 3 vols (Havana: Instituto Cubano del Libro).

—— 1980. *Obra poética, 1922–1958* (Havana: Letras Cubanas).

——1981. *Sóngoro cosongo y otros poemas* (Madrid: Alianza).

—— 1985. *Obra poética*, 2 vols (Havana: Letras Cubanas).

—— 1994. *New Love Poetry/Nueva poesía de amor* (Toronto: University of Toronto Press).

Guirao, Ramón, 1938. *Orbita de la poesía afrocubana, 1928–37* (Havana: Ucar & García).

Gutiérrez-Vega, Zenaida, (ed.), 1982. *Fernando Ortiz en sus cartas a José M. Chacón: 1914–1936* (Madrid: Fundación Universitaria).

Hall, Stuart, 1980. 'Encoding/Decoding', in *Culture, Media, Language*, ed. Stuart Hall (Birmingham: University of Birmingham), pp. 128–38.

Hart Davalos, Armando, 1981. 'Homenaje a Don Fernando Ortiz', *Revista de la Biblioteca Nacional José Martí*, 23.3 (Sept–Dec): 5–19.

Hebert, Christopher, 1991. *Culture and Anomie: Ethnographic Imagination in the Nineteenth Century* (Chicago: University of Chicago Press).

Helg, Aline, 1995. *Our Rightful Share. The Afro-Cuban Struggle for Equality, 1886–1912* (Chapel Hill: University of North Carolina Press).

Heller, Ben, 1989. 'Lectura marginal de un texto marginado: *Respirando el verano* de Héctor Rojas Herazo', *Revista de Estudios Colombianos*, 6: 21–6.

Herskovitz, Melville, 1938. *Acculturation: The Study of Culture Contacts* (New York: J.J. Augustus).

Hess, David J., 1991. *Spirits and Scientists: Ideology, Spiritism, and Brazilian Culture* (University Park, PA: Pennsylvania State University Press).

Hickman, Charles A., and Manford H. Kuhn, 1956. *Individuals, Groups and Economic Behavior* (New York: Dryden Press).

Hill, Errol, 1997. *The Trinidad Carnival: Mandate for a National Carnival* (London: New Beacon).

Hilliard, Asa G., Larry Williams and Nia Davali (eds), 1987. *The Teachings of Ptahhotep: The Oldest Book in the World* (Atlanta: Blackwood).

Hodge, Merle, 1970. *Crick Crack Monkey* (London: Heinemann).

Holmberg, Arthur, 1982. 'Carlos Fuentes Turns to the Theater', *New York Times* (6 June), p. 1.

Holton, Gerald (ed.), 1965. *Science and Culture: A Study of Cohesive and Disjunctive Forces* (Boston: Houghton Mifflin).

hooks, bell, 1994. 'Postmodern Blackness', in Williams and Chrisman (1994), pp. 421–7.

Hultberg, John, 1991. *A Tale of Two Cultures: The Age of Science of C.P. Snow* (Gothenburg: University of Gothenburg).

Hulme, Peter, and Neil Whitehead (eds), 1992. *Wild Majesty: Encounters With Caribs From Columbus to the Present Day* (Oxford: Clarendon Press).

Hutcheon, Linda, 1988. *A Poetics of Postmodernism: History, Theory, Fiction* (London: Routledge).

Ibarra, Jorge, 1990. 'La herencia científica de Fernando Ortiz', *Revista Iberoamericana*, 56: 1339–51.

Iglesias, César Andreu (ed.), 1977. *Memorias de Bernardo Vega: contribución a la historia de la communidad puertorriqueña en Nueva York* (Río Piedras, PR: Huracãn).

Iznaga, Diana, 1989. *Transculturación en Fernando Ortiz* (Havana: Editorial de Ciencias Sociales).

Jackson, Richard L., 1976. *The Black Image in Latin American Literature* (Albuquerque: University of New Mexico).

James, Conrad, 1996. 'Patterns of Resistance in Afro-Cuban Women's Writing: Nancy Morejón's "Amo a mi amo"', in *Framing The Word: Gender and Genre in Caribbean Women's Writing*, ed. by, Joan Anim-Ado (London: Whiting and Birch) pp. 159–68.

James, George G.M., 1985. *Stolen Legacy The Greeks Were Not the Authors of Greek Philosophy, but the People of North Africa, Commonly Called the Egyptians* (San Francisco: Richardson).

Jáuregui, Julio, 1980. 'Las aguas profundas de su cuerpo', in his *Tercera sangre* (Caracas: Monte Avila), pp. 53–63.

Jiménez Muñoz, Gladys M., 1997. '"So We Decided to Come and Ask You Ourselves": The 1928 U.S. Congressional Hearings on Women's Suffrage in Puerto Rico', in Negrón-Muntaner and Grosfoguel (1997), pp. 140–65.

Johnson, James Weldon, 1995 [1912]. *The Autobiography of an Ex-Colored Man* (New York: Dover).

Johnson, Roberta Ann, 1980. *Puerto Rico: Commonwealth or Colony? (New York: Praeger).*

Kaplan, Cora, 1987. 'Deterritorializations: The Rewriting of Home and Exile in Feminist Discourse', *Cultural Critique* 6: 187–98.

Knight, Franklin W., 1990. *The Caribbean: The Genesis of a Fragmented Nationalism*, 2nd ed. (Oxford: OUP).

Kubayanda, Josaphat B., 1984. 'Afrocentric Hermeneutics and the Rhetoric of *Transculturación' Latin America and the Caribbean, Geopolitics, Development and Culture* (Proceedings of the October 1983 Conference of the Canadian Assoc. for Latin America and Caribbean Studies), ed. Arch R.M. Ritter (Ottawa, Ontario: Canadian Assoc. for Latin America and Caribbean Studies), pp. 226–41.

Kutzinski, Vera M., 1987. *Against the American Grain*: *Myth and History* in William Carlos Williams, Jay Wright and Nicolás Guillén (Baltimore: Johns Hopkins University).

Kuznesof, Elizabeth A., and Robert Oppenheimer, 1985. 'The Family and Society in Nineteenth-Century Latin America: An Historiographical Introduction', *Journal of Family History*, 10.3: 215–34.

Lakoff, George, and Mark Johnson, 1980. *Metaphors We Live By* (Chicago: University of Chicago Press).

Lafourcade, Enrique, 1976. *Tres terroristas* (Barcelona: Pomaire).

Latour, Bruno, 1993. *We Have Never Been Modern*, tr. C. Porter (Cambridge, MA: Harvard University Press).

León, Argeliers, 1984. *Del canto y el tiempo* (Havana: Letras Cubanas).

Leps, Marie-Christine, 1992. *Apprehending the Criminal: The Production of Deviance in Nineteenth-Century Discourse* (Durham, NC: Duke University Press).

Levin, Harry, 1965. 'Semantics of Culture', in Holton (1965), pp. 1–13.

Levine, Barry B., (ed.), 1987. *The Caribbean Exodus* (New York: Praeger).

Lezama Lima, José, 1957. *La expression american* (Havana: Instituto Nacional de Cultural).

——1966. *Paradiso* (Havana: Unión), rev. ed. Julio Cortázar and Carlos Monsiváis (Buenos Aires: Ediciones de La Clor, 1968), tr. Gregory Rabosson as *Paradiso* (New York: Farrar Straus and Giroux; London: Secker and Warburg, 1974).

Lionet, Françoise 1989. *Reading Women Writing* (Ithaca: Cornell University Press).

Lippmann, Walter, 1922 (rpt. 1956). *Public Opinion* (New York: Macmillan).

Liscano, Juan, 1973. *La fiesta de San Juan el Bautista* (Caracas: Monte Avila).

—— 1992. 'La tradición transculturada', *Revista Bigott*, 21 (Jan–Mar): 6.

Llaya, Pedro, 1977. 'El tema negro en la literatura venezolana', *Imagen* (Caracas), 110: 34–8.

López, Ana M., 1991. 'Are All Latins from Manhattan: Hollywood, Ethnography, and Cultural Colonialism', in *Unspeakable Images: Ethnicity and the American Cinema*, ed. Lester D. Friedman (Chicago: University of Chicago Press), pp. 404–24.

López Bauzá, Juan, 1995. 'En torno a la más joven narrativa puertorriqueña', *Diálogo* (San Juan, PR: University of Puerto Rico): 51.

López Jiménez, Ivette, 1979. 'Julia de Burgos: los textos comunicantes', *Sin Nombre* (San Juan, PR), 10.1: 47–68.

—— 1993. 'Cortando distancias: Julia de Burgos una vez más', in *Actas del congreso internacional Julia de Burgos*, ed. Edgar Martínez Masdeu (San Juan, PR: Ateneo Puertorriqueño), pp. 274–82.

López Sánchez, José, 1986. *Ciencia y medicina: historia de la medicina* (Editorial Científico-Técnica).

Losa, José de la, 1994. 'Biotechnology Continues to Advance', *Granma International* (28 Dec): 4.

Lotman, Jurij, and Boris Uspenkij, 1979. 'Sobre el mecanismo semiótico de la cultura', in *Semiótica de la cultura*, ed. Jurij Lotman and Escuela de Tartú (n. pl.: n. publ.), pp. 67–110.

Ludmer, Josefina, 1984. 'Tretas del débil', in *La sartén por el mango: encuentro de escritoras latinoamericanas,* ed. Patricia Elena González and Eliana Ortega (Río Piedras, PR: Huracán), pp. 47–54.

Lumsden, Ian, 1996. *Machos, Maricones, and Gays: Cuba and Homosexuality* (Philadelphia: Temple).

Maldonado Denis, Manuel, 1976. *Puerto Rico y Estados Unidos: Emigración y colonialismo.* (Mexico City: Siglo XXI).

—— 1979. *Puerto Rico: mito y realidad*, 3rd ed. (San Juan, PR: Antillana).

Mañach, Jorge, 1991 [1927]. *La crisis de la alta cultura en Cuba – Indagación del choteo,* ed. Rosorio Rexach (Miami: Universal).

Mannheim, Hermann (ed.), 1960. *Pioneers in Criminology* (Chicago: Quadrangle).

Manrique, Francisco Cabrera, 1971. Historia de la literatura puertorriqueña (Río Pedras, PR: Editorial Cultural).

Mansour, Monica, 1973. *La poesía negrista* (Mexico City: Era).

Manuel, Peter, 1995. *Caribbean Currents: Caribbean Music from Rumba to Reggae* (Philadelphia: Temple University Press).

——1960. 'En la popa hay un cuerpo reclinado', in *En una cuidad llamada San Juan* (Mexico City: Universidad Nacional Autónoma), pp. 69–81.

Marías, Julián, 1949. *El método histórico de las generaciones* (Madrid: Revista de Occidente).

Marqués, René, 1977a [1960]. *El puertorriqueño dócil y otros ensayos: 1953–71,* 3rd ed. (San Juan, PR: Antillana).

—— 1977b. 'El problema del idioma en Puerto Rico', in Marqués (1977a), pp. 131–49.

—— 1977c. 'El puertorriqueño dócil: literatura y realidad psicológica', in Marqués (1977a), pp. 151–215.

Márquez, Roberto, 1996. 'De boricuas, jíbaras y jibaristas: Memory, Memoir, and Mimicry', *Latino Review of Books,* 2.1: 30–3.

Martí, José, 1963–73. *Obras completas,* 28 vols (Havana: Nacional).

Martín Barbero, Jesús, 1993. *Communication, Culture and Hegemony: From the Media to Mediations,* tr. Elizabeth Fox and Robert A. White (Newbury Park, CA: Sage).

Martin, Gerald, 1989. *Journeys Through the Labyrinth: Latin American Fiction in the Twentieth Century* (London: Verso).

Martínez, Lourdes, 1990. *Para una semiótica de la mulatez* (Madrid: Porrúa).

Martínez Masdeu, Edgar, 1992. *Cronología de Julia de Burgos: 3 cuadernos del Congreso Internacional Julia de Burgos* (San Juan, PR: Ateneo Puertorriqueño).

Mattos Cintrón, Wilfredo, 1993. 'The Struggle for Independence: The Long March to the Twenty-first Century', in Meléndez and Meléndez (1993), 201–14.

Mbiti, John, S., 1970. *African Religions and Philosophy* (Garden City, NY: Anchor/ Doubleday).

McLuhan, Marshall, 1964. *Understanding Media: The Extensions of Man* (New York: Mentor).

McMurray, George, 1977. *Gabriel García Márquez* (New York: Fred Ungar).

Mead, George Herbert, 1934. *Mind, Self and Society from the Standpoint of a Social Behaviourist,* ed. with an introduction by Charles W. Morris (Chicago: University of Chicago Press).

Medina, Jorge Luis, 1986. 'Conquistadores were misunderstood, says Acevedo', *San Juan Star* (27 August), p. 11.

Medrano, Marianela, 1994. 'El ombligo negro de un bongó' (tr. Daisy Cocco de Filippis), presented at a conference entitled 'Dominican Literature at the Turn of the Century: A Dialogue between a Diaspora and its Nation' (30 June), at the City University of New York's Dominican Studies Institute. Forthcoming proceedings ed. Daisy Cocco de Filippis. The poem has been anthologized bilingually in *Sisters of Caliban: Contemporary Women Poets of the Caribbean,* ed. M.J. Fenwick (Falls Church, VA: Azul), pp. 210–12.

Meléndez, Edwin, and Edgardo Meléndez, (eds), 1993. *Colonial Dilemma: Critical Perspectives on Contemporary Puerto Rico* (Boston: South End).

Melis, Antonio, 1987. 'Fernando Ortiz y el mundo afrocubano: desde la criminología lombrosiana hasta el concepto de transculturación', in *En Cuba: Geschichte-Wirtschaft-Kultur,* ed. Titus Heydenreich, *Lateinamerika Studien,* 23: 169–81.

Meltzer, Bernard N., John W. Petras and Larry T. Reynolds, 1975. *Symbolic Interactionism* (London: Routledge).

Menton, Seymour, 1978. '*Respirando el verano*, fuente colombiana de *Cien años de soledad*', in his *Planetas y satélites* (Bogotá: Plaza y Janes), pp. 247–80.

Molloy, Sylvia, 1986. 'Dos proyectos de vida: *Cuadernos de infancia* de Norah Lange y *El archipiélago* de Victoria Ocampo', in *Femmes des Ameriques* (Toulouse: Travaux de l'Université de Toulouse Le Mirail), pp. 178–9.

—— 1991. *At Face Value: Autobiographical Writing in Spanish America* (Cambridge: Cambridge University Press).

Monsiváis, Carlos, 1993. 'Mexican Cinema: Of Myths and Demystifications', in *Mediating Two Worlds: Cinematic Encounters in the Americas*, ed. John King, Ana M. López and Manuel Alvarado (London: British Film Institute), pp. 139–46.

Morales, Ed, 1994. 'Madam Butterfly: How Julia Alvarez Found Her Accent', *Village Voice Literary Supplement,* 130 (Nov): 13.

Mordecai, Pamela, and Betty Wilson, (eds), 1989. *Her True-True Name: An Anthology of Women's Writing from the Caribbean* (London: Heinemann).

Morejón, Nancy, 1967. *Richard trajo su flauta y otros argumentos* (Havana: Instituto del Libro).

—— 1974. 'Conversación con Nicolás Guillén', in her *Recopilación de textos sobre Nicolás Guillén* (Havana: Casa de las Américas), pp. 31–61.

—— 1982a. *Nación y mestizaje en Nicolás Guillén* (Havana: Unión).

—— 1982b. *Octubre imprescindible* (Havana: Unión).

—— 1995. 'Towards a Poetics of the Caribbean', lecture at the 4th Caribbean Women Writers Conference, Wellesley College, MA. Trans. Alan West with some editorial intervention by John Perivolaris.

Moreno, José, 1971. 'From Traditional to Modern Values', in *Revolutionary Change in Cuba*, ed. Carmelo Mesa-Lago (Pittsburgh: Pittsburgh University Press), pp. 471–97.

Moreno Fraginals, Manuel, 1977. *Africa en América Latina* (Mexico City: Siglo XXI)

Moya Pons, Frank, 1995. *The Dominican Republic: A National History* (Hispaniola Books, CUNY Dominican Studies Institute).

Mullen, Edward J., 1981. *The Life and Poems of a Cuban Slave: Juan Francisco Manzano 1797–1854* (Hamden, Connecticut: Archon).

Navarro Garcia, Luis, 1992. *La independencia de Cuba (Madrid: MAPFRE).*

Negrón-Muntaner, Frances, 1997. 'English Only Jamás but Spanish Only Cuidado: Language and Nationalism in Contemporary Puerto Rico', in Negrón-Muntaner and Grosfoguel (1997), pp. 257–85.

Negrón-Muntaner, Frances, and Ramón Grosfoguel (eds) 1997. *Puerto Rican Jam: Essays on Culture and Politics* (Minneapolis: University of Minnesota).

Nettleford, Rex, 1990. 'The Caribbean Imperative and the Fight Against Folksy Exoticists', *Caribbean Affairs*, 2.2: 29–44.

Noguera, Carlos, 1979. *Inventando los días* (Caracas: Monte Avila).

Nye, Robert A., 1984. *Crime, Madness, & Politics in Modern France: The Medical Concept of National Decline* (Princeton: Princeton University Press).

O'Callaghan, Evelyn, 1993. *Woman Version: Theoretical Approaches to West Indian Fiction by Women* (London: Macmillan).

Olazagasti-Segovia, Elena, 1996–97. 'El sueño de América: sobrevivir la pesadilla' [On Esmeralda Santiago's first novel (1997)], *Latino Review of Books,* 2.3: 54–5.

Oramas, Joaquín, 1995. 'A Broad Movement Producing Dynamic Solutions', *Gramma International* (3 Jan): 3.

O'Reilly Herrera, Andrea, 1997. 'Women and the Revolution in Cristina García's *Dreaming in Cuban'* (unpublished article).

Ortega, Julio, 1991a. *Reapropiaciones: cultura y nueva escritura en Puerto Rico* (Río Piedras: EDUPR).

—— 1991b. 'Dos versiones barrocas: Sarduy y Rodríguez Juliá', in Ortega (1991a), pp. 63–5).

—— 1991c. 'Edgardo Rodríguez Juliá', in Ortega (1991a), pp. 123–62.

Ortega y Gasset, José, 1923. *El tema de nuestro tiempo* (Madrid: Revista de Occidente).

Ortiz, Fernando, 1906. *Hampa afro-cubana. Los negros brujos (apuntes para un estudio de etnología criminal)* (Madrid: Librería de la F. Fé). 2nd ed. (Havana: n.publ., 1917). Republished in 1973 (Miami, FL: Ediciones Universal).

—— 1911. *La reconquista de América: reflexiones sobre el panhispanismo* (Paris: Librería Paul Ollendorff).

—— 1914. 'La filosofia penal de los espiritistas', *Revista Bimestre Cubana*, 9.1–5, 10.1. First published in book form as *La filosofía penal de los espiritistas. Estudio de Filosofia Jurídica* (Havana: La Universal, 1918).

—— 1919. 'Las fases de la evolución religiosa', *Revista Bimestre Cubana,* 14.2: 65–80. Also published separately as *Las fases de la evolución religiosa* (Havana: Tipografia Moderna, 1919).

—— 1926. *Proyecto de Código Criminal Cubano*, with a prologue by Enrique Ferri (Havana: Librería Cervantes).

—— 1939. 'La cubanidad y los negros', *Estudios Afrocubanos,* 3: 3–15.

—— 1940. *Contrapunteo cubano del tabaco y el azúcar*, with an introduction by Bronislaw Malinowski (Havana: J. Montero; republished in 1963, Havana: Universidad Central de las Villas; also republished in Caracas in 1987, Biblioteca Ayacucho). Trans. Harriet de Onis as *Cuban Counterpoint: Tobacco and Sugar* (New York: Knopf, 1947, republished 1996, Durham, NC: Duke University Press).

—— 1950. 'Los espirituales "Cordoneros del Orilé", *Bohemia*, 3: 20–2, 118–19, 122–3.

—— 1950. 'Una moderna secta de Cuba', *Bohemia,* 5: 8–9, 137–9.

—— 1975. *El engaño de las razas* (Havana: Editorial de Ciencias Sociales).

Oviedo, José Miguel, (ed.), 1992. *Antología critica del cuento hispanoamericano del siglo XX (1920–1980),* 2 vols (Madrid: Alianza).

Padrón, Julián, 1939. *La madrugada* (Caracas: Elite).

—— 1957. 'Este mundo desolado', in his *Obras completas* (Mexico City: Aguilar).

Palés Matos, Luis, 1978. *Poesía completa y prosa selecta* (Caracas: Ayacucho).

—— 1995. *La poesía de Luis Palés Matos: Edición Crítica,* ed. Mercedes López-Baralt (Rio Piedras, PR: University of Puerto Rico).

Parkinson Zamora, Lois, 1989. *Writing the Apocalypse: Historical Vision in Contemporary US and Latin American Fiction* (Cambridge: Cambridge University Press).

Parrinder, Geoffrey, 1973. *African Mythology* (London: Hamlyn).

Paz, Octavio, 1950. *El laberinto de la soledad* (Mexico City: Cuadernos Americanos; rev. ed. Mexico City: Fondo de Cultura Económica, 1959), tr. Lysandar Kemp as *The Labyrinth of Solitude: Life and Thought in Mexico* (New York: Grove; London: Allen Lane, 1967).

Pedreira, Antonio S. [1934] 1942. *Insularismo: ensayos de interpretación puertor-riqueña* (San Juan: Biblioteca de Autores). The most recent edition was published in 1992 (Rio Piedras, PR: Edil).

Pérez Jr, Louis A., 1995. *Cuba: Between Reform and Revolution,* 2nd ed. (Oxford: OUP).

Pérez Firmat, Gustavo, 1989. *The Cuban Condition: Translation and Identity in Modern Cuban Literature* (Cambridge: Cambridge University Press).

Pérez Sarduy, Pedro, and Jean Stubbs (eds), 1993. *Afrocuba: An Anthology of Cuban Writing on Race, Politics and Culture* (London: Latin American Bureau).

Perivolaris, John, 1997. Two entries, respectively, on Luis Rafael Sánchez and his novel, *La guaracha del Macho Camacho* (1976), in *Encyclopedia of Latin American Literature,* ed. Verity Smith (Chicago and London: Fitzroy Dearborn), pp. 749–53.

Peset Reig, José Luis, 1987. *El papel del científico ante la independencia americana* (Madrid: Centro de Estudios Históricos).

Piñera, Virgilio, 1956. *Cuentos fríos* (Buenos Aires: Losada). Trans. Mark Shafer as *Cold Tales* (New York: Eridanos, 1987).

Piquet, Daniel, 1982. *La cultura afrovenezolana en sus escritores contemporáneos* (Caracas: Monte Avila).

Poggioli, Renato, 1968. *The Theory of the Avant-Garde* (Cambridge, Mass.: Harvard University Press).

Pollak, Angelina, 1968. 'El culto de María Lionza', *Zona Franca,* 4.58 (June): 14–22.

—— 1984. *Folklore y cultura en los pueblos negros de Yaracuy* (Caracas: UCAB).

—— 1994. *Black Culture and Society in Venezuela* (Caracas: Lagoven).

Quintero Rivera, A.G., (ed.), 1979. *Identidad nacional y clases sociales* (Rio Piedras, PR: Huracán).

—— 1981. *Conflictos de clase y politica en Puerto Rico,* 3rd ed. (Rio Piedras, PR: Huracán).

—— 1986. *Conflictos de clase y política en el Puerto Rico del siglo XIX,* 5th ed. (Río Piedras, PR: Huracán).

—— 1988. *Plebeyos y patricios: burgueses, hacendados, artesanos y obreros: las relaciones de clase en el Puerto Rico de cambio de siglo* (Río Piedras, PR: Huracán).

Rama, Angel, 1982. *Transculturación narrativa en América Latina* (Mexico City: Siglo XXI).

Ramos Guédez, José Marcial, 1980. *El negro en la novela venezolana* (Caracas: Universidad Central de Venezuela).

Randall, Margaret, 1982. *Breaking the Silences* (Vancouver: Pulp Press).

Reed, Ishmael (1996) [1972]. *Mumbo Jumbo* (New York: Simon & Schuster).

Reingold, Nathan, and Marc Rothenberg (eds) 1987. *Scientific Colonialism: A Cross-Cultural Comparison* (Washington DC: Smithsonian Institution Press).

Rezendes, Michael, 1993a. 'Puerto Ricans Say No', *Boston Globe,* 'National/Foreign' section (15 Nov): 1.

—— 1993b. 'Puerto Rico Vote Defies Momentum', *Boston Globe,* 'National/Foreign' section (16 Nov): 8.

Ríos, Palmira, N., 1993. 'Export-Oriented Industrialization and the Demand for Female Labour', in Meléndez and Meléndez (1993), pp. 89–101.

Rivas, Vladimiro, 1972. *Las huellas crecen así* (Caracas: Tiempo Nuevo).

Rodríguez, Marcial, 1976. *Relatos de la Revolución* (Caracas: La Viesa Inprenta).

Rodríguez Beruff, Jorge, 1988. *Política militar y dominación: Puerto Rico en el contexto latinoamericano* (Río Piedras: P.R.: Huracán).

Rodriguez Demorizi, Emilio, 1978. *Poesía popular dominicana,* 3rd ed. (Santiago, Dominican Republic: Universidad Católica Madre y Maestra).

Rodríguez Juliá, Edgardo, 1989a. *El cruce de la Bahía de Guánica* (Río Piedras, PR: Editorial Cultural).

—— 1989b. 'El cruce de la Bahía de Guánica y otras ternuras de la medianía (25 de julio de 1983)', in Rodríguez Juliá (1989a), pp. 9–49.

—— 1989c [1988]. *Puertorriqueños: album de la sagrada familia puertorriqueña a partir de 1898,* 2nd ed. (Madrid: Playor).

Rodríguez Vecchini, Hugo, 1995. 'Cuando Esmeralda "era" puertorriqueña: autobiografía etnográfica y etnografía neopicaresca', *Nómada* (San Juan, PR), 1: 145–60.

Rohter, Larry, 1989. 'García Márquez: Inveterate Cineaste', *San Juan Star* (27 Aug): 9.

Rojas, Rafael, 1995. 'La política como martirio: sacrificios paralelos', *Nómada* (San Juan, PR), 2 (Oct): 11–17.

Rojas Herazo, Héctor, 1962. *Respirando el verano* (Bogotá: Faro).

Roy-Fequiere, Magali, 1994. 'Contested Territory: Puerto Rican Women, Creole Identity, and Intellectual Life in the Early Twentieth Century', *Callaloo,* 17.3: 916–34.

Safa, Helen, 1995. *The Myth of the Male Breadwinner* (Boulder, CO: Westview).

Said, Edward, 1993. *Culture and Imperialism* (New York: Knopf).

Saldaña, Excilia, 1967. 'Ogofuyi', *Pájaro Cascabel* 5 & 6: 43–46.

—— 1982. 'Autobiografía' in Margaret Randall (1982), pp. 200–2.

—— 1987. *Kele Kele* (La Habana: Letras Cubanas).

—— 1991. *Mi nombre – Antielegía Familiar* (La Habana: Ediciones Unión).

Sánchez, Luis Rafael, 1976. *La guaracha del Macho Camacho* (Buenos Aires: Ediciones de la Flor). Trans. Gregory Rabassa as *Macho Camacho's Beat* (New York: Pantheon, 1981).

—— 1988. *La importancia de llamarse Daniel Santos* (Hanover, NH: Ediciones del Norte).

—— 1997a. *No llores por nosotros, Puerto Rico* (Hanover, NH: Ediciones del Norte).

—— 1997b. 'No llores por nosotros, Puerto Rico', in Sánchez (1997a), pp. 193–214.

—— 1997c. 'Abrazos, prejuicios y fronteras', in Sánchez (1997a), pp. 31–8.

Sánchez Korrol, Virgina E., 1993. *From Colonia to Community: The History of Puerto Ricans in New York City* (London: University of California).

Santana Cooney, Rosemary, and Alice Colón, 1980. 'Work and Family: The Recent Struggle of Puerto Rican Families', in *The Puerto Rican Struggle: Essays on Survival in the US,* ed. Clara E. Rodriguez, Virginia Sánchez Korrol and José Oscar Alers (Maplewood, NJ: Waterfront), pp. 58–73.

Santiago, Esmeralda, 1994a [1993]. *When I Was Puerto Rican* (New York: Vintage).

—— 1994b. *Cuando era puertorriqueña.* Tr. with introduction by Esmeralda Santiago (New York: Vintage).

—— 1997a. *America's Dream* (London: Virago).

—— 1997b. Interviewed in Carmen Dolores Hernández's *Puerto Rican Voices in English* (Westport, Conn.: Praeger), pp. 156–69.

Santiago-Valles, Kelvin A., 1994. *'Subject People' and Colonial Discourse: Economic Transformation and Social Disorder in Puerto Rico* (New York: New York State University Press).

Sarduy, Severo, 1972. *Cobra* (Buenos Aires: Sudamericana).

—— 1978. *Maitreya* (Barcelona: Seix Barral).

—— 1984. *Colibrí* (Barcelona: Argos Vergoa).

—— 1986. *La simulacíon* (Caracas: Monte Avila).

—— 1987a. *El Cristo de la rue Jacob* (Barcelona: Mall).

—— 1987b. *Nueva inestabilidad* (Mexico City: Vuelta).

—— 1988. 'Un heredero', in the critical edition of José Lezama Lima's *Paradiso,* by Cintio Vitier (Madrid: UNESCO), pp. 590–5.

—— 1990. *Cocuyo* (Barcelona: Tusquels).

—— 1993a. *De donde son los cantantes* (Madrid: Cátedra).

—— 1993b. *Los pájaros en la playa* (Barcelona: Tusquels).

Scarano, Francisco A., 1993. *Puerto Rico: cinco siglos de historia* (San Juan, PR.: McGraw Hill Interamericana).

Schoijet, Mauricio, 1991. *La ciencia mexicana en la crisis* (Mexico City: Nuestro Tiempo).

Sención, Viriato, 1991. *Los que falsificaron la firma de Dios* (Santo Domingo: Taller). Trans. by Asa Zatz as *They Forged the Signature of God* (Willimantic, CT: Curbstone).

—— 1994. *La enana Celania y otros cuentos de Viriato Sención* (Santo Domingo: Taller).

Senna, Orlando, 1990. 'Cine y literatura en la experiencia brasileña', talk delivered at the School of Communications, University of Puerto Rico, 17 Oct.

Simons, Marlise, 1982. 'Interview: A Talk With Gabriel García Márquez', *New York Times* (5 December): 7.

Simpson, Amelia, 1994. *Xuxa: The Mega-Marketing of Gender, Race, and Modernity* (Philadelphia: Temple University Press).

Smart, Ian I., 1990. *Nicolás Guillén, Popular Poet of the Caribbean* (Columbia, Miss.: University of Missouri Press).

Smith, Sidonie, 1993. *Subjectivity, Identity and the Body* (Bloomington: Indiana University Press).

Smith, Verity, 1993. 'Masks and Voices of the Female Hero: *Tania la guerrillera* as Testimonio', paper presented at the 17th annual conference of the British Society for Caribbean Studies, St Stephen's House, Oxford (July).

Sojo, Juan Pablo, 1943. *Temas y apuntes afro-venezolanos* (Caracas: La Nación).

—— 1972 [1943]. *Nochebuena negra* (Caracas: Monte Avila).

—— 1986. *Estudios del folklore venezolano* (Los Teques, Venezuela: Biblioteca de Autores y Temas Mirandinos).

Solá, Maria M., 1986. 'La poesía de Julia de Burgos: mujer de humana lucha', in Julia de Burgos (1986), pp. 18–19.

Sommer, Doris, 1991. *Foundational Fictions: The National Romances of Latin America* (Berkeley: University of California Press).

Sotomayor, Aurea María, 1995. 'Genealogías o el suave desplazamiento de los orígenes en la narrativa de Manuel Ramos Otero', *Nómada* (San Juan, PR), 1: 42–106.

Stallybrass, Peter, and Allon White, 1989. *The Politics and Poetics of Transgression* (Ithaca: Cornell University Press).

Stam, Robert, 1989. *Subversive pleasures* (Baltimore: Johns Hopkins University Press).

Swift, Molly, 1997. '*Dreaming in Cuban and Gringo viejo:* Case Studies in Intra-American Interpolation', paper presented at the 113th Modern Languages Association Convention, Toronto (29 Dec).

Terdiman, Richard, 1989. *Discourse/Counter-Discourse* (Ithaca, Cornell University Press).

Thompson, Robert Farris, 1983. *Flash of the Spirit: African and Afro-American Art and Philosophy* (New York: Random House).

Tobin, Patricia, 1978. *Time and the Novel: The Genealogical Imperative* (Princeton: Princeton University Press).

Toledo Benedit, Josefina, 1994. *La ciencia y la técnica en José Martí* (Havana: Editorial Científico-Técnica).

Toro González, Carlos del, 1996. *Fernando Ortiz y la Hispanocubana de Cultura* (Havana: Fundación Fernando Ortiz).

Torres, Carmen L., 1989. *La cuentística de Virgilio Piñera* (Madrid: Pliegos).

Torres-Saillant, Silvio, 1994. Presentation of Viriato Sención's 1994 book *La enana Celania y otros cuentos de Viriato Sención*, at the National Library, Santo Domingo. To be included in the proceedings of the conference, 'Dominican Literature at the Turn of the Century: A Dialogue between a Diaspora and its Nation', ed. Daisy Cocco de Filippis, forthcoming.

Torres-Vidal, Nina M., 1995. 'A Dominican Voice Rises Again' [Review of *In the Time of the Butterflies*], *Latino Review of Books*, 1.2: 38–40.

Toulmin, Stephen, 1990. *Cosmopolis: The Hidden Agenda of Modernity* (Chicago: Chicago University Press).

Trabulse, Elías, 1983–92. *Historia de la ciencia en México: estudio y textos,* 5 vols (Mexico City: Fondo de Cultura Económica).

Tsvietáieva, Marina, 1991. *Carta a la Amazona y otros escritos franceses* (Madrid: Hiperión).

Ureña de Henriquez, Salomé, 1989. *Obras completas,* vol. 7 (Santo Domingo: Corripio, Biblioteca de Clásicos Dominicanos).

Urfé, Odilio, 1984. 'Music and Dance in Cuba', in *Africa in Latin America: Essays on History, Culture, and Socialization* (New York: Holmes & Meier), pp. 170–88.

US Department of Labor, 1974. 'The New York Puerto Ricans: Patterns of Work Experience', in *Puerto Rico and Puerto Ricans: Studies in History and Society*, ed. Adalberto López and James Petras (New York: Schenkman), pp. 347–83.

Uslar Pietri, Arturo, 1951. *Las nubes* (Caracas: Edime).

—— 1967. *Obras selectas* (Caracas: Edime).

—— 1970 [1931]. *Las lanzas coloradas,* 7th ed. (Buenos Aires: Losada).

—— 1994. *Del cerro de Plata a los caminos extraviados* (Caracas: Norma).

Valdés Cruz, Rosa E., 1970. *La poesía negroide en América* (New York: Las Américas).

Vallejo, César, 1988. *Poesía completa* (Havana: Arte y Literatura).

Vázquez Arce, Carmen, 1994. *Por la vereda tropical: notas sobre la cuentística de Luis Rafael Sánchez* (Buenos Aires: La Flor).

Veloz Maggiolo, Marcio, 1984. *De abril en adelante* (Santo Domingo: Taller).

Ventura, Roberto, 1991. *Estilo tropical: historia cultural e polemicas literarias no Brasil, 1870–1914* (Sao Paulo: Companhia das Letras).

Ventura, Miriam, 1987. *Trópico acerca de verano* (Santo Domingo: Gente).

Vicioso, Sherezada (Chiqui), 1985. *Un extraño ulular traía el viento* (Santo Domingo: Alfa y Omega).

—— 1994. Untitled presentation at a conference entitled 'Dominican Literature at the Turn of the Century: A Dialogue between a Diaspora and its nation (30 June), at the City University of New York's Dominican Studies Institute. Trans. Daisy Cocco de Filippis with some editorial intervention by John Perivolaris.

Vitier, Cintio, 1970 [1958]. *Lo Cubano en la poesía,* 2nd ed. (Havana: Instituto Cubano del Libro).

Vucinich, Alexander, 1970. *Science in Russian Culture 1861–1917* (Stanford: Stanford University Press).

Wade Chambers, David, 1987. 'Period and Process in Colonial and National Science', in Reingold and Rothenerg (1987), pp. 297–321.

Wagner, Roy, 1981. *The Invention of Culture* (Chicago: University of Chicago Press).

Watson, David, 1994. 'Against Forgetting', *Utne Reader* (Mar./Apr.), pp. 112–115.

Waugh, Patricia, 1992. 'Postmodernism', in Wright (1992), pp. 341–5.

Weil, Eric, 1965. 'Science in Modern Culture', in Holton (1965), pp. 199–217.

Williams, Gareth, 1993. 'Transition and Mourning: The Cultural Challenge of Latin American Testimonial Autobiography' *Latin American Literary Review*, 41: 77–99.

Williams, Lorna Valerie, 1982. *Self and Society in the Poetry of Nicolás Guillén* (Baltimore: Johns Hopkins University Press).

—— 1994. *The Representation of Slavery in Cuban Fiction* (Columbia: University of Missouri Press).

Williams, Patrick and Laura Chrisman (eds), 1994. *Colonial Discourse and Postcolonial Theory: A Reader* (London: Harvester Wheatsheaf).

Williams, Raymond L., 1991. *Novela y poder en Colombia: 1844–1987* (Bogotá: Tercer Mundo).

Wint, Carl, 1995. 'Lip Service Being Paid to Science and Technology', *Jamaican Weekly Gleaner* (28 Apr–4 May): 18.

Wolin, Merle Linda, 1990. 'Hollywood Goes Havana', *New Republic,* 202.16 (16 April): 17–20.

Woll, Allen L., 1977. *The Latin Image in American Film* (Los Angeles: UCLA Latin American Center).

Woll, Allen L., and Randall M. Miller, 1987. *Ethnic and Racial Images in American Film and Television* (New York: Garland).

Wright, Elizabeth (ed.), 1992. *Feminism and Psychoanalysis: A Critical Dictionary* (Oxford: Blackwell).

Wright, Winthrop R., 1993. *Race, Class and National Image in Venezuela* (Austin, TX: University of Texas Press).

Zapata Olivella, Manuel, 1989. *Las claves mágicas de América: raza, clase y cultura* (Bogotá: Plaza & Janes).

Zavala, Iris M., & Rafael Rodríguez, 1980. *Intellectual Roots of Independence* (New York: Monthly Review Press).

Zea, Leopoldo, 1972. *América como conciencia* (Mexico City: UNAM).

Zenón Cruz, Isabelo, 1974–5. *Narciso descubre su trasero: el negro en la cultura puertorriqueña,* 2 vols (Humacao, PR: Furidi).

Index